# Borícua Muslims

# Borícua Muslims

## EVERYDAY COSMOPOLITANISM AMONG PUERTO RICAN CONVERTS TO ISLAM

Ken Chitwood

University of Texas Press *Austin*

Printed in the United States of America
First edition, 2025



♾ The paper used in this book meets the minimum requirements of ANSI/NISO Z39.48-1992 (R1997) (Permanence of Paper).

Library of Congress Cataloging-in-Publication Data

Names: Chitwood, Ken, author
Title: Borícua Muslims : everyday cosmopolitanism among Puerto Rican converts to Islam / Ken Chitwood.
Description: First edition. | Austin : University of Texas Press, 2025. | Includes bibliographical references and index.
Identifiers: LCCN 2024050261 (print) | LCCN 2024050262 (ebook)
ISBN 978-1-4773-3243-6 hardcover
ISBN 978-1-4773-3244-3 paperback
ISBN 978-1-4773-3245-0 pdf
ISBN 978-1-4773-3246-7 epub
Subjects: LCSH: Puerto Ricans—Social conditions | Puerto Ricans—Ethnic identity | Muslim converts—Puerto Rico | Muslim converts—United States | Islam—United States
Classification: LCC E184.P85 C475 2025 (print) | LCC E184.P85 (ebook) | DDC 305.868/7295008297—dc23/eng/20250311
LC record available at https://lccn.loc.gov/2024050261
LC ebook record available at https://lccn.loc.gov/2024050262

doi:10.7560/332436

The University of Texas Press gratefully acknowledges the Joe R. and Teresa Lozano Long Endowment in Latin American and Latino Art and Culture for its support of this publication.

*To my mother, for all the encouragement, love, and Franzia.*

# Contents

# Illustrations

# Preface and Note on Language

THIS BOOK EXTENDS MY PREVIOUS work on Latinx Muslims, their reversion narratives, and their place within American cultures. My interest in these topics began as I reported from a *masjid* in Houston, Texas. A chance meeting one balmy autumn day led to a profile in the *Houston Chronicle* and an introduction to a broader world of Latinx individuals who converted—or "reverted" as can be their preferred terminology—to Islam due to a complex mix of personal, political, and societal factors. At the time, I was interested in researching and writing on *both* Latinx religious cultures *and* Muslim communities in the US and its borderlands. Thus, I cultivated relationships within the Latinx Muslim landscape, where I began to appreciate the immense influence Puerto Ricans had on broader shared narratives of Latinx *Islamidad*. While I considered writing about Muslims in Cuba, Mexico, or in the US/Mexico borderlands, I ended up pursuing a story about Puerto Rican converts—individuals whose lives are shaped by a range of marginalizations, who are strangers in their own lands, and yet find new ways to be and belong in an age marked by increasing, and competing, diversity and difference.

Along the way, I met numerous colleagues who asked why I felt Hatillo, Puerto Rico, and Union City, New Jersey, were ideal places to study what it means to be Muslim or inhabit a place we call "the Americas" in the late-modern world. Questions about wider applicability, representativeness, and numbers are valid. This is, after all, how ethnographers extrapolate from encounters "in the village" to weave a broader narrative about what it means to be human. Although I do not treat Puerto Rican Muslims' lives as a testing ground for academic debates—and firmly believe their lives are a local story informed by particular people, places, and perspectives—I hope their narratives help us (re)consider much larger issues associated with the late-modern, issues that have global significance. Principally: How is it that we live together in a world where relationships are increasingly defined by generative frictions?

Specific places in Puerto Rico or New Jersey, Florida, and Facebook play an illustrative role in this book, as they anchor my discussion of broader issues relevant to understanding American religion, Latinx and Caribbean cultures, Puerto Ricanness, and global Islam. Just as AmeRícan Muslim stories are embedded in specific spaces and embodied in concrete relational lattices, so too are my ethnographic explorations rooted in particular narratives. Thus, I focus on Puerto Rican converts' everyday experience, but with a view to other settings where their narratives might be illuminating. Though I do comparative work, I emphasize that anything that can be said about being or becoming a Puerto Rican Muslim is informed by these real lives in real times and real places. Thus, using thick description to describe people, events, and spaces in detail serves to remind me and you—writer and reader—how everyday, embodied, and material experiences play a role in shaping our view of the wider world. At the same time, global dynamics have a say in shaping local lives. The dividing lines, then, between the AmeRícan Muslim experience and that of broader Puerto Rican, Muslim, American, and AmeRícan narratives is permeable, even blurry. The task is not merely to apperceive why, what, and how these porous boundaries exist, but to examine their meaning in an age defined by the simultaneity of the global and local in daily life.

One telling piece of evidence of Puerto Rican Muslims' permeable experience is the code-switching and multi-lingualism found throughout this book. The intermingling and (re)mixing of Spanish, Arabic, "Spanglish," and English should not be read as the author's privileged appropriation of phrases and vocalisms, or a racially tinged employment of "mock Spanish." Their use merely reflects the ways my interlocutors conversed with me. Mixing languages was, no doubt, informed by my native English and whiteness. But it was also informed by my conversant knowledge of Spanish and my study of Arabic. I am not a master in either, but neither were many of my respondents. Few were fluent in Arabic or felt comfortable articulating their faith in it. Some commented on the fact that I knew more Arabic than they did. Several interlocutors also spoke little to no Spanish, others little to no English; still others were comfortable in both. Some who could not speak Spanish expressed shame at the fact. Some who spoke only Spanish took pride in not speaking English at any point in our exchange.

For Puerto Rican Muslims, language is a contested and poignant inflection point in broader discussions about being and belonging. Thus, although most of the narrative and quotes in this book are in English, I intersperse Spanish, Arabic, or "Spanglish" at various intervals either a) as it was spoken to me or b) to reflect my interlocutors' multi-lingual heritage and practice. The way this book is written, in other words, reflects the conversations and interviews themselves.

An additional note on foreign-language transliteration: Terms or phrases in Arabic, Spanish, German, and Latin are shown in simplified, transliterated text, using English letters. They may or may not adhere to the strictest translation and/or transliteration standards (my wife, who specializes in teaching Arabic, groans audibly at this), but the simplified forms presented here are meant to reach a wider audience than specialists in particular languages. Please, forgive any apparent errors or oversimplifications.

# Borícua Muslims

# Introduction

## AMERÍCAN MUSLIMS IN A COSMOPOLITAN AGE

we gave birth to a new generation,
AmeRícan salutes all folklores,
european, indian, black, spanish
and anything else compatible

TATO LAVIERA

WALKING DOWN BERGENLINE AVENUE AND crossing 31st Street in Union City, New Jersey, I steal a glance to my left. From that vantage point, I can just make out Midtown Manhattan's gleaming mass through the morning mist. It is a muggy late-May Monday, and I am on my way to meet Imam Wesley Lebrón at Noches de Colombia, a restaurant on Bergenline serving slow-cooked meats and pan–Latin American fare. Making my way on foot, I reflect on how here, just west of the Lincoln Tunnel, with a view to Hell's Kitchen across the Hudson River, the Americas come together with remnants left from previous European, Asian, and Middle Eastern migrations. During the latter half of the twentieth century, Cubans, Puerto Ricans, Mexicans, and Colombians migrated to the Union City area searching for stability and economic opportunity. In some towns in northern Hudson and southeast Bergen counties, between 75 and 90 percent of the people identify as "Latino" or "Hispanic"—their impact so evident that the area is sometimes referred to as "Havana on the Hudson."

This palpable Latinx[1] presence is particularly visible along Bergenline, where Puerto Rican, Mexican, Peruvian, Ecuadorian, and Dominican flags hang proudly in front of *botánicas*, *mercados*, and *restaurantes*. Privately operated hail-and-ride minibuses buzz past pedestrians walking the busy thoroughfare cutting through Union City, transporting the predominately working-class residents to work in La Ciudad. Signage and language are often bilingual or multilingual. The area not only features Latinx migrants but also showcases an undeniable miscellany of migrant communities—Polish, Italian, Greek, Chinese, Syrian, and Pakistani—who arrived, established themselves, and built up diaspora networks over the years, shaping the community and its character since the mid-nineteenth century.[2] In 2018, 58.2 percent of Union City residents identified as foreign-born, more than four times the US average (13.7 percent).

In the midst of the area's heterogeneity and resultant hybridity lies the North Hudson Islamic Education Center (NHIEC). Established in 1992, NHIEC can be found just off Bergenline on the corner of Cottage Place and 47th Street. Located in a landmark building with four towering doric columns making up its façade, the 13,500-square-foot NHIEC has hosted the annual "National Latino Muslim Day" since 2004, bringing together Latinx Muslims from across the New York City metro area and the US for an annual celebration of the community's robust history and diversity.

One morning, a NHIEC board member, Ameer Abuawadeh, showed me around. Dressed in a tailored blue suit and shiny brown shoes, Abuawadeh gave me a tour of the converted bank building, proudly pointing out the mosque's multicultural membership. Of its nearly 2,000 members, Abuawadeh said 500 are Latinx. Abuawadeh also highlighted the various programs the center offers for Latinx community members, including Arabic as a Second Language courses. Moreover, he said, they are raising money through *zakat* and *sadaqah* for relief efforts in Puerto Rico following Hurricane María and earthquakes in Southern Mexico. "We are working with our Muslim brothers and sisters in these places," he said, "and Puerto Rican contacts we know here in New Jersey to raise support and fill containers with food and supplies to send to San Juan." As we headed to the main prayer hall for *jummah* prayers, past streamers and flags from all twenty-one majority Spanish-speaking countries, Abuawadeh told me he will be giving the *khutbah* that day and referencing these relief efforts. He said, "The donations will be going to Muslims and non-Muslims, you know. It's important to remember that Islam is not only for Muslims, Islam is for humankind."

Journalist, activist, and self-described "proud Puerto Rican *muslimah*" Wendy Díaz says the NHIEC acts as a significant node and centrifugal hub in the broader Latinx Muslim landscape. She wrote, "NHIEC is the home to one of the largest Latino Muslim communities in the nation and has been catering to their growing needs by providing simultaneous Friday sermon Spanish interpretations, an annual Hispanic Muslim Day for the past two decades, and continuous educational programs specially geared toward Spanish-speakers and new Muslims of Hispanic heritage." She continued, "NHIEC offers *iftar* events catered by local Latino restaurants, like the Peruvian eatery, Fruit Punch, or the Arab/Hispanic fusion buffet called Fiesta" during Ramadan. Outside of Ramadan, the NHIEC also hosts potlucks, in which converts and lifelong Muslims alike share dishes from their family's heritage.[3] From its location on Bergenline Avenue, the NHIEC joins locales in New Jersey and New York, Texas and Florida, California and Puerto Rico, Pennsylvania and Connecticut, and online (e.g., the "Latino Muslim Facebook Group" or "Boricuas Embraced by Islam") that make up this Latinx Muslim landscape. Together, these sites and spaces form a complex matrix within which Puerto Rican converts[4] to Islam craft notions of being and belonging alongside Muslims of various ethnicities and backgrounds.

Lebrón is one such Puerto Rican Muslim. Dressed in baggy jeans, a red polo shirt, and a blue-white-and-red Puerto Rico baseball cap and sporting a long black beard with a striking strip of scraggly white creeping in, Lebrón is all smiles when he greets me in front of Noches de Colombia. As we step in, the windows are dripping with the day's humidity. After ordering, we take a seat near the kitchen and start discussing his recent comments on "The Deen Show"—a popular YouTube program hosted by Eddie Redzovic. Responding to disparaging comments toward Muslims tweeted by then Miss Puerto Rico, Destiny Vélez, Lebrón said in the video that Ms. Vélez would be welcomed by the Muslim community, but she needed to show more "Borícua pride" and needed a "history lesson" about Islam in Puerto Rico. He said:

> If she is a true Puerto Rican, true to the Puerto Rican pride, and proud of her culture, proud of where she came from, then I would ask her to go back and read about how Puerto Rico came about being the country that it is now after being colonized. We see that our people weren't really a people of Christian faith and Christian belief.

Pushing back on those who frame Puerto Rico as a "Christian nation," Lebrón outlined Muslim contributions to mathematics, science, education, technology, and navigation. He harkened back to Andalusian and Caribbean history, claiming his Puerto Rican family boasted Taíno, African, and Andalusian roots. "My great-grandfather used to speak in a language my family didn't understand," he said. His grandmother mimicked the words to

Lebrón once and he believes they're Arabic. He then talks about thousands of Spanish words with Arabic roots and Puerto Rican culture's entanglement with the Middle East's. Referencing Puerto Rican popular music, Lebrón claimed, "'La Bamba' even has Muslim roots." Looking at the camera, he challenged Miss Puerto Rico to "see how our people are connected to Islam, especially through our Borícua culture."

Finishing our breakfast and continuing our conversation, Lebrón tells me about his personal journey to Islam in the 1990s. He says he meandered his way through "street life" before attending a meeting of the Universal Zulu Nation, an international hip-hop awareness group formed and formerly headed by artist Afrika Bambaataa.[5] As part of their mission to inspire solidarity and "ghetto transformation," many Nation of Islam (NOI) members and Five Percenters (from the Five Percent Nation, or FPN, an NOI break-off often considered heterodox)[6] joined these meetings in the 1980s and 90s. Through contacts in the Zulu Nation, Lebrón initially fell in with Five Percenters and later, with members of an all Latinx, and particularly Puerto Rican, community in El Barrio called Alianza Islámica. He took the *shahadah* in 1998 and by 2001 was studying in Medina, Saudi Arabia. Today, he serves as an imam in the greater New Jersey/New York metro area. Reflecting on his story—and that of many other Puerto Rican Muslims—Lebrón says, "You could call Puerto Rican Muslims the 'original gangstas' of Latino Islam. Literally, we started in gangs and then we started the Latinx Muslim community."

## AMERÍCAN MUSLIMS IN THE LATE-MODERN WORLD

In his poem "AmeRícan," Jesus Abraham "Tato" Laviera richly portrays the positives and protestations of biculturalism, bilingualism, and the broader borderlands experience of Nuyoricans like Lebrón and other Puerto Ricans living in the continental US. Part of their circumstances, Laviera wrote, involves developing the skills, sensibility, and artistic ability to (re)create new identifications and socialities out of the marginalized miscellany that is their intersectional, multiracial, and bifurcated lives. In general, Laviera's poems wrestle with themes like cultural identification, race, language, and the persistent sense of estrangement and precarity that being "AmeRícan" represents. Interwoven throughout his works—of which "AmeRícan" is perhaps prototypical—is the constant feeling of belonging neither *here* nor *there*, in one's country of residence or homeland, in one's adopted sociality or that of their birth. Or, as Puerto Ricans who feel like foreigners wherever they are and who seek a place for themselves like to say, they are "*ni de aquí, ni de allá*." But, as the portion of the poem above emphasizes, Laviera also finds hope in the outworking of this imposed, yet inclusive, inventiveness.[7]

In choosing the title "AmeRícan" to refer to the Puerto Rican Muslims whose stories I share, I invoke Laviera's poem to highlight converts' sense of never feeling *quite* at home and yet drawing on variegated lineages to make peace with their multiple heritages and marginalizations. This sentiment pervaded my encounters with AmeRícan Muslims, who are quadruply minoritized as Muslims among Puerto Ricans, Puerto Ricans among Muslims, and *both* Puerto Ricans *and* Muslims in the shadow of American empire. In other words, this book tells the story of how Puerto Rican converts to Islam navigate diversity and difference and transform their minoritizations into new identifications that are simultaneously local and global, Puerto Rican and Muslim, American and AmeRícan, and somewhere beyond and in between. Although they are marginalized within each community they claim membership in ("ni de aquí, ni de allá"), they also believe, belong, and co-create each of these constituencies to one degree or another ("pero de aquí y allá"). Their feelings of being hidden, betwixt, absorbed, digested, and disparaged alongside those they call family, friends, co-religionists, and neighbors form the core of this book's narrative. But this book is also the story of how they "spit out in malice . . . stand, affirmative in action, to reproduce a broader answer to the marginality" that threatens to "gobble" them up.[8] It is, in short, the story of how AmeRícan Muslims take the "accent from the altercation" through *generative frictions*[9] with Others, reshaping their understanding of what it means to be Puerto Rican, Muslim, and AmeRícan all at the same time.

### *The Latent Challenges of the Late-Modern*

While I focus on Puerto Rican converts, this book is also about the ways in which humans of various identifications navigate diversity and difference in the late-modern world. AmeRícan Muslims are far from alone in not feeling at home while living at, across, or between borders, both literal and figurative, individual and social. The late twentieth and early twenty-first centuries are a time of highly developed, and interconnected, globalized neoliberal capitalist societies and the increasing privatization of life brought on by revolutions in information, communications, and travel technologies along with a general compression of time and space.[10] As geographer Doreen Massey put it, the reality of contemporary life is that things are simultaneously and ceaselessly "speeding up" and "spreading out."[11] The process of modernity and its forces of individualization, urbanization, and secularization only intensified in recent decades—at faster rates and more comprehensively than before. This is not to say we have left this thing called "modernity" behind. Instead, in the late-modern, individualization becomes further stratified according to class and power,[12] unequal and overlapping urbanizations, and more fractured and pluralized secularizations.[13]

The challenges associated with the late-modern are manifold. In this book, I focus on the everyday negotiation of diversity and difference from a position of marginalization. The late-modern is defined by a confluence of the legacies of colonial exploitation, the cross-border processes, patterns, and problems that mark neoliberal capitalist globalization, the growth of massive metroplexes as cosmopolitan hubs, and the networks of communication and travel linking them. As a result, media, money, materials, identities, and ideas flow across the world at frightening speeds and increasingly intersect with, and influence, one another according to the contours of class, power, gender, labor, and seemingly given loyalties of ethno-national belonging.[14] Layers upon layers of peoples, cultures, histories, philosophies, religions, and bodies bump up against one another, come into conflict with each other, or fuse together into new coalitions or combinations as they compete for social, cultural, political, and economic capital.

In other words, in the late-modern era of globalization, even if you wanted to, you cannot escape "the Other." The Other—the person, place, idea, or thing you imagine as *different* than you—is constantly *there*. Or, rather, They are *here*. Whoever "They" are—or, more accurately, whoever we define "Them" to be—they are on our television screens, our social media feeds, in our e-mail inboxes. They are sitting next to us on the airplane, detained at the border, working in our fields, handing us our paychecks, serving us our meals, moving in next door, occupying our media screens, entering our worship spaces. As sociologist Peter Berger, one of the progenitors of the "secularization theory," wrote:

> Modernity is not necessarily secularizing; it is necessarily pluralizing. Modernity is characterized by an increasing plurality, within the same society, of different beliefs, values, and worldviews . . . there are "all these others," not just in a faraway country but right next door.[15]

In effect, if pluralization was a latent process and product of modernity, it is more extensive, fluid, and energetic in the late-modern. It is the pluralization of modernity in flowering bloom. And in modernity's spring, no conceptual, physical, or religious space is immune from the involuntary juxtaposition of, and encounter with, Others. This leads to what sociologist Ulrich Beck called "banal cosmopolitanism": the experience of "globality" embedded in the mundane experiences of everyday life.[16] As a result, our ideas about being and belonging (what a "place" or who our "people" should or could be) are constantly in flux. This is the *process* of cosmopolitanization, wherein we try to navigate the simultaneity of the global and the local in our everyday lives.

### *Cosmopolitanism and Cosmopolitanization*

On both a popular and scholarly level, cosmopolitanism is often presented as a world-embracing moral, political, social, or economic ethic aimed at achieving an equal, pluralistic, and liberal international order, or telos. In recent decades, the principles and postures of cosmopolitanism were revisited, and given the pervasive and intense nature of human interconnection and the moral questions it demands, the concept found reinvigorated relevance. As part of that resurgent attention, cosmopolitanism was theorized in three ways: 1) as an ethical disposition and set of values involving a posture of openness toward other cultures and people from different backgrounds and traditions (or "doctrine of culture and the self" according to political philosopher Samuel Scheffler);[17] 2) as a practical and political platform upon which to build a world order of peace and mutuality among, and between, states and other international actors (or "doctrine of justice");[18] and 3) as a social-science methodology examining the global and the local from a "cosmopolitan" perspective.[19]

While personally committed to cultural cosmopolitanism as a moral and political ethic, it is not my main concern here. Instead, I rely on theorizations of vernacular,[20] critical,[21] or rooted[22] cosmopolitanism; or, as I prefer, processes of cosmopolitanization "from below,"[23] which call into question, interrogate, and redefine our notions of local/global, Us/Them, and cosmopolitan/tribal. Specifically drawing on Beck's notion of "banal cosmopolitanism," I treat cosmopolitanization as a situated social process to be analyzed rather than a moral or political philosophy to be applied or achieved.[24]

### *What of "Muslim Cosmopolitanism?"*

This requires re-orienting our understanding of what constitutes "Muslim cosmopolitanism." For cosmopolitanism to be a useful frame for understanding the assemblages that mark Islamic late modernity, we must move away from moralistic and political idealizations of cosmopolitanism[25] and instead focus on cosmopolitanization as a *social process*.[26] The majority of works on Muslim cosmopolitanism try to find, and make a case for, individuals, institutions, or socialities who exemplify certain characteristics of a perceived cosmopolitan character.[27] In general, as Mara A. Leichtman and Dorothea Schulz wrote, this kind of cosmopolitanism denotes, "a certain outlook on the world, a social and cultural condition, a political project, a political subjectivity, an attitude, and finally, a practice or competence."[28] This "considerable conceptual indeterminacy"[29] means the idea—or *ideal*—of cosmopolitanism is applied in numerous, sometimes quite divergent, ways by sociologists, political scientists, anthropologists, and theologians.[30]

In this book, I follow sociologists[31] and anthropologists[32] who approach cosmopolitanism not as an ideal to be reached, but "a social reality, however distorted, which has to be explored."[33] In particular, I am interested in the social conditions and connections existing for people who are Puerto Rican and who draw on Islamic thought and practice to give voice and verb to their navigation of cosmopolitanization.[34] Doing so offers the opportunity to look at what cosmopolitanization looks like in the negotiated realities of everyday life, as AmeRícan Muslims move back and forth (and forth and back) between the local and the global,[35] weaving together a new form of identification entangled with multiple, networked lineages across time and space.[36]

Thus, I situate the too-often lofty idea(l) of "Muslim cosmopolitanism" in the chaotic, ambiguous, and sometimes unexceptional realities of life "between mosque, school, kitchen, sports club, shopping and fieldwork."[37] In the Puerto Rican context, the Muslim cosmopolitan idea(l) comes to grips with the banal reality that different people coming from different perspectives and different places have varying interests, emphases, histories, desires, and practices.[38] AmeRícan Muslims' way through this world is guided by who they are *and* simultaneously the "Other" people around them. Along the way, the give and take occurring in the intimacies of daily life changes AmeRícan Muslims' stories about themselves, as well as their notions of being, belonging, and becoming.

### *Entre Tu y Yo/Between You and Me*

In addition to treating cosmopolitanization as a social process, I operate on the premise that cosmopolitanism is less defined by a sense of "feeling at home" wherever one goes (or whomever one encounters), but more by feeling increasingly *un*comfortable and out of place in places that feel like, are, or we assume should be "home." In other words, we increasingly feel like strangers in our own lands. Far from being the experience of particular elites or narrated primarily through highly regarded principles and privileged institutions, cosmopolitanization is quite the quotidian concern, expressed in the habitus of manners, tastes, gestures, and relationships, all formed and shaped by local forms of hierarchy and power.[39] Cosmopolitanism in this sense—as a critical dialogue of life involving a polyphony of voices in multicultural, multireligious, multiethnic societies across the world—is the norm, not the exception.

In this book, I look at cosmopolitanization's more ambivalent, and I would say *constitutive*, tensions. As cosmopolitan expressions of being and co-becoming metamorphosize, there is no one-to-one monovalence or reduction of complexity. Instead, the complexities compound, the tensions multiply, and the intersections of identification take on increased uncertainty. AmeRícan Muslims are torn between relating to their current locative associations *and* their increasing interconnectivity with different places and peoples. Moreover, they live in the tension between local rootedness *and* extended, transnational networks of entanglement. In other words, AmeRícan Muslims are drawn back and forth betwixt uniformity *and* diversity. For them, the process of cosmopolitanization is messy, full of tension, and contingent.

Cosmopolitanization also involves both pluralization and particularization. Or, as Kwame Appiah put it in conversation with Thomas Thiemeyer, "the cosmopolitan mixes unfamiliarity and recognition. The cosmopolitan is engaged but always slightly uncomfortable, even at home . . . [and] the cosmopolitan's own world and its surroundings become themselves objects of inquiry and selfhood."[40] By focusing on the material, sociospatial, temporal, and power-related ways in which AmeRícan Muslim lives exist within these tensions, I allow for the complexities of, and interferences within, these ambivalences to shine through.

At the same time, my aim is to make sense of these big, abstract forces by paying attention to the ways they meet and collide in AmeRícan Muslims' everyday lives. By focusing on how Puerto Rican Muslims navigate the process of cosmopolitanization in what Ada María Isasi-Díaz calls *lo cotidiano* (the everydayness of life),[41] I weave theories about globalization in with intimate stories of everyday existence, highlighting firsthand perspectives that give voice to Puerto Rican Muslims' daily navigation of being and belonging in the midst of late-modern diversity and difference. Furthermore, by paying attention to what Anna Tsing called, zones of "awkward engagement" or "cultural friction"[42] in the everyday, I show how cosmopolitanization is a disruptive experience, but one wherein Puerto Rican Muslims take the "accent from the altercation" to produce new, hybrid identifications out of otherwise mundane miscellany and mixture.

***Isn't Cosmopolitanization Just Creolization?***

Though I use the terms cosmopolitanism and cosmopolitanization throughout the book, the terms could also be seen as codes for the Caribbean process of *creolization*—or *post-diaspora hybridity*.[43] According to postcolonial literary theorist Bill Ashcroft, the Caribbean is often imagined as a dysfunctional product of colliding colonial claims and legacies.[44] But in part because of its painful past—as well as the region's persistent, neocolonial present and the ongoing development of underdevelopment in the region[45]—it is also a vibrant example of anti-colonial imagination and possibility. Owing to the diversity of a region with over a thousand islands, twenty-eight countries, several European colonial legacies and spoken languages (e.g., French, English, Spanish, Dutch, Hindi, Mandarin, Creole, patois, etc.), and histories founded on the transatlantic trade in enslaved persons as well as the resultant creolization and hybridity all this produces, the Caribbean has often been at the forefront of innovation in culture, arts, and political thought. One of its most potent capacities is the ability to "future think,"[46] according to Ashcroft. This Caribbean intelligence, Ashcroft writes, allows for "a transformed world reality, a world of constant arrival and potentiality."[47]

Thus it is for AmeRícan Muslims. Marginalized within every community they claim membership in, pushed to the edges by systems, structures, and communities of power they simultaneously rely on, all while remaining (neo)colonial subjects under the umbrella of American empire, Puerto Rican Muslims are embodiments of the essential paradox that is the Caribbean: that they are most Caribbean when they are most *Other*. This is the "certain way" of the Caribbean as formulated by Cuban novelist and cultural critic Antonio Benítez-Rojo, where the shared, colonial "Plantation" experience inscribed in the "Peoples of the Sea" a propensity toward generative frictions with the "confrontations, truces, alliances, derelictions, offensive and defensive strategies, advances and retreats, forms of domination, resistance and coexistence" that define Caribbean life.[48] Rather than producing a disorienting, disjointed, or chaotic sense of self, the experience that is resistance to being made *Other* creates not only an ordering principle for Caribbean culture but also an organizing, life-giving force for Caribbean ways of being and becoming.

Therefore, AmeRícan Muslims' cosmopolitanized identifications and cosmopolitan assemblages can also be seen as reflections of broader Caribbean dynamics and problematics. Though their stories are situated within the particularities of a Hispanophone, American, and Muslim material context thereof,[49] theirs is still essentially a Caribbean cultural and post-diaspora process of being and becoming through inversion and hybridization in late-modern contexts of political and social exclusion. Their creole, cosmopolitan, and hybrid identifications—as Puerto Rican, American, Muslim—are a way of pushing back against the dominance of any one voice, one canon, one mode of thought, one community, one identity, or one history in defining who they are, might be, or might find solidarity with. At the same time, those identifications are the byproduct of the dominating discourses (Puerto Rican, American, Muslim) that simultaneously marginalize them. They reveal those dominant discourses' ambivalence, subvert them based on that uncertainty, and invert them in their (re)identifications. But as Homi K. Bhabha reminds us, the hybridity itself emerges out of the dominant forces at work upon them.[50] Therefore, theirs is a distinctly Caribbean story.

As such, it is also a story for a (post)colonial world defined by the proliferation of diasporas and the experience of globality embedded in the experience of everyday life. Thus, there are lessons for us all in this Caribbean story. In the words of Jamaican-British sociologist Stuart Hall, the more we know and see of the struggles of those on the periphery making "something of the slender resources available to them, the more important we understand the questions and problems of cultural identity to be in that process."[51] In this way, their story, emerging as it does from a Caribbean archipelago and its diaspora, adds what I like to think of as an *archipelagic accent* to broader discussions of cosmopolitanism and cosmopolitanization.[52]

## AMERICAN RELIGION MEETS GLOBAL ISLAM

If this book situates theories of cosmopolitanism and cosmopolitanization within Caribbean registers, it also puts American religion and global Islamic studies into productive conversation, making three interrelated interventions: 1) I contend that further integrating the study of Islam and Muslim communities in Latin America and the Caribbean helps us better appreciate the multivalent and intersecting nature of American religion and the ways in which it is intertwined with issues like race, ethnicity, and politics; 2) emphasizing AmeRícan Muslims' multilocal lives sheds light on the changeability and transregional entanglements of religion in the US and Latinx and Muslim socialities in the Americas; and 3) centering the Americas as one of global Islam's representative sites helps us better grasp how Muslims across the world develop and implement strategies to negotiate diversity and difference through what I call *cosmopolitan assemblage*. The following sections discuss these interrelated interventions in more detail.

### *The Diversity and Fluidity of "American Religion"*

This book presupposes that religious actors are part and parcel of the narrative of the Americas' past, the making of their present, and their emerging future(s).[53] Thus, I situate the story of AmeRícan Muslims within the broader narrative of "American religion," hemispherically speaking. This means I not only place them within past and present dynamics in the US, but also contextualize their narrative as part of dynamics in Latin America, the Caribbean, the Atlantic World, and the transregional dynamics occurring at, across, and between them. Moreover, I treat "religion" as a socially enacted, politically inflected, and mundanely expressed aspect of AmeRícan Muslims' everyday lives. Following anthropologist Samuli Schielke, who posits there is too much "Islam" in the study of Islam,[54] I do not examine religion (or *deen*) as such but analyze it as a category employed by my interlocutors who identify as Muslim. In particular, I am interested in how they employ Islam to navigate the interstices of their multiple marginalizations alongside other markers of identification like "Puerto Rican," "Nuyorican," "American," "Latinx," and "AmeRícan."

In recent decades, the study of "American" religion grew to appreciate a broad diversity of religious cultures and thus challenge dominant narratives about European Christianity's influence in the region. This meant a move beyond standard denominational histories, religious diversity surveys, and other "master narratives"[55] about American religion. It also cleared the way for other stories to be told—those of Africans and African Americans, indigenous peoples, women, Jews, Catholics, Buddhists, Hindus, practitioners of modern Paganism, members of new religious movements, the "spiritual-but-not-religious," and Muslims. Eschewing dominant narratives about Christianity, scholars are now more attuned to how diversity—and all of the debates, power dynamics, and tension that come with it—has long been one of the distinguishing features of American religious life. Telling stories from various geographic and social locations and focusing on themes of contact, borderlands, and exchange,[56] such imaginative scholarship showed how the juxtaposition of religious groups fosters conflict but also creates new mixtures.[57] In other words, de-centering white, European Christianity and de-centering the US in our study of American religion helped produce more nuanced and expansive understandings of the topic than ever before.

It is not coincidental that this scholarly re-engagement emerged coterminously with an increasingly "diverse and extremely fluid"[58] religious landscape in the latter half of the twentieth century. Thanks to the compounding effects of an expanding religious marketplace, urbanization, globalization, multicultural discourses, and individualizaion of religious identifications,[59] the reality of American religion—and our appreciation and apperception of it—shifted significantly. Despite the *longue durée* of religious diversity in the US, the nation underwent a marked, extensive, and intense diversification in religious expressions over the last six decades. Principally, the 1965 Hart-Celler Act opened the way for a wide swathe of newcomers, many from South Asia and Southeast Asia. Even as these newcomers met xenophobic resistance, their physical imprint grew, and they found footholds in business, politics, and wider society. As their networks and infrastructure grew—and Christianity's hegemony waned—mosques, gurdwaras, and temples proliferated, transforming the US's religious landscape and concomitant public discourse around religion and diversity.

Simultaneously, the social realities of, and scholarly attention given to, religion in Latin America and the Caribbean also expanded. This expansion included a recognition of increasing diversity as well as the ways in which transatlantic encounters and hemispheric interactions came to shape religious traditions, socialities, identifications, and practices across the hemisphere. Following the disestablishment of religion in the nineteenth and twentieth centuries came the concomitant "growth" of non-Catholic religions in the region. These traditions were already present, but after disestablishment,[60] the enforcement of orthodoxy was no longer tied directly to the state, and "non-Catholic religions were able to emerge and expand."[61] While the Catholic Church still maintains a place of privilege—remaining "the single most influential force"[62] in Latin American cultures—and the processes of disestablishment vary, Catholicism declined from around 90 percent of the region's population in the mid-twentieth century to only 70 percent by the late 2010s.[63] Social, political, and civil unrest contributed to the rise in pneumatic or spirit-centered Christianity and the "Protestantization" of Latin American religion[64]—including conversion to both Protestantism and Pentecostalism[65] as well as Charismatic Catholicism.[66] These shifts have been concomitantly compounded by a more general, global movement of people, ideas, technologies, finances, and media.[67] Religious streams that "have left traces, transforming peoples and places, the social arena and the natural terrain" are an integral part of these "flows" of globalization.[68] This led to a revolution in religious practice; the emergence of new religious movements; increases in public identification with and practice of alternative Christian devotions, New Age religions, Afro–Latin American and Caribbean traditions like Santería, Candomblé, and Obeah; and affiliations with Buddhist, Hindu, and Islamic traditions.[69]

Although cross-fertilization and creolization have long been features in the region—along with a related desire to impose orthodoxy on such miscellany—the scope and intensity of the region's religious mix have recently been exacerbated at local, national, and hemispheric scales. These juxtaposed processes are occurring against a backdrop of global exchange and movement, which produces tensions between beliefs, systems, symbols, and practices, as well as even more creative recombinations of various religious fragments in everyday experience.[70] They also reflect what ethnographer of religion Kristy Nabhan-Warren wrote is a reality simultaneously marked by skin color, social marginalization, victimization, and empowerment,[71] which contributes to a general, "melancholic condition" that American studies scholar Alissa Schmidt Camacho says plagues migrants and trans-bordered peoples.[72]

### *AmeRícan Religion*

As hinted at in the opening anecdote from Union City, Puerto Rican Muslim narratives emerge out of the confluence of these American histories, flows, and contexts. Theirs is not simply one story or another, but a watersmeet of many—a circulating convergence and swirling braid of diverse encounters and circumstances. Whether within the US urban landscape or in the Caribbean, AmeRícan Muslims can neither imagine nor experience a life of cultural homogeneity.[73] They live, argue, ignore, marry, fight, laugh, collaborate, cohabitate, and commiserate with the social, economic, political, ethnic, and religious "Other"—as well as inhabit that moniker, depending on their social location. Difference is an inescapable fact of their lives. As a result, their identifications and notions of belonging are also shaped by living in places where religious diversity is a fact of life.

Since the colonization of Puerto Rico by Spanish forces in the sixteenth century, the archipelago has been predominately Roman Catholic. However, in the nineteenth century, thanks in large part to an influx of European migrants, and then in the twentieth century, following colonization by the

US beginning in 1898, many non-Catholic denominations arrived in Puerto Rico or came seeking converts, ranging from Seventh-Day Adventists and the Assemblies of God to Lutherans and the Church of Jesus Christ of Latter-day Saints.[74] Today, surveys indicate a majority (56 percent) of Puerto Ricans identify as Catholic and a third as Protestant, with half of the latter identifying as "born-again Christians."[75] According to research by Ennis B. Edmonds and Michelle A. González, nearly a quarter of Puerto Ricans identify as Pentecostal.[76] There is also a robust practice of Afro-Cuban traditions (e.g. Santería or Regla de Ocha, Regla Lucumí, or Lucumí),[77] Espiritismo,[78] or Santerismo (a merging of the two),[79] often in combination with Catholic or Protestant identifications and practices in both the archipelago and in the US.[80] Small numbers of people also associate with traditions like Judaism, Buddhism, or Rastafari.[81] Puerto Ricans in the US generally match prevailing trends in Latinx religious affiliation and practice. Despite increasing numbers of unaffiliated, or "nones,"[82] four in ten Puerto Ricans born in the US (42 percent) identify as Catholic and just under a third as Protestant (30 percent), of which an overwhelming majority (80 percent) identify as born-again.[83] Among island-born Puerto Ricans, however, trends mirror the archipelago, with a majority (53 percent) identifying as Catholic and a third as Protestant, most of whom (62 percent) say they are born-again or evangelical.[84]

Others have focused on the increasing share of Latinx individuals in the US Catholic Church,[85] evangelicals and Pentecostals in the Latinx population,[86] or the general importance of religion *and* race in Puerto Rico's historical trajectory.[87] I focus on Puerto Rican Muslims as a subculture through which we might interrogate and more minutely explore traditional markers of what counts as "American religion" and associated conceptualizations of ethnicity, Puerto Rican subjectivity, or claims to belonging and citizenship. Recognizing that there are whole aspects of the American experience not yet in books but shared and told through legacy and individual lives, I provide a case-specific analysis from a "relatively unfamiliar Caribbean and diasporic culture"[88] to continue to reframe the "shifting relation between Muslim identities and ethnicity"[89] and "de-naturalize or de-essentialize"[90] notions of American religion and its racialized norms. Furthermore, I focus on more mundane and material aspects of my interlocutors' identifications and processes of co-becoming, showing how they are intolerant to the erasures of their history, adopting and adapting a more supple set of identifications in response to everyday conundrums, ostracisms, and questions of belonging.

### *Latinx Muslim Flows*

The Latinx Muslim community has a long and robust history stretching back to at least the 1920s.[91] More recently, significant growth occurred in US urban spaces like New York City and Newark in the 1970s and 80s or across the US through media-rich Latinx-specific outreach efforts in the 1990s and in the age of new media in the shadow of 9/11.[92] Subsequently, scholars have examined the origins, narratives, and significance of the Latinx Muslim community in the US, investigating aspects of gender,[93] race and "connected histories,"[94] law and policing,[95] immigration and transnationalism,[96] and media.[97] Chief among them is Harold Morales, who in his introductory text on Latinx Muslims in America, firmly places the emergence, consolidation, and growth of this sociality firmly within the diverse and fluid American religious landscape described in the previous section.

In particular, several researchers did well to situate Latinx Muslims within a wider nexus of Black and Asian Muslim communities in the US, an anti-imperial idiom among marginalized urban minority youth, prison and gang populations, and as a "new American minority" emerging within broader conceptions and discussions of race and ethnicity in the US.[98] Others told the story of Latinx Muslim *reversion* as part of a wider narrative of conversion(s) in the West or as part of the stream of (im)migrant religion in the US.[99] Still others mapped the landscape of the Latinx Muslim sociality, touching on its historical development, ethnic makeup, socioeconomic composition, and, most notably, motivations for conversion from the narratives of Latinx Muslims themselves.[100] The majority of attention is given to "conversion causeways"—the ways in which converts discovered Islam and decided to convert, situated within their spiritual, social, and societal contexts—though several researchers in the field feel such analysis is overdone and under-theorized.[101] Overall, the above research helps provide a textured picture of the Latinx Muslim population and their search for an authentic Islamidad—an identification that mutually reinforces both their Latinx and Muslim identities.[102]

The research also reveals how, along with other Latinx Muslims, Puerto Rican reverts seek to become more fully themselves—in all their hyphenated complexity—through various affective and practical means. In other words, "to make sense of their decision [to convert] and their condition of being in-between,"[103] AmeRícan Muslims actualize their hyphenated identifications in routine, intimate, everyday practices of cultural and religious belonging and co-becoming. As anthropologist Omar Ramadan-Santiago argued, they "make use of music, art (movement and visual), language, culture, religious doctrine, and self-education to rewrite their histories and create for themselves new identities that challenge existing stereotypes they refuse to fit."[104] This, in turn, further reveals "ethnic and religious categories to be fluid sites of contestation"[105] and helps scholars further critique "popular assumptions about race, religion, and ethnicity" or "the fixed nature of identity" as a whole.[106]

Making up almost a quarter of the Latinx Muslim population in the US (22 percent),[107] Puerto Rican Muslims play a significant role in developing and sustaining a broader Latinx Muslim sociality and sentiment—both on the Puerto Rican archipelago and in the diaspora. And yet, Puerto Rican specific aspects of this Islamidad can potentially get lost in broader treatments of the Latinx Muslim community. This book provides more nuance, texture, and transregional perspective to our understanding of Latinx Islamidad by illustrating how such a sensibility and self-perception take shape in specific, material, and embodied practices across, at, and between ethnic, racial, religious, and national boundaries.

### *De-centering Islam in the Americas*

This also helps tell a different kind of story about Islam and Muslims in the Americas and around the globe. Aliyah Khan, in her literary study of the significance, influence, and changeability of Muslims in the Anglophone Caribbean, argued we must do more to de-center the US in the study of American Muslim communities.[108] Alongside efforts by numerous other scholars,[109] she cited the need to expand our inquiry into stories of Islam and Muslims throughout the region. The promise being that when we dive into the details of any particular narrative, what results is a range of intimacies and complexities hitherto unseen or underappreciated. One of the places she recommended beyond the scope of her research in the Anglophone Caribbean as "ripe for more inquiry" was the Hispanophone Caribbean, including "Puerto Rico, the Dominican Republic, Cuba, Haiti, and other countries in the Caribbean—and continental Latin America."[110]

Such a suggestion makes sense, as Puerto Rico maintains "a peculiar status among Latin American and Caribbean countries" due to its simultaneous existence between, within, and beyond multiple states, orders, regions, and areas.[111] On the one hand, it is a US colonial territory that "belongs to but is not part of the United States." In fact, the US Supreme Court described Puerto Rico as "foreign to the United States in a domestic sense" in 1901. On the other hand—and although US culture pervades the archipelago (e.g., fast food and drugstore chains, Protestant and Pentecostal churches, the use of English)—Puerto Rico remains a distinctly Spanish-speaking, Afro-Hispanic-Caribbean nation situated within Latin American and Caribbean racial, religious, economic, and social politics.

Moreover, as a "nation on the move" via (im)migration, cultural imagination, colonization, and social contact, Puerto Rico "ethnically and ethically extends"[112] into other locales, including Spain, West and North Africa, the wider Caribbean, Latin America, and the US. Historically, Puerto Rico is imbricated in a broader "Atlantic World" that includes indigenous Taínos, the Spanish, other Europeans, and Africans. In more recent years, immigration and emigration brought dispersed Puerto Ricans across the US (and elsewhere) into contact with other populations, creating new solidarities and tensions. Puerto Rico also sees its own share of migrants who transverse the "liquid borders"[113] of the Caribbean, challenging the region's "paradise" trope as well as tripartite notions of "Puerto Rican identity" by including their own agency, creativity, resilience, self-determination, and stories of mobility as part of the nation's cultural narrative (this includes Dominican, Haitian, Chinese, Arab, and other migrant populations on the archipelago).[114] As Puerto Rican scholar Jorge Duany wrote, growing diversity on the archipelago and in the diaspora challenge "the idea that the nation can be defined as a singular territory, birthplace, citizenship, language, culture, and identity."[115] These debates about what it means to be American, to be Puerto Rican, or to be religious in such contexts are reflected (and inflected) in the AmeRícan Muslim experience.

Thus, this book heeds Khan's call to expand inquiry in the Hispanophone Caribbean and its diaspora. As a result, what it means to be an "American Muslim," or for that matter a "Latinx Muslim in the US," is reimagined and re-situated.[116] Bringing more networked frames to the study of Latinx Muslims and their connections with other Muslims in the hemisphere, we can better understand how this community is not constituted solely by individuals, organizations, and concentrations in the continental US. Instead, the community is co-produced through a range of cosmopolitan entanglements, connections, and interactions with people, institutions, and material cultures spread across places such as Puerto Rico, Mexico, Trinidad, or in broader networks across the "Muslim Atlantic."[117]

### *De-centering Global Islam*

Even with the rise of "global Islam," the study of regions and populations beyond the Middle East and North Africa remains underrepresented. As historian Scott S. Reese noted, the academy long "emphasized the dominance of the so-called Arabo-Persian 'Islamicate' center" to the neglect of other communities beyond the scope of this narrow geocultural focus.[118] Despite the many and various attempts by scholars to expand our understanding, a paradox still lies at the heart of the study of global Islam, with the preponderance of research still geared toward a fairly narrow geography. If the coherence of "the world of Islam is essentially ideological, a discursive representation,"[119] then that representation continues to skew toward a narrative where the key dramas, actors, ideas, rituals, and impetus come from a MENA core and then disseminate outward through various networks and technologies of globalization. The reality, as I and others suggest, is much more complex, intersectional, and multinodal. Thus, there remains a pertinent need to further—and farther—*globalize* the study of global Islam.[120]

In this book, I tell a different story about global Islam *through* the Americas, centering the hemisphere as a representative site wherein to study currents in global Islam as a whole. I focus on AmeRícan Muslims' everyday lives to help us better grasp how Muslims in the late-modern world develop and implement strategies to negotiate diversity and difference both *among* Muslims and *between* Muslims and non-Muslims. It is a case-specific analysis of how global Islam's difference and multiplicity take shape across territorial, ethnic, racial, and intradenominational boundaries. Specifically, it offers a perspective on how Islamic late modernity exists not despite transregional discourses and encounters but is constituted by such flows and counterflows.

Beyond its analytical weaknesses, there are serious intellectual, social, and political dangers to delimiting the area of the so-called "Muslim world" to restricted geographies and particular mappings. Not only do these constructions belie colonial designs and potential platforms for political denigration, but they also ignore vast swathes of Islamic history and influence across the world. In particular, scholars researching on the so-called "periphery" or "edges" of the Islamicate world found such models fail to address the complex and networked ways in which Muslims themselves understand and live their lives. This range of scholarship challenges the politics of area-ization[121] and the "politically-informed-defining and 'scaling' of localities, ethnicities, languages, religions, and cultures"[122] that long dominated Islamic studies. Pushing back against the "gridded landscapes" we use to imagine global Islam, this scholarship instead emphasizes transregional networks,[123] rhizomes,[124] assemblages,[125] intertwined spaces,[126] "frictive intertwining," "dialogic interdependence,"[127] and processes of cosmopolitanization[128] in places like Europe and Asia, sub-Saharan Africa and Oceania, Latin America and the Caribbean. These works help "render a deeper and more encompassing view of what Islam is and what Muslims do by centering those who occupy the geographic, pedagogical, social, political, queered, embodied, reproductive, and doctrinal margins of the world of Islam."[129]

Embracing the margins in the study of global Islam brings various benefits. Foremost, it allows us to move the focus of Islamic studies away from specific theological discourses, political visions, institutions, cultures, or geographies to better acknowledge and analyze a multitude of actors and socialities, as well as their interconnected perspectives and practices across contexts and boundaries of different kinds and degree.[130] By moving away from center-periphery models, we better see and study the lateral networks, ill-fitting incidents, and unexceptional encounters—such as those of AmeRícan Muslims—than our previously established frameworks and rubrics of study allow.[131] In other words, taking a broader view allows us to consider "Islamic that which was previously not seen as such"[132] and understand late-modern Muslim life "through the complex interactions of globalization."[133]

### *Cosmopolitan Assemblages*

In particular, I suggest AmeRícan Muslims provide a ripe opportunity to (re)consider Islamic modernity through *cosmopolitan assemblage*. As introduced by Gilles Deleuze and Félix Guattari, the notion of *agencement*—or assemblage—refers to a "collection of things which have been gathered or assembled."[134] Theories of assemblage treat social complexity, identification, and bodies as flexible, fluid, and volatile. They also help us analyze the reconfigurations of identification vis-à-vis global forces.[135] In the late-modern, identification is a highly mobile, de-centered, fragmentary process of piecing together dispersed, intermingled, and multiple aspects of being and belonging scattered across fields of governance, class, art, digital technology, gender, mass media, race, and religion.[136] Furthermore, given Puerto Rico's colonial status and Caribbean location, it is a locus of global encounter and displacement. On the archipelago and in the diaspora, Puerto Ricans' story is an assemblage of overlapping colonial histories and resistance, marginalization and survival. Thus, I find it helpful to think through the lens of assemblage to consider how AmeRícan Muslims engage in mobile, transient, and fragmentary processes of identification.[137] Simultaneously moving back and forth between the global and the local, they challenge fixed notions of similarity and difference, defy the boundaries often placed on them, resist assimilation, and celebrate their roots even as they create new relations.

By looking at these processes in quotidian detail, I believe we come to a better appreciation of the capaciousness of Muslim being and co-becoming in late modernity.[138] Working with the daily debris of AmeRícan Muslim lives creates space to think both intimately and empirically about each in fresh ways. Grabbing at those pieces of AmeRícan Muslim lives that are sidelined or deemed to hold less value helps us make better sense of the co-constitutive connections and contrasting contexts making up late-modern Islam. Whether they be geographic, ethnic, or ideological, it also helps us test these connections' progeny, their endurance, and their makeup.[139] The result is that Islamic late modernity is no longer viewed as a contained, monolithic whole but as an ongoing process and expansive network of bodies, socialities, and traditions that is messy, unstable, and full of "divergent affective tendencies."[140]

Thus, I analyze how AmeRícan Muslims craft *cosmopolitan assemblages* out of the flotsam and jetsam available to them from their position on the margins of each sociality they claim membership in. This process involves their (re)creative use of historical lineages inherited from across time and place (chapter 1); remixing normative notions of Puerto Ricanness through material and affective encounters with family, language, architecture, and food (chapter 2); swimming in multiple streams of global Islam as part of an *ummah en vaivén* (chapter 3); navigating generative frictions with other Muslims, which fosters a sense of "fighting togetherness" among Puerto Rican converts I call *asaBorícua* (chapter 4); or contesting the politically inflected realities of American empire (chapter 5) to form new imaginaries and practices of being and belonging that are Puerto Rican, Latinx, AmeRícan, and Muslim all at the same time. Together, these assemblages not only undermine Western colonial notions of what cosmopolitanism is, or could be, but also reimagine and reposition marginalized Muslims as fellow cosmopolitans coming to terms, and struggling, with the daily challenges of diversity and difference in the late-modern.

## A MORE-OR-LESS *MOFONGO* METHODOLOGY

I first learned how to make *mofongo* with Juana in Urbanización Roosevelt, a neighborhood in Hato Rey, in 2015. One of the more widely known and celebrated Puerto Rican dishes, mofongo is made by smashing fried green plantains with a *pilón* (mortar and pestle), mixing in garlic, olive oil, fat or butter, and chicharrón (fried pork skin).[141] Often formed into a bowl or mound and topped with meat, vegetables, and garlic sauce, historian Cruz Miguel Ortíz Cuadra explained how mofongo's origins lie with the Angolans forcibly captured, enslaved, and brought to Puerto Rico in the 1500s. It is possible the word mofongo itself stems from the Angolan Kikongo term *mfwenge-mfwenge*, meaning "a great amount of anything at all."[142] In looking for a metaphor for my decidedly ethnographic—yet mixed—approach to understanding AmeRícan Muslims' lived realities, I often return to that cooking lesson with Juana. As she taught me how to mash my way to a passable mofongo, she repeatedly emphasized the importance of a dense, consistent mixture.

Although ethnographic, I drew on a variety of experiences, inputs, techniques, and sources during the course of my research and writing. This involved a "back-and-forth" methodology involving numerous trips to multiple fields of research (New York/New Jersey, Puerto Rico, Texas) as well as multiyear engagement with Puerto Rican Muslims where I was based in Gainesville, Florida. It also involved ongoing digital engagement and correspondence. Beyond conversing with individuals and institutions, I also consulted art, literature, history, material culture, and poetry to help elucidate some of the experiences Puerto Rican Muslims shared with me or some of the encounters I had "in the field." I also relied on my work as a journalist, not only employing journalistic methods as part of my ethnographic practice,[143] but also publishing popular pieces from Puerto Rico and New York, which solicited additional feedback from the community itself.[144] These "non"-ethnographic elements of research helped create more contextual knowledge and encourage slower thinking than so-called "traditional" fieldwork. In what follows, I describe this mofongo-like methodology,[145] discussing my tendencies to reach for a great amount of anything at all and to mix and compound my way toward a more-or-less consistent representation of the Puerto Rican Muslim experience.

### *No soy musulmán*

It is difficult to determine exactly when my research began—or, for that matter, if it has ended.[146] All the same, spending time among Puerto Rican reverts as a California-born, non-Muslim, and non–Puerto Rican researcher with a white, middle-class background brought a particular generative friction to my ethnography. For good reason, I was asked several times by interlocutors why it was I was doing this research. Given Puerto Ricans' historical oppression, and observation, by colonial authorities[147] and the documented infiltration and surveillance of Muslim communities in the US,[148] multiple individuals inquired about who I was, what I was doing, and why I was interested in spending time with Puerto Rican Muslims in their homes, mosques, schools, social media pages, and neighborhoods.

One such individual was Khadijah. An activist, artist, and documentary filmmaker in Newark, New Jersey, Khadijah is a Puerto Rican revert and the mother of a son killed by gang violence. My first conversation with her took place in the back of a quiet café in downtown Newark, near Rutgers University. In the café, she sat across from me with a mug clutched in her hands. She radiated energy, wrapped in layers of vibrant, colorful clothing. Setting her coffee cup down, she looked me directly in the eyes and said:

> My husband said about you, "Oh, he's probably just another crazy missionary trying to convert us." And I said, "Ok, let's see who this crazy person is." And then we read your work for hours. I'm grateful that you're here, to interview me, to talk to us, to help tell our story. That way, they can know we are just like anybody else, it just happens that we speak Spanish and we are Muslim.

Khadijah's exchange with me—an individual made legible to my interlocutors as a journalist, ethnographer, and Lutheran—was marked by an array of intersecting identifications and experiences. While our encounter was one where my work opened up a conversation, there was the latent possibility my identifications, vocations, and associations could harm Khadijah, stall or stop the conversation, or cause some other insurmountable issue in the neighborhood where she lives, works, and prays. And yet, what she found out about me through her preliminary googling was an individual in pursuit of understanding and mutual exchange in a world of diversity and difference.[149]

Such conversations required interrogating the wants, needs, interests, and scripts of influences bringing me to this research. As I often told those who asked, I think this journey started when I was growing up in the Los Angeles metroplex. Much to my mother's chagrin, my family relocated from a quaint bedroom community in the San Francisco Bay Area to the seemingly chaotic mass of California's "big city" when I was eight years old. I became shaped by LA's multiethnic reality and the tensions and hybrid creations it produced, from the unrest around the Rodney King trial to the creative cultural productions of the city's "bohemians" and "Baja

California *fronterizos*" and "borderlanders."[150] In particular, I was touched by the metropolis's religious miscellany, vividly experiencing it within my own social networks. In high school, my friends identified as Iranian and Italian, Korean and French, Swedish and Mexican. They were evangelical and Catholic, Wiccan and Buddhist, agnostic and Jewish, Mormon and Muslim. Raised in an evangelical Lutheran household with tenuous connections to a mixed-European heritage, I had the opportunity to learn about religious and cultural traditions other than my own through relational networks and everyday interactions with my friends and neighbors.

In the course of my studies, I continued to encounter and engage with traditions, rituals, and teachings other than the ones I was habituated in. I wrote about my experiences, first on a travel blog and then later as a religion reporter. During an assignment for the *Houston Chronicle* at Masjid At-Taqwa in Sugar Land, Texas, in 2012, I met Imam Isa Parada. It was a chance meeting that changed the course of my life and career. At first, I profiled Isa for the paper.[151] Growing up in New York and Houston with Salvadoran roots, Isa was an altar boy and active Catholic before reverting to Islam in 1996. When I met him, he was involved with an organization called IslamInSpanish, which later birthed Centro Islámico—a Latinx-specific masjid in Houston—in January 2016. Isa was the first Latinx Muslim I met. He was far from the last. After my profile appeared, I decided to make Latinx Muslim conversion pathways the subject of my master's thesis, which I was working on at the time.

It was while researching alongside Latinx Muslims in the US that I first came to appreciate the distinct and significant role Puerto Ricans played among them. My introduction to Puerto Rican Muslims came in 2013 via Imam Daniel Abdullah Hernandez. At the time, Danny was imam and director of religious affairs at the Pearland Islamic Center, a suburban masjid overseen by the Islamic Society of Greater Houston (ISGH). Born and raised in the aforementioned Union City, New Jersey, area, Danny identified as a "Puerto Rican American Muslim" and invited me to dip my toes into the AmeRícan Muslim world by visiting his masjid. There, I sat at his feet as he told stories of trying to build an outreach center in Moca, Puerto Rico, or how Puerto Ricans formed a core of both the earliest Latinx Muslim organizations (e.g., Bani Saqr and Alianza Islámica) and more contemporary organizations like the Latino American Dawah Organization (LADO) and IslamInSpanish. After my visits, Danny introduced me to people who helped me further listen to, and learn from, a broader AmeRícan Muslim network across the US and Puerto Rico.

***No soy Borícua***

If there were questions about why I, as a non-Muslim, was doing research in mosques and Islamic centers, there were also skeptical inquiries regarding my ethnic and national identifications. As intimated above, the colonial relationship between the US and Puerto Rico—and the concomitant abuse and betrayal of trust by US academics and researchers who investigated, studied, and researched Puerto Ricans in support of the colonial cause—gave some interlocutors pause when I reached out. Rightly so. Despite my best intentions and reliance on ethnographic best practices, I humbly recognize my contact with Puerto Rican Muslims and Puerto Rican "culture" is mediated, collateral, and contingent. It is also affected by inequalities in power and knowledge. Nonetheless, I sought throughout my research to listen deeply and engage in nonexploitative learning.[152] I tried to see how the world looked, felt, and acted according to the Puerto Ricans[153] who became more than interlocutors, but instructors and friends. Throughout, I sought to protect their agency and wellbeing by defaulting to the narrative nonfiction norm of using first names (stating full names when I reference public work or when explicit permission was given to me), seeking out gatekeepers to enter particular communities (especially online), as well as making myself and my intentions known at every stage of research.[154]

Even so, Puerto Rican readers deserve to know more about my positionality vis-à-vis the archipelago, its inhabitants, and the diaspora. Puerto Rico first came onto my radar in 2004, when I watched Carlos Arroyo and the "basketball warriors" of *Borikén* pick apart the US "Dream Team" in an act of athletic defiance.[155] It was then that I started to learn about Puerto Rico's status as an *estado libre asociado* ("free associated state") and its place within the wider American empire. Although I did not revisit Puerto Rico's status in serious detail until a decade later, I came back to the subject having lived and worked in New Zealand and South Africa, where I was apprenticed in the critical importance of decolonial thought and the multiple manifestations and entanglements of imperial power.

With these lenses in place, I leaned into an array of literature, resources, and educational experiences to better apperceive the Puerto Rican milieu. This process involved engaging deeply with a wide array of literature, from histories written by the likes of Fernando Pico, Christina Duffy Burnett and Burke Marshall, José Trías Monge, and Laura Briggs to poetry, theater, music, and narrative art (including Tato Laviera, Bad Bunny, Pedro Pietri, Calle 13, Rosario Ferré, René Marqués, and Quiara Alegría Hudes). I also turned to the immense resources, collections, and archives of institutions, museums, and colleagues at Centro de Estudios Puertorriqueños at Hunter College New York, Museo del Barrio in East Harlem, el Centro de Estudios Avanzados de Puerto Rico y el Caribe in San Juan, Universidad de Puerto Rico Río Piedras, and Museo de Arte de Ponce. These encounters and experiences were not only informative but also formative in my development as a researcher.

It must also be said that my research occurred against a dramatic backdrop of immense challenges and momentous changes in Puerto Rico and its diasporas, including the declaration of bankruptcy by the island's government, an ensuing financial crisis, and creation of the colonial Puerto Rico Oversight Management and Economic Stability Act (PROMESA) in 2015 and 2016; the Pulse Nightclub shooting in Orlando in June 2016; student strikes, demonstrations, and occupations of Universidad de Puerto Rico campuses in 2017; death and destruction from Hurricanes Irma and María in 2017 and the mismanagement of their respective responses; a renewed US-public interest in Puerto Rican culture and people through popular media like Luis Fonsi's "Despacito" and the work of Lin Manuel Miranda; scandal and ensuing protests bringing an end to Governor Ricardo Rosselló's tenure in 2019 (*la revolución más corta*); a series of earthquakes in 2019 and 2020; the continuing degradation and collapse of the archipelago's infrastructure; the COVID-19 pandemic; and ongoing debates and discussion around gentrification, neocolonialism, and the complicated and contested issues involving housing markets, tax incentives, vacation rentals, and economic development on the archipelago.

Throughout these historic events, which punctuated and shaped my fieldwork, I sought to humbly listen and learn, to reflect *with* and not *on* my interlocutors, and come to conclusions that not only contribute to multiple publics' understanding of an underappreciated sociality but also resonate with their experience and lived reality. I wrestled with the relationships formed, the dynamics of power shaping our conversations, and the resultant impact such forces had on this book.[156] In the end, this is my attempt to "speak in such a way that [I] will be taken seriously by" Puerto Rican Muslims.[157] I hope my consistent, compassionate-yet-critical presence gives my writing authenticity and makes my conclusions ring true to their experience.

Nevertheless, this book still privileges my own interpretation of the material, rather than the perspectives of Puerto Rican Muslims or the material itself. I cannot claim to *represent* Puerto Ricans or Muslims. As an outsider, my descriptions are neither neutral nor objective, but rather conditioned by my social positions, perspectives, and privileges. Along the way, I made choices about what practices and materials to focus on and which to ignore. In book form, my interlocutors will not always agree with my choices. These were not only theoretical and methodological considerations but also political ones—weighted with the reality of American empire and my embodied presence of seeing and being in the field. Our interactions were not neutral. They were not always smooth or "professional." Instead, they were performative, and I made missteps and mistakes. I share some of these in the following pages to be honest about what Elaine A. Peña calls ethnographic fieldwork's "pitfalls and possibilities."[158]

## Quesitos, Mezquitas, *and a Mosaic of AmeRícan Muslim Experience*

Given Puerto Ricans' geographic dispersion, I drew on the example of other ethnographies that adopted multilocal, multisited, or traveling approaches to go beyond studying people in only one place to instead trace their connections, associations, and relationships across space.[159] Thus, I interviewed, interacted with, and observed Puerto Rican Muslims in New York, New Jersey, Florida, Puerto Rico, Texas, and online, simultaneously recognizing and analyzing the networks connecting them as well as the distances separating them. This meant my fieldwork consisted of spending time in places where Puerto Rican Muslims are located in higher concentrations (San Juan, New York City, Orlando, Newark, Bayamón, Miami, or Vega Alta), where I sought to understand their relational dynamics alongside, and in interaction with, other socialities of interest (Houston, Jayuya, Gainesville, Aguadilla, Tampa, or Mayagüez), and in the context of the "chains, paths, threads, conjunctions, or juxtapositions" existing between them.[160] The advantage of a multisited approach allowed for the analysis to better trace and elucidate the complexity of cosmopolitanized lives. Specifically, I believe it helps us better understand AmeRícan Muslims within the broader context of Puerto Rico and its diasporas, the transnational *ummah*, and the overlapping, entangled webs of American empire.

The stories and experiences shared in this book are the product of 111 semistructured, relational interviews as well as innumerable hours of participation and observation conducted in Texas in 2014, Puerto Rico in 2015, 2017, and 2018, New York/New Jersey in 2016 and 2017, Florida between 2015 and 2019, along with concomitant digital ethnography from 2014 to 2018, and subsequent follow-up interviews online from 2019 to 2021, during the midst of the COVID-19 pandemic.[161] Furthermore, I collaborated on a mini-documentary on AmeRícan Muslims with filmmaker

Khadijah Taylor in early 2022[162] and with others on two special publications in 2023 and 2024.[163]

Altogether, I introduce readers to fifty-two interlocutors whose stories reflect the diverse, diasporic, on-the-move, and transregional nature of AmeRícan Muslim lives. Participant observation, informal conversations, and interviews took place in various contexts: in local *mezquitas* and community centers (e.g., MAS Queens, Masjid Alfaruq in Vega Alta, or the Islamic Center of Gainesville); "going along"[164] with interlocutors and walking the city streets in search of vestiges of Andalusian architectural influence, chowing down on *pasteles* and *tripletas* at dinner tables and diners, and sitting cross-legged in quiet spaces set apart for private prayer or devotion; at significant festivals and celebrations (e.g., Eid al-Fitr in San Juan, the Fiesta de Santiago Apóstol in Loíza Aldea, or National Latino Muslim Day in Union City); or via digital discussions about how to convert popular Puerto Rican recipes into permissible products for consumption. In each context, I not only observed but also participated via dance, conversation, cooking, inside jokes, uncomfortable silences, unreturned text messages, long phone calls, and other normal activities of human interaction. I spent time with the people featured in this book in their homes and neighborhoods, aided in ritual and nonritual contexts, pitched in to put out plates and prayer rugs, played with interlocutors' kids, all while engaging in conversation in English and Spanish laced with occasional *inshallahs* and *mashallahs*.

Because I got to know many of my interlocutors relationally and over shared meals, I opted for more informal conversations or lightly structured interviews in most cases, believing this would reap more fruitful results. Thus, whether it was a *cafecito* and *quesito* in Fort Lauderdale, a midday mofongo in Isla Verde, falling asleep on someone's couch after eating a slice of pie in Staten Island, or snarfing down home-cooked *picadillo* in Ponce, I found myself learning from my interlocutors not only through what they were telling me but also through what we were doing together, what we were preparing, who we were doing it with (or not), and how we were engaging with the food in front of us, the people around us, or the place we were in.[165] While I was frequently invited into interlocutors' homes, I also had the honor of inviting them into my own in Gainesville, Florida, where we experienced firsthand the navigation of relationships across boundaries. For example, I remember quite well when one interlocutor went to pray *maghrib* while I was doing dishes only to come back into the room with a concerned look on his face. While he said he appreciated the Qur'an and prayer mat (*sajjāda*) I provided, he wondered if I might remove the statue on my bookshelf before he prayed. It was, it turned out, a representation of Shiva given to me as a gift in Houston. Shiva was put in another room, he prayed, and we continued our conversation into the wee hours of the morning over a fire in the backyard, frogs chirping in the background all night long.

My reflections on being and belonging, religion and cultural identification, minoritization and empire, assemblage and adaptivity flow from these relational interviews and the narratives shared with me. Theirs are relatively small stories from marginalized places, told by people who may appear to be minor actors in the major dramas of the late-modern. But, I argue, their stories matter as we consider the cosmopolitan processes at work in our world. In fact, they make them come alive in textured detail. As both a journalist and ethnographer, I hope this book reflects their experience and my maxim that the best stories make a good argument, and the best arguments tell a good story.

With that maxim in mind, I present a kaleidoscope of vignettes from AmeRícan Muslim lives, rather than a panoramic perspective of a certain whole. And though this book remains decidedly ethnographic, I chose to present many of these stories in a more journalistic fashion. This is not coincidental. By default (as a working journalist) and design (as a form of "ethnographic journalism"),[166] I used this approach to vividly evoke the lived experience of a sociality lacking centralized institutions, established authorities, or a critical mass in any particular place. At times, I also found a journalistic writing style better delivered the narrative force I was looking for. Influenced by my reporting background, I also sought to verify and fact-check an individual's stories as much as possible. Knowing there was going to be slippage in some of their stories, I shared a number of dubious claims anyway (noting them as such along the way). The end result is a mosaiclike image of the AmeRícan Muslim experience. Together, these discrete, fragmented glimpses summon the colorful, variegated, cosmopolitan atmosphere of their existence and present a cohesive, if not comprehensive, impression of their overall experience. If individual narratives become collective memories when entered into an archive, then may this book be an archive of AmeRícan Muslim experience.

### *Whither the Digital Field?*

My direct participation and involvement in the relationships of difference that largely define AmeRícan Muslims' lived experience also occurred in the digital "hypertext."[167] Because of their vast geographic dispersion, AmeRícan Muslims frequently find, connect, and interact with one another online.

Though there is no Puerto Rican masjid in the Bronx or majority Puerto Rican mezquita in Puerto Rico, there were Facebook pages like "Puerto Rican Muslims" (ca. 1,800 members at the time of writing) and "Boricuas Embraced by Islam" (ca. 780 members).[168] Such pages act as significant connective tissues, tying together a geographically scattered Puerto Rican Muslim sociality from New York to Puerto Rico, Texas to Florida, Saudi Arabia to Sweden, and places beyond and in between.

In fact, there was one poignant moment when I was talking to an interlocutor in Newark, and we were discussing a mutual friend and some of the interreligious work she does in Puerto Rico. I talked about celebrating Eid al-Fitr with her family and the good times we shared eating *pinchos* (meat skewers) under the palm trees dotting the shoreline of the Piñones lagoon in Loíza Aldea. As we got into an elevator to leave the interlocutor's office and grab a coffee down the street, she said to me, "It's so cool that you got to meet her." I cocked my head at this comment and asked incredulously, "You *haven't* met her? You seem to know her so well!" To which the interlocutor replied, "No, I only know her online." Her confessing she had no "onground"[169] contact with another interlocutor whom she felt she knew deeply underscored for me the importance of online spaces, interactions, and culture in the formation of AmeRícan Muslim peoplehood.[170]

Viewing digital spaces as another "ethnographic place"[171] like a mosque or a street festival, I did not treat digital ethnography as a method in and of itself, but as a way to expand the field of research by applying the various tools of ethnography in a digital context. Agreeing with Christine Hine that "[w]hatever it is that people do, an ethnographer would generally want to be observing them doing it, and wherever possible doing it with them"[172] I took the perspectives, postures, and practices of ethnography into the digital realm, substituting the discernment between "winks and twitches" for one between "likes and emojis."[173] Appreciating the "blurred boundaries"[174] between on/offline lives, I paid attention to the fluidity and interplay of "place, movement, and sociality" in the "messy web."[175] I approached the digital spaces where Puerto Rican Muslims frequented as embedded, embodied, and everyday aspects of their lives[176] and participated accordingly—liking, commenting, sharing, recording notes, archiving, coding, and analyzing what I came across through my digital fieldwork. In the end, my digital ethnographic methods reflected my general approach to this research, looking to "a great amount of anything at all" to make sense of being and belonging among AmeRícan Muslims in a context of diversity and difference.

# 1
# *Coyunturas* and Contingent Lineages
## ARCHIVES OF AMERÍCAN MUSLIM MEMORY

> The great force of history comes from the fact that we carry it within us, are unconsciously controlled by it in many ways, and history is literally present in all that we do. . . . [I]t is to history that we owe our frames of reference, our identities, and our aspirations.
>
> JAMES BALDWIN[1]

STATEN ISLAND CAN SEEM A world away from New York City's other boroughs. Despite the distance, I made the trek to the far-removed bedroom community one crisp November morning in 2017 to hang out with Abdullah. I first met Abdullah at an event in Queens, where he introduced himself as a "Puerto Rican Muslim ninja [who lives] all the *waaaay* out in Staten Island." Intrigued, I promised to followup with a visit to his karate dojo in the city's "forgotten borough."[2] A month later, that's where I find myself after traveling by bus, train, ferry, and foot for almost three hours from my apartment in Queens. The journey, other than testifying to Staten Island's far-flung feeling, underscores the Puerto Rican Muslim community's dispersion across New York, New Jersey, and the northeastern US. That is if you can call it a "community" at all. Puerto Rican converts are spread across a vast area including northern New Jersey, all five boroughs of New York City, in cities like Providence, Rhode Island, and Hartford, Connecticut, as well as urban centers in Pennsylvania, Ohio, Massachusetts, Delaware, and beyond.

Back on Staten Island, I walk up dimly lit stairs to Abdullah's apartment above the dojo. The smell of ammonia and damp wafts from the stairwell. I catch a glance of security cameras positioned outside the front door. Before I can knock, Abdullah calls from inside. The door is unlocked, and he saw me coming on the cameras. As I enter, I find Abdullah sitting in a black office chair in the middle of his living room. He is being attended to by a visiting nurse, getting his blood pressure checked. He recently suffered a series of strokes and told me he struggles with diabetes, water retention, and high blood pressure. "I'm getting old," he says, "and I am only sixty-seven!"

Despite his age and ailments, Abdullah is a sixth-level black belt and weapons master who runs the dojo—he calls it a "ninja society"—below. As I sit and watch the nurse go about his work, I notice Abdullah's apartment is amply furnished, well lived-in with a comfy sitting room, two bedrooms, a kitchen, and a shared bathroom for him and his roommate. The décor is an eclectic mix of calligraphy, images of the Kaaba, Japanese art, and a menagerie of karate weapons. His roommate is Muslim too, as are his neighbors, from Bangladesh and Pakistan, respectively. Apparently, Ahmed Sattar—the "Post Man" who was convicted of terror-related charges and connections to the "Blind Sheikh" Omar Abdel Rahman and al-Jama'a al-Islamiyya—used to live next door. I am not sure if Abdullah told me this as a point of pride or just in terms of general interest.

Abdullah is straightforward and speaks his mind. Over the course of four hours, he shares with me his views—and tall tales—on religion, politics, business, relationships, and life. With a wry smile, he says he converted to Islam in 1970 when he was twenty years old, "for the ladies." As a Puerto Rican, he was just a Puerto Rican. "As a Puerto Rican Muslim? Damn, now that's interesting. A wider field of play, ya' know?" In keeping with these hopes, he went on to be married three times and has thirteen children. His wives were "Puerto Rican, African American, and British, in that order," he says. He also claims to maintain good relationships with his ex-wives, paying child support and providing other financial assistance as needed. Hence, he says, the need to share his apartment with a roommate. Undeterred, he is currently in the market for wife number four. He says:

> A woman recently came by who sought me out because she heard I am a "Salafi." You see, she is so keen to marry a Salafi because her current husband, a Puerto Rican brother, is dedicated to the deen,[3] apparently. But I am not Salafi. I just follow the *Sunnah* and the

**FIGURE 1.1** *Abdullah shows off his dojo in Staten Island, New York.*

Salaf. There shouldn't be any "Salafi" label. All Muslims should follow the way of the Salaf, no exceptions.[4]

Growing up, Abdullah was connected to the Latin Kings—the largest and most well-known of the Latinx street gangs in the US, founded by Puerto Ricans in Chicago in 1954. Though he no longer calls himself a King, his dojo's colors are decidedly black and yellow, and he continues to draw clients from among their membership. Abdullah first came to faith through the NOI. But he says:

> I never bought into their teaching fully. They had a lot of ignorance back then—and some still do—but they didn't have a lot of knowledge like we do now. The good thing is, they had intention and put Islam into practice as best they could. That's the opposite of a lot of kids today. They are nice kids, they're trying, they're serious, but although they have knowledge they don't always go out into the streets and put it to work.

Reflecting on his early Muslim experience in the 1970s, he remarks it was hard to learn and grow because everyone was suspicious of everyone else and resources for further learning were hard to come by:

> Back then a Qur'an cost thirty-five dollars. It was hard to gain knowledge. Now they give the books away. There are Qur'ans everywhere

> in every language and color: green and red, black and blue, Spanish and Arabic, English and everything else. So, kids have access to the knowledge, but they just don't use it.

The suspicion, he insists, is still there:

> I got into corrections at Ryker's, on the legal side of things as a corrections officer, but I didn't tell anybody at the mosque. Everyone thought we were being watched by the CIA, FBI, the White House. And they were right, we were. Today, it's the same feeling. 9/11 didn't change anything, it just reminded us that we are always outsiders in America.

To underscore the point, he shares a story about the Egyptian Sheikh Muhammad Syed Adly. Adly is a popular Salafi cleric with YouTube videos and a spectral presence in numerous online chatrooms. He is also Abdullah's brother-in-law from a previous marriage. Abdullah says:

> Back in the day, Adly came to a meeting at a brother's home where everyone was packing heat. Death threats had been made. But Adly didn't carry anything in. I did, but he didn't know that. He just came to teach Islam, to correct innovations. He didn't care who you were, where you came from, or what label you chose—he just came to correct the innovations and errors. He came with Islam as his weapon.

Abdullah once had Adly as a guest on his former local-access television program, "Muslim Topics USA."[5] Telling him I'm intrigued, he pulls out some old VHS tapes and we start watching. He is particularly proud of one program called "Islam Is." It opens with Abdullah silhouetted against a green background. A gunshot rings out and then Abdullah spits a spoken word poem:

> Islam is not communism, socialism, Marxism, or Zionism. Islam is not nationalism, Africanism, Arabism, or Nazism. Islam is not bigotry, hatred, Five Percenters, or Dr. York. . . . Islam is not Marcus Garvey, Drew Ali, or the Nation of Farrakhanism. Islam is not Shiism, Ahmadiyyism, Wahhabism, Sufism, or terrorism . . . Islam is against all forms of slavery, pimping, and/or prostitution. Islam is not a compromising religion and yet we are the solution.

He tells me the video was a response to all the "innovations" Adly and others like him were preaching against. "All of this was here in the Muslim community in New York and among Puerto Ricans. People were confused and someone had to set them straight. Who better than a Puerto Rican Muslim ninja?"

After the video screening, we head out for a Staten Island tour. Along the way, he shares points of local interest—a mosque here, a mosque there, a Latin Kings–owned grocery store, an Arab restaurant, a Polish sandwich place. After about twenty minutes of cruising in Abdullah's minivan, we pull up at the Masjid Al Noor Islam Society where he often prays. Tucked into a docking and shipping area, the masjid faced complaints about the man who owns the property using the dock, mosque, and adjacent apartments to smuggle in supposedly dangerous immigrants without documentation. Abdullah tells me:

> We had spies, we had informants, we had people wondering if we were connected to "The Post Man," but it's actually just the opposite. We work with the government, we've done safety training here, and the FBI had some training operations here in the docks. We are against violence of any kind—Black Panthers, Latin Kings, Young Lords, or Islamic extremists.

He then gives me a tour of the mosque where there are a few people hanging about: Adam, a local Staten Island convert with a strong accent and an Irish background; Muhammad, a Black Muslim currently looking for work; and a man and his wife from Sudan who pray together but didn't interact with us much. Before making my way back to Queens, Abdullah poses for a few photos in the mosque and then gives me some books from Darussalam Publishers and International Islamic Publishing House. Based in Riyadh, both publishers have been labeled as Salafi and/or Wahhabi. "Still," Abdullah says as he hands me the books, "they might help you." Not able to resist another rhyme, he says as I walk away, "Allah's peace be with you and hear what I have to say, do not die unless you're a Muslim today."

Despite the personal contingencies at play, Abdullah's narrative reflects some key inflection points in the wider AmeRícan Muslim historical repertoire. Predominately Black Muslim organizations like the NOI and the FPN, transregional scholars from the Arab world, Muslim *dawah* organizations and paramosque communities founded by diaspora groups, street gangs, government surveillance, and Islamophobia all shaped Abdullah's experience.

Furthermore, Abdullah's history emphasizes the global scope, and yet simultaneously grounded locality, of the institutions, individuals, and trends shaping Puerto Rican Muslim converts and communities. As reflected in Abdullah's story, the influence of the New York City area is hard to overstate in the formation of Puerto Rican Muslim being and belonging. However, as important as such a place is, the territorialization of their experience must be held in tension with their connections to other geographies and histories, most notably the experience and narrative of Muslims on the Puerto Rican archipelago itself. As my visit with Abdullah in Staten Island shows, Puerto Rican Muslims' notion of self simultaneously involves relational networks that span national boundaries and geographic borders as well as the everyday stuff of lives largely played out in particular places. It is important to emphasize *both* in the AmeRícan Muslim story, moving back and forth and in between mobile narratives, interpersonal linkages, and the many places where AmeRícan lives are lived.

Thus, in this chapter, I review the entangled, contingent lineages that make up AmeRícan Muslim's historical repertoire. Using Juan Caraballo-Resto's *coyunturas* (junctures) as a starting point,[6] I contextualize the historical lineages they draw on to navigate their multiple marginalizations in the present. The ways AmeRícan Muslims remember and retell their history are not just about facts and important figures, but the confluence of shifting, overlapping narratives spanning multiple geographies. There is not a single Puerto Rican Muslim "history" per se, but various fragments pieced together to tell a certain story about what it means to be a Puerto Rican Muslim today. In other words, their identifications are not the outcome of a singular narrative but a series of contingent events, individuals, and lineages, each with their own precursors, implications, and interpretations. Moreover, they draw on a transregional repertoire of memory—bodies of knowledge culled from multiple cultures, locations, and genealogies. There is, therefore, a fair degree of historical slippage between various periods and places in this chapter, which reflects the ways in which AmeRícan Muslims remember their histories and make sense of their identifications, crisscrossing their way through time and space.

On that point, the ways in which these memories were related to me were, in themselves, significant. The interviews and conversations I share reflect "the histories that people make for themselves—in the ways that they remember and forget—that best [illuminate] how people make meaning of the world around them."[7] Therefore, I do not presume to tell *a definitive* AmeRícan Muslim history but instead recount history *as it was told to me*. Although I reference historical works in relating these narratives, I regularly turn to the "ideational archives" that Puerto Rican Muslims themselves produce, share, and pass on to others.[8] These malleable archives are constituted by discourses and narratives generating their own "genealogies, ideas, and omissions" in a mix of myth and history, fact and useful fictions.[9] Continuing in the tradition of Centro de Estudios de la Realidad Puertorriqueña (CEREP) and its notion of rethinking Puerto Rican histories "from below" in order to understand Puerto Rican realities by taking into consideration its marginalized groups first and foremost, this chapter centers voices, histories, and experiences often missed within the broader scope of Puerto Rican history. Not only does this ex-centric[10] archive tell a different kind of story, it also points to the potential for new, more cosmopolitan, futures.[11]

Thus, these archives matter, whether or not they are always historically verifiable. They matter because they provide a window into how AmeRícan Muslims utilize such stories to situate themselves in the world and in relation to others. They thus act as "inherited structures" constraining and conditioning their "agency in the present."[12] Drawing on Marx and his discourse on the "tradition of dead generations," Latin Americanist Kevin Funk points out how such lineages weigh on how we act in the present, shaping the choices we make, the people we associate with, and the places we identify with.[13] In this way, the histories in this chapter continue to provide a script of influences for how AmeRícan Muslims live in the present and look to their potential future(s). In other words, reviewing Puerto Rican Muslims' origin stories not only presents the broad outlines of the community's past, but more importantly, it also illustrates how they construct *both* history *and* a sense of being and becoming in the midst of a diverse array of perspectives, interests, and contemporary contexts.

The result is a somewhat fuzzy chronology, including a fair bit of carryover and overlap; interludes and shifts in interpretation; continuities and ruptures; gaps both temporal and transnational. Nonetheless, by giving an account of, and analyzing, these "contingent lineages" both through documented historical evidence and chronicles narrated to me, I highlight AmeRícan Muslims' "world-embracing" network alongside the "cosmopolitan specificities" of their local contexts and crossings.[14] While each of these histories—and their meaning in the lives of my interlocutors—will reemerge in subsequent chapters, this chapter provides an overview of the various coyunturas themselves. By tracing these contingent lineages, I not only contextualize AmeRícan Muslims' contemporary narratives but also do so against a wider background of minoritized groups of Muslim converts seeking to rewrite their historical presence in the Americas.

In fact, the contingent lineages outlined here illustrate the intertwined nature of Muslim histories across the Americas, through the broader "Muslim Atlantic,"[15] and beyond. In that sense, their stories can be viewed as an example of the connective tissues existing among Muslim communities both across the American hemisphere and within transregional networks that include nodes and representative sites of Islam in Iberian Spain, North Africa, South Asia, West Africa, the Balkans, and the Middle East. At each juncture in the chronicle of their past, these entanglements continue to influence, shape, challenge, and inspire AmeRícan Muslims today. As James Baldwin wrote, history "is not the past. It is the present. We carry our history with us. We are our history."[16]

## CRISSCROSSING COYUNTURAS

Although there are no official numbers, there were an estimated 3,500–5,000 Muslims in Puerto Rico (most of them immigrants, predominately from Palestine) before fiscal crises, natural disasters, and colonial neglect forced many to leave the archipelago in the years between 2017 and 2024.[17] There are also an estimated 11,000–15,400 Puerto Rican Muslims across the US.[18] Despite the decline in population, there remain several mezquitas serving the archipelago's community, in places like Carolina, Fajardo, Hatillo, Montehiedra, Ponce, Río Piedras, and Vega Alta. In addition, there are *musallahs* and prayer rooms run by local reverts, community leaders, and missionaries in locales like Aibonito, Aguadilla, Bayamón, Guaynabo, and Jayuya. In the US, there are no Puerto Rican–dominant mosques or communities, but their presence is felt in Islamic centers and neighborhoods from Miami to Massachusetts, California to Connecticut. And according to anthropologist Omar Ramadan-Santiago, though there is a longstanding belief that Muslims first arrived in Puerto Rico in the 1950s and '60s, "Islam was introduced to Puerto Rico as early as 1493." The first were Iberian Muslims (*ladinos*) "who were forced to take on the Christian faith yet remained Muslim in their own right. Then came Africans [*bozales*], who were forced to come to the Americas yet maintained their faith and sense of identity" in the midst of the transatlantic trade in enslaved persons.[19] These populations did not leave behind much enduring evidence of their presence, but they did leave an ongoing legacy that influenced later Muslim arrivals and the growth of Puerto Rican Muslim communities in the US in the twentieth century.

Starting with 1493, Caraballo-Resto frames this history as a series of interrelated and complex coyunturas involving the colonial period, the transatlantic trade in enslaved persons, nineteenth- and twentieth-century immigration, the era of transnational dawah,[20] and local conversions.[21] In the following sections, I outline and add additional detail to our understanding of these coyunturas in the narrative of AmeRícan Muslim memory. I thicken and expand this historical narrative in two ways: 1) by showing how these contingent lineages of history are interwoven into the contemporary, everyday experience(s) of Muslims in Puerto Rico and the diaspora and 2) by putting the history of Puerto Rican Muslims in the US in conversation with that of Muslims on the archipelago in order to provide a more multilocal and entangled narrative. This is done to emphasize the crisscrossing and connective nature of AmeRícan Muslim lives and the ways their narrative ties together multiple lineages from across Islam's global landscapes. As with Puerto Ricans as a whole,[22] their community is not an insular sociality but a transregionally entangled one situated betwixt and between numerous places, spaces, and histories.

To return to Tato Laviera's poem, this chapter underlines how AmeRícan Muslim lives are defined by movement

> across forth and across back
> back across and forth back
> forth across and back and forth
> our trips are walking bridges![23]

Those bridges are not always secure. Their connections are sometimes tenuous. And yet, they highlight how Puerto Rican Muslims live between multiple worlds *and* in particular places. Those worlds not only are Puerto Rican, Muslim, and American but also involve—or are inspired by—Iberian, African, Atlantic, and Middle Eastern histories. As will be made evident in the chapters that follow, as AmeRícan Muslims craft a notion of who *they* are, and what constitutes *their* history, they move back and forth (and "forth across and back and forth") between these various lineages.

## "O" IS FOR *OJALá*? MORISCOS AND IBERIAN INFLUENCES IN THE SIXTEENTH CENTURY

While perusing a *librería* (bookshop) in the Residencia Armstrong-Poventud building off Plaza Muñoz Rivera in Ponce, I started to flip the pages of *El ABC Boricua*. Edited by Néstor Murray-Irizarry and illustrated by Felipe Cuchí, the children's book introduces the ABCs with a particularly Puerto Rican accent. The words in the book were, according to Murray-Irizarry, selected because of their place in the ongoing dialogue of Puerto Ricans in their daily lives on the archipelago. Each in their own way, the words were chosen because they speak to *lo que es puertorriqueño*—"that something Puerto Rican."[24] For example, to teach "C" Murray-Irizarry uses the common coquí frog and for "Q" a *quenepa* ("Spanish lime"). When I flipped to the page introducing "O," I was surprised to see, "O is for *ojalá*."

Heard on the streets of San Juan and Ponce, Aguadilla and Fajardo, the subjunctive Spanish expression is a means of conveying hope. Or, as Murray-Irizarry put it in *El ABC Boricua*, ojalá "expresses a strong desire for something to happen."[25] The popular perception is that ojalá's origins stretch back some 1,300 years to the arrival of the first Arabic speakers in the Iberian Peninsula. It is believed that over the passage of time, the Arabic phrase inshallah (God willing) eventually morphed into ojalá. However, according to the *Diccionario de la lengua española*, the phrase's roots are from the archaic Andalusian Arabic *law šá lláh* ('si Dios quiere' or "if God wills") and not inshallah.[26] Nonetheless, reverts invoke the word—and broader Andalusian, or Moorish, history—as part of their spiritual lineage. It is one way in which al-Andalus serves as a touchpoint for Puerto Rican reverts' reimagined identifications and reassembled sense of belonging. Searching Puerto Rican history for what they call footprints (*huellas*) like ojalá,[27] they invoke the arts of memory to "cancel the temporal difference between past and present"[28] and ground their contemporary identifications in the fertile soil of a multi-lineage heritage.

That is not to say their search is without substance. Muslims from the Iberian Peninsula and North Africa influenced the development of the Spanish Americas as explorers, colonizers, enslaved persons, and in the minds and imaginations of Spanish Catholics as they encountered and conquered the so-called "New World."[29] Although the Spanish crown attempted to "rid their country of any remnants of Islamic influence and culture"[30] and prohibit Muslims from coming to the Americas in the wake of the Reconquista, Islam and Muslims were inescapably enmeshed with Spanish culture. No combination of expulsions, inquisitions, or laws could eliminate Islamic influence in Iberia or fully forestall Muslims from coming to the Americas.[31]

Nonetheless, starting in 1501, Spain passed a series of laws prohibiting Jews and Muslims in the Americas, looking to restrict their influence in the newly conquered lands. Treating their American settlements as ideological extensions of their effort to eradicate Moorish power and presence in Iberia, as well as check and circumvent Ottoman ascendancy,[32] the Spanish Crown sought to prevent their American colonies from becoming "another theater of war in their protracted and costly struggle with Islam."[33] In one of the earliest regulations, given to the first governor of Hispaniola, Friar Nicolás de Ovando decreed:

> As we with great care have to carry out the conversion of the Indians to our holy Catholic faith: if you find persons suspect in matters of the faith present during the said conversion, it could create an impediment. Do not consent or allow Muslims or Jews, heretics, or anyone reconciled by the Inquisition, or persons newly convert to our Faith to go there, unless they are black slaves . . . who were born in the power of Christians, our subjects and native inhabitants.[34]

In another decree in July 1556, rulers in the Spanish Indies were ordered to "repatriate to Spain all Muslims" while at the same time acknowledging—with a certain amount of frustration, it seems—that Muslims and Moriscos were finding their way to the Americas despite previous laws barring them from doing so.[35]

Such laws were put in place not only as a bulwark to protect the Christianization project underway in the Spanish Americas but also as part of the construction of more extensive Spanish racial categories emerging at the time. In particular, the concept of *limpieza de sangre*—"purity of blood"—was used to bar many from emigrating to the Americas. For example, a prerequisite for arrival was some form of proof of not having recent Muslim or Jewish ancestry. These laws and prescriptions even overrode desires to bring Moriscos to the Americas as slaves, interpreters, or artisans.

Despite the authorities' efforts, Moriscos arrived anyway. In the face of multiple pressures and prohibitions, many outwardly practiced Christianity in an act of dissimulation, while privately maintaining and practicing their Islamic faith as best they could in private. Because of this, many Moriscos—or those accused of being so—were later brought before inquisitorial courts to face charges of "practicing Islam or of being descendants of Muslims."[36] In places like Puerto Rico, where an official inquisition did not exist as there was no religious court maintained on the archipelago, those suspected of continuing to practice Islam under the guise of Christianity were charged and, at times, remanded to regional tribunals elsewhere in the Americas. Sometimes, they were sent back to regional governors in Spain.[37]

Because of these persistent pressures and subsequent prohibitions, Islam was not practiced openly in colonial Puerto Rico. Although we can surmise there were Muslims among the explorers and conquerors who came from the Iberian Peninsula—or at the very least "the Spaniards [who] arrived in the New World were steeped with Muslim culture and religious beliefs"[38]—the vast majority of their names and narratives remain unknown to us. Since Moriscos were not permitted to worship and express their identities publicly in the context of boundary-making statecraft in the Americas, the full impact of their presence in the New World's politics, economy, and religious landscape is difficult to discern.

Beyond their embodied presence, the specter of the "Morisco" came with Iberian colonizers as well. The mental universe of the conquerors was shaped by the ethnic, racial, and religious tensions of Spanish peninsular culture and history. As the Spaniards who came to Latin America and the Caribbean in the sixteenth and seventeenth centuries were still working out their notions of "Spanish" identity after emerging from a series of wars to (re)claim Spain and the entire Iberian Peninsula for Catholicism, they brought these questions and conundrums with them to the "New World." Thus, the specter of the "Moor" traveled with the soldiers and conquistadors,[39] their visages infusing elements of the encounter between Europeans and indigenous Americans like the Taíno, who became representative of the expelled Moors in the minds of explorers and conquerors.

In these ways, the confluence of the European encounter with Puerto Rico and the aftermath of the Reconquista left undeniable echoes on the archipelago and its subsequent history. This leads some reverts to search for "lost" Andalusian lives and legacies, or "vestiges,"[40] in Puerto Rico's contemporary culture and built environment. They probe Puerto Rican cooking, architecture, and language for fodder to claim *seamos Moros*, or "we are Moors!"[41] Similar to how global imaginaries of Islam and dreams of al-Andalus galvanized racial authenticity for Black Muslims in the 1960s and '70s, Puerto Rican reverts look to Andalusian Spain to define, establish, and defend their dual identitification as Puerto Rican *and* Muslim.[42] This "imagined diaspora" sentiment[43] is a reaction to their multiple marginalizations and a way to re-center and re-locate their identifications amid rupture, loss, and exile.

Mutah Wassin Shabazz Beale, better known by his rap name "Napoleon" and by his association with Tupac Shakur's group "The Outlawz," is one such revert. The hip-hop artist, who grew up in Newark, New Jersey, traveled to San Juan, Puerto Rico, in September 2022 searching for evidence of Andalusian influence on the archipelago. He shared his revelations on Facebook, referencing how "amazing" it was to see echoes of Islamic influence in Puerto Rican art, culture, and society.[44] For people who feel marginalized, he wrote, it is encouraging to find footprints in popular and sanctioned expressions of Puerto Rican history.[45]

For reverts like Beale, al-Andalus serves as a prime historical matrix in the search for a grounding identification. Islamic Spain, in other words, becomes a centrifugal reference point in the process of identity reconstruction.[46] Drawing on historical narratives and connections—often, no matter how tenuous or tangential—AmeRícan Muslims claim Puerto Rico's Moorish heritage renders their affiliation with Islam a *reversion* as much as a conversion. Crafting currents of connection to Morisco forebears not only gives them a sense of continuity with Islamic history and connection to the broader ummah but also empowers them with a model for navigating the realities of living as reverts and quadruple minorities in an increasingly diverse late-modern world. Even if some traces are disputable (or even spurious), this does not stop Puerto Rican Muslims from imagining a direct link between their present-day sociality and the Iberian Muslim emirates of the past.

## BLACK MUSLIMS' ENDURING LEGACY

AmeRícan Muslims also call on their African forebears.[47] Kemal, a twenty-something revert whose family does not yet know he is Muslim, says he does so when he searches out a place to pray. Over Skype, as he sits on the front porch of a family member's home, Kemal speaks quietly, for fear his family might overhear:

> When [my family] go to sleep, I am able to pray. But during the day, I go . . . I'm going to show you [he turns the camera on his phone around and shows me a small mountain covered in trees] I literally go, you see that mountain over there. There's actually an entrance through the trees. That's where I go to pray. . . . I can't do it at home with my

> family living here. I can't do it outside. I can't go to the mosque. So, I'm like, "I guess I have to go into the mountain to do this."

He says reverts "are suffering, we need to have a mosque that is open and available to everyone." This is why he wants to build his own. "I want this mosque to be a sanctuary for the reverts and converts that are hungry for the deen and are being deprived of such. . . . I have a possible location for such a masjid, and I have possible sponsors and donors," he tells me. He even created possible designs. "Something like this would be nice," he says as he pulls up an image of a "small and simple mosque . . . capable of holding at least eighty to one hundred people." Surrounding the mosque is a small mountain, like the one he retreats to for prayer. The building itself is yellow and brown, with a tall white minaret, a small front porch with arched porticoes, and a ridged roof. The design is reminiscent of a small masjid in rural sub-Saharan Africa. The mosque, he acknowledges, is more of a dream than a reality. But, he adds, his desire is to build a place for himself and other converts. "A place of our own," he calls it.

In the meantime, he makes do with what he has at hand. Until he can move forward with his hoped-for mosque, Kemal retreats to the mountain where, he says, he is reminded of his African Muslim ancestors. Kemal says:

> They used to pray in the forest. When they were on plantations, when they were suffering or when their fellow slaves and their owners didn't understand or wouldn't allow them to pray, they snuck away at night to the forest to pray. To be alone with Allah, to find a spot in the trees and pray. So, in that way, I am like other Puerto Rican Muslims before me.

Although there is no direct lineage of converts connecting Kemal to the bozales who brought Islam to Borikén, Kemal imagines a link to them as part of formulating his sense of being and belonging in the face of pressure from family, neighbors, and friends. This feeling of continuity with African Muslims who came before him not only helps him "try and understand where I came from" but also confront the multiple marginalizations he faces—at home, in the mosque, and in society in general.

As far back as the sixteenth century, African Muslims were part of the American story, navigating enslavement, inequality, and numerous misrepresentations and marginalizations in the region for five hundred years. The rapid colonization of conquered territories in the Americas and the drive by those who colonized them to acquire and conquer precipitated a centuries-long trade in enslaved persons from West Africa, leaving a permanent imprint across the Atlantic World. Ships would leave European ports like Nantes and Bristol, pack their cargo holds with enslaved Africans from the Senegambia, Gold Coast, and Central Africa, and arrive at American ports in Brazil and Barbados, St. Domingue (present-day Haiti), and South Carolina. Over time, the transatlantic trade in enslaved persons became the single largest coerced movement of people in the history of the world, leaving an indelible mark on the Atlantic World's demographics and dynamics.

In the words of historian Greg Grandin, this trade also served as the "back door" by which Islam arrived in the hemisphere. Although the exact number is not known, scholars estimate some 5 to 15 percent of the roughly 12.5 million Africans enslaved in the Americas were Muslim. Once here, they became part of New World debates over identity, policy, and the ideals of empires and emerging nation-states.[48] Historian Ayla Amon wrote, "African Muslims were caught in the middle of complicated social and legal attitudes from the very moment they landed" on American shores and came to play a remarkable part in creating America as we know it, mapping its cultural and political contours and fighting against colonial rule.[49] Legal documents, slaveholders' records, and abiding cultural traditions point to African Muslims' significant presence and ongoing influence across the hemisphere. Recently, scholars scoured these sources, revealing stories of resilience and resistance, creative adaptation, and attentive conservation. As scholar Michael Gomez wrote, "The Old World context and set of circumstances molding and impacting Muslim life in Africa and Europe continued to inform conditions in the New World and clearly influenced the ways in which the colonial project unfolded."[50] Today, their enduring legacy influences thousands of Muslims like Kemal in places like Hispaniola, Costa Rica, Venezuela, Mexico, Panama, and Puerto Rico.

African Muslims first arrived in Puerto Rico following the decimation of the local Taíno population through harsh forced labor conditions, violence, and disease (e.g., smallpox, malaria, the plague, influenza, measles, and others).[51] This loss in labor led Spanish colonizers to request royal permission to bring Africans "to supplement the diminishing labor force since they had already built up a natural immunity to the same diseases that plagued the indigenous."[52] Thus, enslaved Africans were brought to Puerto Rico to work on sugarcane plantations no longer supported by Taínos who provided the original labor for the emerging Caribbean sugar economy. At the time, Puerto Rico's population of enslaved persons included "undercover Muslims" (ladinos) from Iberia,[53] as well as West African and non-Spanish-speaking slaves (bozales), from the Wolof, Mandigo/a, and Fula/ni tribes.[54] Among the thousands of enslaved Africans forced onto the archipelago between 1510 and 1873[55]—and despite numerous laws barring Muslims from being forcibly brought to Puerto Rico[56]—there are records of names suggesting enslaved African Muslim presence,[57] evidence that Wolof Muslims rebelled in San Juan in the middle of the sixteenth century,[58] and suggestions that Muslim maroons sought refuge in the island's interior mountains where colonial powers in and around San Juan could not easily extend their reach.[59] Drawing on evidence from what records there are, it is feasible to say Black Muslims were not only present in Puerto Rico but also played a significant part in the Spanish encomienda system, especially as the Taíno population rapidly declined and Africans were brought across the Atlantic to support a struggling sugar plantation economy.[60]

At the same time, there is little official documentation of African Muslim life in Puerto Rico. Partly, this was because they were deemed "inconsequential to the ruling class who perceived them as chattel."[61] In addition, "[t]he prohibition of Islam coupled with African Muslims' severance from their home countries and communities resulted in a steady decline in the number of Muslims in the New World," let alone Puerto Rico.[62] Spanish rule proved "a hostile environment where Christianity was not only favored, but forced."[63] Nonetheless, Muslim presence in the Americas was frequently noted by slaveholders, travelers, journalists, diplomats, and missionaries. They wrote of how, despite the pressures upon them, Muslims continued to pray, maintain halal dietary requirements, fast during Ramadan, engage in dawah, and dress distinctively.[64]

African Muslims in Puerto Rico struggled to maintain their religious practice; let alone pass it down to following generations due to lack of educational institutions (*madrasahs*) or leaders. Even interfamilial mentoring and discipline were made difficult due to how families were often separated and sold to different plantations. Furthermore, the Spanish laws barring the importation or immigration of Muslims made the public practice of Islam dangerous. In addition to Spanish antagonism toward Islam, African Muslim enslaved persons were also minorities—ethnically and religiously—among the enslaved. As a result, and as Luis Mesa Delmonte notes in the Cuban case, "many . . . Muslim migrants were isolated and inserted in small communities with a weak religious life. . . . In other words, there were Muslims but no Muslim institution building."[65] Therefore, the pressure to convert to Christianity constantly, and viscerally, hung over the enslaved person's life to the point where it was often much easier to convert (or fake conversion) than to resist.

Thus, in one sense, early Black Muslim presence appears to have faded over time. There is little evidence of Muslims passing their practices on to subsequent generations in any formal way. Many of their grandchildren and great-grandchildren do not even know their ancestors were Muslim, unless they discover evidence in records, long-kept family heirlooms, or from secondary sources and scholars. What researchers and the Puerto Rican Muslim community in search of historical rootedness are left with are vestiges and hints, historical imagination, and the construction of meaning rather than any direct links.[66]

However, if Islam as a lived religion died out in the Spanish Caribbean, it was passed on in other ways—as a collection of interconnected ideals, symbols, practices, and influences mediated, refracted, and disseminated in culture(s) at large. In other words, beyond their legacy as leaders among the enslaved and those who resisted slavery, African Muslims influenced various material, linguistic, and musical traditions prevalent among Afro–Puerto Rican, Black, and popular American culture(s) today. As Sylviane Diouf documented, Arabic terminology survives in the Gullah language of South Carolina, in Trinidadian and Peruvian songs, in the Caribbean *saraka*, and in the religious diction of Candomblé, Umbanda, and Macumba in Brazil, *vodou* in Haiti, and Regla Lucumí (Santería) and Palo Mayombe in Cuba. Moreover, Islam seems to have influenced musical traditions like the blues and the religious "ring shout" tradition still found in the US South, Jamaica, and Trinidad.[67]

Moreover, Black Muslim movements like the Moorish Science Temple, the NOI, FPN, and various Sunni communities draw on the legacy of their enslaved antecedents to confirm their character as "American" Muslims, encourage others to convert, and espouse the historical longevity of Islam in the Americas. In particular, these groups often call on the history of enslaved Muslims forebears for inspiration and as a rallying cry against the ongoing oppressions their members face in the US and the Caribbean. Whether it be enslavement at the hands of European powers, the struggle for human rights, or the contention that "Black Lives Matter," Black Muslim histories are a critical ingredient in the makeup of Black narratives across the hemisphere.

Although there may or may not be individuals who act as physical links between enslaved African Muslims and contemporary Black Muslim communities, there is a chain of inspiration, connection, and shared vision stretching back across the ages and across geographies. Through groups like the NOI, contemporary Muslims creatively craft a spatial memory that at once recovers and remolds their histories,[68] enabling them to link slave plantations in the US South, Caribbean, and elsewhere to West and North African Muslim traditions, kingdoms, and landscapes. Therefore, at least in some ways, the mosques, temples, and meeting rooms of Black Muslim movements in the Americas are networked with their forebears across the Atlantic to West Africa, the Sahel, North Africa, and the Middle East. Their stories are entangled with one another, and their genealogies and geographies linked across time—materially and in memory.

Too often, many Puerto Rican Muslims feel these stories are forgotten as part of broader status quo cultural frameworks. The "little bit of everything" some Puerto Ricans sometimes use to describe their ethnicity includes Taíno, African, and Spanish heritage.[69] Nonetheless, according to US Census data from 2020, some three-fourths of Puerto Ricans identify as white alone. Just 12 percent identify as Black, even though history and culture would indicate many more Puerto Ricans might be considered so. Though Puerto Rico is sometimes positioned as a "racial paradise, where race is subordinate to national and cultural identity,"[70] Black Puerto Ricans are often forgotten, excluded, or marginalized in popular retellings and representations of Puerto Rican history and culture.

For example, Yeidy M. Rivero analyzed representations of race on Puerto Rican television and radio, showing how Black actors were largely excluded and white actors often portrayed Black subjects with blackface and blackvoice, contributing to the general marginalization of nonwhite citizens in Puerto Rican popular media.[71] Such media are only one aspect of a broader, interlocking lattice of silences,[72] "disappearances [or] excesses" in Puerto Rico's cultural and historical archive.[73] They also contribute to structural racism in Puerto Rico, where Black populations are overrepresented in the archipelago's penal system, are less capable of obtaining upwardly mobile work, and are concentrated in areas with some of the greatest environmental pollution[74] and the fewest resources to deal with issues like healthcare disparity and economic precarity (e.g., Vieques, Guayama, or Loíza).[75] As a result, many Afro–Puerto Ricans choose to "pass" as white when it comes to the national census, in day-to-day interactions, or in their own sense of being and being-in-relation to Others.[76]

This crept into Puerto Rican Muslims' own self-perception, asserts Kemal. Over a meal of *mofongo con camarones* along the Condado coast in San Juan, he told me that is exactly why he and another local Muslim planned on starting a course for "fresh converts." He said:

> It will be a kind of "Islam 101" that helps orient them not only to the basics of Islamic belief and practice but also Islam's historical connections to the island and its people. Starting with Spain, sure, but also pointing out that the first significant Muslim communities were Black, brought to Puerto Rico during the slave trade. . . . Focusing so much on al-Andalus and the Spanish side of our history, we forget the Africanity of our faith. . . . It's the same with other Puerto Ricans forgetting that one part of the *tres raíces* [three roots] of our culture is Africa. . . . We are Black. Whether from Morocco or the Gambia, the first Muslims here were Black. We are still Black Muslims today.

For Kemal, orienting the contemporary AmeRícan Muslim community to what he sees as its essential Africanity helps not only to correct omissions in popular Puerto Rican narratives of identification, but also to resist imperialism and racism today. "They are our ancestors in the struggle," he said, "it's not just about their oppression and omission, but about how they resisted—in big and small ways—the yoke placed upon them by history, by time, by those in power. We can learn from their example today. Or at least we should."

Kemal's comment about being "Black today" is particularly poignant. It not only signals toward efforts to resignify tripartite notions of what it means to "be Puerto Rican"[77] but also what is called "political Blackness."[78] In British contexts, the notion of Blackness as a political symbol was used to galvanize a range of different people groups who are racially abused, insulated, and marginalized (e.g., in the United Kingdom, peoples with origins in Asia, the Middle East, Africa, and their diasporas).[79] Before Black Atlantic theorists like Stuart Hall popularized the notion in the 1980s and '90s, Malcolm X called on Black revolutionaries around the world to resist their masters using a concept of shared Blackness encompassing anyone who was colonized or exploited by Europeans. Malcolm X himself was preceded by W. E. B. Du Bois, who wrote, "The problem of the twentieth century is the problem of the color line; the relation of the darker to the lighter races of men in Asia and Africa, in America and the islands of the sea."[80] In referring to themselves as "Black Muslims," or drawing on the legacy of enslaved African Muslims as part of their historical narrative, AmeRícan Muslims tap into these long-held, if contested, notions of political Blackness to counter what they see as continuing colonial and racist exploitation and exclusive notions of what it means to be Puerto Rican, Muslim, or American.

Thus, despite broader denials of Africanity in Puerto Rican culture,[81] the legacy of enslaved Black Muslims continues to resonate in the lives of AmeRícan Muslims. Dreaming of an "archive unfolded that can be made to answer that which colonialism and slavery has obscured,"[82] their (re)reading of Puerto Rican history fuels and animates their resistance and adaptations today. As they face ostracism because of their religion, they invoke those who faced oppressors in the past not only to instill a sense of pride, but also to feel that being Black *and* Muslim has a long history on the archipelago they call home. It also encourages them to work toward the radical potential of different kinds of "Afro-futurities."[83] Thus, for Kemal and others, the memory of Black Muslims in Puerto Rico and the broader Americas was never fully lost nor did it ever truly die out.[84] Nor is their legacy only one of de-Africanization, oppression, and loss. Instead, the stories of African Muslims in Puerto Rico provide a way for contemporary converts to look back with pride on these "forebears" with an eye toward grounding their reversions in the present and working toward a future when their identifications and contributions to Puerto Rican culture and society will be more widely recognized and celebrated.

## EVERYONE KNOWS SALIM: ARAB MIGRANTS AND GLOBAL MUSLIM DIASPORAS

Perhaps because the number of Muslim diaspora and migrant communities in Latin America and the Caribbean is relatively low when compared to other regions, narratives of Muslim transnationalism in the Americas remain somewhat neglected in scholarly discourse.[85] But in the nineteenth and twentieth centuries, intraregional flows and migration from Asia, the Middle East, and North Africa emerged as important dynamics in the region's formation.[86] Unlike the histories above, which gave shape to early Muslim life in the Americas, these more recent movements of people across oceans and borders are still ongoing. Significantly, these "Muslim diaspora and migrant communities" continue to define how "localized idioms of Islam are embedded and, inevitably, affected by broader global trends" in the Americas.[87] In fact, the communities, infrastructures, and networks they established give shape to the current contours of Muslim life in the region and continue to evolve, grow, and overlap with more recent dynamics and flows.[88] Thus, the case of Arab migrants and global Muslim diasporas in the context of the broader AmeRícan Muslim experience requires consideration.

In particular, the Arab diaspora in Puerto Rico shows how global Muslim experiences are differentiated and diverse according to local context, while also entangled with intraregional and transregional networks. Their stories also problematize the ways we consider diaspora Muslim socialities more broadly. This not only enables scholars to consider South-South connections and stories of diaspora movement and relations but also produces vital insights into how Muslims, or migrants in general, wrestle with, translate, and develop distinct idioms of identification, belief, and practice in conversation with multiple cultural vernaculars.[89] This pushes us to recognize various parts of the globe as loci of lived Islam and thus make the world our framework and method in the study thereof, rather than favoring any one locality, region, or network.

According to the Arab American Institute Foundation, the population of those who self-identify as having Arab-speaking ancestry in Puerto Rico was estimated to be 7,284 (or 0.2 percent of the total population) as of 2015.[90] The largest number of these came from Palestine, Jordan, Lebanon, Egypt, and Iraq. According to the 2010 Census, roughly 47 percent of Arab Americans in Puerto Rico have Lebanese or Palestinian roots. Since 1990, significant increases appeared in the number of Puerto Ricans who are of Jordanian and Iraqi descent. Others claimed Algeria, Bahrain, Djibouti, Kuwait, Libya, Oman, Qatar, Saudi Arabia, Tunisia, the United Arab Emirates, or Yemen as their country of origin. Nonetheless, roughly 39 percent of respondents chose the generic identity of "Arab/Arabic" rather than any country-specific identifier.

Arabs first came to Puerto Rico beginning in the late nineteenth century and continued to arrive throughout the twentieth. Similar to other locales in Latin America and the Caribbean, the vast majority of these early Arab migrants to Puerto Rico were Catholics. Among them were also members of Orthodox, Malakite, Druze, and Muslim communities.[91] Starting at least in the 1950s, more Muslims began to arrive from Palestine, Egypt, and Jordan. They set up businesses or worked as itinerant traders, finding a quality of life they enjoyed enough that they decided to remain or to create cycles of circular migration between the Caribbean and Middle East. Establishing a successful economic foothold in Puerto Rico, Arabs became part of a larger integration process of various immigrant groups there by the mid-twentieth century.[92] Beyond their economic proclivity, Arabs left cultural footprints as well, in language, architecture, music, food, and philanthropy. They also established and built mosques in several cities and municipalities across the archipelago.

For the most part, the Arab–Puerto Rican story is largely predicated upon, and runs parallel to, twentieth-century Palestinian history, occurring in four successive seasons. The first season came in the late nineteenth and early twentieth centuries, amid the decline of the Ottoman Empire (1860–1916). The second occurred under the British Mandate in Palestine between 1918 and 1948. Finally, the last two seasons were a direct result of two significant events: the 1948 Palestinian exodus, when more than 700,000 Palestinian Arabs were expelled from their homes following the creation of Israel, and the Six-Day War of 1967. Although the numbers of Arabs and Palestinians arriving in Puerto Rico before 1948 was quite low, their population rose to 2,000 between 1940 and 1970 (0.07 percent). Due to continued immigration and internal demographic growth, that number rose to an estimated 3,000 (0.09 percent) in 1980; 4,500 (0.13 percent) in 1990; and 5,000 (0.13 percent) in 2010. Today, the population appears to be stagnating, and possibly declining, as subsequent generations either move to the US or back to the Middle East.

Today, the Palestinian community remains perhaps most well-known on the archipelago for their commercial presence. People who identify as Arab have owned and operated gas stations, restaurants, pharmacies, and tourist attractions like the popular butterfly shop in Viejo San Juan. The longevity of the Arab community in Puerto Rico is crucially linked to the vitality of this economic activity.[93] However, while some found success, not all prospered or found it easy to blend into the local context. Likewise, while some Palestinian (and other Arab) immigrants in Puerto Rico are economically incorporated and fairly comfortable, if not coalescent, with local communities, there can remain a sense of distance—particularly between Palestinian Muslims and Puerto Rican reverts. This ambivalent position in Puerto Rican society makes Arabs a "middle-man" minority, linking various geographies, identities, and religious communities together, according to Caraballo-Resto.[94] Although they provide economic and social benefit, there can be the impression that they remain somewhat sequestered from the general population. At times, they have been the object of both subtle and explicit resentment.

While Palestinian Muslims are far from the only Muslim transnational influence in Puerto Rico, their role is hard to overstate. Without them, the community as it exists today would look drastically different. The institutions they built, and communities they constructed, form the formal infrastructure

**FIGURE 1.2** *Salim Electronic Center is not only a prominent, popular store in Jayuya, Puerto Rico, but also a place where locals connect over a cup of coffee.*

of most Muslim practice on the archipelago. The following story is meant to convey a sense of that lived impact, the multiple roles they play in local communities, and how they shape everyday Muslim lives on the archipelago. Furthermore, it illuminates how movement from one region to another brings forth new identifications, new connections, and "expressions of shared struggle and solidarity." [95] In the work of artist Alia Farid, who was born in Kuwait in 1985 and grew up in Kuwait and Puerto Rico, the Palestinian diaspora in Puerto Rico is interwoven into the archipelago's cityscapes, financescapes, and religioscapes. Echoing Farid's work, such stories complicate visions of Palestinians—or other Arabs—in Puerto Rico as aloof and standoffish, disconnected from the community, or cliquish.

Because in Jayuya everyone knows Salim.[96] The famous, coffee-rich community—Puerto Rico's mountain "capital"—is known for its summit-perched globe, its Taíno heritage, and its deep-fried *surullitos* (fried corn balls). And Salim is known for his coffee—his free coffee, to be exact. Founded in 1911, Jayuya only boasts a population of 14,000. It is a small town, and a lot of people know each other. When you walk around Jayuya you notice how friends greet loved ones on the street as if they had not seen them in years, but in reality, it's likely only been a few days. The Muslim community there is likewise close-knit, as I was about to find out. I was following up a lead I was given about a mosque here in the mountains. After a prolonged text exchange with someone on the other end of a phone number I was given at the mosque in Aguadilla, on Puerto Rico's western coast, I was sent the following information: "*Wa alaikum as-salaam.* Go to the Salim electronic store located in the same street as the mosque at 200 meters, the street is Calle Esteves. You ask for Raduan or Salim and they have the key."

After driving up the ever-winding, and slightly perilous, road from the municipality of Juana Díaz, I park a little way down from the electronics store and start making my way through town. As I look up the road to the store, I see two men sitting at the entrance. At first ignoring me, I greet them with peace. One, with a pockmarked face and holding a mobile phone to his ear and yet saying nothing, points to a man I take to be Raduan. Raduan pushes up his gold-rimmed glasses, looks up from an appliance catalog, and tells me to come back in an hour, closer to *dhuhr* (afternoon) prayers, when Salim will be around. I spend the time in between exploring and stopping to eat surullitos before circling back to the store, which I find is packed with just about everything and anything that could be plugged in: stoves and fans, refrigerators and microwaves, blenders and billiards lights.

That is when Salim steps out from his air-conditioned office to join me in "the showroom." A man of some sixty-three years with dark suntanned skin, salt-and-pepper hair, a tooth or two gone missing from his generous smile over the years, and dressed in business casual gray pants and brown suede shoes, with a mess of keys hanging from his belt loop, Salim invites me to the back of the shop for a sip of coffee. I tell him he did not need to go out of his way to make it, but as I find out—Salim's coffee is a bit of an establishment in Jayuya. Proudly pointing out the sign on the front of his building, which reads *Si no hacemos negocio, nos tomamos el café* ("If we don't do business, we drink coffee"), Salim says people know he gives away the coffee, which is locally grown, harvested, prepared, and roasted. He boasts it is some of the best coffee on the island. Sure enough, in my three hours at his shop several people stop by for a cup. While talking with Salim in his office, a man from Jayuya even feels comfortable enough to come in and make his own pot!

Sipping my tooth-sweet coffee, I ask Salim more questions about his background. Born in Ramallah in 1954, he grew up in Palestine and did not leave until he was twenty-one or twenty-two. Seeking to escape the unpredictability of life in Palestine in the 1970s, he moved to Dubai in 1976. After a few years in the United Arab Emirates, he heard from his brother in Puerto Rico that life was good in the Caribbean—there was a moderate climate, safety, and good business opportunities. And so, in 1981 he relocated to Jayuya and joined his brother and family already there. They were the only Muslims in town at the time. Salim started selling clothes door-to-door and making connections in the community. Soon, he built up enough social and financial capital to open his electronics store. It has been a staple in Jayuya for over twenty years. The first day he opened, Salim did not sell anything, but he did give away free coffee. More than a gimmick, the clever courtesy worked, and Salim is one of the most trusted and successful businessmen in town. "I am not a millionaire," he says, "but I have a home, food in my belly, a family to love, and things to do. *Alhamdullilah*." His family—wife, two sons with their own families, and a daughter—all live in Puerto Rico. He also has a cousin in town. Adjoined to his cousin's house, just a couple of blocks down from the store, is the community's prayer room. They built the prayer room as an add-on in 1997. While the Muslim sociality in Jayuya remains small—about ten men show up for jummah prayers on Friday every week—they are tight-knit. When I ask Salim about an imam, he laughs, "If you come this Friday, you could be the imam."

With his US passport and money-making business, Salim is able to travel every year to see his brother, who retired to Amman, Jordan, where he is closer to their 111-year-old father in Ramallah. I ask him if he thinks about moving back to the West Bank. He says, "No, when I moved here, I said to myself, '*Este es mi cementerio*.'" ("This is my cemetery.") He is still proud of his Palestinian roots. As we wait for dhuhr prayers, he ushers me back into his air-conditioned office to show me a video of Mohammad Assaf who, he beamed, won *Arab Idol*. "He is from Gaza," Salim tells me, "it shows everyone that there is more to Palestine than violence. They make beautiful things, music, there too."

With the music still playing—quite loudly—in the background, Raduan returns with the key and a few appliances for delivery. Salim and I help unload a couple of fridges and three washers. As we work, a farmer named Ernesto walks in and greets Salim like an old friend. Salim shouts over, "I've known Ernesto since he was a baby . . . but now he is older than me!" They laugh and Ernesto comes to the back to share a cup of coffee with Salim and me. My hands shaking from caffeine and dreaming of decaf, I strike up a conversation with Ernesto, who tells me the coffee we are drinking—and making me shiver with energy—is from his farm. He tells me it is difficult being a farmer in the current economic situation, amid Puerto Rico's financial crisis. He says he is still able to export coffee, but with locals it is harder. Over three thousand people left Jayuya in the 2010s (about 6 percent of the population). But he keeps doing business with Salim, whom he met as a boy when Salim came around selling clothes at his family's home in the hills. "No one comes out there," he said, "except Salim . . . he's different." Our conversation is interrupted as two women come into the shop looking for a stove. Salim greets them with *besos y abrazos* (kisses and hugs) and welcomes them into the store with coffee. It's a small gesture, but a sure sign of Salim's solidified standing in Jayuya. He is, as they say, part of the fabric of the place. And if people do not do business with him (though it seems they often do), they at least can sip on some of Ernesto's coffee with him.

Salim's story represents a microcosm of the Arab Muslim migrant experience in Puerto Rico. His local entanglements, transregional connections, the impetus for his departure in the calamitous decades of the twentieth century, the economic opportunities that drew him to Puerto Rico, and the community he collected around him represent similar experiences among fellow Palestinian Muslims like him across the archipelago. Although Puerto Rico is often ignored or overlooked in discussions of Arab diasporas, the Palestinians there have left a significant imprint on the local economy and the archipelago's religious life.

In general, Arabs in the Americas share a common narrative of successful merchant ventures like Salim's and showcase a healthy degree of integration into the local community, while at the same time maintaining specific ethnic identities or hybrid practices such as diglossia.[97] As a diaspora sociality, Palestinians in particular have been labeled a people "between assimilation and long-distance nationalism."[98] We see this with Salim as well, who has no plans of leaving Puerto Rico but still maintains visible, strong ties with his patronage. Altogether, Salim's story is a reminder not only of Palestinians' particular presence in Puerto Rico but also of their ongoing influence on the makeup of its Muslim sociality and the experience of local converts who join it.

## THE OGS: ALIANZA ISLÁMICA AND BANI SAKR

Just as Arabs like Salim were arriving in Puerto Rico, so too were numerous Puerto Ricans making their way to the US. Already in the beginning of the twentieth century, Puerto Ricans migrated to Hawaii to work sugar farms. Then, from the interwar years to the post–World War II boom, they arrived in places like New York City and its environs, founding what became known as the "Nuyorican" community. Throughout the course of the twentieth and early twenty-first centuries, they also came in increased numbers—more than 850,000 migrated north between 1940 and 1970 alone—to places like Philadelphia, Pennsylvania; Newark, New Jersey; Chicago, Illinois; Hartford,

Connecticut; and Nashua, New Hampshire.[99] More recently, they have come to Florida—now home to the largest Puerto Rican population in the US.[100] In these locales, they mixed and mingled with fellow migrants and other minoritized populations, including Black Muslims or Muslims from the Middle East, South Asia, and Africa. Slowly but surely, and thanks to daily contact and connections with Muslims in their neighborhoods, workplaces, and local bodegas, pockets of Puerto Rican reverts started to emerge.[101]

In this regard, one urban center in particular stands out from the rest: New York City. It was from its metroplex that the first significant AmeRícan Muslim communities emerged: Bani Sakr and Alianza Islámica. As the first Latinx-specific Muslim organization in the US, Alianza Islámica is appropriately noted as a significant node in Latinx Muslim history. However, its particular Puerto Rican flavor—or *sazón*—receives less attention. And yet, Puerto Ricans played a significant role in giving shape to the Latinx Muslim community emerging around it and across the US in the '60s, '70s, and '80s.[102] Specifically, by exploring some of the memories around the emergence of Alianza Islámica and Bani Sakr, I suggest Puerto Rican Muslims constitute a critical nucleus within the emergence of a broader Latinx Muslim sociality, playing an outsized role in its development and contemporary contours. As Lebrón put it, one could say Puerto Rican Muslims are Latinx Muslims' "OGs." Puerto Rican Muslims not only were Bani Sakr's and Alianza Islámica's core constituents but also served as their leaders, providing inspiration for, and shaping the development of, future Latinx Muslim organizations, both online and elsewhere in the US and Latin America. Thus, to understand Latinx Muslims past or present it is necessary to attend to dynamics among Puerto Ricans in particular.[103]

Similar to Palestinian Muslims in Puerto Rico, the experience of Puerto Ricans involved with Muslim communities in the '70s, '80s, and '90s was simultaneously global and local, not easily delimited by the categories often proposed as frames for American Muslim history. As the Puerto Rican diaspora "contributed to eroding the conventional dichotomy between black and white people that has prevailed throughout U.S. History,"[104] AmeRícan Muslims (and Latinx Muslims in general) also challenge the prevailing split between so-called "indigenous" and "immigrant" Muslims in the US. Their story further complicates the already intricate, interwoven, and intimate currents of contemporary Muslim American identity in the context of a globally networked ummah. They challenge forced binaries that draw strict lines between identifications, illustrating how the formation of identity is a complex process involving imaginative agency, shot through with multivalent discourses and practices embodied in specific, local—and in this case, urban—contexts.

Although they converted for many and various reasons, early Puerto Rican Muslims came to know Islam largely through contact with Black Muslims.[105] The Black Muslims who were their friends, neighbors, and coworkers claimed membership in the Ahmadiyya, the NOI, the FPN, at Sunni mosques, in Sufi *turuq*, Shi'i groups, or the Moorish Science Temple of America in US urban centers like Chicago or New York City's Harlem neighborhood, dubbed "Black Mecca" by religion scholar Zain Abdullah.[106] Through these contacts, Puerto Ricans converted to Islam, often as a means of augmenting and undergirding their broader civil rights struggle.[107] As historian Patrick D. Bowen wrote, while Latinx groups would later emerge to provide mutual aid, organized protests, or supplement religious and social organizations, they tended to be small when compared to Black organizations. Therefore, larger Black groups remained "important loci of resistance to oppression" for Puerto Rican converts.[108]

That importance is reflected in the personal trajectories of numerous early Puerto Rican converts. One was Piri Thomas, who during his incarceration in Comstock Prison in New York in the 1950s "became involved with a group of NOI members after seeing and hearing their unique practices." Another is Benjamin Pérez, who joined the Oakland, California, NOI mosque in 1957.[109] Five Percenters also explicitly sought out Latinx converts, "primarily Puerto Ricans, who were often called 'Power Rules,' following the 'religious'-symbolic alphabet's application to 'P.R.'"[110] Among these early 'Power Rules' Gods were Sha Sha, Armando X (a.k.a. P.R.), and Kendu Islam. Sha Sha became the prime FPN proselytizer among indigenous Americans, and Kendu Islam came to some prominence within the movement due to the fact that he pulled the lever to cremate Clarence 13X, the FPN's founder,[111] and is "reported to have brought the teachings to Puerto Rico."[112] There were others, like a certain Ernesto "Puerto Rican Righteous" Piniella who played a part in establishing an FPN crew's drug distribution network in South Jamaica, Queens.[113] Another prominent example is Brooklyn-born Big Daddy Kane—originally named Antonio Monterio Hardy—who was a 'God' and influential hip-hop artist in the 1980s and '90s.

In fact, FPN influence on Puerto Ricans continued for decades. Orlando, who told me he converted in the late 1990s, said if it was not for the FPN, his own trajectory within Islam would have been radically different. The Queens-born postal service worker said he was running around with some gangs in his teens, searching for a community he could call his own. "That's why I was sucked in by Salafis for a long time." Salafism, a broad, modernist Islamic reform movement focused on purity and clarity of doctrine, appeals to many humiliated, downtrodden, and disgruntled young people—including discriminated migrants or the politically marginalized—like Orlando.[114] He said he was attracted to Salafism as a young man in search of a strong footing, finding in its doctrines and practices a coherence he found wanting in the Catholicism of his childhood, the gangs of his youth, or other religious groups he was looking into at the time.

But Orlando soon tired of the constant focus on purity and the deterritorialized and de-culturized character of the movement,[115] which he felt encouraged him to downplay his Blackness and Puerto Ricanness. When he came across the FPN in Harlem, he at first thought they were "*loco*, absolutely crazy," he said, but soon came to see things from their perspective. In brief, the FPN emerged after an NOI member named Clarence 13X embarked on his own study of the group's insider text, the Supreme Wisdom Lessons, in the 1960s. His conclusions put him at odds with official NOI doctrine, particularly around the issue that Black people are the true and living gods of the universe. He broke away from the NOI, renaming himself "Allah" as a representation of the wisdom he had learned from sources like the NOI's "Lost-Found Muslim Lesson No. 2"—that the 5 percent of the poor, righteous teachers should see God in themselves, so that the 10 percent of the rich and powerful can have no power over them. Orlando said:

> The message was simple, but revolutionary: You're the god. No one else is but you. So, when people try to tell you how to think, who to be, how to express who you are as a Puerto Rican, you ask them to "show and prove." I learned from the Five Percenters that Black people are true living gods. That truth made being Muslim possible for me again after my Salafi sojourn. Fact of the matter is: A man named "Allah" changed my life.

Like others, Orlando found in the FPN a message, strategy, and ideology of survival and resistance. The FPN not only allowed for new religious identifications, but it was also a social reality he found more satisfying than what other formulations like New York street gangs, the Catholic Church, or Salafism offered.[116]

Puerto Rican Muslims such as Orlando played various roles in the development of groups like the NOI, FPN, and other Muslim organizations springing up in US urban centers in the twentieth century. As minorities struggling together on city streets and on the margins of the US Muslim community, Black Muslims of multiple ethnic backgrounds often worked with one another to establish themselves in Islam. Moreover, it could be said that as (or alongside) Black Muslims, Puerto Rican Muslims helped filter Islamic cultural and historical precedents into mainstream Western culture and history through minority societal infusion and discourses.[117] Tapping into general anti-imperial sensitivities across Latin America, Islam provided a new opportunity for Puerto Ricans in the US to counter predominant culture and binary racial categories alongside other Muslims *and* other Puerto Ricans.[118] Without the connections, collaborations, and conflicts emerging from these contacts and conversions, multiple Puerto Rican Muslims say they would not be who they are today.

### *An "Oasis in El Barrio": Alianza Islámica*[119]

Puerto Rican Muslims' resistance discourse and activism flowered in the work of Alianza Islámica in the 1980s. Situated within broader currents of Nuyorican activism, Alianza Islámica's founders John "Yahya" Figueroa, Ramon "Rahim" Ocasio, Mark "Abdus Salam" Ortiz, and Freddie "Ibrahim" González "grew up in a revolutionary center of political activism and the struggle for civil rights."[120] They founded Alianza in 1987 at 1717 Lexington Avenue in the heart of East Harlem. Not "merely interested in starting a new cultural phenomenon of halal tacos and Islamized aguinaldos,"[121] the founders wanted to reach out with the message of Islam and improve their neighborhood and its way of life. Ocasio said the impetus for Alianza came both from their ostracism in local mosques and from being "absorbed into the existing established ethnic communities while maintaining only a token, marginal attachment to their own ethnicity."[122] They did not want to be "spiritually colonized," he wrote.[123] They were also motivated by a deep desire for social justice. He said:

> African Americans back in the 70s would convert and they would go to an African American mosque and wouldn't feel alien. They had a support group. They weren't left out to dry. In contrast with the Latinos . . . they [took] shahadah and blend into what—the greater Muslim mass . . . they start dressing differently and people don't know who they are. How could anybody count Latino Muslims? Go to a mosque in New Jersey, New York City, how could you tell? And after a while . . . some people blend in, survivors, they can take it . . . there are those who aren't surviving. They are leaving.

Ocasio and his fellow founders decided to create something for themselves. Ocasio said, "We wanted to create a safe space where we don't feel alienated, where our culture matters, yet it has an Islamic expression. Alianza created that space."

They also wanted to speak out against racism, struggle in the cause of social justice, and liberate people from what they saw as El Barrio's moral enfeeblement. Ocasio said, "We felt that Islam was the salvation for our family. For our community. For our people. And then for humanity at large." They partnered with prominent cultural institutions like Museo El Barrio, met with New York City Council member Adam Clayton Powell IV (the son of civil rights leader and congressman Adam Clayton Powell Jr. and his third wife Yvette Diago), and modeled their first storefront location on the Mosque of the Islamic Brotherhood's 1970s tea rooms, where they offered a range of programs, including GED and ESL courses, health and nutrition seminars, prison visitations, HIV/AIDS care work, *aqidah* (creedal theology) classes, outreach initiatives, employment assistance, *janazah* (funeral rites) for victims of AIDS, sewing classes, drug and gang counseling, and what they called *la Mezquita del Barrio*—the Barrio's mosque. They also marched in *caminatas*, "where brothers and sisters, even whole families, would walk en masse down 3rd Avenue, Spanish Harlem's main street, to spark attention, curiosity, and, perhaps, some conversation," wrote Ocasio.[124] In their by-laws, they envisioned "central departments" for dawah and public propagation; labor, to provide information and advising for creating meaningful employment opportunities; substance abuse, which "affect[s] the lives of minorities and all problems related"; prisoner affairs, to "maintain active communication with incarcerated [M]uslims"; women's affairs; and publication and translation services.[125] Sharing a language, an ethnicity, a history, a call for social justice, a cosmopolitan outlook simultaneously focused on their local needs, and a religion made Alianza Islámica a hub for Puerto Rican and Latinx Muslims in the city—what they believed to be "the Prophet's ideal institution."[126]

Even today, almost three decades since they first inhabited the building at 1717 Lexington Avenue, the neighborhood still knows their name. Slowly becoming gentrified, the area is no longer the El Barrio of old. And yet, traces of its history remain. Where Alianza Islámica once stood, just blocks from the Spanish Methodist Church occupied by the Young Lords in 1969 and 1970, there is a barber shop and a brewpub catering to the area's newcomers. Just two doors down to the left, however, is an old boutique with a Puerto Rican flag hanging in the window that looks like it has been around for a while. I knocked on the door to find a group of older women inside, chatting, playing cards, and surprisingly beckoning me in. I told them why I was there and one of them smiled as she scanned the cards in her hands, looking for her next play. "I remember la Alianza," she said, "they haven't been here for years, but I remember them from the '90s. They were a big deal in their time and people still know who they are." While you would not know it, their heritage and history remain in a part of the city still known for its activism and deep Puerto Rican roots.

Speaking with some of Alianza Islámica's founders and original members—including Ocasio, Figueroa, and Jorge Pabon—a couple of months later in Queens, we discussed how best to situate the organization's emergence in the 1980s. Reflecting on the "old days," Figueroa told me how he grew up in New York City's *barrios* and encountered various gangs, social activist groups, and religious communities all "vying for your attention and allegiance." It was at this time, he said, a certain Nuyorican and post-colonial Puerto Rican consciousness came of age in metro areas like New York, Hartford, Chicago, Philadelphia, and Boston. Among movements that included the Movimiento Pro Independencia (MPI), later El Comité; the US branch of the Puerto Rican Socialist Party; the Puerto Rican Student Union (PRSU); the Movement for National Liberation (MLN); and the Armed Forces of National Liberation (FALN) was the Young Lords Party (YLP),[127] a political organization representing "the concerns of Puerto Rican urban youth and their commitment to make a difference in dealing with the everyday problems of the inner city barrios."[128]

Originally founded in Chicago as a street gang by José "Cha Cha" Jiménez in 1968,[129] the New York chapter would prove "the most visible and active"[130] within the emerging YLP network. There, Miguel "Micky" Melendez gathered with other like-minded student activists who were also increasingly aware of the social inequality experienced by Cubans and Puerto Ricans in and around El Barrio. Inspired and influenced by the Black Panthers, the Chicano civil rights movement out West, and the anti–Vietnam War struggle, Melendez helped charter the YLP's New York branch, which became a powerful and respected, if controversial, voice of Puerto Rican resistance.[131] From their storefront headquarters in East Harlem (Madison Avenue and 111th Street, now known as "Young Lords Way"), they defiantly fought back against racism, oppression, and injustice through a potent combination of direct action and community empowerment.[132] Involving a multiethnic range of "revolutionist nationalists," they not only offered free breakfast programs, clothing drives, health services, and cultural programs for the community, they also took direct action through takeovers of the First People's Church (the Spanish Methodist Church at the corner of 111th and Lexington) and Lincoln Hospital in 1969 and 1970.[133]

Their work provided an embodied, empowering sense of idealism, anger, and vitality—or Borícua *power*[134]—to Puerto Ricans and other Latinx inhabitants in El Barrio at a time when they were facing increasing economic pressures, lack of educational parity, discrimination, police brutality, gentrification, threats to their cultural identifications, and residential displacement.[135] While the YLP only existed for a few years, they embodied a radical ethos that was part of a broader, anti-imperialist movement, inspiring other organizations through their direct actions.

One such organization was Alianza Islámica. Danny "Khalil" Salgado (also known as al-Portorikani) wrote:

> A product of their times, the surrounding radicalness encouraged some to make the "radical" move on the religious front: embracing Islam. Islam was not viewed as religion, but as a viable answer to society's problems.[136]

Salgado further wrote that Alianza's founders "envisioned themselves" as a movement "that would bring positive change among 'Latinos'" in ways similar to the YLP. Moreover, he argued, they "viewed Islam in terms of a liberation theology," which helped them carry on the legacy of YLP's activist spirit in El Barrio. Salgado quoted Ibrahim González as saying, "We didn't want to give up the struggle, so we looked in different places. Islam represented a place for us to be part of a larger community." Ocasio said they

> saw a smooth transition between becoming Muslim and continuing the same kind of militant social activism that we were engaged in before with the Young Lords Party . . . [e]xcept, now we were doing it "Islamically," and we thought we were doing it in a much more moral, in a much more substantial, much more substantive way.[137]

In Ocasio's telling, groups fostering a rhetoric and modus of resistance reinforced with images of armed revolutionaries were part of the milieu out of which Alianza emerged. He said groups such as the YLP, the Student Non-Violent Coordinating Committee (SNCC), the Black Panther Party, el Movimiento Pro Independencia, El Comité, and the PRSU inspired him and others to offer the people of El Barrio what they felt was "a real and tangible way to build their identities and draw strength in times of hardship."[138] Thus, Alianza built their project on the model of other community activists and civic organizations already operating in the Puerto Rican diaspora for decades.

Another of Alianza's *pioneros*, Yahya Figueroa, became a Muslim in 1973 after being a member of the YLP. There were, however, other influences shaping his role in what Alianza Islámica would become. Along the way to his conversion, Figueroa said he was attracted to the Ahmadis and said they were "influential" in the early formation of Black and Puerto Rican Muslim socialities.[139] "We wouldn't be what we are without them," he said. He said he also used to "go around with the Tablighi Jamaat to lapsed Pakistanis in the city and started thinking, 'Why am I not doing this with my own people?'" He also dabbled as a Five Percenter, he said, "because I was at 112 and Lennox, you had to be. There was no choice." He saw Malcolm X speak in Harlem, he listened to Clarence 13X ("Allah") "teach mathematics lessons to the gods." Along with Ocasio and González, the trio also associated with the Islamic Party of North America (IPNA), a Washington, DC–based Muslim organization, beginning in 1975. They felt it would help them extend their work through disciplined, coordinated activism and civic engagement around issues of poverty and social injustice.

In relation to such groups, these "young Muslim Nuyoricans now faced a new form of possible assimilation and loss of Latino language and culture."[140] This time, Harold Morales wrote, "they worried their Spanish would be displaced by Arabic and their culture by one from a Muslim majority society."[141] Figueroa said:

> They try to tell us that we shouldn't be tribal or have our own culture. All of them do! They are proud of being Saudi, Turkish, Pakistanis, whatever. And we've been behind them. We were out there marching for Palestine before anyone else. We fought [the Jews] to march and protest. We know how to be global; we choose to remain proudly Puerto Rican.

Ocasio and Figueroa, alongside González, founded Alianza Islámica in 1987 with the expressed aim of propagating Islam and offering social service programs for "their people"—bringing "peace to [their] beloved neighborhood."[142] This Nuyorican core sought to draw other Latinx members of their community into the fold and to struggle for justice in a shared and "similar cosmopolitan space in the United States."[143] Influenced by the "revolutionary center of political activism and the struggle for civil rights" they grew up with in New York City,[144] Figueroa, Ocasio, and González drew inspiration from various movements that came before them, from the Ahmadiyya, NOI, and FPN to the Zulu Nation and YLP. They also took cues from a relatively forgotten group of Puerto Rican reverts in 1970s Newark.

### *Bani Sakr*

According to community testimony and reports, Bani Sakr was founded by former YLP members Al-Hajj Yusuf Abdul Rahman Padilla-Alvarez, Yahya Garcia, and Puerto Rico–born Karima Kayyam in Newark in 1972, with "Hajj Hisham Jaber, who led Malcolm X's funeral prayer, as their spiritual guide."[145] Similar to Alianza Islámica, various Black, Latinx, and other ethnic empowerment organizations influenced their community's genesis. But they remained distinctly Puerto Rican. Rahim Ocasio wrote of his visit to Bani Sakr in 1974:

> We were among other Muslims unashamedly Latino, proudly sporting names like Yusuf Padilla and Bilal Arce. A wedding there was a delight, feasting on sumptuous arroz con pollo to a soundtrack of percussive rhythms, tumba y bongó, an expression of ourselves that no longer looked foreign or alien, something our mothers could relate to. We now had a glimpse of what was possible and were determined to make it a reality.[146]

In a piece titled, "A Historical Review of Bani Sakr," later published on the Alianza Islámica blog, Padilla-Alvarez fleshed out the strong Puerto Rican nature of the group in his own biography:

> I was born Jose Angel Padilla-Alvarez, in El Corozo de Boqueron, Cabo Rojo, Puerto Rico in 1954. My family migrated to New York then to Newark, New Jersey while I was still an infant. On the historical side, most Puerto Ricans migrated from Puerto Rico to New York where they settled and work. My uncles Antoline, Santos and another person by the name Fundador were the first Puerto Ricans to move from New York to Newark. My parents followed suit. My mother's two sisters remained in New York and the other brother.[147]

There, among Black residents and Italian, Portuguese, Polish, Turkish, and Central American neighbors, Padilla-Alvarez remembers the early influence of the NOI and the reputation and resonance of Temple No. 25 on South Orange Ave., the first NOI mosque to open in Newark (in 1958). He also recalls the push and pull of gang life in the wider New York City area at the time, with mafiosos in Little Italy, the Tongs in Chinatown, the Latin Kings, and others claiming, and competing for, street corners and neighborhoods across the metroplex.

Lacking any distinct Latinx institutional presence or guidance, Padilla-Alvarez and other Puerto Ricans like him turned to neighbors who already embraced Islam. Many of them were Black Muslims who belonged to groups like the NOI, FPN, or Sunni groups emerging around the city. Padilla-Alvaraz himself said he took the shahadah at the State Street Masjid in Brooklyn—also known as Masjid Dawood or the Islamic Mission of America—founded by Sheikh Dawood Ahmed Faisal and his wife Sayedah Khadijah Faisal in 1939. Of Haitian descent, the pair aimed "to bring immigrant Muslims and new American converts to the faith together in one mosque . . . where Muslims from Pakistan and Morocco prayed shoulder to shoulder with American black converts."[148] Padilla-Alvarez remembers Black, Yemeni, and other Arabs joining together there for prayer in the '70s.[149]

Although not without its tensions, fissures, and silos, the wider New York/New Jersey Muslim community became a multicultural milieu in the 1960s. Muslims from all over the world rubbed shoulders with one another, organizing various outreach groups and communities for study and prayer. Out of that mix, Hajj Hisham Jaber mentored Padilla-Alvarez, who then "preached" to "a chain of relationships" among family and friends in towns like Elizabeth, a suburb of Newark. By the mid-1970s, a small, Puerto Rican Muslim "community" emerged out a core of "bad guys" who bought, sold, and brokered weapons and drugs in what Padilla-Alvarez described as the Newark's "massive ghetto." Padilla-Alvarez wrote:

> We made no open public dawa efforts. We grew organically from within. Others began to come into the ranks. We were young, but we "believed." . . . As we grew and expanded into the predominant Catholic/Pentecostal tightly knit Puerto Rican community, other non-Muslim Puerto Ricans began to take notice and we were not liked, liked, or distantly respected, or not respected at all. There were too many ties of relationships via blood and friendships that were binding everyone together (Muslim and non-Muslim). It was a powder keg. Some traditional families had become divided through religious lines.

In an effort to connect with the broader ummah, they decided to call themselves "Bani Sakr" after Dr. Ahmad Hussein Sakr, a founding member and president of the Muslim Students' Association of the US and Canada, later known as the Islamic Society of North America (ISNA). Sakr was also a founding member of the World Council of Mosques and the first director and representative of the Muslim World League to the UN.

The idea, said Padilla-Alvarez, was to "get warm and fuzzy, 'Rico Suave' style, with the new brother in town, the man with the money." That strategy faltered, along with many other attempts at gaining support from larger Muslim organizations. Padilla-Alvarez said:

> There were many broken promises from so-called Muslim and Arab funding sources, outside support groups, and internal disputes about the actual goals and direction of Bani Sakr. . . . Latin American Muslims in North America were nothing to be given consideration to. We just didn't count or seem to exist. This attitude is still prevalent even unto today.

For this reason, and because of internal disputes and a lack of organizational focus, Bani Sakr slowly dissolved and disbanded. According to Padilla-Alvarez, Bani Sakr's main problem was "looking outside of our own Latin Americans for guidance and leadership." Saying that every American Muslim community had leaders from among themselves, he said, Puerto Ricans and other Latinx Muslims could "cultivate our own as well."

It was this sentiment that inspired Alianza's founders. Burned by larger organizations that they felt demanded they temper their Puerto Ricanness, they sought to explicitly address the realities their communities were facing rather than deal with the vicissitudes of changing interest by larger, transnational organizations like the Muslim World League, ISNA, or IPNA.[150] This point becomes clearer when Alianza Islámica is situated within a wider nexus of politically and socially active young organizations representing the more radical politics of the Puerto Rican diaspora in US cities in the 1970s and '80s. Tired of "second-class citizenship, racism, and poverty, as well as with the United States' continuing colonial domination of Puerto Rico,"[151] Puerto Rican radicalism—including Alianza Islámica—resisted various forms of marginalization through their activism, seeking to overcome the challenges of migration in a colonial context while also creating new alternatives for social connection and collaboration. These groups are another example of a range of activist communities and cliques that "sought to adjust to and mold their new surroundings to meet their needs, as well as to improve conditions for themselves and others, [relying] on social networks, the celebration of cultural traditions, involvement in existing community institutions, the building of their own community organizations, and political activism" to get their work done.[152]

## DOT-COM DAWAH AND CONTEMPORARY ACTIVISM

After being evicted from their "home turf" in El Barrio, Alianza Islámica re-established themselves at 287 Alexander Avenue in the South Bronx in the year 2000. The organization struggled to find its footing in the Bronx, and Ocasio wrote, "torn from its roots, it was never the same."[153] What Ocasio called a "slow, inexorable decline" ended in 2005, when a fire gutted the building's basement space, which they occupied. Nonetheless, Alianza inspired, informed, and influenced second and third waves—or "generations" as Ocasio prefers[154]—of Latinx Muslim organizations and initiatives. As author and community historian Juan Galvan wrote, "Alianza Islamica was more than just a building or a place to gather and worship. It continues to represent a movement."[155] From groups like LADO to the Three Puerto Rican Imams project, each drew on Alianza's legacy and example to celebrate "Latino ways of being Muslim and Islamic ways of being Latino,"[156] provide community-specific dawah, engage in philanthropy, and make contributions to American civil society.

Concomitant with the general Sunnification and Arabization of Muslim communities in the US in the 1990s, multiple organizations grew out of Alianza Islámica, albeit with slightly different emphases. In particular, alongside the "Dot-Com Boom" at the end of the millennium, there was a burgeoning of numerous online communities and chat rooms where Latinx Muslims across the US, Latin America, and the Caribbean (and even as far afield as the Middle East and North Africa) could connect and share experiences. These, in turn, later gave birth to groups like LADO in September 1997,[157] as well as a slew of other organizations in subsequent years. This was, according to Morales, the "second wave" of Latinx Muslim conversion and community development.[158] Through the leadership of the likes of Juan Galvan from Texas and Juan Shafiq Alvarado of New York, LADO produced the periodical *The Latino Muslim Voice* starting in 2002, which provided "discourses and strategies"[159] to help reverts deal with the primary crises and issues of their recent reversion (specifically, the dual ostracism they faced from the Latinx culture on the one hand, and their newly found Muslim community on the other).

Whereas groups like Bani Sakr and Alianza Islámica featured a distinctive Puerto Rican sazón in their work, these later waves of Latinx Muslim conversion and community building were much broader in character and appeal. Overall, the unifying voice of conversion narratives and the culturally creative power of community character created a pan-Latinx Muslim narrative. While still referencing particular heritages and backgrounds (e.g., Mexican, Dominican, Salvadoran, Puerto Rican), the overall emphasis was on an umbrella "Latino" or "Hispanic" culture and its connections to, and correspondence with, broader Islamic cultures. They thus helped create a comprehensive Latinx Muslim ethos, or sense of Islamidad.[160]

These Latinx-specific Muslim organizations emerged to not only meet the needs of their own community but also reach others beyond. Since Alianza Islámica and Bani Sakr paved the way and LADO broadened its appeal and approach, a myriad of other organizations came forth including, but not limited to, IslamInSpanish (a multimedia organization aiming to translate outreach materials and information into Spanish); Why Islam? (a hotline set up by Muslim volunteers to offer Islamic advice and information to people of Latina/o background, including many in Mexico); La Asociación Latino Musulmana de América, popularly referred to as "LALMA" (supporting outreach activities, transitional support, Spanish-language materials, and introduction courses to Islam); the NHIEC (although not specifically Latinx in nature, it has the largest concentration of Latinx Muslims compared to any other Islamic center or masjid in its region and thus engages in Latinx-specific dawah, including Hispanic Muslim Day); Propagación Islámica para la Educación y la Devoción a Alláh el Divino (PIEDAD, a network of women who engage in activities to support Latinx Muslim spiritual development, community building, sisterhood, and educational outreach); and local organizations such as Latino Muslims of Chicago, the Latino Muslim Association of the San Fernando Valley (LMASFV), Alameda Islamica: Latino Muslims of the Bay Area, and the Atlanta Latino Muslim Association (ALMA). Such paramosque organizations expanded the footprint and effectiveness of Latinx-specific dawah and owe much of their inspiration to the initial catalysts among Puerto Rican Muslims in and around New York in the 1970s and '80s.

Having achieved a certain level of understanding, and acceptance, among the Muslim community in the US, many of these organizations are now reconfiguring and consolidating their efforts.[161] According to Morales, the efforts of organizations such as IslamInSpanish and the Los Angeles Latino Muslim Association are shaped

> by political discourses around ISIS, immigration, and the 2016 election cycle. Increasingly negative coverage of Latinos, Muslims, and Latino Muslims within this context has prompted renewed attempts to consolidate the resources of disparate Latino Muslim groups across the nation in order to unite and produce collective responses to hateful characterizations of their identity groups in public discourse.

The result is a dual move with three manifestations. In the first move, Latinx Muslim outreach groups are reaching broader constituencies than before, both within and beyond the Latinx demographic. In the second move, there is a parallel process of re-specification, predicated on efforts to reach particular constituencies within the broader Latinx umbrella. These two moves, in turn, manifest in three ways.

First, there are initiatives to reach people through targeted outreach efforts across Latin America and the Caribbean. This is part of a general trend in which "in a postcolonial world [. . .] Muslim missionary efforts are being recast in a global, multicultural, and multilingual context."[162] Not only are *da'is*—those who invite others to faith, to prayer, or to Islam—finding it necessary to engage in more "soft-sell" forms of dawah in North America, they are also seeing the need to tailor Islam to particular cultural realities and languages. Da'is reaching out to Latinx people in the US and others in Latin American countries realized that Islamic doctrine and practice need to be translated into the Spanish language and local cultures in order for them to come into "authentic" contact with Islam. These Latinx Muslim da'is do so not only in US metro areas where there are large Latinx populations (e.g., Houston, Los Angeles, Miami, San Antonio, Chicago, and New York) but also in places such as Mexico, Puerto Rico, and Ecuador.[163]

Second, recent reporting and research shows how outreach organizations and institutions like Centro Islámico in Houston, Texas, are broadening their appeal beyond the Latinx community. Offering services in both Spanish and English, Centro Islámico reaches a broad swathe of believers, including Arabs, South Asians, Turks, and Black Americans.[164] Preliminary studies also point to how their use of media enables a sociality that crosses ethnic, national, and geographic boundaries. Whether it's a Bangladeshi member from Houston, Latinx Muslims listening in from Arizona, or others in Latin America looking for resources in Spanish, Centro Islámico's local work in Houston serves as a platform for a much broader scope of contact and community.[165]

Third, and finally, there are groups focusing on more specific demographics within the broader Latinx Muslim community. Apropos to this book, numerous organizations with a distinct Puerto Rican leadership and/or focus emerged over the last decade, including Puerto Rican Muslim Facebook groups and the Esperanza Community Hub. There are a number of Facebook groups and pages aimed at Latinx Muslims of various backgrounds and in multiple contexts. Among them are pages such as "Boricuas Embraced by Islam" and "Puerto Rican Muslims." The explicit purpose of both groups is to help "Borícua Muslims" to "get to know each other" and for everyone on the page to learn more about Islam through a Puerto Rican perspective. Members post about traveling to Puerto Rico and looking for halal food recommendations in popular tourist destinations, raise funds for well-building projects in Haiti and Gaza, link to *khutab* from imams in Montehiedra, Puerto Rico, share pictures from Puerto Rican history, or inquire about Islamic schools and mezquitas on the archipelago. Through such posts about everyday piety, sharing memes, digging deeper into the Latinx Muslim "mythos," or debating politics across the ummah, Puerto Ricans are engaged in a complex process of creating a distinct Puerto Rican Muslim sociality.[166]

These examples bring the final—and most contemporary—coyuntura of AmeRícan Muslim history and its meaning in the lives of Puerto Rican Muslims full circle. Initiatives and groups like the Puerto Rican Muslim Facebook pages provide further examples of the "second wave" of Latinx Muslim activism in the US. They also stand out as Puerto Rican–specific cases of "third wave" activism, "characterized by a distinct historical context" including debates around immigration, the public role of Islam and Muslims in the US, and the relation of Latinx Muslims to the country as a whole.[167]

As much as they share similarities with the groups Morales analyzes and the reconfigurations of the Latinx Muslim landscape occurring during the 2010s, they also represent a distinct and notable divergence from a more general "consolidation," which Morales argues marks this "third wave." Although they feature connections and collaborations with other organizations and groups, each is particularly focused on Puerto Ricans' needs, identifications, and specific historical and contemporary context. They may serve broader needs (e.g., by building wells in Haiti or providing halal restaurant information to Muslims visiting Puerto Rico as tourists), but their impetus for existence is addressing the peculiar situation and struggle of Puerto Ricans on the archipelago and in the diaspora. In this, they are more similar to Alianza Islámica, whose mission—while certainly impacted by, and important to, a broad swathe of Latinx and non-Latinx Muslims—emerged out of the particular needs of Puerto Ricans in urban New Jersey and New York in the 1980s and '90s and its founders' motivation to "publicly showcase an expression of a distinctly Puerto Rican Muslim culture and accurately reflected our contemporary cultural reality" with a result that is "novel yet familiar to both Muslims and non-Muslim alike."[168]

## CONCLUSION

Together, the multiple crisscrossing storylines coming together at, in, and between the multiple coyunturas of AmeRícan Muslim historical memory show some of the everyday realities and contextual specificities giving shape to their notions of being and belonging. Furthermore, the accounts of how Puerto Rican Muslims read, understand, and live according to these histories illustrates how these "contingent lineages" help them authenticate certain identifications and their place in particular socialities in the present. Each of these histories—and their meaning in the lives of Puerto Rican Muslims—will reemerge in subsequent chapters. But already in the overview of the coyunturas themselves, we begin to get a sense of how those resources come from a diverse and deep array of temporal and geographic sources. This transregional and cosmopolitan assemblage will only thicken as we turn from historical narratives to focus on contemporary lives, beginning with a stroll along the Paseo de la Princesa in Viejo San Juan.

# 2
# "I will never deny I'm Borícua"
## RESIGNIFYING PUERTO RICAN PEOPLEHOOD

We had to assert our dignity in small ways . . . little details that tell the world, we are not invisible.

ABUELA CLAUDIA, *IN THE HEIGHTS*

IF WALKING DOWN BERGENLINE AVENUE in Union City or spending time in Staten Island evinces one aspect of AmeRícan Muslim peoplehood, a stroll down El Paseo de la Princesa in Viejo San Juan evokes another. This palm-shaded nineteenth-century esplanade, with its antique streetlamps, vendor's carts selling fruit and meat skewers (pinchos), and Sunday-afternoon salsa dancing for septuagenarians is often the starting point for a tourist's stroll through "Old San Juan." Often featured on postcards and posters, it is a stock image for Puerto Rico's cultural imaginary and tourist marketing—a place where tripartite notions of Puerto Rican peoplehood are prominently performed and presented for visitors and local alike.

As one emerges past the infamous "La Princesa"—a prison-turned-tourism-headquarters at the end of the walkway—and into sun-soaked views of San Juan Bay, the Raíces Fountain is hard to miss. Completed in 1992 by architect and artist Miguel Carlo to commemorate the five hundredth anniversary of the encounter between Spanish colonizers and the Amerindian populations of the Caribbean, the bronze statues in the center of the fountain are eye-catching and eclectic. Designed to honor the notion of the three roots (tres raíces) of Puerto Rican culture (African, Spanish, and indigenous cultures) in particular, the statue looks as if it is a ship being steered out to the sea.

It is one of many (re)presentations of Puerto Rico and Puerto Ricans that shape national conceptions of what counts as part of *la gran familia puertorriqueña*—the "Great Puerto Rican Family."[1] Beginning in the nineteenth century and continuing through the twentieth, photographs, music, paintings, posters, literature, architecture, poetry, and films helped *produce* a romanticized and idealized racial triptych of Puerto Rican sameness and national unity that was simultaneously ambiguous, divergent, and paradoxical, as it denied racial and class differences between what José Luis González called Puerto Rican culture's "four stories" (*cuatro pisos*): the Spanish colonial period, an Afro-Caribbean popular base, South American and European immigration, and US colonialism.[2] Along with other theories about hybridity and mixing on the archipelago,[3] such constructions of peoplehood are *products* of situated, material, human labor, which give shape and substance to an idea of who belongs to the Puerto Rican nation. As one of these productions, the statue acts as a tactical and tactile "enunciation of identity"[4] wherein notions of Puerto Rican peoplehood are negotiated, presented, and performed into being to produce an imaginary of sameness, intimacy, and constancy.[5]

Ethnicity, as a variable, imaginative repertoire of belonging, is based on crisscrossing historical, social, and cultural orders. For AmeRícan Muslims, their ethnic "practices of the self"[6] and efforts at "belonging" and "co-becoming"[7] emerge out of the generative friction and co-constitutive dialogue between becoming Muslim and produced notions of *puertorriqueñidad* expressed in places like the Raíces Fountain. Their attempts at integrating both into some kind of unified whole presents both challenges and opportunities. On the one hand, such practices help them fuse their identification as Muslims with conventional, tripartite notions of Puerto Rican identity and re-establish their Borícua bona fides. On the other hand, they also try to integrate their Muslim identification into new, and more cosmopolitan, conceptualizations and practices of Puerto Rican peoplehood. Some even go so far as to add a "fourth root" to what it means to be Puerto Rican.[8] In other words, Puerto Rican reverts seek ways to restore a sense of coherence and selfhood out of the flotsam and jetsam of *both* received notions of Puerto Rican culture *and*, as will be illustrated in later chapters, ideas about what it means to be "Muslim" in the late-modern world. They do not believe there is an innate dichotomy between *becoming* Muslim and *being* Puerto Rican. Allah, they insist, does not make them choose.

That is because AmeRícan Muslims are proud of their Puerto Ricanness. Look no further than a symbol often found on Puerto Rican Muslim Facebook pages. Popping up nearly every month in some shape or fashion, the image features a fist raised in defiance of colonial incursions and social marginalization, emblazoned with the Puerto Rican flag in resplendent blue, white, and red. Above and below are the traditional words associated with this symbol—"Puerto Rican Pride." This image is used by non-Muslim Puerto Ricans, but Puerto Rican Muslims add their own twist. Inserted, somewhat awkwardly, in between the top of the fist and the words "Puerto Rican" is "Muslim" in a false-Arabic font. When a Puerto Rican imam is hired by a mosque in the Bronx, a commenter posts this picture. When Muslims gather for Eid in San Juan, someone shares the image. When Lebrón and others protested the perceived mistreatment of Puerto Ricans in the wake of Hurricane María, the photo was displayed prominently on profiles and in discussions about the issue. It is but one of the "small ways [or] little details," in the words of Abuela Claudia in the popular movie *In the Heights*, that AmeRícan Muslims "tell the world, we are not invisible."[9]

At the same time, being Muslim does require reverts to become Puerto Rican in new ways. While identifying as a "Puerto Rican Muslim" is defined by mobility and divided experiences across borders and boundaries,[10] it is also defined by their interactions with particular places, people, and inherited perspectives on what counts as "Puerto Rican." Thus, AmeRícan Muslims create new modes of agency and affective representation through the spaces, places, people, and materials they encounter or are already embedded in as part of everyday life.[11] In particular, to craft more palpable and pliable "practices of the self," they turn to the tangible, material, and quotidian (e.g., food and foodways, rituals, language, sartorial practices, geography, and architecture) to resignify their identifications through a trans-creative process that subverts generally accepted notions of race, religion, or ethnicity. This includes how Puerto Rican Muslims share recipes for halal *habichuelas*, make much of Arabic's influence on the Spanish language, imaginatively interact with Puerto Rico's physical environment, or engage with vestiges of Islamic influence in local architecture along *avenidas* like the Paseo de la Princesa.

By exploring the material contexts wherein AmeRícan Muslims performatively reinterpret their identification as *both* Puerto Rican *and* Muslim, this chapter facilitates further reflection on what geographic, affective, and physical frameworks constitute *being* and *becoming* Puerto Rican; what social imaginaries and conceptual maps frame Puerto Ricanness; what place the diaspora and other transnational movements have in relating to the archipelago and its worlds; how this impacts ideas of race, ethnicity, and citizenship; and what ways Puerto Ricans of many kinds figure themselves within the thick polyvalence of Puerto Rican architectural, culinary, musical, linguistic, and visual culture. Thus, this chapter speaks to "notions of experience, affect, the unexpected and the sensorial . . . [and] the materiality of landscape" that call into question the "hegemonic archive of scholarly criticism" on the Caribbean(s)—and Puerto Rico in particular.[12] By extension, it also illustrates broader, everyday processes of cosmopolitanization long embedded in Caribbean experience,[13] which helps expand our understanding of what overlapping experiences of religion and ethnicity look, feel, and act like in the late-modern.[14]

Finally, this chapter reaffirms matter and place's ability to reflect and inform the quotidian complexity of late-modern lifeworlds. Applying this specifically to the study of Islam and Muslims, emphasis on matter and place makes "it possible to identify differences in Muslim life realities and appreciate the plurality of their local forms of expression"[15] while also attending to the discourses, texts, and traditions to which Muslims appeal as they navigate such conundrums.[16] This helps further humanize the "Muslim subject" and widen the scope of "Muslim identity" beyond the masjid and madrasah.

By offering personal, affective, and situated accounts, I provide a different take on the ways Muslims are represented and written about. Islamic studies scholar Vernon Schubel once argued that "the discipline of Islamic studies should have at its center the experience of Muslim people."[17] While that can include their encounters and engagement with classical texts, political movements, and elite jurisprudence, "it also includes the experience of ordinary Muslims" in particular places and material contexts, their lives intertwined with forces of time, mobility, and cultural contestation. By "turning to the tangible," such analysis helps us better "grasp Islam and Muslim cultures and societies in an alternate, more comprehensive way."[18]

## *PASTELES*, PLANTAIN STAINS, AND PEOPLEHOOD

Miriam, who has practiced Islam since 2001, had her own journey with what it means to identify as both Puerto Rican and Muslim. For her, being an AmeRícan Muslim is a mix of pilgrimage and pasteles, infectious laughter and living out Islamic law as a proud *puertorriqueña*, listening to the coquí frog in the evenings from the patio of her parents' home outside San Juan and the call to prayer ringing out from a phone app in the early morning hours back home in Houston, Texas. Her heart kindled by the camaraderie, festivities, and blessings of Ramadan each year, Miriam is also drawn to, and caught up in, the annual rhythm of *Día de Reyes* and the *navidades* season in Puerto Rico. She said:

> Since I was a kid, navidades has always produced this particular vibe, this special feeling for all Puerto Ricans. After I converted to Islam, there are many things I gave up—pork, alcohol, of course—but there are some aspects of being Borícua that I can't . . . no, that I won't . . . sacrifice.

In New York and Puerto Rico, Philadelphia and Florida, Puerto Rican reverts find ways to continually ground themselves in their Puerto Ricanness. They discover multiple ways to identify with Puerto Rican culture and history *as Muslims*. And yet, reacting to being minoritized within their own sociality after adding a new identification of belonging, they struggle to convince fellow Puerto Ricans that being Muslim does not negate being Borícua. To that end, they search for, and share, ways in which the two are intertwined. They draw on symbols, traditions, and aspects of received culture to undergird and navigate their faith. In this, they find a means to present their identification as *whole* not only to their family, friends, and neighbors but also to themselves.

"Belonging to a society," wrote anthropologist Francio Guadeloupe, "is a matter of context, degree, structure, agency, and choice."[19] In other words, our notions of who "We" are (and thus, who "They" are) are contingent and active, "grounded in particular environments with objects and others through which we move and with whom we interact."[20] Against a background of ongoing colonial legacies and persistent imperial realities—and with the concomitant reality of increasing diversity and difference brought on by late-modern cosmopolitanization—there is a sustained re-engagement with what it means to be "Puerto Rican." Thus, as Puerto Ricans revert, and reconstitute their identifications and their notions of being and belonging once more, they resignify their *Ricanness*[21] not only through a new religious identification but also in the context of ongoing negotiations of what it means to be Puerto Rican in the twenty-first century. In the process, AmeRícan Muslims wrestle with *how* they belong to Puerto Rico and its cultural heritage and relate to their Puerto Rican families, friends, and neighbors.

The result is an evolution of what it means to be Boricua in the intimacies of the everyday.

***What is that "something Puerto Rican?"***

The aforementioned tres raíces emerged as a popular litmus test for providing a unified sense of cultural authenticity as Puerto Ricans were constructing a sense of national identity in the twentieth century. Drawing on the myths of racial democracy, a cadre of 1930s intellectuals, politicians, and cultural institutions like the Instituto de Cultura Puertorriqueña produced a racial triad that "highlighted Spanish ancestry while folklorizing Blackness and presenting Taínos as biologically fragile."[22] Reproduced in art, tourism posters, and public statuary, the tres raíces were integrated into various understandings of what constitutes authentic "Puerto Rican culture."

Today, the tres raíces tend to dominate institutional and popular perceptions of Puerto Rican "peoplehood": that *lo que es puertorriqueño* that encompasses multiple material and performative aspects of "official" Puerto Rican ethnoracial categories.[23] Moreover, the three roots provide "foundational dimensions" for how Puerto Ricans see themselves and identify as Puerto Rican, "thus denoting belonging in a strong affective manner."[24] Reinforced by "governmental and disciplinary interventions," Puerto Ricans are taught that the tripartite notion of race in Puerto Rico is constitutive of, and coterminous with, *being* Puerto Rican.[25] Thus, the triad continues to serve as a sanctioned and celebrated—if constructed and contested—touchpoint for puertorriqueñidad on the archipelago and in the diaspora. For example, as anthropologist Arlene M. Dávila posits, this "romanticized and harmonious integration" of the three roots of Puerto Rican culture became part of an objectified national imaginary, which contrasts "authentic Puerto Rican culture" against US commercializing and colonizing culture(s).[26] Nonetheless, this framing of puertorriqueñidad is "a positioned narrative that draws on notions of truth to accomplish its political and economic goals."[27]

Although such "official" categorizations of Puerto Rican culture serve as tools to stoke national identity, they also demarcate boundaries of what constitutes being authentically Puerto Rican. In this process, "[s]ome people and certain elements of the culture are valued as part of the community; others are shunned, excluded, and categorized as 'ethnic' or foreign."[28] Therefore, these "emblematic expressions of being Puerto Rican," and "the widely circulated and hegemonic narratives of the Puerto Rican nation" function as "ethnoracial regimes" of knowledge and power that, in turn, "silence, erase, and trivialize alternative interpretations and understandings of Puerto

Rican historical trajectories" and contemporary understandings of people and place.[29] The uncritical instrumentalization of these frames can lead to Puerto Ricans' inability to "recognize [themselves]," writes anthropologist Caraballo-Resto, particularly when it involves hyphenated designations like "Arab–Puerto Rican" or "Puerto Rican Muslim."[30] While "links between the Middle East and the Caribbean are many" and, in Caraballo-Resto's estimation, should be "recognized, named, studied, and at times even celebrated,"[31] they are often ignored, sidelined, or precluded from inclusion in broader Puerto Rican cultural imaginaries.[32] In this way, tripartite notions of Puerto Rican culture and their dominant place in the broader Borícua cultural imagination can "contribute to colonial premises" rather than challenge them, Dávila argues.[33]

In reaction, and as part of broader shifts in the archipelago and diaspora, Puerto Ricans have embraced a range of varying identifications in recent decades, including "mixed race," "Black," Nuyorican, "Afro-Caribbean," DiaspoRican, or "Taíno." Those Puerto Ricans who (re)signify their connections to indigenous Taíno culture and heritage have received particular attention. The people who came to be called the "Taíno" were the pre-Columbian inhabitants of Puerto Rico, along with other Caribbean islands like Cuba, Hispaniola, Jamaica, and the Bahamas. Migrating to the Caribbean from the Orinoco River delta in the Amazon Basin (near present-day Venezuela and Guyana), the Taíno first came to Borikén some six thousand years ago as part of ongoing movements and migrations in, through, and around the Caribbean,[34] flourishing on the archipelago for nearly five hundred years before Spanish arrival.[35] While there was an estimated one hundred thousand pre-Columbian Taínos on the archipelago, the Spanish "conquest's genocidal impulse"[36] and its brutal combination of murder, enslavement, disease, intermarriage, and forced migration decimated the population during the first half of the sixteenth century.[37] Thought to have become extinct, Taíno survived through intermingling and intermarriage with Spanish settlers and African enslaved persons.[38] Others "took to the mountains to live outside the historical archive, where they may have even survived," writes historian Meléndez-Badillo.[39]

Drawing on genetic studies or the broader Neo-Taíno (or "Taíno revival") movement since the 1980s (or, for that matter, the importance of indigenous themes in the nineteenth century as part of an emerging Puerto Rican national consciousness),[40] some Puerto Ricans identify as Taíno descendants, even calling on the government to recognize their tribal status.[41] This revival became particularly notable among DiaspoRicans, with the founding of the Taíno Inter-Tribal Council in New Jersey in 1993 (until 2001) and the United Confederation of Taíno People founded in New York in 1998. Though numerically small, "these self-described Taínos have sought to reconstruct and preserve their ancestors' language, culture, and religion"[42] as part of broader trends in voluntary identification and volitional belonging in the late-modern.[43] Parallel to the emergence of Taíno as a visible social identification among Puerto Ricans are some Nuyorican and Afro–Puerto Rican efforts at re-centering their own identifications, which often critique "the hegemony of a homogenous definition of Puerto Ricannness."[44]

Together, these debates and ambiguities around Puerto Rican peoplehood, according to Feliciano-Santos,

> challenge homogenous narratives that rely on colonial logics of erasure, displacement, and replacement to instead consider the multiple historical possibilities of the past as they become materialized in the present and mark the potentiality of the future.[45]

As intimated above, DiaspoRicans in particular often attach themselves to normative motifs of puertorriqueñidad to push back against persistent notions that those outside the archipelago (*allá fuera*) are not authentically Puerto Rican. If to be Puerto Rican is "to be ever in search of one's self,"[46] and be "in a constant state of transformation . . . with many forms of expression,"[47] then whether they are in Newark or Florida, San Juan or San Antonio, the Middle East or even "the moon,"[48] Puerto Ricans continue to wrestle with popularized notions of where they are, who they are, and what they are supposed to be or represent.

### "*Foreign in a domestic sense*"[49]

Enter AmeRícan Muslims, who often feel their identifications are over questioned by fellow Puerto Ricans in a cultural context where Islam does not stand out as a prevalent identity referent.[50] They say they are treated like foreigners in a society where they feel at home, but where Islam is ignored, forgotten, and viewed as anachronistic at best, antagonistic at worst. Although Puerto Rican Muslims do not report any widespread discrimination, they reference multiple, cumulative "micro-aggressions"—everyday insults and indignities that prove more than just annoyances but deliver a constant reminder that they are "less than" and, apropos to this chapter, not fully Puerto Rican. If culture works through the stories we tell ourselves, the myths we know we are making, both personal and communal, passed down bit by bit over generations, codified into laws, left unsaid in customs, and embodied in everyday practices, then reverts feel "Puerto Rican culture" excludes their mixed identifications. They feel, to borrow words once used to describe Puerto Rico in colonial relation to the United States: "foreign, in a domestic sense."[51]

Take la Fiesta de Santiago Apóstol (The Fiesta of St. James the Apostle) in Loíza Aldea.[52] On the northeastern coast of Puerto Rico, Loíza Aldea is known as a hub for Afro–Puerto Rican culture, music, and dance. There in July 2017 with friend and fellow anthropologist Omar, we were suddenly met with a cacophonic intermingling of the deep beats of *reggaetón* mixes with the music-making of a truck full of *bomba y plena* instrumentalists that suddenly appeared around the corner, along with a procession of SUVs, cars, golf carts, pedestrians, bikes, and parade floats that stretched for miles through the coastal communities that make up the Loíza municipality. At the head of this lively procession was a group of garishly dressed *vejigantes*—bogeyman-looking characters donned in brightly colored, carnivalesque costumes. They wore masks, adorned with horns, handmade from coconuts, and painted in bright and bold orange, yellow, pink, black, and the colors of the Puerto Rican flag. The group leading the procession in Loíza are known as *los diablitos*—"the little devils." They take pride of place at this widely honored multiday celebration, one of the largest public festivals in Puerto Rico.[53] For locals, and according to Puerto Rico's cultural politics, the fiesta is primarily a celebration of Afro-Puerto Rican pride, identity, and religion.[54]

The vejigantes are symbols of Afro–Caribbean traditions' robust strength and adaptability in a place where they are still marginalized or neglected in cultural politics. However, vejigantes can also represent the embodiment of evil, the forces of darkness, the dead, or simply a robust mixture of multiple cultures. At their point of origin, the vejigantes represented a particular, and poignant, people group for the Spaniards who brought the festival to Latin America and the Caribbean. When the festival first arrived, los vejigantes represented the enemies of Catholic Spain. They represented Andalusian Muslims, los Moros—"the Moors." Thus, beyond representing Afro–Puerto Rican culture and invoking images of good-versus-evil, the history of the Fiesta reveals a deeper resonant meaning behind the vejigantes, their masks, and the processions that serve as an easy excuse to dance, sing, gather with friends, and drink sangria from sunrise to sunset. This festival also hints at the role that Muslims—in memory and in body—played in Puerto Rico's colonization, establishment, and cultural development.

Nonetheless, Loíza-based artist Samuel Lind, a local, legendary artist known for producing posters for the annual event, told me, "if you asked

FIGURE 2.1 *A representation of St. James (Santiago Apóstol) riding a white horse over turbaned "Moors" as part of the Fiesta de Santiago Apóstol in Loíza Aldea, Puerto Rico.*

any man in the street, or even someone dressed as a vejigante, they would think they are heroes—not enemies, not Moors." The term los Moros is a historically ambiguous one, which could refer to those from what is now modern-day Morocco or could be used as a broad signifier for "Black" or "dark-skinned" people. This means that over time, the term "Moor" (or el Moro) was used to refer to Africans of many kinds, Muslim and non-Muslim, from North Africa or sub-Saharan Africa. It was also used at times to refer to the indigenous peoples of the Americas[55] and served as a less-than-coded term in what Alejandro Escalante calls the "long arc of Islamophobia" in the Americas.[56] Despite the terminology surviving, Lind said, "The Muslim presence in the festival has been forgotten. Now they solely represent African pride." While acknowledged and noted by scholars and researchers, the Muslim influence on the festival, as Lind said, has long "been forgotten" among the masses. The people of Loíza, of course, can little be blamed for not recognizing much about the Muslim presence in, and influence on, their festival. For them, the story and ritual of the vejigantes and the *caballeros* took on other resonant meanings and their re-casting of the vejigantes as the point of pride in the festival became a critical part of their resistance to white, hegemonic rule.[57]

And yet, as multiple AmeRícan Muslims shared, the festival is another example of how Muslims are left out, forgotten, or—in this instance—trampled underfoot within the broader Puerto Rican cultural imaginary. As Omar put it:

> The people don't recognize the vejigantes as "Muslims" but just moros in a cultural sense, as symbols. Even so, it's sad to see. I mean, [Santiago] is crushing a Muslim. A turbaned, dark-skinned Moor. I wish it wasn't such a big part of Puerto Rican cultural identity. But it is what it is. At least they aren't actually celebrating killing Muslims . . . otherwise, I'd be in big trouble.

Thus, the embodiment and performativity of Islam can become a poignant point of contestation for Puerto Rican Muslim converts, who are constantly answering and reformulating their responses to their everyday political, social, temporal, and cultural context.[58]

Although primarily marginalized because of their religious affiliation, there are other intersecting identities that come to the fore, including race and gender. Presupposing that such markers (e.g., "Puerto Rican" and "Muslim") do not exist independently of each other and that each informs the other, AmeRícan Muslims' multiple minoritizations create a complex convergence of marginalization and adaptation. They work out these minoritizations, and try to reconcile their various identifications, through a search for Borícua Islamidad—a unique Puerto Rican Muslim sense of belonging that resists complete assimilation to Arab cultural norms even as it reimagines and expands what it means to be Puerto Rican *and* Muslim.[59]

That is because Puerto Rican Muslims see themselves and their stories not as exceptional cases, but simply as one of the many stories that can be told about Puerto Ricanness. Cuban novelist and essayist Antonio Benítez-Rojo argued that we need to critically examine what is often taken for granted in Caribbean discourses and explore the multifarious narratives that circulate alongside, and combine with, each other in the region.[60] Taking up his point, and emulating how Feliciano-Santos reconsiders "decolonization narratives not only in terms of Puerto Rico's colonization by the United States but also in terms of the more complicated forms of hegemony that frame the relationships between Puerto Rican elites and the complex of marginalized groups on the island,"[61] I focus on Puerto Rican Muslims' stories and the dissonance they manifest by (re)imagining themselves as part of the Great

Puerto Rican Family. In particular, I pay attention to how they perform and anchor their identifications, which are "not always compatible with or reducible to sanctioned historical narratives." Discarding history books in favor of shared narrative and material expression, they draft their own, "new-but-touching-on-history" stories of survival and Puerto Ricanness.[62]

At the same time, while some of my interlocutors seek to rewrite Puerto Rican history, most are not trying to present an alternative theory of what constitutes puertorriqueñidad. Instead, they address the questions that frustrated—and galvanized—their (re)identifications in the first place: What have we lost as Puerto Ricans by disregarding Islamic legacies and Muslim presence? How might taking our narratives seriously help solidify and strengthen Puerto Rican peoplehood more broadly? As they provide answers, however uncertain and contested, they (re)articulate themselves and their identifications in quotidian, material fashion. In doing so, they contribute to our understanding of how minorities on the archipelago and in the diaspora make meaning within and beyond received notions of puertorriqueñidad in the familiar intimacies of day-to-day life.

## RESIGNIFYING PUERTORRIQUEÑIDAD

Although certain pasts (e.g., African and Taíno) can be simultaneously memorialized as well as marginalized,[63] Puerto Ricans remix what is available to them to produce a different version of puertorriqueñidad by altering the balance of, and adding new elements to, romanticized national imaginaries. As one of my interlocutors, Aminah, put it:

> In some ways, conversion is a loss. I feel like I've lost part of my Puerto Rican identity. But for me, it also reconnects me to certain aspects of my Puerto Ricanness that were lost in history books or in stories passed down through family. It reconnects me with a wider world of being Puerto Rican, rediscovering roots that we didn't know were there.

Aminah's words are a testament to the many ways in which AmeRícan Muslims make manifest their notions of self in the messy and uncertain interstices between *being* Puerto Rican and *becoming* Muslim.

Writing about Puerto Rican Muslim musicians and the ways in which they (re)examine and (re)imagine their identifications through Islam and hip-hop, Ramadan-Santiago noted how Puerto Rican Muslims like him used both cultural and religious influences "to shape the persons they see themselves to be, despite being seemingly at odds with mainstream conceptions of what 'Puerto Rican' means."[64] Expanding on this, I share how AmeRícan Muslims resignify Puerto Ricanness in the context of relationships, architecture, food and foodways, the natural environment, and language. In the process, I show how they re-identify what it means to *be* Puerto Rican and *belong* to the Puerto Rican community through a range of material and affective means. As they learn a new canon and challenge representations of "official Puerto Rican culture"—generating fresh expressions along the way—they draw on authorized versions and their representations to illustrate their puertorriqueñidad. Their efforts are marked by generative frictions with friends and family and continual, if contested, material, ritual, and conceptual adaptations that include an array of clashes, hard-fought distinctions, and affective adjustments. Thus, they serve as critical sites where the ambiguities of, and discourse around, their identifications play out in everyday contexts.

### *"My family don't understand what Muslims is"*

Upon converting, most AmeRícan Muslims begin the process of resignification at home, among family and friends. In the documentary film *New Muslim Cool*, rapper Hamza Pérez shares about his conversion to Islam against the backdrop of the post-9/11 world, government surveillance, prison, drugs, and street life in Pittsburgh, Pennsylvania.[65] At one point in the documentary, Pérez opens up about how his family reacted when he converted. His aunt reflected that it was a "shock" because "we're Catholic ya know? It was a little . . . we would get into our little confrontations, arguments." His mother talked about raising Pérez in a Catholic school, his name being Jason and not Hamza, and the process of his conversion being confusing for her. At the same time, she was happy that he no longer drank, smoked, or was involved with gang life. But in the end, she admitted they struggled with his conversion, because "my family don't understand what Muslims is," he said.

Pérez's story is far from the only one that involves misunderstanding, confrontation, and struggle within the family. The same could be said of other converts I spoke to, like Miguel and Adrián. Miguel—one of the first Ahmadi Muslims in Puerto Rico—faced questions from family and friends when he converted. They asked, "So you're not going to celebrate Christmas no more? Or the fiestas?" They also openly wondered if he was a "terrorist" or was abandoning his Puerto Rican culture to become an "Arab." To this day, some of his friends believe he betrayed his culture when he converted. He said facing the onslaught from his family and friends was "like being a one-man army going against everything. But the thing is, this is my culture, this is what I grew up in. So, the challenge is to not go back to my old ways, but also not be so singled out as a complete stranger." Miguel said, "Puerto Ricans are proud of their culture so it's important that you be at home in your own, even after converting."

In Adrián's case, his family rejected him and his identification as a Muslim in multiple ways. I first met Adrián when he was cleaning the steps leading up to the prayer room at the Vega Alta mosque. He was vigorously mopping the white tiles to get them pearly clean before the community gathered for prayer. A fairly recent revert who grew up Christian, he first became interested in Islam as part of his broader support for the Palestinian political cause. Through contact with Palestinian activists and other anti-colonial agitators, he took the shahadah in 2016. His conversion cost him. When we met in 2017, he was living at his mother's house after going through a divorce. Adrián said that he kept his conversion a secret at first until his wife "caught him praying" and "freaked out." He said, "While she respects Muslims she couldn't convert and we realized our interests, feelings, and outlook were heading in different directions. So, we divorced."

Adrián's family struggles were not limited to his former marriage. When Adrián reverted, his father made fun of him for his religion. "As an old-school Marxist who still thinks religion is the opium of the masses . . . my father doesn't take me seriously," Adrián said. His mother had even stronger words. Reflecting on how Puerto Ricans respond in general to his being Muslim, Adrián said that it could all be summed up in his mother's reaction to the news of his conversion—"You betray Christ," she said, "you betray our culture."

Psychologist and Ponce-based therapist José Osvaldo Reyes wrote that in Puerto Rico, the family continues to be a significant institution for most individuals' psychosocial development. What he called *familismo* has had an outsized impact on the archipelago, shaping its "political geography" and Puerto Ricans' sense of self, he wrote.[66] Furthermore, commenting on Pérez's narrative in *New Muslim Cool*, independent scholar Yamil Avivi highlighted the role mothers, and families in general, play as "bearers of cultural identity" in Puerto Rican contexts.[67] Thus, and as intimated above, these relationships act as the primary quotidian context where AmeRícan Muslims navigate their sense of authenticity and interculturality.

Hamza's, Adrián's, and Miguel's experiences briefly illustrate how conversion can be isolating and disrupting. It is, as the Greek philosopher Diogenes said, a kind of exile—from the comfort of local truths, from the warm, nestling feeling of nationalism, from the absorbing drama of pride in oneself and one's own. In this sense, conversion, which makes possible alternative ways of being, does not offer immediate refuge. While it opens up certain opportunities and creates new associations, it also challenges pre-existing, and quite intimate, relationships that ground an individual's sense of being and belonging. If those ruptured relationships, and the resultant shattered sense of self, cannot be quickly mended, they then lean into alternative sources of belonging and new communities of connection.

This became evident to me while seated around a table on the occasion of Eid al-Fitr in 2017, when Sumayah invited me to her home in Bayamón, southwest of San Juan. There were fourteen people in attendance to celebrate the end of the Ramadan fast. It was an eclectic mix of people around the table: some of Sumayah's non-Muslim coworkers, neighbors, and friends; me, a PhD candidate from Florida; her Puerto Rican mother, her Egyptian husband Muhammad and their two kids, a Puerto Rican revert and her Moroccan husband; Sumayah's best friend and fellow revert Rachel; and Muhammad's good friend and colleague Jonathan from Iran. In between laughter, prayers, and multilingual chatter, each reflected on how glad they were to find one another.

Each of the people at the table felt ostracized in some way from family and friends. Whether because of moving away as migrants, marrying someone outside of their religion, converting, or spending time in interfaith activities, they felt on the margins of communities they still strongly identified with—whether they be Puerto Rican or Moroccan, Catholic or Muslim, Egyptian or Iranian. There were both push and pull factors that brought them together this Eid. While they acknowledged a shared affinity, each of the participants told me they gathered together at Sumayah's Bayamón home instead of at the nearest masjid because they felt unwanted or judged by others: unwanted because they refused to conform to certain cultural markers embedded within the local Muslim community or judged because they sought to fuse their Puerto Rican sense of self with their religious sensibilities and practice. Furthermore, their non-Muslim families and friends were largely not open to celebrating Eid with them. Still, when asked if they would change a thing, they all heartily replied that this table constituted a life of connections with people who redefined for them what it meant to be Puerto Rican, Egyptian, Iranian, or something else in between.

Taking a break from the food and stepping out onto the street, where a Pentecostal church service was just letting out across the road, I talked to Jonathan about these things. Born to a Puerto Rican mother and Iranian father, Jonathan operates a restaurant and food truck featuring what he brands "el mejor comida del Medio Oriente en Puerto Rico" ("The best Middle Eastern Food in Puerto Rico"). The food truck represents a fusion of his heritage, he said, a meeting between "East and West" in plates that represent his own journey. Jonathan primarily identifies as Puerto Rican and claims the archipelago as his home. This identification is not always easy, however. As a kid, he was picked on at school for "not being Borícua enough." His neighbors, although friendly, still make jokes about him being "half Puerto Rican, half Muslim." Over the years, he found himself having to continually reassert his puertorriqueñidad to friends and neighbors, coworkers and customers. The result, he said, is that he seeks out "third places" like this iftar, where there are other people stuck "between and beyond" the ways family, friends, or others frame what it means to be Puerto Rican or Muslim. "Here, we are family. Around this table, with all of our identities, all our stories, all our pasts and presents, all our ethnicities, we are *una familia*."

### *"No Victor but Allah": Puerto Rico's Islamic Built Legacy*

Where new families and tables are not so easily found, AmeRícan Muslims go in search of other places to secure their multifaceted identifications.[68] For example, Kemal, in addition to the mosque project mentioned in the previous chapter, wants to build a museum of Andalusian history in Puerto Rico. During the early days of the COVID-19 pandemic in 2020, he scoured the streets of San Juan, his hometown Hatillo, and other municipalities in Puerto Rico for vestiges of Moorish influence and examples of how the architecture of "Muslim Spain" shaped Borikén. He found inscriptions on doorways in Viejo San Juan; neo-Moorish buildings like the Residencia Gómez in Mayagüez; the courtyard of the Casa de España on Avenida de La Constitución; furniture pieces he argues date back to the sixteenth century and might have been spoils from Spanish Catholics' defeat of "los Moros" during the Reconquista. Determined, Kemal said he is on a mission to locate every piece of Andalusian heritage in Puerto Rico—"to find my roots," he said.

Kemal does not feel like he can find those roots in the many places for prayer across the island. The oldest among these is Centro Islámico de Puerto Rico in Río Piedras (established in 1981) and the first purpose-built mosque is Masjid Alfaruq in Vega Alta (construction completed in 1997). There are also purpose-built mosques in Hatillo (Mezquita Al Madinah),

**FIGURE 2.2** *Various* mezquitas *(mosques) from around Puerto Rico.*

Fajardo (Islamic Center of Fajardo), and Ponce (Centro Islámico), the archipelago's second largest city. In addition to these, there are publicly available prayer rooms in Aguadilla and Jayuya, along with an Ahmadiyya Community Centre in Carolina. At each location, local converts can be found praying, partaking in services, and participating in community initiatives. But Puerto Ricans are always in the minority—sometimes overwhelmingly so—and rarely, if ever, found in leadership positions.

Instead, the leaders are Palestinian, Egyptian, Pakistani, Nigerian. Most imams are brought in from outside Puerto Rico, although there have been a couple of "home-grown" leaders from Puerto Rico with Palestinian or Egyptian heritage. Kemal thinks this is significant, as these mezquitas often act as Islam's "public face" on the archipelago. Particularly prominent is Masjid Alfaruq in Vega Alta, situated in the hills overlooking the busy intersection of Puerto Rico's Highway Two (PR-2) and the Expreso José de Diego tollway, or the mezquita in Río Piedras, just steps away from the busy Plaza del Mercado de Río Piedras. Thus, those who visit or observe them might walk away with the impression that the Muslim community is only made up of immigrants or members of the global Muslim diaspora. The perception, local converts like Kemal told me, is that Islam still tends to be seen as a "foreign" religion *in* Puerto Rico rather than one *of* Puerto Rico and Puerto Ricans.

Kemal wants to challenge this status quo. That is why he emphasizes his roots in the history and legacy of al-Andalus:

> I always sensed some connection to al-Andalus, from the very first time I learned about it. But I always wondered, where did the people go? Where did the places and culture go? I thought about doing DNA testing, but then I noticed that Andalus didn't go anywhere. It's still here. In me. In the buildings. All over Puerto Rico. So, I went in search of my own lineage. To make my own mythology.

He plans to keep combing the streets of Arecibo, Fajardo, Hatillo, and the districts of San Juan to find his "lineage," to show how palpable and present Andalusian Islamic influence remains in Puerto Rico. "I have a lot left to discover," he said. This search for roots, as anthropologist Ramadan-Santiago noted, is vital to understanding Puerto Rican Muslims' "identity construction and validation."[69] It is, he wrote, a search for authenticity and a means of answering the tantalizing and tense question of "Who has the right to claim something as their own?"[70]

In architecture, reverts find a rich repository. Across Latin America, architect and author R. Brooks Jeffery wrote there is a "profound legacy of Islamic architectural characteristics in the Hispano-American built environment [. . .] still evident today."[71] Andalusian and neo-Mudéjar aesthetics and architecture—what has been called "Latin America's 'Alhambrismo'"[72]—emerged out of the confluence of immigrants' desires to "incorporate memories of their homeland when they commissioned architects" to build spaces and places for them in the Americas and a certain "predilection for Orientalism" that was prominent among "architects who both trained and travelled in Europe and whose designs, on occasion, reflected the territorial surroundings that inspired them."[73] Influenced by Orientalist paintings, architectural journals, and travel narratives like Washington Irving's *Tales of the Alhambra,* Latin American architects copied or drew inspiration from the Alhambra and other examples of Andalusian architecture—influenced as it was by Maghrebi, Umayyad, Byzantine, Visigothic, and other sources—and adapted their elements, features, and motifs to local conditions, needs, and lifestyles. Raphael López Guzmán and Rodrigo Gutiérrez Viñuales wrote, "This meant that, on occasion, what featured in an interior in Granada may have appeared on a facade, or what was without colour in the walls of the Alhambra may appear as a rich chromaticism typical of the Caribbean."[74] Not only speaking to the "global 'romantic' significance" of Andalusian architecture, this trend also emerges as part of Puerto Rican perceptions of national and local peoplehood.

Indeed, the lasting influence of Spanish colonial architecture is apparent in the narrow, meandering streets of Viejo San Juan, with its blue-tinged cobblestones known as *adoquines* (brought from Spain as ballast for ships) or in the numerous pastel, tile-roofed buildings with ornamented balconies and substantial wooden doors opening on inner courtyards commissioned by the Spanish. More common, however, after five centuries' worth of degradation and change, are buildings built in the early twentieth century under the influence of an eclectic mix of styles, including art deco, neo-Romanticism, and neo-Mudéjar. This last style, as part of the broader Moorish Revival, emerged out of Madrid and Lisbon in the late nineteenth century and came to influence locales across the Spanish Americas.

Featuring glazed tiling and mosaics, horseshoe arches, arabesque windows, mosque-like galleries, and other elements that recall the Mudéjar manner of colonial Spain, the style's proliferation in Puerto Rico is exemplified in a wide range of buildings: el Teatro Fox Delicias in Ponce (Francisco Porrata-Doria, 1931), the maternity ward of Hospital Auxilio Mutuo in Hato Rey (Rafael del Valle Zeno, 1908), el Edificio del Periódico 'El Mundo' y 'Puerto Rico Ilustrado' in Viejo San Juan (Francisco Roldán, 1923), la Penitenciaría Estatal de Río Piedras (Francisco Roldán, 1926), Mercado de las Carnes (a.k.a., "la Plaza de los Perros") in Ponce (Rafael Carmoega, 1926), el Torre de la Universidad de Puerto Rico Río Piedras (Rafael Carmoega, 1937), the exterior façade and interior Nasrid plasterwork of el Ateneo Puertorriqueño in San Juan (Francisco Roldán, 1922), the courtyard and the Alhambran "Fountain of the Lions" at the nearby Casa de España (Pedro Adolfo el Castro, 1934) or el Parque de Bombas in Ponce (Máximo de Meana y Guridi, 1882).[75] Beyond these more prominent buildings—many of which serve as symbolic references points for aspects of Puerto Rican peoplehood—there are also numerous, more mundane, examples of Spanish renaissance and Moorish Revival influence on the archipelago, found in homes and private buildings across the archipelago's urban centers, but particularly in areas such as the Bayola district of Santurce or the home of Enrique Calimano in Guayama, built by Pedro Adolfo de Castor in 1928.

Many of these buildings, and more beyond, are featured in Kemal's growing corpus of photos. He hopes to one day publish them together or feature them in the museum. He told me:

> I'm still learning, but I want to provide a way for people to acknowledge their roots. I want people who are starting to question themselves

> because of their current religion or because of their ancestry, a way to see with their own eyes who they really are. I don't want them to only listen to my words, I just want them to see the evidence available.

The evidence, he said, points to a rich Andalusian legacy at the heart of Puerto Rican culture. As far as he is concerned, his project is nothing less than rewriting Puerto Rican history. This "passion project," he said, aims to re-center Islam and Muslims at the heart of the Puerto Rican story and center Puerto Rico within the story of global Islam. Pointing the finger at government officials in the US and Puerto Rico from 1898 forward, he said of this history and built legacy, "They don't want people to see it. So, I just have to fight right now to find this. To trace the shape of our lineage, our *real* history."

Kemal is not alone in making meaning through the tangible interfaces and atmosphere[76] of Puerto Rico's Andalusian and neo-Mudéjar architecture. Going along with converts on the streets of Viejo San Juan or Ponce, they frequently interrupted the flow of conversation to point out an inner courtyard, an arched gallery, or a blue, ochre, and emerald glazed tile to make sure I understood just how pervasive the perceived "Islamic" influence was on their archipelago. In fact, one of my earliest interviews with José—a self-identifying Black Haitian and Puerto Rican Muslim working in information technology, married to a Dominican with whom he has one daughter—was held in the shade of the "Roosevelt Tower" (popularly known as "la Torre") at the Universidad de Puerto Rico Río Piedras, where he invited me for coffee and conversation. As we sat on a bench in its umbrage, he pointed out his intentions in meeting me here:

> I wanted us to have this conversation with an appropriate setting. You see that [pointing to the tower]? Every day I walk past here, on my way to a lecture or on my way to the [Río Piedras] masjid for prayer, or just driving by or on the bus, I see this tower and I'm reminded that I belong. That we belong. That being Muslim isn't foreign, it's part of our culture, our buildings, the best university we have.

Even away from Puerto Rico, the significance of Andalusian and neo-Mudéjar architecture in Puerto Rican Muslim self-fashioning is evident on social media. From time to time, Puerto Rican Muslims post pictures of themselves making a "pilgrimage" to significant places on the archipelago that further intimated the sentiments expressed by José and Kemal above.

Puerto Rican Muslims from Florida, New Jersey, New York, and Texas post photos and galleries of themselves visiting some of the numerous institutions mentioned above, and two in particular: la Casa de España and el Ateneo Puertorriqueño.

For example, in May 2017, Willy—a middle-aged revert who was active in dawah both in Florida and in his hometown of Aguadilla—posted a picture of himself in front of the glazed-tile mosaic in the lobby of the Ateneo Puertorriqueño, a cultural institution that offers conferences, classes, and contests for an elite slice of Puerto Ricans interested in the archipelago's artistic, literary, and musical heritage. While the interior halls are off-limits for members of the public, the lobby is open to visits, and numerous Puerto Rican Muslims like Willy make their way inside to point with one finger at the inscription at the top of the tile. It reads:

> ولا غالبَ إلا الله
> Wa la Ghalib Illa Allah
> No hay vencedor excepto Allah.
> There is no victor except Allah.

Featured hundreds of times on the walls of the Alhambra in Granada, Spain, it can also be found on the façade of the Andalusian-inspired building at 311 Calle de Fortaleza in San Juan. The saying was the so-called "motto" of the Nasrid, the last Muslim dynasty to rule in Spain before being finally defeated and driven out of the Iberian Peninsula in 1492, a year before the conquest of Puerto Rico by the same Catholic Spanish empire.

By posting this picture, and by pointing to it with a single finger representing *tawhid*—the oneness of God—Willy and others like him signify their pride in being both Puerto Rican *and* Muslim, finding in architectural motifs copied from the Nasrid a means of unifying both aspects of their identification. Reverts also post similar messages and sentiments at the Casa de España, a building near the Ateneo Puertorriqueño. There too, reverts like Wanda—a mother of three who said she takes her children to Casa de España, Parque de Bombas, and the Ateneo to "teach them a lesson in their history"—posted a picture of the Ateneo's lobby and a carving in the Alhambra Palace side by side on Facebook and wrote, "This is part of the rich history of our island, but few know about these cultural gems hidden sometimes in plain sight. #nuestraherencia."

These "dreams of al-Andalus,"[77] embodied and affectively engaged with through Puerto Rico's architectural legacies, illustrate how AmeRícan

Muslims fashion themselves as an "imagined diaspora" in reaction to their multiple marginalizations. It is a way to re-center and re-locate their identifications amid rupture, loss, colonization, and exile. Utilizing and engaging the "post-modern arts of memory"[78] in order to recapture and reconstitute their past, these imagined antecedents affirm not only their Puerto Rican peoplehood, but also their Muslimness *as* Puerto Ricans. Moreover, this reconstructed narrative of the past transcends colonial identities, freeing them from the hegemony of imperial categories and exclusionary practices by those in power. Influenced by Black Muslims' own appeals to al-Andalus, wherein they sought to ground their identifications in a deeper Islamic past,[79] and broader memories of al-Andalus in contemporary Arab and Latinx narratives,[80] they look to Andalusian Spain as a mythohistorical homeland. They yearn, as with other diasporas, to return. However, this return is not necessarily geographic, but chronographic. Through architecture, AmeRícan Muslims collapse history and reclaim a centrality and majesty within widely accepted symbols and references points in Puerto Rico's cultural imaginary, not otherwise possible given their marginal position within Puerto Rican society as a whole.

### *"They sneak pork into everything here."*

They make a similar move with Puerto Rican cuisine and culinary practices.[81] For example, Yvonne Maffei is the founder and publisher of *My Halal Kitchen*—originally a cooking blog, now available as a printed cookbook. Half Sicilian, half Puerto Rican, she was born and raised in "small-town Ohio," from whence she took her homebred curiosity across the world. Along the way, she picked up cooking methods in Mexico, Spain, Italy, and Morocco. Today, Maffei is passionate about pursuing what she called "the culinary arts within a halal context." While emphasizing nutrition, food freedom, local sourcing, and "wholesome homemaking," her efforts focus on how to make global culinary traditions accessible, organic, and, most importantly, halal. "Unfortunately," she said of those who share her Puerto Rican background, "that's not always an easy thing to do."

One area where most Muslims, and non-Muslims, engage with Islamic legal traditions in their day-to-day lives is in relation to food consumption. Muslim food traditions are derived from the Qur'an and *hadith*. Both sources of Islamic law speak to the meaning, significance, and permissibility of food and the manner of its preparation and consumption. Textually speaking, food is seen as a divine blessing (Q. 80:25–32). The fairly well-known term "halal" designates any object or action that is permissible according to

Islamic legal traditions. Halal stands in juxtaposition to that which is *haram*, forbidden or off-limits, and distinguished from that which is compulsory or obligatory (*fard/wajib*), recommended (*mustahabb/mandub*), and disliked (*makruh*). These terms are used to designate multiple facets of life as unlawful or legitimate. Depending upon regional contexts, doctrinal debates, and judicial authority, terms like halal, makruh, and/or haram are applied to investments, pharmaceuticals, or makeup. Most often, however, such terminology is used by scholars and practitioners to classify products as either forbidden or allowable for consumption or use in cooking. These distinctions are applied to prohibit things like pork or alcohol, but also to other foods, the treatment of animals, and their slaughter.

While legal interpretations differ, food is considered halal if it is not prohibited by the Qur'an or hadith and is free from anything that is prohibited, and has been raised, processed, produced, made, kept, or prepared by using methods, machinery, or means that are considered clean. Haram items include, but are not limited to, alcoholic drinks and intoxicants, pork and pork products (e.g., lard), blood, carrion, carnivorous animals (e,g., hawks, falcons, lions, and even crocodiles), human body parts (e.g., hair), or gelatin (save for fish gelatin, which is halal). Most designations are explicit, but there is debate about classifying certain foods or products as either halal or haram. Some of these items are referred to as *mashbuh*—in doubt or questionable. Most scholars agree that these items are best avoided, but there is no grievous harm caused if they are consumed or used on accident. Others are disliked (makruh), and abstaining from them is recommended and will be rewarded (e.g., eating fresh garlic). Food that is good and wholesome is often described as *tayyib*. These are general examples, and it is important to point out that regional understandings of halal practices can differ depending on various social, cultural, religious, or economic factors.[82]

Both contributing to, and as a product of, the cosmopolitanization and intensifying entanglement of continental economic exchange in the era of post–Cold War globalization and neoliberalism, the global halal industry grew to accommodate an increasingly diverse array of Muslim dietary and lifestyle practices. While globalization precipitated this phenomenon and made the cartography of consumption more complex and differentiated, it also made navigating it a possibility—albeit a fraught one. In Muslim minority contexts, traditional *fiqh* authorities may not be familiar with local food offerings, and the sources of Islamic law may not be clear on whether or not a food is permissible (e.g., with certain seafoods). Sometimes food choices in such contexts can serve as grounds for intense discussion and debate, with legal opinions varying widely. Legal opinions and debate over halal practices can also be implicated in delimiting the boundaries of a community.[83] Thus, "the question of determining whether or not a particular food is halal can be more complex than simply checking a list."[84]

On the practical side, Maffei said that through *My Halal Kitchen*, she wanted to

> create a platform for readers (regardless of religious or ethnic background) where I would be able to showcase the tasty recipes I've learned to make or that others share with me, all of which are tested to ensure accuracy. Additionally, it was created to share kitchen tips, stories about cooking, thoughts on food, information on what's happening in the food industry and where you can find all the same things I do to create my halal meals.

A significant aspect of this desire emerged from her own biography. Maffei sought to adapt the Sicilian and Puerto Rican recipes she grew up with and remake them to conform to her halal lifestyle. Making meatballs and homemade pizza was one matter. When it came to Puerto Rican food, it was another. But Maffei met the challenge of pork, alcohol, and other debatable or disliked (makruh) products featuring prominently in the culture's cuisine.

One such recipe was for habichuelas, or pinto beans, a popular side dish in the Hispanophone Caribbean, particularly Puerto Rico and the Dominican Republic. Very often cooked in lard, or pork fat, Maffei was determined to cook up a halal substitute using olive, vegetable, or grapeseed oil. Still featuring the popular and unmistakable flavors of achiote seasoning and *sofrito*, Maffei's halal habicheulas seem to be a relatively simple fix when it comes to the conundrums of how Puerto Rican Muslim converts learn how to consume their cultural heritage according to the laws of their religion. Other adaptations and negotiations in the food practices of Puerto Rican Muslim converts are not so straightforward.

Similar to converts in other American minority contexts,[85] one of the principal means AmeRícan Muslims attempt to (re)mix their cultural identifications is to consume food that is halal, Borícua, and *both* at the same time. While other scholars have pointed out how performative politics are visual, sartorial, or auditory, the foods consumed, prepared, and shared by AmeRícan Muslims illustrate another aspect of their sense of being and belonging. I suggest it is part of how they seek to make being Muslim not simply something that exists *in* Puerto Rico, but something that is *of* Puerto Rico. As they wrestle with what it means to be Puerto Rican *and* Muslim against the backdrop of the archipelago's cultural politics, their foodways form a significant part of how they perform their remixed identifications *as* Puerto Ricans.

These choices are complex, full of tension, and part of an ongoing process of negotiation with place and context, culture and individuality. They are, in many ways, resistant responses to built-in mechanisms of power that both exclude and tangentially include Muslims in the Puerto Rican cultural imagination. This hybridity is not some blanket, elite, or de-historicized conception of culture,[86] but a specific, and nuanced, response to the simultaneous local and global encounters of the late-modern world typified by AmeRícan Muslim experiences. It is an outcome of the generative frictions that occur between various identifications, loyalties, relationships, encounters, and entanglements, that make up their cosmopolitanized worlds. It is, to riff on the work of W. E. B. DuBois,[87] the result of a "quadruple consciousness" and the painful incompatibility between how AmeRícan Muslims see themselves and how other Puerto Ricans, Muslims, and Americans see them in terms of their race and religion.

Many elements of Puerto Rico's culinary culture—including beans, corn, cassava, tannier, sweet potatoes, plantains and bananas, yams, pork, beef, and salted codfish—were introduced and refashioned by individuals and socialities who adapted former traditions to a new environment over time, against a backdrop of successive colonial societies. In concluding how "Puerto Rican cuisine and food-ways" came to be, Cruz Miguel Ortíz Cuadra references the tres raíces, citing the "knowledge and experience of the archipelago's indigenous population," the desire of "Spanish settlers to duplicate a familiar gastronomy in an unfamiliar land," and the "thousands of African slaves and large contingents of soldiers" who came to add their own flavors to the mix—a mix known locally as "la Cocina Criolla" (the Creole Kitchen).[88] He also calls attention to how Puerto Ricans are inclined to identify themselves as Puerto Rican "through the agency of food" and the practices that surround it as a means of claiming "authenticity" as Puerto Ricans.[89] Thus, eating an "authentically Puerto Rican diet" is a means of expressing a certain "food nationalism."[90] Ironically, this is done even though the archetype of "Puerto Rican cuisine" is severely influenced by US colonialism and the commodification of "Puerto Rican food," with Krispy Kreme and Burger King almost as likely to feature in a Puerto Rican diet as *arroz con pollo*.

To unpack how Puerto Ricans become "Puerto Rican" through the agency of food, take, for example, the place pork holds in the Puerto Rican cultural imagination. First brought by the Spanish in the early period of colonization, pork soon took on a character of its own on the archipelago. The meat became particularly popular with the proliferation of the *orejano*, a feral pig found in the highlands and prized for its lean meat. The swine were readily available and there was a robust trade in both wild pig and cattle in the early colonial era. This, in part, led to a general *carnivorismo* (love of meat) on an island where every Saturday on roads through the countryside you can smell the sweet smoke of a *lechonera* on your way to the beach with family.

A further aspect of the love of pork has to do with Spanish identity and society. Ortíz Cuadra commented that the Spanish deliberately populated Puerto Rico with meat to recreate the Peninsular associations of meat consumption with "distinction" in Spanish society and "a confirmation of one's religious faith and heritage." Ortíz Cuadra writes that eating pork was a way to reinforce and consolidate "an individual's power and his social and religious associations."[91] Why? While meat in general was a luxury in Spain, pork came to be a symbol of distinction among Christians over and against their Moorish enemies. This practice was recreated in Puerto Rico and left its stamp on the culinary culture of the archipelago and its people. Namely, it was a way to establish Puerto Rico's "Catholic" and "Christian" heritage over and against the specter of Jewish and Muslim inhabitants of the Iberian Peninsula, whom the Spaniards feared would come and populate the Spanish Americas as well.

Obviously, for AmeRícan Muslims looking to maintain a halal diet, the prevalence of pork can prove an intricate impediment. Over a meal at El Pavo Asado—a restaurant focused on using turkey and chicken in, and alongside, traditional Puerto Rican dishes—Miguel tells me how when he converted to Islam as a university student in the US, some friends thought he was betraying Puerto Rican culture. In part, this was because he stopped eating pork. "Puerto Ricans are proud of their culture and part of that culture is pork," he says, "sometimes I thought my friends were just joking about it, but it's not that funny." In the end, however, he knew he must find ways to adapt. He reiterates how pork is put into almost everything in Puerto Rican food. On top of that, he says, "Nowadays, bacon has made its way into things that didn't even have pork before. Bacon is treated like it's gourmet," he grunted, "it's not gourmet. Please. Worse off, it's not halal." Pointing down with his fork at his turkey meat loaf, rice, and pink beans (*meat loaf de pavo con arroz y habichuelas rosadas*), he says, "As an Ahmadiyya Muslim, part of our religion is being at home in our own culture and so I find ways to eat like a Puerto Rican as a Muslim, not in spite of being a Muslim." Drawing on *Surah al-Ma'idah* (5:5), which permits the consumption of food prepared by "People of the Book" (Jews, Christians), Miguel said he eats meat other than pork, knowing "Puerto Rico is mostly a Christian country, that means I can be confident that the meat is lawful, even if it is not killed according to the Islamic way." Scraping the last bit of his meal from his plate, he exclaimed with a smile, "Mmmm, I forgot how good these rice and beans are!"

Although Miguel enjoyed his last bite of rice and beans, there is often a potent sense of loss that accompanies such dietary negotiations. Arjun Appadurai makes the point that "authentic" cuisines and their attendant cultures (cookbooks, menus, etc.) are marks of nostalgia that can evince feelings of exile and a sense of loss.[92] So it is with AmeRícan Muslims, who eschew or adapt certain aspects of Puerto Rican eating and drinking culture, steering their mouths, stomachs, and food choices through a real-world setting that only offers a certain array of options. Some, like Maffei, regularly said how difficult it is to navigate Borícua cuisine and maintain halal consumption standards. Maffei said her mother "struggled to avoid the lard in pasteles" or leaving the meat aside when making sazón for arroz con habichuelas. "Pork, after all, is just a flavor, right?" seemed to be Maffei's mother's attitude. However, Maffei said that just as much as halal could divide and confront, it also led to new combinations. She said:

> I bonded with Muslims through food. A good friend of mine [in college] came from Yemen, and going into her household was an experience. I was let into their world and was so curious about how the women in her family lived. What is the secret? Why do they hold things so sacred? And then I met Sudanese, Qataris, Indonesians, and Palestinians all in the span of a couple of years. And I thought, Wow their food is all halal. It's all different, but carries the same message.

This cosmopolitan encounter inspired Maffei to rework dishes from her culinary heritage and interest (Puerto Rican, Sicilian, American, French). In this way, she said, "Finding substitutions for those foods I love is me saying, *I have respect for how I was raised, for where I come from*."

Maffei's blog, cookbook, and speaking schedule are dedicated to sharing her "halal kitchen" and its multiple influences—including Puerto

Rican—with a wider network. Puerto Rican food writer Von Díaz writes that the cookbook "has some pretty brilliant hacks for cooking without alcohol" and "workarounds for not using pork" and that "it's an incredibly useful cookbook for home cooks, Muslim or not, who have diverse communities of friends and loved ones."[93] For Von Díaz, Maffei's creativity in the face of food conundrums offered an opportunity to craft a cosmopolitan cookbook that others—Muslim and non-Muslim, Puerto Rican or not—can enjoy. Inviting readers into her "halal kitchen" becomes a means for Maffei to invite readers into multiple culinary lineages and socialities.

However, for al-Ishbili, a recently married Puerto Rican revert in Florida, the fact that pork frequents so many Puerto Rican dishes can make it hard for Muslims to feel like they "belong." He said:

> Pork is so important to Puerto Rican culture, with Muslims not being able to eat it, it contributes to a non-Muslim Puerto Rican narrative that says, 'Muslims don't belong, they don't fit into the overall Boricua identity.

But, he contested, through a mouthful of *plátanos maduros fritos* (sweet friend plantains), "I can be Puerto Rican and not eat pork." As he then sunk his teeth into chicken and vegetable pasteles, he said, "You don't have to use pork lard or bacon in every dish. Really, you don't." While he questioned the primacy of pork in Puerto Rican cuisine, al-Ishbili never questioned the prohibitions against its consumption. Hoping to serve as an imam and having studied fiqh in California, he admitted that many Muslims found it difficult to express why pork is forbidden—some name health risks, others that it is a "filthy animal"—he referred to prohibitions against its consumption in the Qur'an. Along with other *ayat* about not questioning the commands of Allah (4:65; 33:36), he quoted *Surah al-Baqarah*, 2:173. Expounding about its prohibitions against carrion, blood, pig's meat, and "animals over which any name other than God's has been invoked" and its note on exceptions in special cases, he said:

> This isn't about going over to *abuela's* house and there only being pork pasteles around, then you eat it. No, no, man. It's not like that. This has to be you starving, on the edge of death, then maybe you can eat pork. That's a general rule in Islam, that if it is dangerous or of necessity, there is mercy.

Speaking against certain Muslims who feel they can eat pork or drink alcohol because it is provided by Christians, al-Ishbili appealed (like Miguel) to verse 5 of the appropriately titled *Surah Al-Ma'idah*—"the Feast" or "the Table Spread with Food"—which permits eating the food of the Ahl al-Kitab, or "People of the Book." Al-Ishbili said that such a verse must be understood according to 6:121, which reads, "Do not eat unless Allah's name has been taken and this [not taking Allah's name] practice is transgression." Al-Ishbili explained, "We can eat with them and they with us," and referring to our shared meal together he said, "just like we are doing here." Al-Ishbili clarified, "that doesn't make this food halal per se, it's just that it's okay for me to consume it. As long as it's not pork. That's never allowed. It's absolutely forbidden. Like, haram, haram."

Other respondents reiterated the prominence of pork, the difficulty of avoiding it in pursuit of a halal diet, and how that contributes to—or problematizes—their sense of belonging. One was Ahmad, who confirmed al-Ishbili's opinion that pork is almost ubiquitous in popular Puerto Rican dishes. Meeting up with the father of three at a café in Guaynabo, I observed how he navigated the "pork problem" in everyday life. As the waiter finished scratching down our orders on a small notepad, Ahmad asked the server if there was any pork in the dish he asked for. The waiter replied that there was no pork in the dish, but Ahmad wanted to verify. He asked again, with a hand raised awkwardly for emphasis, "There is absolutely no pork in this dish, correct? I'm allergic." Appearing rushed, the waiter shook his head and promised Ahmad that it would be a pork-free plate. As the waiter walked away, Ahmad turned to me and, with a wry smile, said, "You have to be careful, they sneak pork into everything here." Indeed, with mainstays such as succulent slow-roasted pork (*lechón asado*), mashed deep-fried green plantains mixed with garlic, salt-cured pork, pork crackling, and perhaps even lard (mofongo), green banana *masa* or yuca stuffed with stewed pork (pasteles), or popular sandwiches filled with either lechón or roasted pork shoulder (*pernil*) and ham on top of grilled steak with fries and toppings (*la tripleta*), all frequently washed down with a cold Medalla Light, Puerto Rican cuisine can present an assemblage of challenges.

When it comes to carnivorismo, AmeRícan Muslims show an ability to simultaneously avoid pork and adapt their consumption of authentic Puerto Rican cuisine, all the while striving for a holistic sense of being *both* Puerto Rican *and* Muslim. It is not easy. They sometimes must conceal their Muslim identity and consume the effects of Islamophobia and the ridicule and reticence to accommodate "otherness" that it produces.

Yet, the experiences shared above illustrate how Puerto Rican Muslims endeavor to find a way to maintain halal practices in a markedly non-halal environment—each in their own way. Ahmad, al-Ishbili, Maffei, and Miguel each made their peace with pork and Puerto Rican culinary culture. While they reject the pork, they understand the meaning and importance of it in Puerto Rican cuisine. Overall, they feel that consuming pork is part and parcel of being Puerto Rican and that it is not others who should be expected to adjust, but themselves. Moreover, they find ways to work around it and maintain halal standards while simultaneously honoring fixed ideals of what it means to eat like a Puerto Rican (al-Ishbili, Maffai, and Miguel finding alternatives, Ahmad ordering traditional Puerto Rican dishes *sin cerdo*). They place the onus on themselves and accommodate colonial culinary heritage, occasional discomfort, or xenophobic humor, knowing that their choice is an unfamiliar, and perhaps unsettling, one in their local context. In the end, their adjustments and adaptations make for a hard-fought, and negotiated, expression of their multivalent identifications.

### *La cultura borracha*

Perhaps pork is the most obvious, and most ubiquitous, challenge to maintaining a Borícua halal diet for Puerto Rican reverts. But AmeRícan Muslims said there were numerous hurdles they had to navigate in their quest to maintain halal standards in a culinary culture that was far from premised on the same standards. Interlocutors told me about the popularity of *frituras* and *empanadillas* with conch, crab, and octopus meat, questions surrounding the permissibility of consuming iguana meat, and avoiding sofrito-based dishes on Fridays because ingredients like garlic and onion can be considered makruh (not recommended/to be avoided) on a day of prayer. And a strict line is often drawn when it comes to what several respondents referred to as *la cultura borracha*.

The topic of *borracha* culture first came up with Pedro, a college student from San Juan, in our conversation after jummah prayers at the Centro Islámico del Caribe in Montehiedra. As he told me his conversion story, he related how he was trying to escape la cultura borracha. For Pedro, this is shorthand for

> the ills of our society, the haram nature of most of Boricua culture—women, sex, dirty language, reggaetón, all of it. But most of all, the drinking. The beer mixed in with everything we do here; the beach, the home, after work, on the weekends. Everywhere. All the time.

Pedro made a point that he wanted to break out of this routine and that he found his escape in Islam. "I love my culture, my heritage," he said, "but I must leave the haram aspects of it behind." For him, that means no drinking, no women, no dancing.

Ahmad echoed Pedro's sentiments about la cultura borracha. After our *tortillas españolas* (Spanish omelets) arrived—thankfully, without pork—at the café in Guaynabo, he said:

> The main issues I face in communicating the message of Allah to Puerto Ricans comes down to things like pork, beer, and dancing. They put pork in everything. Puerto Ricans drink beer like water down here. And, if you want to dance with your wife, fine. Just get a room. Do it in your home. Don't make a public festival of it.

All of these things—pork, beer, dancing—he argues, stem from Puerto Rico's colonial past. He said:

> Christian missionaries and governments used these things to keep the people dumb and submissive, docile. Islam is here to decolonize Puerto Ricans, to set them free. Puerto Ricans struggle with giving these things up, but what they don't realize is that giving these things up will actually allow them to fully live. They are distractions.

For others, struggling with la cultura borracha produces gray zones in their simultaneous pursuit of piety and puertorriqueñidad. Sighing as he put down his ice-cold Medalla Light, the sweat trickling down the gold-tinged can, forming a wet ring on the table, Hector—an intermittently employed, middle-aged man with family in the US and Puerto Rico—told me that the problem with la cultura borracha is not necessarily the drinking, but the drunkenness. "Being a Muslim is about being a real human being. I try to live like a real human being. If everyone in my family or friend group is toasting and they offer me a glass of wine, I will have it because I am not going to get drunk." Referring to verses from the Qur'an about not praying while intoxicated (4:43) and that there is both profit (Spanish: *provecho*) and harm (Spanish: *perjuicio*) in alcohol (Arabic: *khamr*) even if, "su perjuicio es mayor que su provecho" (its harm is greater than its benefit), Hector said there is debate about alcohol in some schools of Islamic thought. Invoking traditions within the Hanafi school (*madhab*), Hector insisted that only certain kinds of alcohol are strictly prohibited in the above verses and in the

Qur'an (5:90–91). "Certain Muslims teach that drinks made from things like barley or wheat are only haram if you get drunk or as long as you're not coming to prayer under the influence," Hector said. For him, this means beer is in the clear. Sipping again at his cold can of mid-summer refreshment, Hector sighed, "Especially Medalla Light, that's mostly water anyways and it's good to drink on a hot day on the beach."

And yet, Hector understands many Muslims—and even most Hanafis—would not agree. There are tensions in his choices. Hector said:

> Then I'll hear the "But Muslims don't drink!" Well, that's a different story. When I am in front of Allah we will straighten that out, but right now I am going to enjoy a bit of wine with my neighbor or maybe a beer. There is a difference between a bit of wine and a full borracha lifestyle, and that's what a lot of people don't understand.

Not only does Hector face accusations from Puerto Rican friends who hold him to their image of what "Islam" is, or what "Muslims" are supposed to do or don't do, he also faces pressure from fellow Muslims. He said:

> I've been seen in public with a beer in my hands and been challenged by my brothers, but I'd rather be comfortable in the hot sun with a cold beer than drink the junk that's in a Coke can. For them, it's cut and dry: "Arabs don't drink." But for Puerto Ricans it is so much of who we are and what we do, beer is mixed in with everything. I'd be denying my culture without enjoying a beer with friends. It's not that simple.

Pedro, Ahmad, and Hector feel that la cultura borracha is haram, but they each employ different ways of navigating this reality in light of their multivalent sense of belonging. Each adapts in their own way, illustrating again how such choices are mediated and messy. For Puerto Rican Muslims wading through la cultura borracha, this is an ongoing process of becoming, of different adaptations, accommodations, and, at times, "divergent affective tendencies."[94] These negotiations do not fall outside the pale of Islamic history and tradition. They are not unique or wholly exceptional. When compared to other Muslims across time and space, Puerto Rican reverts are not outliers. Rather, they are part and parcel of the process of how Muslims coming to terms with the paradox and pressures of everyday interactions with non-Muslims and their fellow faithful in a diverse and differentiated world. In and through these historically contingent encounters and negotiations, such structural tensions (as opposed to explicit "contradictions"[95]) show how Muslims the world over—not only along the so-called "edges" of global Islam—are involved in a persistent parlay between diversity and difference, orthodoxy and power, social dynamics and the pursuit of a seemingly consistent sense of self.

### *Borícua halal*

A few days after the iftar where I met Jonathan in Bayamón, I was making my way to Paseo Tablado de Piñones for a distinctly Puerto Rican Eid feast. Past Playa de Isla Verde and Luis Muñoz Marín International Airport and along the winding roads toward Loíza and Carolina, to the north of Canóvanas, one cannot help but notice Piñones's sights, sounds, and succulent offerings. Along the beach, there are various *kioskos* tucked in between the palm trees that dot the shoreline of the Piñones lagoon. Wisps of BBQ smoke, reggaetón, and the sumptuous scents of *arroz con jueyes* (crab and rice), *alcapurrias* (stuffed fritters), pinchos (meat skewers) and *pastelillos* (a smaller version of an empanadilla) swirl around you as you try to find your way to a table along the water.

Waving the smoke out of their faces as we pass by the kioskos, Muhammad and Jonathan say that seafood can be tricky to navigate. There is an almost dizzying array of legal opinions on the permissibility of meats of the sea, with some saying that all food from the sea is halal (for example, the Maliki school), while others provide more specific rulings about scaled fish and shrimp being permissible (Shi'i) or scavengers, bottom feeders, and carnivores like sharks being impermissible or some Shafi'i rulings on things like seahorses that are not permissible because their terrestrial counterpart (the horse) is haram. That means that while Puerto Rican favorites like *bacalao* (cod) and *chapín* (trunk fish) are permissible, other common selections such as *camarones* (shrimp), *jueyes* (crab), or *pulpo* (octopus) are haram or makruh, depending on which legal tradition you adhere to. It is hot, and our stomachs grumble loudly, so we immediately start hankering for the various foods on offer: *pastelillos de chapín, mofongo con camarones, arepas de coco,* and *piña coladas* (*sin alcohol*). As we snarf down our food, we excitedly share our favorite snacks and talk about how Muslims navigate such a feast.

Jonathan says he finds food separates him even further from his fellow Puerto Ricans. He shares that while out on the job, he might be eating with new colleagues and "they'll offer me pork and I will say, 'no, thank you.' And they'll ask if I am sick or allergic. When I tell them it's because of my faith, they'll confront me and say things like, 'Aren't Muslims terrorists? Aren't they violent?'" As Freidenreich writes, religious laws about food consumption—Muslim, Christian, Jewish, or otherwise—can be used both to divide and unite, maintain boundaries and mend fences between "Us" and the "Other."[96] This can happen both within religious communities and without.

And yet, new fusions can also seek to transcend those boundaries, combine traditions, and make the "Other" (whether it be their food or their history/culture/tradition) part of "Us." Such is the case with some Puerto Rican Muslims' explicit attempts at creating foods that are Borícua halal. Rachel, one of Sumayah's closest confidantes and friends, tells me as she finishes her arepas de coco that she tries to avoid the obvious—no ham in your *croquetas* for example—but does not make much fuss about anything else. "I am here to celebrate breaking the fast, not make more rules than necessary." Like Hector, Sumayah and Rachel are critiqued by fellow Muslims because of the lack of emphasis they put on culinary purity. Instead, they said, they opt for enjoying Puerto Rican food in all its rich diversity, including questionable creations such as *empanadillas de pulpo* or being seen sipping on a piña colada in hijab in public—even if it is alcohol-free.

This blend of foods is something Sumayah and Rachel are particularly proud of. Leaning back in their chairs after eating their fill, Sumayah and Rachel gesture at the food they consumed and discussed their two Eid meals, in Bayamón and Piñones, respectively. Excitedly going back and forth about recipes, they share that they hope to open a halal Puerto Rican food truck in the future. Already, they invite women over to their homes to show them how to cook what they call "Borícua halal." Sumayah and Rachel said they are trying to create a new culinary community by merging Middle Eastern and Puerto Rican cuisine. That is why they regularly gather with friends to make halal versions of traditional Puerto Rican dishes. Rachel says, "This is why we want to open our own halal Puerto Rican food truck. The food is delicious and so many Muslims avoid it because they are afraid that it is not halal." Rachel shares that they even want to try their hand at making halal beer to serve with the food. Echoing Hector's sentiments quoted earlier, she says, "Beer is like water here in Puerto Rico. If you can make piña coladas without alcohol, why not nonalcoholic halal beer?" Looking over at Sumayah, they both smile, dreams of their halal food truck beginning to gleam in their eyes.

### *A jíbara in jannah*

"Fuck, it's cold, isn't it?" asks Juan incredulously as we walk across the bridge connecting the neighborhoods of Washington Heights in Manhattan and Highbridge in the Bronx. We are on our way to his apartment after meeting in front of a local recreation center. It is, indeed, a fairly frigid November morning. As we cross the bridge, Juan smiles and asks another rhetorical question: "Not much like la isla del encanto, no?" Referencing how I transitioned from fieldwork in Puerto Rico in August to the New York City metro area in September, he asks how it was to adjust to the drop in temperatures and the less-than-tropical environs after a summer in the sun. Equivocating a bit, I turn the question back on him. Juan tells me he migrated to New York from Puerto Rico when he was in his early twenties. The change was a shock, he says:

> This place. This is not Borinkén. I thought I owned a jacket, hermano, but it turns out I didn't know what a jacket is. It was so cold. So different. Look at this damn bridge. All bolts and metal and rust. The city: concrete on top of the asphalt on top of the metal on top of dirty water. Not like back on the island. Nothing like that at all. Puerto Rico is beautiful, pure, and warm.

Now, in his late thirties, Juan says he has adjusted. "It took a while to adjust and learn to live here. Now I have a jacket," he says as he pulls his varsity-style collars a bit tighter over his neck and shoulders, "but, it still gets friggin' cold. I'll never get used to that."

Like other Nuyoricans, Juan transitioned from an initially hostile perception of New York—and a concomitantly romanticized, idealized, and enchanted image of Puerto Rico—to a begrudging adaptation to his new environs. Similar to poet Virgilio Davilá, Juan pitted Puerto Rico and New York against each other, using atmospheric conditions to underscore the differences between them. In "Nostalgia," Davilá writes how Puerto Rico calls him ("¡Mamá! ¡Borinquen me llama!") and how the US is not his home ("¡Este país no es el mío!"). For Davilá, the archipelago's warmth ("¡Borinquen es pura flama") is contrasted with the quelling cold of New York ("y aquí me muero de frío!").[97] Puerto Ricans, especially those in the diaspora, display what María Acosta Cruz called "a deep and abiding love for . . . the scenic beauties of the land," which is in turn tied to "nationalist emotions, to patriotism" and what she argued is a "dream nation."[98]

In the nineteenth century, as part of Creole elites' attempts to stir up "a national imaginary as part of their resistance to colonial rule by Spain,"[99] they sought to inspire a romantic return to the land. Later, in the face of US political intervention[100] and as Nuyorican and wider DiaspoRican[101] populations grew in the twentieth century, that feeling morphed into a romantic return to the island itself. The island—"la isla del encanto"—became a central site of self-fashioning for Puerto Ricans in the diaspora. There are expressions of lyrical love for, and commitment to, the Latinidad of New York locales like Loisaida (the Lower East Side) or El Barrio (East Harlem)[102]—and a new category of literature and art that deals with the traffic jams, roads, overcrowding, vehicular lifestyles, technology, and commercial enterprises of twenty-first century Puerto Rican life. But more prominent is a long history of literature and artistic representations like Davilá's that present an "Edenic vision of Puerto Rico"[103] as a "native nest" (*patrio nido*) of true puertorriqueñidad as a salve to counteract the uncomfortable weather in the United States or structural inequalities and xenophobia in its metropolitan cities.

Tapping into this desire for the archipelago, some popular parlance and literature can even evince a quasi-spiritual experience with the land. In *My Broken Heritage*, author Quiara Alagría Hudes speaks of her own experience of "revelation" about her cultural identification and belonging. Wrestling with her puertorriqueñidad as a daughter of a Puerto Rican mother and Jewish father living in "Philly" (Philadelphia, Pennsylvania), Alegría Hudes wonders, "Was I not Puerto Rican enough?" During a Quaker meeting, waiting in silence, open to inspiration, and looking for the Light Within, images of Puerto Rico came to her in a vision. With her knees and shoulders quaking, she stood and shared a word with the congregation:

> Puerto Rico. Its vistas stretched before me. I could finally imagine them because I had visited at last. . . . Plunged headfirst into Luquillo Beach's turquoise waves. Tasted calabaza ice cream from los chinos. Seen the cement house [my mother's] papi built and the farm across the road, which had become a nunnery. . . . Gulp down the mountain air, taste its crisp citrus dew. All that greenery, a verdant drape, as if the island were a king who wore these mountains for robes.[104]

Alegría Hudes wrote, "the images soothed me, pulled me toward a focused silence." In Hudes's imagination, Puerto Rico itself becomes a spiritual divulging, a possession, a vision, an unveiling.

Others shared similar experiences, specifically linked to the island and the physical experience thereof. In poetry and song, authors and artists wax eloquently about that "post-stamp island in the Caribbean," expressing a deep longing for the place and its presumption of peoplehood. Especially for DiaspoRicans, this longing is a potent mix of nostalgic memory, globalized identifications created in the midst of—and as a result of—migration, and transnational homemaking.[105] For example, Juan Rodríguez Calderón called Puerto Rico the island of "happy fame" and his "blithe sanctuary."[106] Santiago Vindarte also waxed lyrically in his poem "Insomnia":

> And see you there beneath its shady foot,
> a wondrous garden where blooms so lushly grow
> where April lives, my Siren, in each root?
> Well, that garden's name is Puerto Rico.[107]

Indeed, as Adrian Florido reported, "within the canon of popular Puerto Rican music, there is no shortage of songs" that express a particular "nostalgia for the island itself, often written by or for or about people who have had to leave Puerto Rico for one reason or another, but who yearn to return."[108] One of the oldest and most enduring of these is Noel Estrada's "En Mi Viejo San Juan" ("In My Old San Juan"). Written in 1943 and first recorded by El Trio Vegabajeno in 1946, it is about a man who leaves his beloved island with a plan to return, but finds himself unable to: "Adiós, adiós, adiós Borinquen querida, tierra de mi amor" (Goodbye, goodbye, goodbye, beloved Borinquen, land of my love). Similar to other diasporic peoples, Puerto Ricans look back to what has been left behind with "nostalgic reminiscence."[109]

Together, these artistic expressions speak to DiaspoRicans' melancholic[110] desire to ground their notions of being and belonging, to glimpse and perhaps grasp their self's source, in Puerto Rico itself—to know "peoplehood" by taste and feel, sweat and sweets, sights and sounds, music and mountains. Such a move is vital, in many ways, to (re)connect those in the diaspora to a place and an idea that stands at a distance through colonization, displacement, and geopolitical, linguistic, and cultural fragmentation. The social identification of race in particular is a key aspect of national identity-building in Puerto Rico and its diaspora.[111] The celebration and (re)imagination of their home's geology, ecology, and climate become ways to traverse distance and contest dislocation forced upon them by racialized colonial, political, and social orders and *become* Puerto Rican again. Thus, these remembrances should not be framed "as a debilitating form of escapism." Instead, their "nostalgia offers valuable insights into their present condition of disenfranchisement" as it "not only functions as active critique but is also instrumental" in their "desire for equality and empowerment."[112] In effect, it is a tool for cultural resiliency, restoration, and—in the AmeRícan Muslim case—resignification.

Geography, after all, is more than charts and maps. Instead, it is "an expansive field" that incorporates "space, place, scale, materiality, emotions and affect, and human and environment interactions."[113] Thus, geography offers a critical lens through which to further examine the ways in which Puerto Rican Muslims conceptualize their peoplehood. In complex interaction with Puerto Rico's physical and human environment, which is "often gendered but also intersected by age, race, class, and sexuality amongst other social locations; and depicted in mainstream culture, which in turn influences social-spatial discourses and practices,"[114] AmeRícan Muslims express a deep connection to the island *alongside* and *as part of* their profession of Islamic faith.

AmeRícan Muslims frequently reference "la bella Isla" or "la isla del encanto"[115] and appeal to its lush beauty, profound fecundity, and picturesque white sand beaches. For example, Adrián remarked to me as we drove on PR-2 west of San Juan how the mosque in Vega Alta was prominent with its white walls and coral minaret, but that its true beauty lies "in how it is surrounded by the essence of Puerto Rico—the beautiful trees, colors, and sounds of coquí frog." What made this mosque distinctly "Puerto Rican" to Adrián is that it was enveloped by the island's natural splendor. Similarly, others use the image of the coquí frog in logos and posts, reference its ubiquitous sounds in their poetry, and even use it as a metaphor for practices of Islamic piety. In a post on Facebook, Lebrón once linked listening to the coquí frog back in Puerto Rico to listening to recitations of the Qur'an. Both, he said, are a means of being bathed in the sound of "home," which in turn reduces anxiety, brings tranquility, and focuses the mind on Allah—his gifts, benefits, and blessings.

In her work, "Muslim and Boricua (Puerto Rican)" poet and journalist Wendy Díaz put it this way: that while she remains proudly Muslim, she would never deny her puertorriqueñidad. "I am Boricua to the core, no one can change that fact," she wrote, "I can choose to call god Allah while my origin stays intact." She also wrote nostalgically of "la isla del Encanto," linking Puerto Rico to the notion of *jannah* (paradise)—the final abode of the righteous in Islam, writing, "The Island of Enchantment is where I was born; And I pray that in Heaven I find a similar abode (I will never deny that I am Boricua)." In Díaz's reading, la isla del encanto acts as a temporal foretaste of paradise, the southern coast and hillsides around Salinas previews of the promised splendor of heaven. To her, there is no other comparable earthly beauty she would rather dwell in for eternity.

Moreover, Díaz writes she will "always be a *jíbara.*" A *jíbaro/a* (or *jibarito/a*) refers to Puerto Ricans who farmed the land in a traditional way. Now, they serve as a representation of the roots of modern-day Puerto Ricanness and are used to symbolize the strength of puertorriqueñidad, with its links to the land and the countryside in particular.[116] For Díaz, she longs to be a jíbara in jannah, enjoying paradise like she enjoys her time back home in Puerto Rico—reposing under large trees who shades are ever deepening, walking through lush, green mountains, and enjoying the peaceful presence of rivers—whether they be like the Euphrates or the Río Nigua. In this, Díaz joins others in longing for the island as a means of returning from the hinterlands of Hoboken, New Jersey, or Hartford, Connecticut, to ground themselves in Puerto Rico as both a real and imagined place. Those living on the island do so with proud pleasure; those elsewhere with diasporic longing.

These longings, reflecting their puertorriqueñidad and refracting their Muslimness, evince another aspect of their search for community from a position of marginalization from "la gente y la isla." Interlaced with Islamic references and language, these nostalgic remembrances act as a means of imitating, dwelling in, and yearning "for a future realm of as yet unrealized communal possibilities and potential."[117] In these formulations, the island of Puerto Rico, its flora, and its fauna become more than a place of ethnic belonging, but of religious self-fashioning and situating. It becomes a place where AmeRícan Muslims seek to imprint themselves upon the land and Islamize it.[118] Through this process, the "topographical and ecological particularities" of Puerto Rico become "more than empty canvases for human activities" but affect and shape the formation of a certain peoplehood, which on the one hand is locally emplaced and on the other hand transcends local boundaries.[119] Fusing their peoplehood with physical places and past remembrances, this peoplehood is "not merely an exclusively religious category but something encompassing both ethnicity and religion as foundational dimensions, thus denoting belonging in a strong affective manner."[120] Thus, in ways similar to their invocations of the island's architecture, their expressions are attempts to mix Islam—and their own Muslimness—into Puerto Rico's lush beauty, green forests, and golden beaches.

### *"Ahlan wa sahlan. Mi casa es tu casa"*

Another means of pointing to the past to situate identifications in the present is found in AmeRícan Muslims' appeal to the influence of Arabic on the Spanish language.[121] Although not all Puerto Rican Muslims, nor all Puerto Ricans, speak Spanish, it is an important point of pride in their understanding of what it means to be Puerto Rican. As it turns out, it is also an important node in their self-understanding as Muslims. Since ethnic identity and linguistic identity are mutually imbricated, the questions of who speaks what languages, how many, and where, are all relevant for considering the idea and reality of cosmopolitanism.[122] For AmeRícan Muslims, it means being proud of their Spanish language and pointing out how Arabic influenced the language and thus, by extension, Puerto Rican peoplehood. There are also practical dimensions when it comes to what languages they speak, which languages are spoken at the mosque, how theologies, ideas, and materials are translated into new languages, or the ways that individuals navigate the diversity of languages in the context of local communities.

Many Puerto Rican converts I interacted with do not speak Arabic beyond what recitations, phrases, prayers, or words they memorized from the Qur'an or discourses of Islamic tradition. There are notable exceptions to this rule, with some having studied Arabic in Saudi Arabia, Egypt, or online. Nonetheless, the primary languages spoken among and between AmeRícan Muslims are Spanish and English. Most are bilingual. Only relatively few could speak only one or the other. Regardless, most evinced a pride in the Spanish language and viewed it as a primary marker of puertorriqueñidad. Even those who could not speak Spanish—most of whom were second- or third-generation Puerto Ricans in the US—believe it is an important aspect of being Puerto Rican and often expressed remorse over not learning Spanish in the course of life.

Language is a crucial aspect of Puerto Rican cultural identification. On the archipelago, Spanish remains the primary, functionary language, and English has not penetrated deeply into the nation's daily life, despite 125 years of US colonization. Part of the process of "Americanizing" the US's new colonial holding in the Caribbean was the Official Languages Act in 1902, which mandated that English and Spanish be used indiscriminately. In practice, English was the sole language used by the military government from 1898 to 1900, and education in government schools was overwhelmingly conducted in English as "education was considered an instrument for the assimilation and Americanization of Puerto Ricans."[123] Proud of their language, history, and heritage, teachers and students resisted, affirming their puertorriqueñidad by conducting classes in Spanish.[124] Beyond the classroom, the use of Spanish remained ubiquitous across the archipelago, and the maintenance of the language became a form of resistance to what was perceived as foreign incursion by nationalists and other Puerto Ricans who did not want to abandon their language and culture at the behest of colonizing powers.[125] Over a century later, the Spanish language's survival "has become inextricably linked for many with the survival of Puerto Rican identity and that of the Puerto Rican nation itself."[126] Speaking Spanish can even be treated as an act of resistance[127] wherein "every Spanish word represents a refusal to capitulate to English ethnocentricity."[128] In effect, the preference for Spanish among Puerto Ricans serves as a marker to represent and to scrutinize the majority and the discrimination and dispossession that the community suffers.[129] Thus, over time, loyalty to the Spanish language is, in some respects, a litmus test—albeit a contested one—for a more general loyalty to Puerto Rico and puertorriqueñidad as a whole.[130]

Yet, some Puerto Ricans disagree about the importance of the Spanish language for politics, education, and cultural identity. As studies show, Spanish language use does not necessarily "correlate with the feeling of group membership and the development of a clear cultural identity" among all Puerto Ricans.[131] For example, within the Puerto Rican diaspora, Spanish is adopted as a symbol of Puerto Ricanness, but it is not always maintained in practice. As education scholar Edwin Lamboy wrote, "Puerto Ricans in the United States, like most other Latino groups, do not perceive being proficient in Spanish as a co-requisite for identifying with the Puerto Rican culture and way of life."[132] Puerto Rican Muslims can often speak *both* English and Spanish, but maintain a definitive pride in the Spanish language. This is particularly true in the diaspora, where Puerto Rican Muslims are proud of their Spanish language ability (if they have it).

In fact, many AmeRícan Muslims—on the archipelago and in the diaspora—point with pride to their Spanish language skills and Arabic's influence on it. For most, this helps them underscore how being Muslim is not in opposition to being Puerto Rican. Some go one step further, claiming that it makes them even *more* Puerto Rican by having a connection to one of the Spanish language's antecedents. Lebrón, for example, in his aforementioned rebuke of Miss Puerto Rico, referenced the debt that the Spanish language owes to Arabic. Lebrón claimed there are some "two thousand to three thousand Hispanic words derived from the Arabic language." He even went so far as to posit that his grandfather spoke "words that sometimes that [his family] could not understand." He said that when his grandmother vocalizes them, "they sound as if they are Arabic words."

Lebrón is not alone in making these assertions or pointing this out as evidence as a means of connecting Islam and Puerto Rican culture. Soraya Asad Sánchez identifies language as one of the "footprints" left by Arabs on Puerto Rican peoplehood.[133] She wrote that up to 20 percent of Spanish words bear the imprint of Arabic, perhaps up to four thousand in all,[134] including agricultural, architectural, astronomical, topographical, and mathematical terms and phrases.[135] Based on this, Sánchez even asserted, "we can point out that the Arab was the fourth ethnic group to integrate into our culture. That is to say, Arabic is a fundamental part of it."[136] Many AmeRícan Muslims would share this sentiment, roused by the possibility of including Arabic as an integral aspect of Puerto Ricanness.

Although this may function as an instrument of defending and grounding their sense of being and belonging in Puerto Rican cultural histories and practices, how does the use of Arabic and Spanish get worked out on the ground and in their local communities? For example, what are the linguistic contexts at the mosques where Puerto Rican Muslims pray, learn, and connect with other Muslims? While the lingua franca on the streets in Puerto Rico is overwhelmingly Spanish, it is sometimes hard to come by Spanish in the archipelago's mosques. One gets a sense of this in the environs around the mosque in Río Piedras. The first mosque established in Puerto Rico, it is situated in a lively part of the city just south of the University of Puerto Rico's largest, and most well-known, campus. The neighborhood also has a robust commercial history still evident in the bustling market down the road from the mosque. Arab immigrants came into the area in the twentieth century and set up their own shops in and around the market. Then, in 1981, they converted one of the buildings in the neighborhood into a masjid.

One day during my fieldwork, I walked into the home-goods store across the street from the mosque and was greeted in Spanish by a Palestinian man. He seemed to be running the show and explained that he imports Palestinian and Jordanian goods he often sells to local Arabs, making sure he is well-stocked on Fridays as many people will come and buy things after prayer. The man thanked me for coming into the store, and then I followed him to the mosque as the *adhan* sounded out along the street. When I entered the mosque, there was a young man who had an assortment of literature spread out before him in Spanish and English, the basic pamphlets explaining Islam to the curious seeker. He was reading them enthusiastically. Later, I joined him and a small group of Puerto Ricans (and other visitors) where a man named Yusuf translated the khutbah from Arabic into Spanish. While the majority were able to follow the Arabic khutbah, a small minority huddled in the back needed to have it summarized and translated into their vernacular. There were two men there who recently reverted and were struggling to learn Arabic. There was also Alejandro, whom I met at Montehiedra the year before and who was translating the Spanish into English for a visitor from Pakistan. There was also a man from Bangladesh I met the previous week at prayers in Vega Alta. All told, we were a group of eight. Of some seventy to eighty men there to pray, most were Palestinian. There were others as well—a man from West Africa and a small group from Indonesia—but Palestinians predominated.

This scene is oft repeated at mosques across Puerto Rico. In fact, there is an ongoing, lively discussion among local Muslims about which mosques offer Spanish translation, Spanish summaries, or that have the khutbah delivered in Spanish. At various times, I was told that *this* mosque or *that* mosque had a Spanish khutbah or a summary read from the front. Often, these places were lauded, their leaders praised among Puerto Rican reverts. This is how someone like Imam Zaid Abdelrahim, who served in Montehiedra, came to be so respected during his tenure there. He gave the khutbah in both Arabic and Spanish. Those places that either did not offer a translation at all or expected individuals to gather in the back as we did in Río Piedras were disparaged or were mosques I was discouraged from attending. Various AmeRícan Muslims told me that they felt that they were not treated like "real Muslims," but were "ghetto-ized" into the back of the mosque because they could not speak Arabic.

Others critiqued the mosque leaders for "not being here to preach to Puerto Ricans, just to other Arabs."[137] Miguel, mentioned earlier, shared that it can be tough for Puerto Rican converts, "because, like I said, they're not interested in spreading the message. So, you can go to the mosque, and they won't kick you out, but they are not going to preach to you either. So, you're Puerto Rican, and you go into Islam, but you have to do everything on your own." He compared imams like Zaid who speak, and preach in, Spanish with those who "don't even speak Spanish," praising his own imam because he was making the effort to learn and deliver his messages in Spanish. The overall concern was that Puerto Rican Muslims would otherwise not feel "welcomed or that they belong," he said. Without Spanish in the mosque, Miguel said Puerto Rican Muslims were staying home or seeking out other communities online because "they don't feel like [the mosque is] their community, but an Arab social club they can't join. So, they are on their own."

Some Puerto Rican Muslims deal with this tension by endeavoring to learn Arabic. Taking courses in Egypt, Saudi Arabia, enrolling in ASL (Arabic as a Second Language) courses at mosques in North Hudson, Carolina, Montehiedra, or online, they want to learn Arabic for a feeling of authenticity, respect, or authority. While not fluent, Lebrón shared with me that in New York, a lot of Latinx Muslims find it difficult that "there is a clear lack of services for Latinos and a discrimination factor even among and within the Arabs." He said, "There's a little bit of tribalism there too." He said he would see "a clear change in demeanor" when he started speaking Arabic. People would automatically start paying attention to him, he said. "They gave me respect that maybe I don't deserve because I don't know it all. But I'll take it." With this in mind, some imams offer ASL courses. Benny, a recent revert at the mosque in Ponce in the south of Puerto Rico, said that he was learning Arabic not only to feel more integrated in the local Muslim community, but as a means of access to a wider world. He said that he was taking an ASL course in Montehiedra to "learn part of a new culture" and come to understand the messages at the mosques where everyone else is Palestinian. "I am the only Puerto Rican here," he said, "so I have to change. I have to learn a new culture even if I am not giving up my own." Individuals like Benny view Arabic as a portal to authority and authenticity in their religious communities.

Others feel differently, however. Rahim Ocasio, one of Alianza Islámica's founders, said when he went to mosques, "back in the day" all he would see "were Arab men sitting around talking Arabic . . . there was no place for a young Nuyorican like me." He sought a more varied mosque community, "to enjoy the diversity that Islam has to offer." Seeing Latinx Muslims as an "underserved minority" in American Islam, he and others endeavored to translate outreach materials, messages, and other Islamic literature into Spanish. This was sometimes supported by official publishing houses or outreach organizations and sometimes not. Sumayah told me that while the materials are being translated into Spanish, YouTube videos are being made, and podcasts produced, it is not enough. She lamented that when you walk into mosques, Spanish-language materials "are often hard to find or located on a disheveled and dusty bookshelf not touched in a long time." The desire, she said, is to see more organizations like IslamInSpanish working on producing Spanish-language messages and materials for Latinx and Puerto Rican Muslim minorities in the Americas.

This issue is one AmeRícan Muslims share with other non-Arab Muslims and reverts, where speaking Arabic is linked to authority and authenticity within the wider ummah. For AmeRícan Muslims, their particular pride in Spanish is also a means of resisting colonization by foreign powers and outside forces. They learn Arabic, but they also fight to maintain their Spanish and underscore its relations to Arabic, its connections to a global Islamic narrative, and its continual use in the Muslim community in Puerto Rican contexts. This process of negotiation and exchange, translation and transculturation mixed with a bit of resistance and critical tension is pivotal to AmeRícan Muslims' cosmopolitan lives. They show an openness to the world but bring their experience as Puerto Ricans to that openness. The generative friction between these two aspects of their lives leads to new cultural expressions and a rereading of previous experiences and markers of identity, but not wholesale abandonment or some form of globalized homogeneity.

Their vernacularization of Islam and its idioms into their own language(s)—or desire to see more thereof—is a tactical reversal of domination and its idioms.[138] It is a means of resistance through appropriation.[139] On the one hand, they are vernacularizing the global language of Islam into their own idiom. On the other hand, they are globalizing their own idiom, positioning it as a means and mode of transmitting Islam. Spanish gains new inflections and significance through this process. Whether in rehighlighting its Arabic roots or elevating it to the language of a khutbah, Spanish becomes something more than it was before—a language of Islam. It is not only a sign of their Puerto Ricanness but also a sign of their inclusion and/or exclusion within the ummah. Although their efforts at translation are still stunted in many respects, the process of vernacularization is an active mode of resistance and appropriation, inclusion and exclusion, the global and the local in dynamic tension. It is a simultaneous process of "carving out space"[140] for Spanish in Islam and among Muslims, as well carving space out for Islam and Muslims in the Spanish idiom that Puerto Ricans pride themselves in speaking.

Although it can be compared to cases of diglossia or the navigation of language and cultural pride and preservation among American Muslim communities in Chile,[141] Colombia,[142] Mexico,[143] or elsewhere in Latin America and the Caribbean,[144] the above vignettes detail the particular contours of the AmeRícan case. They illustrate how AmeRícan Muslims' insistence on Spanish as the language of their faith and their highlighting of Arabic's influence on Spanish is yet another means by which they seek to situate, express, and identify their Muslimness within the vernacular of puertorriqueñidad. In this instance, "lo que es puertorriqueño" is a literal vernacular. But, as this chapter illustrated, AmeRícan Muslims' resignification of Puerto Ricanness is also expressed through relational networks, architecture, foodways, and an array of everyday, material means and affective modes.

## CONCLUSION

AmeRícan Muslims' relationships with popular perceptions and practices of puertorriqueñidad—and the communities and connections they represent—involve both loss and contestation, fresh opportunities and combinations. All the while, they wrestle with their own *Puerto Ricanness*, simultaneously grappling with what it means to be Puerto Rican and what it means to be Muslim in, through, and around the traditional markers of Borícua being and belonging. Their stories reflect how people find a way to live beyond the labels and stories placed upon them.

At the same time, specific places, histories, and stories still matter. Thus, accommodation, adaptation, and artistic resourcefulness are commonplace in their everyday lives as they attempt to merge their Muslim identification with discourses around, and practices of, Puerto Rican culture. On the one hand, this is an opportunity for expanding their notion of being and belonging. On the other hand, it confronts and challenges what is held as more "traditional" Puerto Ricanness, even if those traditions are themselves hybrid amalgamations of various influences from the past (e.g., Taíno, African, Iberian).

For AmeRícan Muslims, choosing certain types of food, engaging with certain kinds of buildings, and interacting with their place in the world in certain ways are a means of making sense of a contingent and multilineaged past, in the midst of a cosmopolitanized present, so that they might lean into a more integrated future, one where their identifications are not limited according to imaginaries that exclude parts of their sense of self. Through processes of resistance and transformation, they co-opt hegemonic frames of puertorriqueñidad in order to craft a new narrative of the possible and highlight the thick polyvalence of what it means to be "Puerto Rican." Nonetheless, the tactics they employ are not the answer to such concerns and questions, but the conundrum itself. They are caught in a process of constantly working out who they are through what they do in the context of everyday life—at a café in Guaynabo, on the beach drawing henna tattoos, or shopping at the local Coop *supermercado* as they prepare for family dinner. As shown, there is no singular approach to these quandaries. Instead, there is ambiguity and miscellany to be found in a multitude of practices and efforts at belonging and co-becoming.

Moreover, the resignification of Puerto Rican peoplehood is just *one* facet of their cosmopolitan complications. Another, and perhaps broader, resignification occurs in the context of their religious identification. In the next two chapters, I consider how AmeRícan Muslims navigate the generative frictions that exist in their everyday lives as Puerto Ricans within the context of a global ummah.

# 3
# An *ummah en vaivén*
## AMERÍCAN MUSLIMS, GLOBAL TRADITIONS

The opportunities of globalization have enabled an increasing number of religious actors to promote not only different versions of Islam, but rival claimants to religious authority. [. . .] If this cacophony of rival versions of Islam seems bewildering, that is because this is precisely the collective character of global Islam.

NILE GREEN[1]

ILYASS IS A TWENTYSOMETHING MAN with a fair complexion, paper-thin black mustache, and goatee. One night, as evening draws in around us and the sound of cane frogs croaking echoes from the swamp next door to my condo in Gainesville, Florida, he and I sit on the back patio under Spanish moss hanging from the oaks above. I light a match to spark the kindling for a fire, and Ilyass opens up about his youth in Tampa—two hours southwest of Gainesville. "I was into drinking and chasing after girls, that was everything to me," he says. When he converted at eighteen, he says he struggled to give up drinking. That was, he says, until he met a Salafi Muslim at a mosque in Philadelphia when visiting family. "He set me straight," says Ilyass, "I learned so much from him about how to control my urges . . . not to mention a lot of other things about what to eat and not eat, what's just makruh and what's actually haram or halal. For example, did you know that some kinds of mozzarella aren't halal? Who knew?"

This leads us into a discussion of orthodoxy, authentic Islamic praxis, and varying opinions and applications thereof by different Muslim groups. Identifying as "Hanafi in fiqh [jurisprudence], Ashari in aqidah [creed], and Qadiriyyah in *tariqa* [ritual practice]," Ilyass shares some strongly worded opinions about other streams of Islamic thought and practice:

> Everyday-practicing Shi'i who just go about their prayers and try to live their life according to the Prophet (PBUH) are probably Muslim, but you can't actually know Shi'i creeds and theology and pretend to be an authentic Muslim. Like, you can't curse the *sahabah* [companions of the Prophet Muhammad] and remain orthodox.

An equal-opportunity critic, he also has stern words for feminist jurisprudence and Islamist groups like the Muslim Brotherhood. "A true Muslim does not confuse what the world is interested in with what Allah wants from us," Ilyass says. He also says he's met Sufis who, when he challenged them to recite al-Fatiha (the first *surah*, or chapter, of the Qur'an, often regarded as its essence and summation), they could not. "Not Muslim," he says of such Sufis. On the Salafis in Philly in particular, he says, "They're too intense for me. They know the Qur'an, but they're . . . kind of scary, to be honest. They crowd up and get all intense with themselves, each other, other Muslims." Then, after returning from his *isha* prayers in my upstairs office, Ilyass tisk-tisks as he opens the sliding door to the back patio, warning me that the *muska* (*tawiz*, or amulet) given to me by a Bosnian Muslim in Mostar and displayed on one of my bookshelves, is "pure *shirk*, man. But you're Christian, so I guess it's not the worst of your problems."

We both smile, enjoying the banter and ignoring its more serious implications in favor of the friendship developing between us. After a beat or two, staring into the flames and getting lost in our own thoughts, I press Ilyass a bit more about the tension between orthodoxy and Muslim unity. He then cites a hadith, reported by Nu'man bin Bashir: "The believers in their mutual kindness, compassion and sympathy are just like one body. When one of the limbs suffers, the whole body responds to it with wakefulness and fever." He says:

> We can debate fiqh, we can argue over particulars of practice and even call each other *kharijis*, but we have to believe we are part of one ummah. The things that divide us are not feminism or talismans,

> philosophy or politics, it's just sectarianism. Tribalism. This group and that group, being Puerto Rican or being Egyptian, Bosnian or Botswanian . . . I don't know. People in most mosques are divided along ethnic and linguistic lines. Sometimes, I think there is less tribalism in the world than there is inside a mosque!

This, he says, can be a bit depressing. When I ask whether his strong opinions about different sects and socialities might contribute to such disunity, he looks at me long and hard, twirling a cup in his hand, before turning his eyes up to the Spanish moss and the few stars he can make out through the smoke swirling up from the fire below. "I don't know, Ken," he sighs, "I'm just trying to find my own way."

If AmeRícan Muslims struggle to find their place as Muslims among Puerto Ricans and within established notions of Puerto Rican peoplehood, they also grapple with being Puerto Rican on the so-called "margins" of global Islam. In the following two chapters, I share how they navigate the various landscapes, traditions, and communities of global Islam from the margins. In this chapter, I explore their fealty to various traditions. Then, in the following chapter, I examine the strains between AmeRícan Muslims' localized identifications and the ideal of unity within the worldwide ummah. Along the way, I address built-in mechanisms of power, which include and exclude Puerto Rican Muslims from Islamic institutions and academic discourse(s). In this chapter, I share how AmeRícan Muslims navigate some of these tensions, evaluating how they "find their way" within traditions and in particular socialities based on a web of relational contexts, life experiences, and embodied, affective encounters.

While I will return to the generative frictions between AmeRícan Muslims and their fellow faithful, this chapter looks at four narratives from across the spectrum of AmeRícan Muslim allegiance and identification: from a searching Sufi in Harlem to the fledgling Ahmadiyya community in Puerto Rico; a budding Puerto Rican politician who aligns with the "Qur'an only" movement; and a man named Jesús looking for a place to call home in New York City. Together, these stories illustrate how Puerto Rican reverts variously acquire new religious languages, practices, and imaginations, drawing them from, and adapting them to, their affective needs, sociopolitical contexts, and relational networks. More broadly, it shows global Islam to be a living, breathing network of divergent affective tendencies, socially reimagined at multiple scales: personal and communal, national and regional, familial and academic.

## WHAT IS THIS THING WE CALL "GLOBAL ISLAM"?

Constituting a quarter of the world's population, Muslims believe distinct things, act in different ways, and hold varying kinds of relations with one another across the globe. Nevertheless, if you were to look at certain maps,[2] survey the news,[3] or analyze a cross-section of academic publications, positions, and presentations,[4] you might not know it. Instead, you would be led to think that most—if not all—Muslims live within a certain geographic subset of the world, speak a certain language, and hold a certain worldview in tension with popular perceptions about "the West" or the "modern."

The reality, however, is that most live outside the Middle East and North Africa. Muslim communities are found in significant concentrations from Asia to the Americas and many places beyond and in between. Moreover, the vast majority of contemporary Muslims are not fluent Arabic speakers but speak Persian, Urdu, Turkish, English, or Spanish. Lastly, only a sliver of a subset of Muslims are scholars, jurists, or trained theologians. Most of what we call "Islam" is lived, not learned in a formal sense. And yet, the preponderance of publications on Islam and Muslims continue to favor particular geographies (the Middle East and North Africa), focus on particular kinds of texts (Arabic), and fix on the finer points of doctrinal debates or elite, so-called "orthodox" norms.

There is, of course, pushback against these just-so narratives about, and mainstream understandings of, the who, what, and where of global Islam. Studies in sub-Saharan Africa, Southeast Asia, the Balkans, East Asia, South Asia, the Americas, and the spaces that connect them, along with explorations of groups (e.g., Alevi, Ahmadiyya, Sufi, Shi'i, Black Muslim movements) and practices (e.g., tattooing, magic, dance, alcohol consumption, etc.) often deemed unorthodox all help highlight the "other sides of Islam" that are not as "Other" as they might first appear.[5] Such studies illustrate how the realities of Muslim lifeworlds—whether they be Sufi poets or feminist scholars, Muslim Marxists, or imams with southern accents[6]—are shaped less by orthodoxy than by things like "pragmatism, creativity and poetry."[7] The question these works ask, as Edward E. Curtis IV wrote, is what might happen "if we put Muslims who are socially, culturally, theologically, and politically marginalized at the center of our understanding of Islam and Muslim communities?"[8] By emphasizing the complexity, capaciousness, and seeming chaos of Islamic traditions and socialities across time and space, these works offer more textured and nuanced portraits of Muslim lives across geographic, sectarian, and ritual divides. They are not without their blind spots, but they make evident "that by paying attention to the margins of Islam, we learn a much more inclusive and accurate version of the religion and its many interrelated communities."[9]

In this book, I offer a distinctive contribution to this ongoing conversation. By paying attention to Muslims who are politically, geographically, doctrinally, culturally, and socially marginalized, yet not without important perspectives, I add another layer of shading and distinction to our increasingly complicated portraits of global Muslim lifeworlds. Specifically, this chapter focuses on AmeRícan Muslims' experiences of religious belonging, their communal identifications, and the constitutive contextual and relational dynamics thereof. These relations include cooperation and connection, but also conflict and confrontation. Together, they provide a window into what Muslim identification, community, and practice look like in the late-modern.

Such perspectives are too often minoritized in our imaginings of global Islam. I center them here with the conviction that smaller parts build to a bigger whole, that their relational and contextual narratives offer a rich storytelling space that simultaneously reflects *and* shapes broader currents. By focusing on the mundane and routine, the coincidental and the seemingly inconsequential, the inspiring and the idiosyncratic in AmeRícan Muslims, lives, I believe we come to a richer, more contextualized, and networked understanding of what constitutes Islam around the world and across history.

It will become clear that traditions, groupings, and practices that emanate from geographies more often associated with "Islam" and "Muslims" (the dominant "discourses" of global Islam, if you will)[10] find concrete, if complex, expression in AmeRícan Muslim lives. However, this discourse is inadequate to fully account for the marginal adaptations and minoritized experience that constitute their lifeworlds. Although AmeRícan Muslims cannot escape these wide-ranging flows, they also cannot be fully reduced to them. Instead, like "branches of a river that separate and meet, merging with other rivulets and accumulating meaning"[11] as they run their course through particular communities and contexts, global traditions take on the sediment of AmeRícan Muslims' everyday lives and relational landscapes. In other words, looking at global Islam from the AmeRícan Muslim perspective requires doing so from the varying urban, diasporic, and insular milieus of Puerto Rican life.

In the next two chapters, I show how within the "infinite multiplicity of discourse"[12] that is global Islam, AmeRícan Muslims find a countervoice that unsettles large patterns of description, domination, and discrimination.[13] This countervoice will be the particular focus of the following chapter. In this chapter, I focus on how Islamic traditions are subjectivized, interpellated, and embodied in the AmeRícan Muslim experience in order to emphasize how they are not peripheral to a perceived global Islamic center but representative of it. In other words, it shows how they "participate in [global Islam's] flows and dynamics,"[14] intimately involved in its debates and decidedly part of determining its contemporary contours.

## AN *UMMAH EN VAIVÉN*

AmeRícan Muslims' experiences with global Islamic traditions are marked by complementary forces of *subjectivity* and *interpellation*. First, the sense of belonging they feel (or do not) to particular traditions is shaped by personal affect, tastes, or opinions that are simultaneously subject to the contours of power and the particular relations through which that power is expressed. Affects, tastes, and opinions like Ilyass's could be said to be the *subjectivity* of AmeRícan Muslim lives. But that subjectivity, that sense of being Sunni or Shi'i, Ahmadi or Sufi, *this* kind of Muslim or *that* kind of Muslim, is not solely a matter of individual agency or personal proclivity, but the result of *interpellation*—that is to say that AmeRícan Muslim identifications and ideologies emerge out of the particular political, social, economic, and relational context(s) in which they are situated, within which they live, and out of which they make meaning. In other words, while AmeRícan Muslims feel they choose the traditions with which to identify (and subsequently the socialities with which they associate), they are also *interpellated* by certain outlooks and positioned as subjects within the world of Islam by particular social contexts and constructions. These subjectivities and interpellations define what is knowable and experienceable. Moreover, they facilitate not only AmeRícan Muslims' religious, political, and social present but also their potential futures and the ways they view their past.

The overlapping vicissitudes and uncertainty of their search for a sense of being and belonging within the wider ummah means AmeRícan Muslims associate with a range of communities, organizations, and streams of Islamic thought, jurisprudence, and practice. Schools of Islamic traditions have long traveled extensively and encountered one another at various junctures in time and place. Furthermore, schools of thought within Islam are not necessarily mutually exclusive (i.e., Muslims may follow a hybrid approach that draws from multiple schools of jurisprudence) and the prevalence of these schools can vary within different countries and regions. But there remains a tendency for traditions to be concentrated in particular geographies and Islamicate contexts or to predominate among particular communities (e.g., Hanafi in Turkey, the Balkans, Central Asia, and South Asia; Hanbali in Saudi Arabia and the Persian Gulf; Maliki in North Africa and West Africa; Shafi'i in Eastern Africa and Southeast Asia; various kinds of Shi'i in Iran, Lebanon, Turkey, and Iraq).[15]

AmeRícan Muslims, however, do not pledge fealty to any one madhab or *mawla*, one sect or succession of teachers.[16] Though many may be Hanafi-adjacent, one can debate finer points of fiqh related to dogs with Maliki practitioners in Queens, break the fast with Ahmadis in Guaynabo, eat pumpkin pie with a Nuyorican Salafi in Harlem, practice *dhikr* with a Puerto Rican *sheikha* in Mexico City, or talk about Shi'i theology and shirk next to a bonfire on the back patio under oaks decked with Spanish moss in Gainesville, Florida. All of these encounters were with AmeRícan Muslims during my fieldwork, with individuals who, in their quest for a sense of home on the margins of the so-called "Muslim world," associate with a range of traditions from across the diversity of Islamic history, habit, and heritage. This is, I suggest, another way that AmeRícan Muslims attempt to take the "accent from the altercation" and, in striving to reproduce a broader answer to the marginality they face from their fellow faithful, imagine a new, more cosmopolitan sense of Islamic being and belonging.

The diversity of allegiances that AmeRícan Muslims claim is, similar to other junctures in the historic spread of Islam across the globe, a matter of contact and contestation, encounter and exchange. Trade, missionary efforts, political expansion, caravans, groups of travelers, educational networks, and local leaders all played roles in the spread of Islam—and its various traditions—into specific places and among particular people groups across the world. For example, trade networks helped expand the Shafi'i madhab in port cities and their inland networks across the coasts of East Africa and Yemen and into Indonesia and Malaysia. Elsewhere, caravan routes across the Sahel helped bring people into contact with Maliki thought across North and West Africa, and Sufi networks connected disparate locales in Baghdad, Iraq, to Ajmer, India, and Jaghbub, Libya; or Bukhara, Uzbekistan, to

Padang, Indonesia, and Trebizond on the Black Sea.[17] As Aaron Hughes succinctly explained:

> [Muhammad's] message spread into various (unbordered) regions. Modern nation states would only arise much later. And each of these areas was already in possession of its own set of religious, legal and cultural traditions. The result was that Islam had to be articulated in the light of local customs and understandings. This was done, in part, through the creation of legal courts, a class of jurists (ulema; mullas in Shiʿism), a legal code (sharia) and a system of interpretation of that code based on rulings (fatwas). Many local customs arose based on trying to understand Muhammad's message. And these customs and understandings gave rise to distinct legal schools.[18]

In the modern and late-modern eras, flows of capital, information, media, symbols, technology, and migration produced three interrelated effects in the spread of these schools and traditions within and along global Islam's constituent networks and interconnected nodes: 1) the dispersed and widespread distribution of various traditions across the world; 2) increased contact, competition, and contestation between them in areas of mixed concentration; and 3) the variegated allegiances of more recent convert communities in places where Islam did not historically predominate.

The Americas are, in some ways, quintessential exemplars of these recent trends. Through the arrival of indentured servants from India and Indonesia in the nineteenth century, immigration from the Ottoman Empire's Arab provinces in the nineteenth and twentieth centuries, and through increased missionary activity, trade, political allegiances, and ongoing migration and movement in the twentieth and twenty-first, Latin America and the Caribbean showcase a menagerie of adherence, with Sufi lodges in the Chilean interior, Ahmadiyya outreach centers in Guatemala and Belize, a Salafi center in Mexico City, and Deobandi schools in Trinidad, Guyana, and Haiti.

In one community alone, on the outskirts of San Cristóbal de las Casas, in Mexico's southernmost state of Chiapas, a community of local Maya converted to Islam in the 1990s. Initially associated with the Murabitun World Movement—itself a Sufi network with connections to Scotland, Spain, and South Africa that derives its lineage from the Darqawi tariqa in Morocco—the converts later split into various communities. Today, there are four mosques in town, variously associated with the Murabitun World

Movement, a Mexico City-based Salafi organization, as well as Sunni and Ahmadiyya traditions.[19]

Such kaleidoscopic concentrations are a result of what I call an ummah en vaivén.[20] This is an ummah not only on the move (through the flows outlined above) but also alternating, in fluctuation, and sometimes moving in multiple, frictive directions through the everyday, relational contexts and processes of cosmopolitanization. This, as others put it, is Islam as *verb*,[21] not bound by particular persons, places, or things, but an evolving set of actions, states, or occurrences engaged with the discursive frames of tradition in dynamic, generative tension. And as Islam continues to be defined and redefined by crisscrossing population movements, languages, traditions, political ideologies, economic interests, and mediatized discourses, so too the idea of an ummah also remains an elusive (yet persistently important) concept by which Muslims label, and identify with, the collective community that forms around it. This collective community is not an ephemeral concept, but a consequence of embodied, interpersonal relationships.

Among AmeRícan Muslims, who themselves are a people *en vaivén* between the US, Puerto Rico, and the wider Caribbean, in search of a national identification that remains ambiguous, diasporic, and always "on the move," the variation and uncertainty compounds. Thus, whatever traditions AmeRícan Muslims claim allegiance to are a result of the dispersed, but nevertheless particular, contexts wherein their conversion occurs; the identifications they make upon reversion a result of the specific diacritics of the situations and relations they find themselves in at the time; the communities they choose, remain in, or, more often, switch to, a consequence of the subsequent twists, turns, and deeply personal and contextual encounters of everyday life.

The following four ethnographic vignettes help illustrate this dynamic in textured, relational detail. They reveal how AmeRícan Muslims navigate various traditions within global Islam. They also illustrate the complex and contingent amalgam of relations, circumstances, and affective, individualized interpretations that led them to particular constellations of being and belonging, identification, and *communitas*. This is not a positivist or representative approach to the demographics of the AmeRícan Muslim community, but a subjective and qualitative one, reflecting the everyday and embodied aspects of their journeys through various traditions. But by looking at these statistically small, but categorically complex narratives, we get a better sense of the unexpected changes and variations that the ummah is undergoing in the late-modern world. The result is an intricate lattice of narratives that reflect the complexity of the real world—and real humans in the social, political, economic, gendered, and class-based contexts that define their lifeworlds as well as guide the trajectory of their allegiances to one tradition or another. By centering their stories, we better understand the vicissitudes not only of AmeRícan Muslim experience(s), but those of global Islam as a whole.

### *Miguel: Puerto Rico's only Ahmadi*

I'm late, but Miguel (briefly introduced in chapter 2) graciously greets me with a smile and a handshake as I make my way through the doors at El Pavo Asado, a cantina on the busy Avenida Jesús T. Piñero thoroughfare in San Juan, just west of Parque Luis Muñoz Marin. A stocky man in his early thirties with a close-cropped flattop and dark goatee, Miguel is dressed business casual as we meet during his lunch break from work as a data analyst at a health care company. As he orders his *albóndigas de pollo con arroz y habichuelas guisadas* and I my *pastelón con arroz cilantro y habichuelas* with a *jugo de parcha* (a solid selection, as far as Miguel is concerned), he tells me he was one of the first Ahmadis in Puerto Rico. And for a time, he was the only one. Though it was not always easy, Miguel is particularly proud of the fact. "It was like being in a one-man army, going against everything," he says, "Puerto Ricans who did not understand what being Muslim means—let alone an Ahmadi—or Muslims who didn't accept me as one of their own."

Originally from Guayanilla, a town on the Caribbean Sea in Puerto Rico's southwest, Miguel was raised Roman Catholic, attending Catholic school from fifth grade to high school. He says:

> My family mainly just celebrated the holidays, the fiestas, and I remember somebody in the family was always reading the Bible, but I was always more spiritually inclined than my family or my compañeros. You could say I was the most devoted in my class. I even thought about becoming an altar boy, but . . . nah. I couldn't stand the fact that priests couldn't get married. I wanted to serve, but I was like, "No, that's not for me."

After graduation, Miguel studied physics at Recinto Universitario de Mayagüez, about thirty miles from where he grew up. "Studying physics was hard, like really hard," Miguel says, "I wanted to get out of the program and study something else. It wasn't working out for me. I wanted something new." Two friends from Guayanilla were studying architecture at the University of Wisconsin Milwaukee (UWM) via an exchange program through Universidad Interamericana de Puerto Rico. Miguel quit his physics program, booked a flight, and flew to Wisconsin. For three months, he slept on his friends' couch. He then enrolled in the Mathematical Sciences Department at UWM and started studying statistics. Laughing as he reminisces, "It was cold, crazy weather . . . and then too hot and humid. But I liked it. I was young and was ready for an adventure. So that's how I came to the United States, which ended up forming me into who I am today." To get by, and to get off his friends' couch, Miguel worked two jobs: one as a math tutor for other students and the other at a university cafeteria.

It was while working as a tutor that he met an Ahmadi Muslim. Miguel tells me:

> The Iraq War was going on at the time—we're talking about 2003—and I was following it really close. I read like every news article I could find. I wanted to know what was going on. The terrorism. Why are these people doing this in the name of God. It doesn't make sense to me. So then it didn't take too long for God to answer that. He sent me an Ahmadi to the tutoring section I was in. So I was talking to him about the war and said, "Man, you're a Muslim? Oh good, 'cause I have some questions. What about all these terrorists?" And then he started talking about his sect and proved to me that it wasn't true that all Muslims were terrorists. I was like, "These guys sound different. Hmmm, tell me more."

The conversations continued from there, with Mujid, an Ahmadiyya missionary, coming almost every week to discuss Miguel's questions and share literature from his community. Beyond his concerns about the Iraq War and terrorism, Miguel says he started to explore some of his misgivings about Catholic theology—particularly the idea of Jesus's death and resurrection. Among the literature Mujid had were books about how Jesus did not die on the cross but traveled east to Kashmir in search of the Lost Tribes of Israel, eventually dying a natural death in the Khanyar quarter of Srinagar city.[22] After reading the first Ahmadiyya literature he was given, Miguel could not put the books down. He says it was like his eyes were opened to another world of possibilities. If what he thought he knew about Jesus was not true, Miguel had even more questions.

Thus, he connected with the local Ahmadiyya imam, Rashid. Not only could Rashid answer Miguel's questions in more detail, but the two also connected as friends. "We thought a lot alike. I liked him. We made this instant connection when we met on the quad one day for lunch," Miguel says. Encouraged, he decided to visit the local Ahmadiyya mosque the following Friday. When he arrived, he found Rashid was not the only person he could connect with. Miguel says, "When I got the mosque, everyone was so nice to me, and we also connected really quickly. There was a bond there. A real connection. Right away." Persuaded by their convictions and drawn by their friendliness, Miguel says that there was never any question whether he would convert. "After that first visit, I never stopped going," he says.

In 2006, after finishing graduate school in the States, Miguel returned to Puerto Rico as the only Ahmadi on the archipelago. Miguel says he struggled to remain true to his beliefs without a community of support around him:

> This is the place I grew up in, so it was strange not to revert back to how I was before. Eating pork. Celebrating Christmas or the other fiestas. Whatever it was, I had to fight to not go back to my old ways, but at the same time be in the sort of position where you're not singled out as a kind of stranger. Puerto Ricans are proud of their culture, so I had to endure being a bit different and being called out for it by friends. They would make fun of me (and they weren't really funny). To this day, some friends think that I betrayed the culture or Catholicism or something. Only some were open-minded, saying "whatever makes you happy." I respect them.

For the next seven years, Miguel remained alone. He went to the *jalsa salana* (formal annual gathering of the Ahmadiyya Muslim Jamaat) in Pennsylvania in 2008, but only once because of a lack of finances.

In the meantime, he went to Sunni mosques in Ponce, Montehiedra, and Vega Alta. For a while, the people at the mosques were nice enough, Miguel says:

> But it didn't fill me up. What they do is not for Puerto Ricans. It's that simple. The sermon is in Arabic. The imams can't speak Spanish. They only care about their community, maintaining their culture. They're not interested [gesturing outside the window] in this place. They at least offer to teach you Arabic and that's great, which is nice. But it's not enough to make me feel comfortable.

When they found out he was Ahmadi, he says, the debates began, and the hospitality turned to cold shoulders and even hostility. At a small musallah in Yauco, a mountainous town not too far from where Miguel grew up, he says he ended up in an argument with someone about Jesus. Feeling threatened, he started going to the masjid in Vega Alta. Then, one time when he was wearing a bracelet with the Ahmadiyya motto—"amor para todos, odio hacia nadie" (love for all, hatred for none)—he saw two guys staring at him while he was making *wudu* before prayers. "All I picked up was 'hamadiya' or something like that in Arabic," Miguel says, "and the next time I went up there for prayer, I was told I was no longer welcome."

Then, in 2013, he received an e-mail from the Ahmadiyya community in the US telling him: "There is a new convert in Puerto Rico. You should contact him." His name was Bilal, and he lived in Isabella, about an hour's drive from Cabo Rojo where Miguel was working at the time. "We tried, but we never found a time to connect," he says. Then, he started talking with a woman at work who had questions about Islam—much like himself back in Milwaukee. She converted in 2015. It would not be until 2017 when the community would grow to four when they welcomed a new imam—Imam Ahmad Salman—to Puerto Rico in 2017. Miguel says he was overjoyed:

> When they told us a new imam would be arrive, I thought, "Oh great! We can finally be in unity. We can connect with each other." When you have an imam, you gather around him. He unites us. It's like how it is with the *kalifa*. All these people around the world. All these mosques. They all unite around him. It's the same here with Ahmad. We finally have some who will unite us. He is our shepherd.

More than that, Miguel says he found a friend in Ahmad. "He and I are the same age, and, in that sense, I am very grateful because we have connected not only religiously, but as friends," he says, "I can get to know [him] man to man."

Miguel gave me Ahmad's number, and we met up a few days later in Carolina, just east of San Juan. Another day, another diner, which was becoming my modus operandi for interviews and meet-ups. Born in Pakistan and raised in Canada, Ahmad already served as an Ahmadi missionary in Ghana, Canada, and the San Francisco Bay Area of California. Married to a Gujarati convert, he has two kids—ages two and five. Fluent in Urdu, Punjabi, Arabic, and English, Ahmad is trying to pick up Spanish, but it is still early days.

FIGURE 3.1 *Imam Ahmad Salman and a member of the Ahmadiyya community in Puerto Rico meet with the then governor Ricardo Rosselló. (Image courtesy of Ahmad Salman)*

Ahmad only recently arrived in Puerto Rico and is brand new to the work. His enthusiasm is palpable, and he spends the first hour of our time together selling me on the Ahmadiyya. With pamphlet after pamphlet, he makes clear to me that his aim was for converts "to remain loyal to their country of residence. To be Borícua *and* Ahmadi." Some of his pamphlets are emblazoned with the Puerto Rican flag and, when he hands me a white gummy bracelet (similar to Miguel's), he points out the Ahmadiyya motto "amor para todos, odio a nadie" printed on it in blue and red—reflecting the colors of the Puerto Rican flag. At the time, Ahmad says, the small Ahmadiyya community was meeting in Parque Luis Muñoz Marin (near where I met Miguel for lunch), but Ahmad wants to purchase a property in Guaynabo that is convenient for members as far apart as Hato Rey and Isabella to meet at.

For now, he is getting to know local leaders, including the mayor of Aguadilla, the assistant to the governor for religious affairs in Puerto Rico, Puerto Rico's governor Ricardo Rosselló (2017–2019), the mayor of San Juan, Yulín Cruz, and a representative of the Puerto Rican historical society in San Juan. He is trying to get Humanity First operations running on the archipelago as well. Humanity First is the humanitarian, philanthropic arm of the Ahmadiyya Muslim Jamaat and, as researchers S. Alejandra Sotomayor and Rolando Macías note, one of the prime means of community connection employed by Ahmadi missionaries across the globe—as well as in Latin America and the Caribbean.[23] Ahmad also runs Arabic and English classes out of his living room to help connect with people in the neighborhood. "I am often the first Muslim these people meet," Ahmad says. On the one hand, he finds that quite astonishing, since there are thousands of Muslims already living in Puerto Rico. On the other hand, he says he is not surprised. "So far, I've found that the local mosque leaders have very little to do with the community. I plan on changing that." Though his community is small, Ahmad takes pride in one thing above all else: "The best part is we are almost 100 percent Borícua. Outside of me and my family, all of our members are local Puerto Ricans."

### *Angelica: Running with the Qur'an Only*

I am, once again, in a restaurant on the outskirts of San Juan, about to meet up with a local Puerto Rican revert. This time, I'm grabbing brunch with Angelica at the Bistro Café, which straddles the dividing line between Carolina and San Juan. Angelica arrives with her adolescent daughter, who orders a juice and settles into playing a game on her iPad as her mom and I chat.

Angelica is wearing a black headscarf and matching black lipstick—"I'm like a Puerto Rican Muslim punk," she laughs, "but not *that* punk." Angelica also tells me that most of her outfit is from Old Navy (gray long-sleeved maxi dress with black leggings and stylish, cat eye black-rimmed glasses). She says, "I just wear normal clothes and shop at normal stores. It's not like I go to Muslims 'R' Us!" Sometimes she goes out with nothing on her head. To the beach she goes with a turban and shows her neck. If she gets pushback, even from her husband, she will reply by referencing the diversity of what Muslim women wear (or don't wear) across the world. "I'm an independent thinker, to be sure," she says.

Born in Mayagüez, Angelica lived for a time in Bayamón and now resides in Ceiba on Puerto Rico's east coast. She runs an air taxi company between the islands of Vieques and Culebra with her husband, who is a pilot. Her husband is Colombian and of Palestinian descent. His father was born Muslim, but converted to Catholicism after living in Colombia and even carried an image of the Virgin Mary around his whole life. He regularly went to Mass but, Angelica tells me, confessed Allah as the one God and Muhammad as his prophet on his deathbed. That's when his son (Angelica's husband) reverted, along with his first wife, who was Colombian. Angelica's husband left Colombia to avoid compulsory army service and met Angelica not long after he arrived in Puerto Rico. The head of a mixed household, they have four children from his previous marriages and one from Angelica's previous relationship. Angelica says her husband is more of a "mainstream" Muslim than she is. When I ask her what she means, she replies, saying he is Sunni, but on the whole "a little more traditionalist and conservative." She continues:

> But he is willing to change his views. He just wants to be faithful and practice Islam "rightly." We may have different opinions and perspectives, but we figure it out. Sometimes, it's a struggle, but it's worth the relationship.

Angelica claims no allegiance to any particular group or sect. "I'm definitely not mainstream," she says. Although she took her shahadah among Sunni Muslims in Montehiedra, she left after what she called "conflicts" with the imam and others over women being separated during prayer. "It was unfair that women had to pray separately or that if they had children they were told to pray at home," she says, "it seemed sexist and not in keeping with the equality evinced in the Qur'an or practiced by the Prophet." She also criticizes imams on the archipelago for interpreting the Qur'an or quoting hadith about the permitted abuse of women.[24] She says, "You can't talk about those things in Puerto Rico where we have such a domestic abuse problem. You have to know your context."[25] For these reasons, she says, she won't call any imam on the archipelago a sheikh. She says, "They don't deserve my respect if they don't give us respect."

In general, Angelica thinks most Puerto Rican reverts are tempted to stricter interpretations, mentioning Salafism in particular:

> All these Salafists. ¡Ay, Dios mío! It's this "colonized mindset" that Puerto Ricans carry around—just wanting to be told what to do. And the Arabs are more than willing to colonize them with their cultural version of Islam. If the Salafists were a little better at dawah they would have the Puerto Ricans eating out of their hands!

That is why Angelica says she identifies most with the "only Qur'an,"[26] but independently so.

The Quraniyya movement generally holds that traditional religious clergy corrupted the religion, and divine law should be derived solely from the Qur'an. (Re)interpreting Islam according to their Quranic readings, the noncentralized "movement" challenges what constitutes "authentic Islam." Some among them believe problems in global Islam stem partly from traditional elements of hadith and Sunnah traditions, rejecting those teachings in favor of more modern interpretations. For her part, Angelica says she pays no heed to hadith and only reads and recites what she calls "progressive translations" of the Qur'an. When I ask for an example of a "progressive translation," she mentions *The Sublime Quran*, translated by Laleh Bakhtiar. Of particular importance to her is the translation of al-Nisa, 4:34 in Bakhtiar's edition of the Qur'an, which reads:

> Men are supporters of wives because God has given some of them an advantage over others and because they spend of their wealth. So the ones who are in accord with morality are the ones who are morally obligated, the ones who guard the unseen of what God has kept safe. But those whose resistance you fear, then admonish them and abandon them in their sleeping place, then go away from them; and if they obey you, surely look not for any way against them; truly God is Lofty, Great.

Also in her library are several books on Islamic feminism and how to read the Qur'an as a woman (we talk about amina wadud's *Qur'an and Woman*, Asma Sayeed's *Women and the Transmission of Religious Knowledge in Islam*, and Omid Safi's *Progressive Muslims*). She also has Islamic children's books she says she read to her daughter when she was younger. Angelica says, looking over at her daughter who is preoccupied scrolling through Snapchat:

> I guess I just want to make sure she has the right influences in her life. I don't care if she grows up to be a Muslim or not. I am totally okay with what she decides. "There shall be no compulsion in religion," the Qur'an says. No one who is born Muslim is criticized for having a Muslim child, but for some reason people get concerned that a revert like me is going to "brainwash" my daughter. I am not. I want her to make her own decisions. With the right sources. The right influences.

All of this, Angelica says, is an attempt to adapt Islam to her Puerto Rican cultural context. Riffing on the theme of contextualization, especially in West Africa, where she believes Islam was thoroughly adapted over the centuries, Angelica says she had what she calls an "intellectual journey to Islam," through independent reading and investigation. Beyond the books in her library, she says she was moved by media—watching *The Stoning of Soraya* and *New Muslim Cool*. After watching the latter, Angelica says, "I saw in Hamza how I could be both Puerto Rican *and* Muslim. His story resonated with me, and I realized I could be both, authentically and fully."

Further complicating her relationship with local Muslims and their interpretations of Islamic tradition, Angelica also has a diverse group of friends—including Wiccans, atheists, Catholics, evangelicals, and Santeros. "One friend even sent me a message about becoming a Dionysian where I could just drink and be indulgent [she laughs]. Dios mío, I was happy for her and all, that she, like found her path . . . through a bottle of wine!" She then tells me about a transgender Muslim friend of hers. "He inspires me every day. He is brave for being Muslim, being trans, and for pursuing his path no matter what." She draws on her friends for strength, she says, because she has no real connection with most Puerto Rican Muslims. "It's sad, but I am sure you know more Puerto Rican Muslims than me. I feel somewhat isolated in Ceiba, but I have my community online." That community is stretched between New York, Chicago, Orlando, and Philadelphia—"It's like Puerto Rican Muslims have our own diaspora in another diaspora," she jokes. Angelica also has connections with Black Muslims in the US, saying she feels for them, because their situation is "similar to ours, pushed out and downtrodden, not appreciated among the faithful." Although she draws parallels between their experiences, she is careful to add that they are not the same. "They've had more time to come to terms with Islam as it is and their culture. Puerto Ricans are different. We are still figuring out our own path right now," she says, "we can learn from them, but we have to find our own way."

In a way, Angelica is a bit of a pathfinder herself. She received widespread publicity as the first Puerto Rican Muslim to run for public office. In 2016, she ran for a local senate seat in Carolina as part of the erstwhile Partido del Pueblo Trabajador (PPT)—a party founded in 2010 by a broad coalition of trade unionists, environmentalists, and feminists like Angelica.[27] For her part, Angelica styles herself a socialist. "I wanted to run as a woman representing my Puerto Rican people first," she says, "but also as a muslimah." She says she caught slack from both sides in the process:

> People attacked me because I am Muslim. They said some pretty horrible things, but nothing I hadn't heard before. But then Muslims attacked me for not being a "Muslim candidate." . . . By that, they meant I wasn't conservative enough or not the right kind of Muslim. They told newspapers and television stations I didn't count as a "real" Muslim.

Even so, some organizations and individual Muslims reached out to support her campaign. She did not accept their money, she says, because she knows her progressive views would not match up with "mainstream Muslim opinion." She says, "If me and my husband can't agree, I'm not going to try and run a campaign with other Muslims. That'd be a joke! I know I'm on the margins. I'm okay with that. It's where I *want* to be."

### *Jesús: "Kind of a nondenominational Muslim"*

After exchanging several Facebook messages and texts, Jesús invites me to join him for jummah prayers one Friday afternoon in October at the Islamic Cultural Center of New York (ICCNY). Located in East Harlem at 1711 Third Avenue, between East 96th and 97th Streets, the ICCNY was New York's first purpose-built mosque (originally located on Riverside Dr. on the Upper West Side) and, in its new location, remains one of the city's largest.

With emerald-blue skies and a crisp autumnal coolness in the air, I walk from my apartment, down through Morningside Park and across to East Harlem, skirting Central Park's perimeter and passing Museo del Barrio along the way. I come across a Caribbean shop selling DVDs of Martin Lawrence stand-up, flags from places like Trinidad, Puerto Rico, Cuba, and Costa Rica hanging in the windows alongside flyers advertising a visit from Turkish president Recep Tayyip Erdoğan, an Indo-Pak halal meat bazaar and grocery store, and a steady stream of present and former places of prayer and community connection: Sopey Shaykhul Khadeem Mosque on 116th, A-Salam Islamic Center of Harlem, the bold brick, yellow, and green-domed Masjid Malcolm Shabazz a little further east, and Alianza Islámica's original location on Lexington Avenue. Just one block east and a few streets down, in the borderlands between Harlem and the Upper East Side, I arrive at ICCNY. Even with so many mosques around, Jesús told me via text that many Latinx Muslims gather there for prayer, as it is large and conveniently located near El Barrio, not far from the 96th Street Metro Station.

As I approach the turquoise-domed, *kufic* script–inscribed, modernist mosque surrounded by high-rise apartment buildings, worshippers are streaming in on foot, getting dropped off by yellow cabs, and perusing tables on the sidewalk outside with books on topics as diverse as *salah* for children, *dua* for contentment, and the life of Muhammad or the "*hajj* made simple." Taking in the soundscape around me, I hear a mix of French and Urdu, Spanish and Arabic. A spectrum of sartorial manner and modes of expression can be found across the complex. Some are sporting track suits, others business suits. A guy with an ankle monitor on is making wudu in the downstairs bathroom next to a police officer on lunch break. Tourists are taking salah-selfies in the main prayer hall. There are women with headscarves in almost every color and style and men with henna-dyed beards, others with dreadlocks. Underneath the circular lamps and in front of the layered glass and gold metal *mihrab*, the masjid is packed for jummah prayer. I struggle to jostle for space in the back and decide to head outside, to make room for others, only to find rugs being rolled out on the mosque's patio for overflow. Built in 1991 at a cost of $17 million (USD), the mosque can accommodate up to 1,000 in the main prayer hall and an additional 328 in the auxiliary prayer rooms. Today, it is at capacity.

Amid the crowds, Jesús and I are not able to find each other before prayers. Instead, we meet up afterward at a halal food cart set up along a table for NYC Social Services volunteers handing out one-pagers about Donald Trump's "Travel Ban" in English and Arabic. Other merchants sell rugs, clothes, incense, books, prayer beads, and snacks on the sidewalks surrounding the ICCNY—a microcosm of the "Muslim world" in the midst of Manhattan. After we eat our samosas and enjoy a bit of informal chitchat, we decide to grab a coffee and talk a little more in-depth about Jesús's path to Islam.

A thirty-two-year-old contract laborer and security guard at a local shopping center, Jesús is a fairly recent convert. Born in Washington Heights on Manhattan's northeast side, Jesús kept his given name after reversion (instead of changing it to "Isa," for example), referring to other Puerto Rican and Latino Muslim reverts who Islamicize or Arabize their names as "typical Latino nonsense—always looking to be someone else, or from somewhere else, as if that will give us more authenticity or better standing in the community. Nonsense." Jesús says he is proud to keep the name of one of Islam's most prominent prophets, as it is, in Spanish. He is also proud of where he comes from and the role it played in his journey to Islam:

> When I was growing up in the Heights in the eighties, people were converting all around me. Mostly, it was the Nation of Islam. That was the introduction for many Latinos. They definitely converted more Latinos than [any] other Islamic organization I can think of in America. They were even stronger in Harlem . . . [there] they called Latinos out of discrimination and racism, empowered them as a people of color. . . . Oppression shapes Latinos, for good and for ill. Whether it's crime or poverty or religious practice, every Latino comes from this background.

Asking if he was familiar with Alianza Islámica back in the '80s and '90s, he does not recall but knows some Puerto Rican Muslims still reference the organization. "I never heard of it before," he says.

Jesús grew up in a single-parent household with his mom, who was a fairly nonactive, nondenominational Christian:

> My mom was the most religious among us, and I rarely saw her pray. We did not go to church all that much either. But she did talk about Jesus (PBUH) . . . but she wasn't a dedicated Christian, I guess you could say.

His father, who visited from time to time, was a nonactive Catholic who viewed "religion as a family tradition as opposed to a relationship with God." His *abuelitas* on both sides took religion seriously, he says, with daily prayers, saints all over the house, and a consistent presence at Mass. He still finds their example inspiring, even as a Muslim. Looking back on his parents' religiosity, Jesús says he found their practice (or lack thereof) somewhat "depressing" and "disturbing." He says, "Of course, that influenced me growing up. You put God in your back pocket and put everything else first. . . . Your relationship with God should be everything. All else is temporary."

Jesús says he did not become more familiar with Islam and Muslims until after 9/11. His original impression came from the mediated discourse around and about Islam during the heights of the "War on Terror":

> Watching watered-down news, we couldn't think outside the box. We didn't know what Islam was. We had to accept what CNN taught us. I thought of Islam as a new religion and some kind of threat to humanity . . . curiosity about it over time led me to learn more, though.

Never particularly religious himself, Jesús says he "took advantage" of the mercy he heard about from his grandmothers, using their talk of forgiveness to "justify what I was doing as a kid." When asked what kinds of actions he was hiding or justifying, he says he did not want to get too deep into his past life, as much of it was "haram." But he shares this:

> I'm from the streets. I felt I was justified to do what I wanted to do: with girls, with drugs, with alcohol, with other people's stuff. But there's a lot of depression and paranoia that comes with that too. Up until the age of twenty-five, I didn't care if I was going to live or

> die. I woke up every day and didn't care. I just tried to make money and do what I got to do to pass the time. It was a crab in the barrel, "get rich or die tryin'" attitude. I didn't care at all. . . . There's a lot of people on the streets—gang members, drug dealers, pimps—they believe in God. They believe in mercy and blessings. But they also believe the ends justify the means. I got tired of wearing that suit.

Then, after his twenty-fifth birthday, he hit rock bottom. Not wanting to go into details, he says he had to check himself into a local homeless shelter. It was at that time, Jesús says, he started to take a keener interest in religion. "The shelter had a stack of free Bibles and I read it from cover to cover," he says, "it became a matter of life or death for me." Baptized into the Catholic Church at age five, he decided to be baptized again at twenty-five. "I was touched by the story of Jesus (PBUH), it was life changing," he says.

When he moved out of the homeless shelter and back into the Heights, Jesús says he had a hard time applying the Bible stories to everyday life on the streets. "They just didn't jive," he says, "Jesus and Jerusalem felt so far away from what I was experiencing in the hood or reading in the newspaper every day." He also noticed Christians were conspicuously absent, or just not visibly present, on the street corners and in the local bodegas. Jesús did see, however, members of the NOI, the FPN, or the Black Hebrew Israelites. Claiming that Black Americans are descendants of the ancient Israelites, Black Hebrew Israelites combine elements from Christian and Jewish traditions, while also exhibiting influences from Freemasonry and New Thought. Not associated with, or accepted by, mainstream Jewish communities, the movement is heterogeneous, with varying beliefs and practices across its various communities (e.g., some also believe that Indigenous Americans are the descendants of Israelites). Jesús says that he had his "look in the book and his feet in the streets" when he started to talk more seriously with members of the Black Hebrew Israelites. While he never formally joined, he adopted their practices as a way of life: "I kept the Sabbath, I stayed away from drugs, and believed homosexuality was a sin." But, he says, he was turned off by the hate he often saw among members. So, he kept his distance.

It was at this time that Islam finally came into his life, he says:

> I think one of the big game changers when it came to me converting to Islam is about a year and a half ago, I'd been practicing Christianity for about five years, and I watched this video on YouTube. It was

> about this professor in Illinois who took a picture with a hijab on. I read all the controversy and condemnation, all the hit pieces and hot takes. But each time I kept coming back to her story . . . it brought me to tears.[28]

Having seen Islamophobia run rampant among Christians, Black Hebrew Israelites, and others in his relational networks, Jesús says he felt a certain sympathy for Muslims at the time. "As fellow oppressed people, it struck a nerve to see all the lies being spread about them and the fear around them," he says. Then, when he saw the video, he thought of solidarity and how he could better stand with oppressed Muslims around the world.

It was also while watching this video that he says he remembers hearing the word "Allah" for the first time. Minimizing the YouTube video, he immediately put "Allah" into Google and read "for the next few hours." He continues:

> What really struck me was that there is no plural. There are no Allahs. There is no son. No spirit. Just the one. People use the term a lot of ways (like the Nation talking about men being "Allah"), but it made sense that this term means "the God"—it specifies the singularity of the one God [refers to Qur'an 32:59].

Around the same time, Jesús started a new job as a security officer, where he would often take over from a guy people called "Sheikh," who wore a *kufi* to work. Jesús and Sheikh would talk between shifts. "He was a Muslim's Muslim and not undercover. I knew he would be a good person to talk to with all my questions," says Jesús, "I was picking his brain every damn day." The unidentified Sheikh was himself a convert. A former nondenominational Christian pastor, Jesús says, "Sheikh taught me how commentaries corrupted the Bible and showed me the connections between all the monotheistic faiths, how they can be compatible—he helped me bridge the gap between where I was and where I am now." As Jesús continued his conversations with Sheikh, he also did his own independent reading of the Qur'an, connecting and conversing with Muslims online. He got to a point where he could no longer believe in the Christian concept of "the Trinity" or that Jesus died during the crucifixion. Three months after meeting Sheikh, on his thirtieth birthday in 2016, Jesús took the shahadah at ICCNY. "I just wanted to rush into it like a Black Friday sale or something," he says, "it answered all my questions."

Nonetheless, Jesús says he is still looking to learn more. To that end, he remains active online, keen to research other paths and people. He's not ready to settle with one interpretation or tradition within Islam. With all the different influences around him, both online and off, Jesús says he is trying to be cautious with whom he associates and how he identifies. Doing his own "independent research" and reading multiple versions of the Qur'an in Spanish and English, Jesús says:

> There are so many different sects and schools of thought in Islam. You have to be careful. Like the Nation and the Five Percenters, they're offshoots of original sects. The Wahhabis are trying to sneak their teaching into every book, every mosque, every Qur'an. You have to watch out.

He continues:

> I'm looking hard at the Ahmadiyya. I'm even into the Bahá'í. . . . I'm not locked down ideologically. I don't know what sect of Islam I'll cling to the most. Right now, I guess I am mostly Sunni. But I don't consider every Sunni hadith to be authentic and that's a problem for a lot of Sunnis. My relationship with the Sunnis is changing. They're very judgmental. They claim they're "orthodox," but they're a sect like everyone else. They remind me of Christians with judgmental mindsets saying who is in and who is out. Islam is simply surrender to one God. It's not saying, "Yo, I'm this or that Muslim." It's a way of life. To me, non-Trinitarian Christians are Muslim. Jewish people are Muslim as hell. And plenty of other monotheists too.

Going on for almost another hour on the theme, Jesús reviews various groups, communities, and ideologies—from Hezbollah and the Shi'i to *al-Dawla al-Islamiyya* and the Mu'tazilah. None of them, he says, is absolutely wrong nor wholly right. "As I look through all these different varieties of Islam, as I read the Qur'an, as I try to apply hadith to my daily, I'm logical, like the Mu'tazilah," he says, "trying to use my brain to figure out Islamic theology." In the end, he says, "I guess I'm kind of a nondenominational Muslim."

These explorations, Jesús says, are also influenced by the people he interacts with, most of whom are online. "I'm making more friends than I'm losing," Jesús says, "it doesn't matter to me where you come from or what you believe. I just want to learn. There's people online who I've never met who've taught me so much. I'm much closer to them than even some members of my family." When I ask about what mosques he frequents, Jesús says he often ends up at ICCNY. Sometimes, he goes to a masjid in the Bronx with a core group of Latinos, he says. But in general, Jesús is not too connected to other Latinx, or Puerto Rican, Muslims. Even so, he says,

> there is a clear lack of services for Latinos in the mosques. That's obvious. There's a discrimination factor there, for sure. There's a little bit of tribalism. I see a clear change in demeanor when I'm talking to Arabics [*sic*] and they hear my accent. They want to keep a distance. That impacts mosques all over New York. . . . The majority of Muslims here are South Asian or Black. A lot are immigrants. They're very segregated. . . . But there's not enough Latinos to make a mosque of our own. So, if you don't speak Arabic or Urdu, Bengali or English, there's limited space. People who only know Spanish, good luck. . . . Maybe in New Jersey, I heard of a place that reaches out to Latinos. They learned Spanish. They care. I've not seen any of that in New York.

In general, Jesús says he likes mosques with more racial diversity. That is why he goes to ICCNY, which is also where he met other Latinx Muslims in person for the first time. But they were visitors, and he only stays in touch with them online. He would love to be part of a Latinx-specific mosque. But for now, he says:

> I am isolated from the Latino Muslim community in New York and New Jersey. Not online, it doesn't feel that way. But in everyday interactions, it's just me. We are too spread out to have a place of our own. I've met plenty online from Atlanta, Philly, Houston (that's the strongest community in the US). Here in New York, though, there's no predominately [Latino] Muslim masjid. It just doesn't exist.

With all his searching, Jesús says he hopes one day to find a place of his own. "I am still trying to find a place to call 'home,'" he says, "inshallah, I'll get there."

### *Frankie: A Searching Sufi in the City*

A few weeks later, I meet up with Frankie at an IHOP in Harlem one damp autumn evening. As I am sipping my coffee, waiting for him to arrive, I scribble some notes about the area I walked through on the way. The IHOP is located at the corner of 135th Street and Adam Clayton Powell Jr. Blvd.,[29] just up the street from the Muhammad Ali Islamic Center and not far from what was the epicenter of the Black Muslim movement in the 1960s and '70s (or, for that matter, where Alianza Islámica would be founded by three Puerto Rican reverts in 1987). Walking east from my basement apartment on 135th Street, I made my way down the steep steps in St. Nicholas Park, descending from Hamilton Heights into the heart of Striver's Row. Passing by a Jamaican restaurant on my right and an Ethiopian establishment on my left where the woman at the counter smiled and waved as I walked by, I also noted three mosques in as many city blocks: Masjed Alfalah, Masjid Al-Firdaus, and the Murid Islamic Community in America, the latter a branch of the Muridiyya order, founded in Senegal in the 1880s by Sheikh Ahmadu Bamba M'Backe. As I am wrapping up my notes, Frankie—or "Faruq" as he sometimes goes by—arrives straight from work at a local nonprofit where he is a case manager. As he sits down, I share my notes. Frankie says he visited them all. Masjid Alfalah, he says, is a tight space, but "mashallah, the community is multicultural and caring"; Masjid Al-Firdaus, "predominately a place for West Africans and other Black Muslims from the area"; and the Murid center, "a Sufi spot, but not my crew."

When Destiny, our server, comes to the table, Frankie tells me about his journey to Islam. A slight, gentle man with a generous smile and bright eyes, he is wearing an emerald-green kufi and dark blue jacket. Frankie says he grew up in a Roman Catholic, Puerto Rican household in Harlem. Although they went to Mass every Sunday, Frankie's family "weren't too religious," except perhaps his abuela, who he says practiced Santería or Espiritismo—he did not know which—and whose basement was filled with images and altars featuring "Native Americans, St. George slaying a dragon, and slaves."[30] An altar boy at thirteen, Frankie says he started using drugs and getting into trouble with friends during high school. "The trouble ended up being fairly serious, because I ended up in Rikers Island [New York City's largest prison] when I was 17," he says. Frankie also says he was "spiritually dead" at that point—not inspired to turn to the Catholic faith of his youth for solace or to adopt Santería, which he says, "freaked him out." He dabbled with various spiritual practices picked up from fellow inmates but says he didn't know what he was doing. Nothing helped. And everything hurt.

Then, in 1995, a guard who was a member of the Nation of Islam approached him in the yard at Rikers. He was interested in what the guard said but was put off by some of the Nation's political perspectives. He was also intimidated by the NOI faction in the jail. "I didn't like the strong racial aspect to it all," he says. So, he sought out other Muslims behind bars and met a man named Hakim, who was Sunni. Not long after, Frankie took the shahadah.

> At first, it was an emotional thing for me, you know. Just feeling like I belonged. Like I had something to follow. Then, slowly, it became an intellectual journey and I went deeper. I didn't know enough at first, but that changed.

Diagnosed with a learning disability as a child, Frankie said he never had a problem reading and understanding the Qur'an or memorizing hadith. After reverting, his cognitive abilities improved, he says. Then, he started experiencing visions and dreams—what he called "visualizations"—of the desert, of the Prophet. "I was still in prison, but in my mind, as a Muslim, I was free." Frankie also found community, protection, and a higher meaning among his fellow Muslims in Rikers. "There was this one kid in there who would give the adhan and it was so beautiful that when he sang it, everyone—Muslim or not—would stop and listen."

Upon his release, Frankie visited different Sunni mosques in Harlem and Brooklyn, where he connected with Pakistani and Albanian Muslims who befriended him. At the same time, he met his first wife, a British Muslim with "African roots," who he says "opened up the world to me." They traveled to the United Kingdom to meet her family and went on both *umrah* and hajj together. Nonetheless, Frankie says he was largely dissatisfied with what he saw among Muslims in other parts of the world:

> I would watch people read about God (SWAS) and learn about him, but never experience him, ya know? And I was like, "Oh no, here we go again, it's like being a Catholic all over."

Then he heard about Sufis. Drawn to the promise of "direct contact with God," Frankie found some Naqshbandis meeting in a nineteenth-century church building on 9th Avenue in Manhattan.[31] This got him in contact with a Naqshbandi order, the Osmanli Naksibendi Hakkani, which operated out of a *dergah* (center) in Sidney Center, a small town in the Catskill Mountains about 150 miles northwest of Harlem. Widely regarded as one of the more vigorous Sufi orders, the Naqshbandiyya originated in fourteenth-century Bukhara and feature a strict adherence to *shariah*, a sober devotional practice, and a rejection of music and dance in favor of silent dhikr, or devotional practice of remembrance. "I was pretty gung-ho, pretty serious, pretty strict. And so, I was attracted to a strict sheikh," Frankie says of his affiliation with the Naqshbandiyya.

Originally from Cyprus, Frankie said the sheikh was stern in his tutelage. As a result, Frankie says he "put the whole shariah on. I was walking around with a thick beard and a turban. I wore these rings, bought all these clothes, it was a lot. I did it, and I loved it, but it kind of became overwhelming." In particular, Frankie says he struggled with balancing the tension between the demands of his practice with the life "of a Borícua in Spanish Harlem, ya know, with all the *jahiliyyah* that goes on here—music and dancing and all." As he was starting to question his own allegiance, he was in conversation with the dergah's leader, Sheikh Abdul Kerim al-Kibrisi, one day. As they were sitting together, Frankie was surprised to hear the sheikh reprimand him for his outward appearance. "He looks me and, laughing, says, 'What are you doing? You look like an Afghan, not a Puerto Rican!' He was right. Something had to change."

Thus, Frankie left the order, met a Latina Muslim from Houston, Texas, and moved to Chicago. In Houston and Chicago, Frankie met other Latinx Muslims and started to get a sense of what he called a broader "Latino Muslim world and outlook." At the same time, he said he was skeptical of how big the Latinx Muslim tent became. Some people who claimed to be Muslim, in his opinion, were far from authentic versions of Islam. "I met this Puerto Rican 'brother' in New York who didn't really know who the Prophet (PBUH) was or who Allah was, but was sprouting a big beard, a kufi, and people were treating him like a true Muslim even though he didn't know the basics." His own brother, Omar, joined the Five Percent Nation. Frankie was not a fan. "The FPN aren't Muslim. They may use Islamic words, they may talk about Allah, but they're all about themselves. Omar and Frankie would regularly argue about their perspectives on what Islam is and is not, and after a particularly big fight one night, they've never spoken to each other again. "I hope he's become more orthodox. *Rahimahullah* ['God have mercy on him']."

Marrying his third wife, this time a Latina Muslim from Union City, New Jersey, he came in contact with Imam Abdullah "Danny" Hernandez and says, through him, he met "a ton of other Latino Muslims in Jersey." Some of them told him about an old "Puerto Rican masjid" in the Bronx, called Alianza Islámica. But Frankie says that after he visited, he was not sure he could trust whether it was "legit" or not. "They were located in a basement [referring to their entrance below street level on 287 Alexander Avenue in the South Bronx] and all they had was a low-hung sign. It felt like a secret society." Noting that Imam Danny was an exception—with his extensive knowledge and educational background (having studied at al-Azhar)—Frankie feels that too many Latinx Muslims "don't know enough or don't take Islam seriously enough."

In search of authenticity within, and connection to, the broader ummah, Frankie went looking for another community. At first, he fell in with the Nimatullahi order. Originally a Sunni tariqa, the Nimatullahi spread from southeastern Iran in the fourteenth century, gradually becoming a Shi'i order in the fifteenth. Expanding to Europe and the Americas in the mid-1970s, they emphasize silent dhikr and ethical engagement with the world. "Unfortunately, I didn't vibe with their martyrdom complex, the silence, and the general sadness in their meditation," Frankie says, "the meditation didn't bring the joy I used to experience. It depressed me." He also became disenchanted after Javad Nurbakhsh, the order's then leader, died in 2008. His son, Alireza Nurbakhsh (a.k.a., Reza Ali Shah) then became the Master of the Nimatullahi Order and brought in changes Frankie says he did not care for.

Frustrated, he started scouring the internet for other orders nearby. On Meetup.com, a social media website for hosting and organizing in-person and virtual events for people and communities of similar interests, Frankie came across the Madaniyya. The Madaniyya were founded in 1909 by Sidi Mohammad al-Madani in Tunisia, who was influenced and trained in the reformist Darqawiyya (Shadhiliyah) tradition under the tutelage of Abu Abbas Ahmad ibn Mustafa al-Alawi of Algeria. Frankie was encouraged to start his own circle. "I invested a lot of time and money into it and then, when it launched, seven people showed up," he said. When I say to Frankie I did not think the turnout was that bad, he backtracks a bit, saying, "I know, I know, but it left me empty. It left me depressed again. It wasn't enough of a community."

Frankie then returned to the internet in search of something more joyous and meaningful. He came across a video of Sufis dancing on YouTube and looked up their background. It turned out they were from the Tijaniyyah order, founded in the Maghreb by an Algerian—Ahmad al-Tijani—in the late eighteenth century. Another tariqa that rejects popular Sufism in favor of more ascetic practices, Frankie said he finally feels at home among the Tijaniyyah. A largely Senegalese community that meets at a small mosque on 127th Street in Harlem (I never was able to identify the exact location),

Frankie says their practice is "a middle road of Muslim mysticism. They're not too extreme in their approach or strange with their dhikr. They're focused, not fuzzy like some Sufis who are too spiritual." Frankie says, after researching numerous orders, he appreciates their moderation and, he chuckles, "their willingness to translate things into English for people like me, which helps."

Although he feels at home as a Tijani, Frankie would love to see something for his "people." Thinking back on his own biography, his own struggles, to find "a spiritual home," he says:

> I don't know. I feel like things are different these days. People are looking for something and they need guidance. Drugs, gangs, teen pregnancy, school dropouts. These are all distractions that Puerto Ricans in New York need to take care of, need to address. A nice mosque, for them, would go a long way to help. Somewhere in Manhattan, a central-enough locale.

The problem, he says, is that "Puerto Rican Muslims come from all over the ideological spectrum of Islam. That is a constant issue in trying to unify them or bring them together for anything." He thinks Sufism might help.

> It might be the thing that could unify them. I don't want to exclude anyone—and Senegalese, Pakistani, or whoever are all welcome—but I just think it should focus on Puerto Ricans and their particular social needs. It's just like other mosques that have a focus. So, we can come together and be like-minded, build a community center for Puerto Ricans, other Latinos, to serve the whole community. Some will gravitate to it. Others won't. It just needs to be a place where people don't have to give up their culture or ethnicity to become Muslim but bring them together into one. Maybe I'll try to start one and see.

## CONCLUSION

Together, these vignettes reflect the scripts of influences that shape AmeRícan Muslim lives, their reversion experiences, and their association with, or dissociation from, specific socialities. What we discover in these narratives is that the measures by which we determine what constitutes the ummah are not fixed and immutable. Instead, they are subject to adaptations and debate among, and between, individuals in specific, if still transregionally informed, relational contexts. Even though the sense of an Islamic peoplehood—or Muslim identification—has proven persistent across the years and multiple geographies, there continue to be constant fluctuations and frictions that challenge Muslims to (re)consider what it means to be an ummah in *this* time, in *this* place.

Each narrative testifies to an ummah en vaivén between Spain and Saudi Arabia, Baghdad and the Bronx, Puerto Rico and Pakistan, but also between Sufis and Shi'i, Sunnis and Salafis, the Nation of Islam and the Quraniyya. Thus, if "what Islam is" is a question of who is defining it, this chapter was an exploration of how AmeRícan Muslims do so from *their* place, decidedly on the margins of multiple socialities and Islamic geographies, but central to the late-modern making of Islam.

At the very least, their perspectives help "render a deeper and more encompassing view of what Islam is and what Muslims do," while not reifying Islam/Muslims as either alien to "the West" or the "modern" (or late-modern).[32] In our efforts to understand global Islam, it is increasingly important to pay attention to such experiences, embodied as they are in particular lives and specific places. Historian Ulrike Freitag wrote that "while Islam creates bonds of solidarity or is used to invoke such bonds, these are not standardised to create one 'world of Islam.'"[33] Instead, a range of specific interpretations, religious organizations, and ethnicities coexist and cross-pollinate, undermining the tendency to generalize by using adjectives like "Muslim" or "Islamic." "If too general," Freitag wrote, "[such adjectives] can obscure important specificities."[34] Specificities, I suggest, like those of AmeRícan Muslims, which reveal a kaleidoscope of practices, preferences, and perspectives on Islam, subjectified and interpellated by a range of local and transregional factors. As Dietrich Reetz noted in his research on madrasah graduates from India and Pakistan in the Malay archipelago, becoming more aware of the intense, individualized, and yet interpellated transfer of religious knowledge, social connections, and practical associations helps us better apperceive the "the global dynamism of Islamic actors and institutions" that shape their own version of late modernity and cosmopolitan identifications—or in Reetz's reading, "alternate globalities"—formed as they are picking through the flotsam and jetsam of crisscrossing, global Islamic networks.[35]

However, as is evident in the preceding vignettes, various contingent factors identify AmeRícan Muslims as part of the ummah, even if they find themselves in fairly consistent contestation with it. In other words, they feel simultaneously *at home* and *out of place* within the ummah.[36] On the one hand, AmeRícan Muslims notions of self, their feelings of being and belonging, are founded in the ummah and its various facets and traditions, practices and associations. On the other hand, they experience evident discordances, divergences, and debates resulting in alternative social formations. To further explore these generative frictions, I return to Ilyass and pick up his story after he delivered the khutbah at an Islamic center one summer afternoon in Florida.

# 4
# Between *ummah* and *asaBorícua*

## GENERATIVE FRICTIONS ON THE MARGINS

Friendliness does not abolish the distance between human beings, but brings that distance to life.

WALTER BENJAMIN

SITTING ACROSS FROM ME IN a white *lungee* (an Afghan-style turban) and long, gold-fringed *thawb*, Ilyass had just delivered the khutbah at the Islamic Cultural Center of Gainesville, Florida. It was a couple months after we sat on my back patio, when Ilyass first told me how he turned to Islamic tradition and sought out scholars to help him navigate his new sense of being and belonging after conversion. At the time, he said, there was immense pressure to prove himself as a "real" Muslim by conforming to certain cultural expectations. "People at the mosque were telling me to dress a certain way, look a certain way, speak a certain way," he says, "and I wasn't having any of it."

Frustrated by feelings of ostracism within the very communities he at first found so welcoming, Ilyass looked to alternate spaces or different Muslim communities beyond his local masjid for a sense of belonging and connection. Floating around online, Ilyass found and connected with the Ta'Leef Collective. Described as a "third space" beyond the home and the mosque where people can experience "Islam as it is,"[1] the Ta'Leef Collective—a spiritual and social gathering space for young Muslims, with campuses in Chicago and Fremont, California—has also been labeled an American "Sufi counterpublic."[2] While it is true that the Ta'leef Collective aims to discipline and motivate members toward supposedly "purer" and more ethical forms of Islam[3] to contest the retreat of Islam from the public sphere, they also challenge what they see as limited, "ethnicized" visions of Muslim community. In part because of this latter emphasis, Ilyass fell in with the Collective. Soon after finding them online, he was traveling to training sessions in California and Illinois.

During his training, Ilyass was particularly drawn to the notion of "Islam and the cultural imperative." Outlined by American neo-traditionalist Uma Faruq Abd-Allah, and evinced by others like Ta'leef founder Usama Canon[4] and European Sufi leader Abdallah Bin Bayyah, the central idea is that Muslims are to consciously establish and renew unique cultural identities within the contexts of their daily lives. They are, in Abd-Allah's words, to lay down roots and "reflect the good in the world's diverse races and ethnicities." Despite many Muslims' misgivings about "creating a Muslim American culture," Abd-Allah argues Islamic civilizational history and jurisprudence provides numerous examples and guidance to harmonize "indigenous forms of cultural expression with the universal norms" of Islamic law.[5] Applied in the US, he wrote this would "engender a Muslim American culture that gives us the freedom to be ourselves."[6]

Ilyass took Abd-Allah's words to heart. "When [Abd-Allah] wrote, 'Islam must reflect the good in the world's diverse races and ethnicities' he tapped into the core of Muhammad's message," Ilyass tells me. "The Prophet (*sallallahu alayhi wa sallam*) and his message were sent to perfect the character of the people, not to destroy their culture," he says. For Ilyass this is as much a personal imperative as it is an obligation placed on all the faithful. He continues, "Muslims do not have to discard their culture to become Muslim. It is a process of give-and-take." Quoting Muhammad and a hadith in which the Prophet is supposed to have said, "No Arab is better than a non-Arab,"[7] Ilyass sits up in his chair across from me, saying enthusiastically:

> What happened?! While Islam used to shape, and become shaped by, the culture it came in contact with, this is no longer true. Islam is now enforced and imagined as some monolithic culture of universal rules and regulations.

Inspired by Abd-Allah, when Ilyass does dawah he strives to make sure people know they do not have to abandon their culture to become Muslim. Reflecting Abd-Allah's words, Ilyass says, "Islam is like a river; wherever the river flows it reflects its bedrock." By this, he means that Islam takes shape in the fluid and dynamic interaction between its cultural context and its historic tradition. Each is shaped and changed by the other as they come into visceral contact with one another. "There are uniquely Chinese, Indian, African, or Mediterranean flavors of Islam in their contexts," he continues, "wherever Islam has flowed, it has taken on some of the character of the culture and its people in that context." Sadly, he reflects, this seems to no longer be the case. Appealing to his reading of Islamic history and its encounter with other cultures, Ilyass hopes Puerto Rican Muslims like himself would lead the way in shaping a truly "American Muslim culture," he says.

Ilyass's message in the Islamic Center of Gainesville that hot and heavy summer day in 2016 flowed out of such sentiments. Just two days before the beginning of Ramadan, he made an appeal for Muslims in Gainesville to follow the call for Islam to be a "middle nation" (an "ummat-an wasat-a" in *Surah al-Baqara*, 2:143). He used this as a platform to critique what he saw as the creep of inappropriate custom and culture into the community's practices. He warned against allowing "old ways" to become "*the* ways," especially among Muslims in Western contexts. He advised instead, Islam in the US should be like "water flowing across rock"—shaping the culture around it even as the tradition picks up bits and pieces of its new context, adding it to the mix of what came before.

Ilyass's khutbah had an impact, just not the one he hoped. It was not well-received. After prayers, complaints riffled back and forth between senior members of the community. Standing around after jummah, some said of Ilyass, "He doesn't know what he is doing!" or "He is too young!" or "Give him time, he just has to learn." The fallout lasted for weeks, and, in the end, Ilyass was removed from the *minbar* rotation.

Meeting up with him a couple months later, he complains to me that he was taken off because of the very "tribalism" he preached against. He tells me, "I am not treated fairly because I am Puerto Rican. I am held to a different standard than others that do not know as much as me." Because of this tribalism, Ilyass says, he lost his regular stint at the mosque and was forced to find work at a local hotel. He laments that "most mosques I've been to are divided along ethnic and linguistic lines." He complains that the Gainesville community was no different and that they completely missed the point of his sermon on the essential call for Muslims to unite around their diversity and differences, not divide over the false ideal of unity based on conformity. Asking if he sees much hope for the future, he says, "We don't know what it is to be an ummah. Even non-Muslims do it better than us, man. There is less tribalism and division at my job at the hotel or where I go to school than at my mosque. That isn't how it should be!"

## GENERATIVE FRICTIONS

Similar to those in Puerto Rico, converts in New York and Florida, New Jersey and Texas often feel ostracized and overquestioned by Arab and South Asian Muslims, who predominate in local mosques.[8] The promise that the ummah is colorblind[9] does not hold true in their day-to-day experience. Tensions exist, they say, between Muslims of different ethnic identifications and racializations. These tensions, similar to other communities in the Americas, are further exacerbated by border problematics and attendant issues of power and class.[10] In this chapter, I examine how AmeRícan Muslims navigate these tensions, adopting a "critical cosmopolitan" posture—asaBorícua—to do so.[11]

I focus on how these tensions operate as generative frictions in AmeRícan Muslim lives. What I mean is that while AmeRícan Muslims aspire to be fully formed members of a global Muslim community (ummah), their connections to it "come to life in 'friction,'" or in "the grip of worldly encounter" as anthropologist Anna Tsing called it.[12] In "the sticky materiality of practical encounters," AmeRícan Muslims carve out their corner of the global stream of Islam, inserting their own genealogies "of commitments and claims" in the process.[13] In Laviera's styling, they once again take the "accent from the altercation"—this time on the margins of the ummah, generating new notions of being and belonging in the process. As they do so, they confront built-in mechanisms of power, revising and renaming, adapting and conforming their minoritarian identifications while remaining in productive tension with majoritarian affiliations.[14]

In describing these tensions, I do not want to reify labels and identifications like Puerto Rican, Palestinian, or Arab as sui generis racial categories. Nor do I want to reify religion as an independent variable separate from notions of race and ethnicity. While the nouns "race" and "religion" are often used to denote distinct phenomena, in practice people have long used the underlying concepts in intertwined and twisted ways to categorize people and rank them. None of the identifications in this chapter can be reduced to either the biologizing terms "race/ethnicity" or the spiritualizing label "religion." Instead, I view each as categories that are mutually inflected by the other and recognize the multifaceted nature of being and the fluid, circumstantial dynamics of group belonging(s) in the late-modern world.

Writing from an Indo-Caribbean context in Trinidad, anthropologist Aisha Khan demonstrates how "the intersectionality of race and religion is always a simultaneous process."[15] While one or the other might be foregrounded in a particular historical or social context, "they are always and necessarily in a state of mutual definition, even as [they are] variously construed."[16] This goes to show how our identifications and notions of being and belonging to one race or religion or a combination thereof are not inherent or given. Instead, Khan shows how "race" and "religion" are "complex forms of agency that orient modes of identification (of ourselves and others)."[17] Or, in other words, they are open-ended questions for us to locate ourselves "in relation to the earth and to the cosmos" and our myriad contextual interactions and relations in the present.[18]

Thus, identifications like "Arab" or "Puerto Rican" within the ummah are not possible without notions of difference, constructed as they are in "diffracted and complex relationship with others"[19] at various scales.[20] As Khan reminds us, assumptions about racial and ethnic identity or metaphors of encounter and mixing are "generated within certain kinds of power relations, rather than as prescriptive, predicting a priori what those relations ought to be."[21] Within Caribbean (or, for that matter, Islamicate) contexts and diasporas, those power relations are defined by colonial legacies and lingering racial (white) and religious (Christian) hegemonies, which function as the point of reference for boundary inscription and maintain both Arab and Puerto Rican Muslim identifications in a state of "alterity." Accordingly, it is important to keep in mind how race and religion form what Khan calls an "articulated discourse" wherein such "categories are meaningful and possess agency only in conjunction with one another."[22]

Furthermore, to understand human socialities in the late-modern requires coming to terms with the messiness, paradox, and tensions of identifications that are the inevitable result of being human in relation to other humans in a (post)colonial world. Islamic studies scholar Ali Mian wrote that the "contradictions, tensions, and [divergent affective tendencies]" that constitute such relations "are historically contingent and thus call for case-specific analytical frameworks."[23] Therefore I focus on the affective, relational dimensions of these dynamics, further illustrating AmeRícan Muslims' "multiple experiences of disparity, marginalization, and oppression" while at the same time avoiding "settler-colonial and [w]hite supremacist logics that pit marginalized groups against each other."[24] Moreover, I acknowledge both

Puerto Rican and Arab Muslims' heterogeneous experiences and the ways in which they struggle as differently colored and identifying social actors despite sharing a similar "discursive and ideological environment and context,"[25] looking at a diverse range of dissonant-yet-resonant generative frictions that exist between them. I also look at how, in the styling of Walter Benjamin, their intimate contact with one another, "does not abolish the distance between [them], but brings that distance to life."[26] Consequently, this chapter offers an alternate approach to situating *difference* within Islam, rejecting stereotypes about ethnic or sectarian identities to instead highlight the interplay of being and belonging in conjunction with, and opposition to, relations between ordinary Muslims in the context of empire.[27]

Through the complexities, ambiguities, and nuances of life together, what emerges is what one of my interlocutors called "asaBorícua." As a response to their marginalization within the ummah, asaBorícua is a formation that stands in contrast to its majoritarian surroundings (e.g., "Arabness," "Arab Muslims," or "South Asian Muslims") and in turn establishes its own social boundaries. These demarcations of difference are neither simply given, nor can they be taken for granted.[28] Instead, they are formed in specific places and at particular times. In this chapter, they are shown to be the result of the ways in which immigration, ethnicity, economics, religion, and racialization intersect in AmeRícan Muslim lives.[29]

Furthermore, the making of this minoritized identification should not be viewed in contrast to the processes of cosmopolitanization, but as part and parcel of them. As historian of religion W. C. Smith wrote, religious actors often disagree with one another, often over fundamental aspects of the tradition they share. These disagreements, he argued, do not tear apart the community, but often constitute it.[30] As Muslim minority identifications are formed and re-formed, defined and re-combined, asserted and adapted, in myriad places across a world marked by diversity and difference, they contribute to emergent cosmopolitan formations[31] of being and belonging—formations like asaBorícua.

## *ASABORÍCUA*: A "FIGHTING-TOGETHERNESS"

Several days after my midday meal with Ilyass, I remained intrigued by his interpretation of the allegorical notion of Islam as "water flowing across rock." In particular, I was struck with how his vision seemed to resonate with my interpretation of cosmopolitanization—that it is a process of generative friction, wherein the conflict, resistance, and tensions experienced in the encounters between diverse peoples, ideas, customs, and technologies in the late-modern (re)produce new notions of belonging and co-becoming. His vision of what Islam might look like among AmeRícan Muslims was that the streams of Islamic history and tradition flowing across time and space for centuries were now converging in a new context, coursing across a fresh landscape. As Islam poured over AmeRícan foundations, Ilyass imagined a process of abrasion and mutual formation that simultaneously transforms the sediment itself and shapes the course of the river that flows across its surface. In other words, as more and more Puerto Ricans converted within the AmeRícan context, both Puerto Rican culture and Islam itself would be changed and rearranged.[32]

Central to this process is a negotiation of difference, tension, and living together in collaboration and conflict. Or, at least, this is what I proposed to Ilyass the next time we meet, this time at a falafel restaurant where we sit scrunched up in the back corner near the restaurant's bathroom. As we wipe our fingers free of the oil coating the crispy mashed chickpea balls, Ilyass shares yet another creative adaptation of Islamic tradition to elucidate what he feels the AmeRícan Muslim experience to be. "This whole situation reminds me of Ibn Khaldûn," he says, "he was writing about tribalism hundreds of years ago and nothing's changed. Just the characters. Not the roles they play." Ilyass was referring to Ibn Khaldûn's ideas of ummah and *asabiyah,* and over the course of the conversation to follow, he would adapt and reapply the concept to the AmeRícan Muslim condition.

Ibn Khaldûn (1332–1406 CE) was a renowned administrator, historian, and judge originally from Tunis. Writing on the themes of unity in the context of historical processes and social realities, Khaldûn developed a theory concerning what he saw as the cyclical nature of dynasties and political power in Iberia, North Africa, and the Arab Middle East, identifying two antithetical societal groupings: rural tribes and urban populations. Although he believed that all people were born the same, he thought growing up in an urban context and growing up in rural areas produced different social sensibilities. On the one hand, he posited that rural societies were by nature (or *tabiah*), "morally pure, socially cohesive, and militarily tested." City peoples were, on the other hand, "morally corrupt, socially atomized, and militarily inexperienced."[33] He placed these juxtaposed populations in a "framework of a cyclical, dialectical model that explained, he said, the chronic political instability and persistently anemic culture."[34] Arguing that in order to survive and thrive human societies had to create forms of community and organization (*ijtima*), Ibn Khaldûn theorized the concept of asabiyah.

Asabiyah is variously defined as "social solidarity" or "communal identity," with an emphasis on group consciousness, cohesiveness, and unity. The term became popularized with the publication of Ibn Khaldûn's Muqaddimah, or "Introduction" to history. Most likely drawing on an earlier sense of clannishness or tribalism within Arab society, Ibn Khaldûn elevated asabiyah to the level of "fundamental principle of social solidarity"[35] and viewed it as a natural power generated through a combination of common descent, kinship ties (either physical or fictive), and common everyday experiences. Ibn Khaldûn wrote, "asabiyah produces the ability to defend oneself, to offer opposition, to protect oneself and to press one's claims."[36] In effect, Ibn Khaldûn believed that societies, tribes, or communities with strong asabiyah possessed a certain tenacity, bravery, and toughness that gave them a will to power. Over time and in the context of cosmopolitan cities, he believed, asabiyah weakened until dynasties collapsed, typically victim to the power of another tribe or nation with stronger asabiyah.[37] Although, in principle, Islamic social ethics are opposed to local solidarities that privilege some ethnicities over others, Ibn Khaldûn's theory came to play a critical role in Islamic intellectual and political history over the centuries, often combined with and adapted to more modern theories about ethnicity, minority identification, and kinship.[38]

Ilyass became one of the latest Muslims to take up and reapply Ibn Khaldûn's theories—this time in reference to dynamics at work between AmeRícan Muslims and the ummah they interact with and see themselves as part of but marginalized from. While he agreed it was wise to heed the caution to not make Ibn Khaldûn say things for our time that he could not, or perhaps would not,[39] Ilyass believes the concept of asabiyah is relevant to the conversation around AmeRícan Muslims and the idea(l) of Muslim cosmopolitanism today. He says:

> Puerto Rican Muslims feel caught between the ummah and their own asaBorícua. While we all want a unified ummah, we are faced with a sense that being Borícua doesn't fit within preconceived categories of what that ummah looks like or how it is supposed to act, pray, or speak.

Echoing Ilyass, other AmeRícan Muslims shared how they felt Arab Muslims communicated in word and deed that there is no way to be a "good

Muslim" and remain proudly Latinx or Puerto Rican. As a young Mexican-Puerto Rican activist in Detroit, Hazel put it this way in a post shared on Facebook:

> Being Puerto Rican Muslim is hard . . . we gotta prove to the Puerto Ricans how Borícua we are. And we gotta prove to the Muslims how Muslim we are. We gotta be more Borícua than Puerto Ricans. More Muslim than the Muslims. All at the same time.

In Hazel's styling, AmeRícan Muslim lives exist at the juncture of multiple, competing cultural contexts, with that of Puerto Rico on one side and global Islam on the other, exposing them to sidelining and misunderstanding from both.

Listening to interlocutors like Ilyass and Hazel, I make the case that as they face pressure and ostracism from family, friends, and their fellow faithful, AmeRícan Muslims retreat into the strength of their own asaBorícua to assert their Muslim identifications and simultaneously challenge the prevailing power that they feel forces them to be something they are not. I suggest their sense of asaBorícua emerges out of being in those hinterlands, those places between worlds—real, imagined, and possible. As they envisage it, the very process of marginalization and the harshness of sentiment and strength of solidarity this engenders allows for AmeRícan Muslims to produce a creative, adaptive way to manage minoritization in multiple directions, but primarily among their fellow Muslims. Thus, asaBorícua offers Puerto Rican Muslims a sense of solidarity, of fighting-togetherness against those with power over them. In effect, it provides AmeRícan Muslims a means to "defend themselves, offer opposition, and press their claims"[40] within the felt distance between them and the constructed majority paradigm.

In one sense, asaBorícua might also be called "Borícua Muslim pride." This was an often-expressed sentiment among Puerto Rican reverts, which evinces a sense of group consciousness, cohesiveness, and solidarity shared between AmeRícan Muslims as a means of pushing back against the marginalization they face in the ummah at large and in specific, local communities. In another sense, however, asaBorícua is a specific attempt by Puerto Rican reverts to center their selves, stories, and sense of belonging at the center of the ummah and its late-modern manifestations. Ernest Gellner, in his formulation of Ibn Khaldûn's theory, posited that asabiyah rests on two pillars: "Leadership exists only through superiority, and superiority only through group feeling (*asabiyya*)"[41] and that only tribes bound together by asabiyah can subsist in the desert and resist the seemingly superior, concentrated power of the cities. When related to AmeRícan Muslims, their formulation of asabiyah (asaBorícua) also works in two directions: to assert a sense of superiority over other Muslims and to foster a micro-level solidarity that allows them to exist, subsist, and contest their place on the margins, in the hinterlands of global Islam.

Dealing with their place on the perceived margins—geographically, religiously, and culturally—AmeRícan Muslims turn to asaBorícua to reassert their agency, gain recognition, and perform an alternative, more cosmopolitan sense of being and belonging within the majoritarian discourse(s) of global Islam. To do so, they not only draw on a sense of Puerto Rican cultural pride (see chapter 2) but also engage with broader debates going on within and across the ummah over ideology, identity, and institutions to make claims for greater autonomy and acknowledgement within it. This is, after all, a central aspect of asabiyah—its ability to translate a will to power into reality[42] or "help in building internal solidarity" in the face of overarching, majoritarian formations.[43]

Therefore, this chapter shows how AmeRícan Muslim cosmopolitanism is not solely a product of forces from outside the ummah, but one that is generated by the very tensions and negotiations involved in their engagement with majoritarian Muslim formations within it. As a central marker of belonging, religious identifications play a significant role in connecting and dividing. They become another tool in the hand of those seeking to demarcate boundaries and generate an emergent identification within the context of a dominant majority. Thus, I show how AmeRícan Muslims employ religious perspectives and practices to construct narratives, counternarratives, and discourses to inform their relations and interactions with Others who they encounter in their everyday lives. These everyday encounters are not uniform. The ways individuals and groups in this chapter relate to one another are multifarious, enabling them to broker or straddle their differences in numerous directions.[44] But by paying attention to the Islamic inflections of this process, I suggest we can better appreciate "Muslim cosmopolitanism" as capable of producing emergent and contingent minority identifications based on the varying contours and cadences of the majoritarian surroundings Muslims of varying racial and ethnic identifications find themselves in.

## NATIONS, TRIBES, AND KNOWING ONE ANOTHER

Over and against the seeming fragmentation of Muslim societies, ideologies, and socialities, Muslims across the late-modern world still aspire to an ummah ideal. This is partly due to how the unity of the ummah functions as the desired social embodiment of tawhid—the oneness of Allah. In this framework, fragmentation and disunity (*fitna*) become signs of Islam at war with itself *and* the Divine. In a way, disunity becomes a loss of one of Islam's central organizing discourses. And yet, with the rise of Islamic modernism alongside the causes of nationalism in the nineteenth and twentieth centuries, there is a vociferous debate about the relationship between local identifications and loyalty to the ummah. As part of this process, the idea of the ummah itself took on more symbolic power than before, especially among minority Muslim communities trying to assert their Muslim identifications over, against, or alongside the majority populations of their respective nation-states.[45] In the thought of some Islamic modernists, nationalism became linked with jahiliyyah, and thus, Muslims were called to leave behind nationalist formulations of being and belonging in favor of a unified ummah.

Found in several places in the Qur'an, the term ummah signifies in multiple, if interconnected, directions. But the different meanings share a similar basis: They express an ideal of essential unity and equality among Muslims across cultural, geographical, and ideological boundaries. Derived from a root "meaning to repair or to direct one's course to a thing to seek with aim,"[46] the ummah idea(l) provides Muslims with a sense of belonging to something *more*, a familiarity and a fraternity in a world often fragmented by various fealties. Said to have been used in pre-Islamic Arabia to refer to pacts set between peoples to regulate access to wells—a precious commodity in arid, desert climates—ummah became an umbrella term for avoiding chaos and delineating a shared understanding for how to divide a scarce, shared, resource that yielded a mutually beneficial outcome. In the Qur'an, the term is extended to apply to those whom Allah sent a prophet or the people who are objects of a divine plan of salvation (for example, Christians or Jews). The idea is that the ummah is a force that attracts disparate elements and individuals together, like a magnet drawing metallic objects.[47] Nonetheless, it is, "a fairly elastic term and is also used in the Qur'an more specifically to connote a religiously defined community, with each umma being distinguished from the others by the degree and content of its collective beliefs and disbeliefs."[48]

The desire for unity in the face of adversity, tribalism, nationalism, or external pressures notwithstanding, the ideal of the ummah remains a multivalent concept. While it might be tempting to think that the ummah exists as a unique lattice connecting the worldwide Muslim community across various dividing lines, it is more of an "imagined community" than anything else.[49] It serves as an ideal, a normative vision for what the Muslim community should, and might possibly, be or become. Throughout Islamic history, there were numerous attempts to reify the ummah and define its boundaries. In the late-modern, Muslims continue to realize and debate its parameters and meaning in the context of globalization, racial identification, kinship ties, and disparate if interconnected geographic locations. Thus, the idea(l) of the ummah is "contested, challenged, resisted, transformed, modified, and remade by Muslim" actors, who showcase individual and collective agency and ingenuity in an ongoing dialogue with(in) a fragmented community across time and space.[50] Although this could be framed in a negative light, I read it as a sign of a shared cosmopolitanism. As will be shown below, the tension between the ummah and local identifications, nationalisms, or "tribalisms" is part and parcel of the process of cosmopolitanization wherein actors seek to make sense of the world and their place in it in the dialogue of diversity and difference in daily life.

### *Souk in a Trunk: Searching for Palestinian Peoplehood in Puerto Rico*

When I first arrived in Puerto Rico for preliminary fieldwork, I knew I wanted to make my way to the Eid al-Fitr celebrations hosted at the San Juan Convention Center. So, and not without a bit of first-day jitters, I made my way to the Convention Center on July 17, 2015. Upon my arrival, the massive convention center seemed empty, and I wondered if I made a mistake or went to the wrong place. Before too long, I saw a man dressed in a thawb and thanked God I seemed to be in the right location. I walked up and introduced myself. He introduced himself as José. While already familiar to the reader from a previous chapter, this was the first day I met José. As I took a seat on some lime-green couches in the foyer and enjoyed the air conditioning in the Convention Center, I was excited to get to know the Puerto Rican convert community in flesh and blood.

Curious, José asked what I was doing there. I told him I was looking to get to know "Puerto Rican Muslims" here and in the US. José quickly corrected me:

> That's not right. You can't study "Puerto Rican" Muslims. There is no such thing. There are only Muslims. There is one ummah. Sure, if

> you go to this masjid or that community, one speaks Spanish and the other speaks Arabic, but otherwise it is a universal faith. What is true about it is global. You misspeak by saying "Puerto Rican Muslims," as if there is such a thing! There are Puerto Ricans who are Muslims, but the ummah is one.

As a testament to his testimony of unity, there were Muslims who claimed heritage or came from such diverse locales as Egypt and Ethiopia, India and Indonesia, Haiti and Hato Rey gathered for Eid celebrations that morning. Given the diverse group gathered for *takbir* and prayers, the khutbah and the announcements were made in a mix of Arabic, English, and Spanish. It seemed to me that everyone there was united in their pronouncement of takbir, their collection of the Eid donations, and their excitement over breaking the fast of Ramadan together.

We then left the convention center rooms where the prayers were held, shuffling into the main hall where over five hundred people were gathered to eat and celebrate. There were bounce houses for the kids to play in, tables full of dates and snacks, a stage set up with a full sound system and disc jockey, as well as tickets being handed out for a fried chicken lunch. Desserts were a mixture of *basbousa*, *kanafeh*, and baklava. As I grabbed some kanafeh and Turkish coffee, I was approached by Abdul. A gas station owner in San Juan, Abdul introduced himself as a "local Palestinian." Born in Caguas—a city to the south of San Juan—Abdul said he grew up in Puerto Rico. However, he lived in Amman, Jordan, and Tampa, Florida, before returning to San Juan. He asked why I was at the event, and I shared the same thing I told José before: I am here to learn more about "Puerto Rican Muslims." Instead of lecturing me about the unity of the ummah, he widened his eyes and said, "That's good, that's good. People don't know much about Puerto Rican Muslims, just us Palestinians maybe. But not much. It is a vibrant, living community. Imam Zaid, he bridges the world between Palestinians and Puerto Ricans. He is respected here. Treasured even."

Abdul then introduced me to friends at his table—Muhammad and Abdullah, Shaquille and Ahmed. We ate and shared stories. Each of them was born in Puerto Rico to parents who came from Palestine in the 1950s, '60s, or '70s. Each had spent time in Jordan, Palestine, or both. Each also considered themselves Palestinian and *not* Puerto Rican. At the end, as we were finishing our desserts and they were about to head to the main stage for *dabke*—a popular Levantine dance—Abdul turned to me and said, "It was great talking to you. Really. But if you want to learn more about the Puerto

Rican Muslims you should head over there." He pointed to a couple of tables in the corner where there were several couples sitting back and looking over in our general direction. Before he walked away, I asked, "Abdul, you were born in Puerto Rico, raised here, have family here, and live here. You don't consider yourself Puerto Rican?" Abdul replied, "No, not at all. I am Palestinian."

These sentiments are in keeping with what Juliane Hammer found in her exploration of Palestinian memory and identification in the diaspora. She found that "Palestinians all over the world have, to different degrees, managed to pass on a sense of Palestinian identity to their children since 1948."[51] Such is the case with Palestinians in Puerto Rico. In their search for a homeland, they find each other. They established connections with one another across the archipelago, forging partnerships in business, marriage, friendships, and religious communities. Fridays at the mosque present an opportunity not only for prayer, but also for connecting with other Palestinians and expressing their sense of Palestinian being and belonging in explicit ways. In mosques decorated with pictures of al-Aqsa or with Palestinian flags or Handala stickers, they spoke Southern Levantine dialect with one another, talked about news from Palestine, discussed potential engagements between daughters and sons "back home" and living on the archipelago. At mosques in Vega Alta, Río Piedras, and Montehiedra, they had the opportunity to buy their preferred Palestinian groceries—both fresh and shipped from "home"—like olive oil, fresh *kibbeh* and *sfiha*, Nakhla brand tobacco for their water pipes and peach-flavored Laziza malt beverages, falafel and *maftoul* mix, cucumbers and *kunafa* in jars. Nevertheless, and as Hammer pointed out, Palestinians in the diaspora live transnational lives and have a "floating sense of 'home'"—meaning they may struggle as they rethink ethnicity and identity in the light of global forces and interests. Often, Palestinians are forced to live between two worlds, two homes, even if they only claim one.[52]

I got a glimpse of these multivalent dynamics at work among the Palestinian community in Puerto Rico when I stuck around one day after jummah prayers in Vega Alta. After talking to a few folks in the air-conditioned environs of the masjid, I stepped outside into the heat to chat with Ahmed, who was selling goods from the back of his van in the parking lot. Showing me the contents of his Aerostar, he said, "It's like a souk in a trunk." There were cans of Al Shark sardines and bottles of olive oil from Nablus, boxes of *maamoul* and *maftoul*, *freekeh* and *foul*, Ziyad brand chickpeas and bags of looseleaf Al Wazah Ceylon tea with cardamom. Poking my nose around,

FIGURE 4.1 *A Palestinian Muslim enjoys a soft drink in front of a "souk in a trunk" outside the mosque in Vega Alta, Puerto Rico.*

Ahmed told me, "people like having a taste of home in Puerto Rico, and I like to deliver it to them." We talked a bit about my travels to Palestine and Jordan and the fact that my wife was soon moving to Amman. He smiled, saying it is important to go and *see* places in person. "That's different than watching it on TV," he said, "you don't feel for the people in the same way if you don't see them face-to-face. It's the same with the problems here in Puerto Rico. People don't see us. Or in Palestine. People don't see us. People don't want to see us."

As our conversation continued, several other men from the mosque joined me at the back of Ahmed's truck—from Palestine and Trinidad, Bangladesh and Puerto Rico. People shook hands, caught up, met each other's grandkids, shared a meal together, all after having prayed side by side. They were not overly intimate, but they were not standoffish or cliquish either. Arabic, Spanish, and English floated in and out of the conversation, and everyone seemed to acquiesce to the language of one's choice (people spoke to me in English, Arabic, and Spanish, making sure I understood and code-switching if I did not). Yet, noticeably, there was a lack of Puerto Rican dishes, customs, and topics of conversation. There were some, but the gist of the impromptu post-jummah gathering was focused on the Middle East. The Palestinians hosting this impromptu group seemed to be hospitable, inviting others into their beloved traditions and giving them a taste of their home, of which they were proud.

### *"That's pure tribalism"*

For some Puerto Ricans, however, it can come off as something else entirely. After meeting José at the Eid celebrations, I catch up with him a few days later in Río Piedras. We talk about the celebration—the prayers, the food, the dancing, Abdul's comment, and Ahmed's truckload of Palestinian and Levantine goods. José balks. Stressing again the unity of the ummah across the globe, he lays divisions in Puerto Rico at the Palestinians' feet. Referencing the dabke and some of the food, he says it was all "pure tribalism." He continues:

> We can eat the food, we could participate in the dances, but that wouldn't be us. That isn't our identity and it isn't Islam. They can get together for their celebrations, to remember they are Palestinian—that's fine! We have our festivals, our celebrations as Puerto Ricans. But we don't mix that with Islam. We don't try to make it one and the same.

These tensions would linger and continue to crop up in conversations throughout my fieldwork over the next few years.

For example, two years after these initial conversations, I found the fissures were still felt and still fresh at the next Eid celebration I attended. Sumayah, married to an Egyptian and a convener of a multicultural group at her home for Friday prayers and special events, joined me at the Eid al-Fitr celebration at the Convention Center that June. Since I last visited, Sumayah says she fell out with the established Muslim community in Puerto Rico. Whereas she used to be seen as a leader for her efforts in doing dawah among Puerto Ricans, she is now widely suspect for her outspoken positions on LGBTQI+ issues and leadership in same-sex wedding ceremonies. She came to the Eid celebrations willingly that day but was wary of her co-religionists at the same time. Pulling me aside just outside the main prayer room, she says:

> We get together every year for this ritual, this celebration, and people gather from all over Puerto Rico. But the thing is—this isn't real

> community. It's "community" without community. I'd rather be on my own, or with my own, than interact with them [the wider Arab Muslim community in Puerto Rico].

As Palestinian music begins to play in the background and several men dance their way to the stage, Sumayah points out that there are not many Puerto Ricans in attendance when compared to years past. Looking around the room of five hundred, she counts twenty at most. I ask if this is just a reflection of the small number of converts, and she retorts, "No, it's a reflection of how they do not feel part of this community!" Her Egyptian husband, Mohammed, interjects to provide more evidence of the ostracism and marginalization they feel are at work at the Eid celebrations. He says:

> For example, the Spanish summary of the khutbah they provide isn't an actual summary. It's not the khutbah. It's probably some printout from the internet they downloaded a few minutes before showing up. Maybe it's based on the same text, maybe not. They don't care.

There are a few others around the table with us who nod their heads and add their own perspectives. Khaled, from Morocco, goes on an extended rant about "the Arabs" and echoes Sumayah's comments about wanting to create a community of their own. He says, "I'd rather invite a new convert to become part of our family. Have dinner with us. Pray with us. We don't need them [pointing to the Palestinians dancing]. We can get together on our own, our kids can play, and we can make a new community." The sad thing, Khaled says, is that this tribalism contrasts with the Sunnah of the Prophet himself. "Meccans in the time of ignorance used to call Friday *yawm-ul-urabah* or the 'Day of Arabness,'" he says. "Muhammad (PBUH) changed it to *yawm-ul-jumaah*, a day of inclusion, togetherness, and gathering. That's the ideal, but that's not the reality we live. There are hierarchies, there are tensions, there's us, and then there's them. We are back in jahiliyyah."

### *A Battle for Peace of Mind*

Back in the US, Lebrón shares that when he entered his first mosque near Passaic, New Jersey, his impression was, "'What did I get myself into?'" He says, "All I saw were Arab men sitting around talking Arabic, and their leader stood in front of them and began delivering a speech in Arabic."[53] Turned off by the overwhelming "Arab" feel of the mosque, he found comfort in another that was more diverse, where there were "African Americans,

Hispanics, whites, Arabs, etc." and even some "brothers" from Puerto Rico and Guatemala, he says. Reflecting on these experiences later, he says:

> Way too often sometimes we hear that people, especially when it comes to converts like myself, people say, "Well, you have to wear thawb all the time, you have to look like an Arab, behave like an Arab, take on the characteristics of an Arab"; but the reality is . . . that Allah (SWT) . . . did not create me to be a Saudi Arabian, Pakistani, Indian, Syrian, Egyptian. He created me [pointing to his Puerto Rican baseball hat] to be from Puerto Rico.

He continues, "Allah (SWT) created me to be a Puerto Rican Muslim . . . Alhamdulillah I can combine the two and it makes something exquisite and beautiful, to accept and speak Islam in the Spanish language."[54] Relating this to when Islam first came to the Arabs, he highlights in his testimony that:

> Allah (SWT) didn't tell the Arabs to change their food, their customs. As long as something didn't go against the Qur'an or the Sunnah . . . then there is no problem. Even the shari'a is founded according to the customs of the people . . . you don't have to become some other than who you are to become Muslim.

This, he says, was how he resolved the tensions in his battle for peace of mind following conversion.

For Lebrón, the tension experienced in conversion—and the collision of culture, traditions, and customs that comes with it—produces new notions of being and new formulations of belonging. This process is not an easy one, but through the confluence of streams from different cultural heritages and the pressures they feel in joining a community that feels pre-formed, a new identification emerges that is both decidedly Muslim and stubbornly Puerto Rican. Puerto Rican Muslims like Lebrón or Sumayah do not feel they must make a choice between the two. Instead, they attempt to merge them, doing so in strategic and creative ways. Not only do they try to conform their Puerto Rican cultural heritage to their new Muslim identity (chapter 2), but they also couch their Puerto Ricanness in Muslim tradition, customs, and teachings (chapter 3).

Their cosmopolitanism is optative in that it allows them to choose between various identifications. At the same time, each of these becomes contested, imagined, and somewhat ambiguous. For Lebrón, that means looking to the foundation of the early Muslim community in the seventh-century Hejaz, in the revelation of the Qur'an, and in the practice of the Prophet Muhammad to express his asaBorícua identity in ways that resonate with his fellow, non–Puerto Rican, Muslims *and* his fellow Puerto Rican Muslims. It also means (re)mixing his clothing, one day wearing a *taqiyah* (a skullcap) and the next day a red flat-bill lid with "PUERTO RICO" emblazoned on the underside of the bill in bold letters with a *jalabiya* on below; mixing a Puerto Rican pride sweatshirt with a *keffiyeh* or *shemagh*. Far from trivial, such sartorial choices help AmeRícan Muslims like Lebrón to recover and remix a more authentic notion of self and signify their membership in multiple constituencies.

In the end, these choices are rooted in a broader desire for authenticity. Paralleling the experience of Black American Muslims in the US, AmeRícan Muslims seek ways to authenticate their ethnic identifications over and against the supposed and inherited authenticity and superiority of the "Arab Muslim" or "South Asian Muslim" experience. Su'ad Abdul Khabeer wrote of this in regard to Black Americans in the US. Because they "cannot claim immediate descent from the 'Muslim world,'" she wrote, they are "presumed to be new to the Islamic tradition, and [their] religious practices and perspectives have to be authenticated."[55] Meanwhile, Muslims of Arab descent are "presumed to have proximity to the Islamic Tradition," and their "religious practices and perspectives are endowed with authenticity simply because [they are] Arab."[56] Likewise, Puerto Rican Muslims look for ways to authenticate their "Islam-ness" without necessarily becoming "Arab."

The tensions that exist between Puerto Rican Muslims and their coreligionists because of this cannot simply be summed up as a contest over tradition or a battle over ethnicity and authenticity. Instead, this relationship is part and parcel of the late-modern experience. Confronted with the world and its diversity—and finding "home" in multiple places, identifications, and socialities—AmeRícan Muslims and those they are in relationship with work out these tensions in multivalent ways. They are at odds with one another but at the same time arguing over shared concepts (for example, the ummah) and wrestling with shared experiences. Even as they argue and contest each other's respective identities and loyalties they also stand in solidarity with one another on various issues (chapter 5). In practice, they quarrel, but they do so together.

While Arab and other majoritarian Muslims possess a certain power over Puerto Rican Muslims and, in turn, Puerto Rican Muslims sense a certain "colonization" of their minds, bodies, and hearts as they join and contest established Muslim communities, there is a simultaneous process where the divides and hyphens between them become fuzzy. Whether in conflict or collaboration, the two are taking on each other's attributes, becoming mutually implicated in the supposed "Others'" lives. Although Sumayah's community of self-described "outcasts" could be aptly described as a counterpublic to the core Palestinian community that predominates in Puerto Rico's mosques—and a prime example of the assertion of asaBorícua minority politics—they are not the only ones wrestling with the ethnic tensions, debates over tradition, and other stresses placed on the supposed unity of the ummah in Puerto Rico. At each mosque I visited in Puerto Rico, I ran into Puerto Ricans, Palestinians, and other Muslims from various places claiming multiple heritages and wrestling with how to live, work, and pray alongside one another.

### *One Mezquita, Three Stories: Adrián, Saber, and Alejandro*

To gain an even deeper appreciation of this process at work, I headed back to Vega Alta's Masjid al-Faruq. Like many others in Puerto Rico, Vega Alta's mosque was founded with funding from Palestinians and other Arabs. Indeed, across Puerto Rico's mosques and Muslim communities, Palestinians possess power and privilege in numbers, leadership, and financial capital. Although there are exceptions, Arab Muslims in Puerto Rico tend to be middle class and economically well-established, owning and operating a range of businesses from gas stations to restaurants, stores to art galleries. They are proud to be "self-made" entrepreneurs after fleeing economic, political, or societal uncertainty in the Middle East. Converts, on the other hand, tend to struggle economically. Many I spoke to were unemployed, seasonally employed, students, working in blue-collar positions, or getting by with menial labor.

For example, Adrián—whom readers met when he was cleaning the steps leading up to the prayer room at the mosque in Vega Alta—suffered not only socially after converting but also financially. His wife supported the household, ironically through her job working for Arab Muslims on the archipelago. When I met him, he was between jobs and keeping busy with his street art. That is why he loves coming to the mosque in Vega Alta. Since moving out of his former home and living between friends' couches and family members' spare beds, Adrián says the mosque became a "second home." And so, he treats it accordingly, carefully washing each nook and cranny of the complex before Friday prayers, resting in its relatively cool interior in the midst of another torrid Puerto Rican summer afternoon, or storing his thawb in the imam's office so that it is not sullied as he goes to and fro on public transportation. During one of our conversations in the cool, maroon-carpeted interior of the mezquita, Adrián says, "the first mosque was the Prophet's home, and now this mezquita is mine." The first night he was forced to leave the home he formerly shared with his wife, Adrián came here and, he says, "I prayed and then I slept, comfortable that no matter what was to happen, Allah would take care of me."

After Adrián's prayers, we are joined by Saber, a member of the mosque's leadership. Born in Amman, Jordan, in 1951 after his parents fled during al-Nakba (the catastrophic loss of Palestinian society and homeland after the establishment of Israel in 1948), Saber came to Puerto Rico in 1974 after spending several years in Kuwait following the fallout from the Six-Day War in 1967. He says his experience was not unlike many other Palestinians in the archipelago. "We had to find some place to live because our homeland was taken away," he says. So, he and other Palestinian newcomers invested into businesses that might help establish them in the community—gas stations and pharmacies, restaurants and shops. "Many people do not know this," he shares somewhat conspiratorially, "but we Palestinians brought IHOP to Puerto Rico!'" Cleaning out a back room at his gas station in 1980 for prayer, a community began to gather there, and over the next twenty years they collected the funds, bought the land, and eventually constructed Puerto Rico's first purpose-built mosque in 2000. Unfortunately, though many Palestinians lived in Puerto Rico, it "can never truly feel like 'home,'" he says, "my heart is never fully whole here."

Saber has been in Puerto Rico for over twenty years, speaks Spanish, and sends his children to Puerto Rican schools or has married them off to Puerto Ricans. "But I still feel split in two," he says, "desirous of being back in Jerusalem, but dedicated to living here." Adding to this is a low-boiling ostracism and anti-Muslim rhetoric in broader American political orders. He shares:

> Some ignorant people don't understand. They call us "Osama bin Laden" or "Taliban." Other times they shout "*terrorismo*" or things like that because they are brainwashed by the media. One time a young man came into my gas station and said something about "you Arabs." I looked at him and asked how old he was. He was thirty. I told him, "I've been here since 1974." That's forty-three years. I speak

> Spanish. I have had five kids here. I own this business and have been part of this community for four decades. I am more Borícua than a lot of Borícuas!

Looking out the window at some place in the distance, he reflects, "Puerto Rico is my home, sure . . . but Palestine is in my heart." Others, he says, moved to Chicago or went back to Palestine but, he says, "no matter where we [Palestinians] go, we are in between."

Saber's story sits in strange tension alongside stories like Alejandro's. Raised in Bayamón, near San Juan, Alejandro had what he calls, "a rough go for a while," struggling with alcohol, crime, and sexual addiction. Raised Catholic and with influence from family members who were Jehovah's Witnesses, he says he went on a spiritual search after a particularly difficult run-in with the law and a short stint in prison. His family members were not helpful, with lists of things he had to believe and had to do to gain redemption in their eyes. "I just wanted to learn how to pray," he tells me. In the end, he says he found that simple spiritual sustenance in Islam and was supported by Muslims who provided a place for him to live as he sought to re-establish himself. But Alejandro says that after an initially warm welcome, there was a steady progression toward exclusion. He says, "The Arabs act as if they are the only ones who are worthy, Puerto Rican Muslims are just add-ons to them." He now does most of his study on his own, likes to go to the mosque to pray when others are not around, and does not want to speak up about his own ideas or raise his own questions.

Alejandro says the tensions between him and the Arabs come down to a fundamental difference in culture and class. "They think I need to be business-successful like them, but they don't know what it's like to be Puerto Rican. The daily struggle." Because of this, Alejandro says he saw multiple Puerto Rican converts come to the mosque over the years and then head out on their own after a while. He assumes the same will happen to Adrián. Responding to these forces and lacking the financial and social capital to construct their own purpose-built mosques, Puerto Rican Muslims often turn to their homes, converted store fronts, and small, shared spaces for places of prayer, connection, and community celebration. These personal prayers spaces reflect the improvisation, innovation, and protest embedded in Islamic infrastructure in the hinterlands. They are the very places where Puerto Rican Muslims feel they can be most fully Puerto Rican *and* Muslim.

### *The Problem with that "Party Spirit"*

Sheikh Yunus, an imam from Nigeria serving the Vega Alta community since 2016, told me he deals with these tensions every day. One of the largest communities in Puerto Rico and with renewed energy after the arrival of their new imam, the Vega Alta community is a prime example of how Muslims in Puerto Rico are navigating the generative frictions between ummah and asabiyah, between Palestinian pride, power, and an emergent asaBorícua discourse.

One afternoon, I sit down with Sheikh Yunus on the patio overlooking the fertile valley that the Vega Alta masjid overlooks along Puerto Rico's Highway Two (PR-2), the main east-west thoroughfare where thousands of Puerto Ricans drive every day. Sheikh Yunus and I talk about his most recent khutbah, entitled, "Islam Forbids Intolerance and Prejudice on the Basis of Family Names, Origin, or Ethnicity." He began his message with the following words:

> Brothers and sisters in I-salaam, the noble religion of I-salaam invites [us] to solidarity among the Muslims worldwide, regardless of differences in color, language, or gender! Are you the type that gets easily offended on the basis of differences in country, party, or other identities? Even Prophet Muhammad (PBUH) rejected being projected as superior over other prophets if such projection arose from intolerance and boastfulness!

He continued by quoting two reports that supported his claim concerning the Prophet, concluding with a portion of a hadith: "He who summons others to party-spirit [asabiyah] does not belong to us; and he who fights based on party-spirit [asabiyah] does not belong to us; and he who dies upholding party-spirit [asabiyah] does not belong to us."[57] As an imam, Sheikh Yunus shares he is concerned about his community and the divisions he sees between Palestinians and Puerto Ricans. He says, "That has no place in Islam! There is to be solidarity among Muslims worldwide and we have to root out the party-spirit, this asabiyah." I ask whether it came from one group in particular, and the imam says:

> No, not one in particular. I understand both, however. I understand. Palestinians have lost their home and so they look to one another to remember where they come from. Puerto Ricans lose their families and friends; they are foreigners in their own home. And so, they look

> to one another as well. But we cannot fight. In the end, our home is Islam.

A couple nights after we talk, Sheikh Yunus brings together a group of people who regularly pray and participate at his mosque to discuss the issue of dawah—how to reach out to the local Vega Alta and Vega Baja communities. Having just received a delegation from the Vega Alta mayor's office the week before, Sheikh Yunus saw a prime opportunity to build bridges between the mosque and the community in which it is situated. Gathered around the table are Saber and Adrián, mentioned above; Yusuf, who was born in New York City but moved back to Puerto Rico with his family after time in Miami and Orlando; Francisco, an older man who lived next to the mosque for eight years and had family in Florida; Elba, an outspoken woman who, with a bit of a wink, insists I speak English with her so that she can "learn the language of my enemy."

Before the meeting could even broach the topic of outreach in Vega Alta, Francisco begins with a salvo:

> The problem with the current state of dawah on this island is that the Arabs are too concerned with their businesses and not taking the message to the Puerto Ricans. They [the Arabs] are in the streets, but they are not of the streets, the barrios. They may own the gas station I work at, but they don't know the people like I do, because I work there, and I am from here.

Saber, the sole Palestinian at the table, responds, saying he understands Francisco's frustrations, but reminds him that it is difficult for Palestinians in Puerto Rico as well. Sharing a bit of his story, he wonders aloud if, as a Puerto Rican who lived between New York, Florida, and the archipelago, Yusuf might be able to understand this a little bit more. Yusuf nods and agrees with Sheikh Yunus, who reminds everyone to "forget nationality, class, and politics because we are together, Muslims." Referencing Francisco's comments about the business efforts of many Palestinians in Vega Alta, Sheikh Yunus says, "No matter what businesses we own or work for, we are in the business of Islam together." Having stayed uncharacteristically silent up until this point, Elba chimes in and shares that she feels part of the ummah, but "here, right now, in the Vega Alta mosque, I don't see a lot of *amor*, *unidad*, or *abrazo*!" Her comments about the lack of love, unity, and embrace inspire another round of discussion about diversity and disunity with multiple accusations and anecdotes.

Sensing that the meeting was headed in a direction he did not want it to go, Sheikh Yunus tries to rein things back in. He reiterates, "It is important that we acknowledge our differences—culture, gender, age, income—but then dissolve them in the melting pot of Islam. In the end we must all speak the common language of our deen, 'Allah said . . .' or 'the Prophet said . . .'" Returning to the business trope, he shares stories of how traders arrived in Indonesia and spread Islam through their different fields of business and their interactions in the marketplaces. He reflects that both Adrián and Francisco came to Islam in part because of connections to local Palestinian-owned companies. "Religion is a business, the business of salvation," Sheikh Yunus concludes, "and we must first educate ourselves on the principles of our business and then sell that in the streets like any other good or service."

When I interview Sheikh Yunus after the meeting, he shares his concern about the divisions and calls it his greatest task as an imam—uniting the ummah as it exists in Vega Alta. He says:

> We are supposed to treat everyone with respect before Allah. That is the ideal. But that is not always the reality. Here in Vega Alta, or in Hatillo and Montehiedra, they struggle with this. We forget that Allah created all nations so that we may learn from each other and instead we turn against each other. Teaching this is my primary business here.

He is concerned that Puerto Rican Muslims are too caught up with the issue of their nationality and that if they only "learned Islam" and "performed their religion" their concerns about clothes and politics, language and culture would "melt away." He continues:

> Asabiyah is associated with jahiliyyah [the time before Islam, or "ignorance" of monotheism and divine law]. People going back to their different groups is not Islam. . . . Solidarity within a group is not a problem, but not at the expense of other Muslims. This basis of stressing difference or intolerance is something that doesn't build peace and Islam is peace. It is I-salaam.

I ask him if he sees this "tribal" solidarity among Palestinians, and he says, "No, I don't see them forming a clique or leaving the mosque or doing their own thing against their Puerto Rican brothers." I ask if this might do with the fact that they are the leaders of the mosques and the primary stakeholders in the community. Sternly, he says, "One-third of Islam is praying, charity, etc. and the other two-thirds is interacting with others. They know this. Maybe, sometimes, they will not speak in Spanish or speak in Arabic only and this hurts people's feelings, but they are trying to perform their religion. That is all."

## CONCLUSION

But "just religion" is never *just* religion. A sociocultural construct of our own making, religion is consistently and constantly embroiled in multivalent orders, both personal and political. As illustrated in the vignettes above, its supposedly essential and eternal ideals (e.g., ummah) are always embodied in contextually contingent communities, in relational contexts, and in everyday encounters across difference where concepts like the ummah unfurl in often unexpected and unstable ways. In other words, whatever the ummah is, it is what Muslims and those they live alongside of make it. As the last two chapters show, it is made in the splintering of various traditions according to relational networks and encounters; it is in the classed, raced, and power-laden frictions that animate local communities; it is in the emergence of minoritized discourses that give verb and verve to constituencies on the margins.

Thus, these stories of religio-racial contestation behoove us to rethink "Muslim cosmopolitanism" through the lens of AmeRícan lives. The interstices of identification where their experience is lived out illustrate how the different conceptions of what the ummah is, or how it should be made manifest, and continue to be worked out in complex interactions between multiple constituencies and divides. Thus, we might even go so far as to say that Muslim cosmopolitanism is *constituted* by these conflictual relationships and the outcomes of the dialogic exchange across borders that occur between, and across, them—what has been referred to as *generative frictions*.

Seeing and appreciating these frictions helps us rethink ideas like "Muslim cosmopolitanism" as expressions of border problematics,[58] where territory, place, and the exchanges and encounters that happen between individuals and communities at, across, and between them produce new notions of being and belonging. In particular, in a world of proliferated borders, of territorialization and de-territorialization and re-territorialization, of unequal power relations embedded in the experiences of everyday life, border problematics produce identifications of resistance similar to asa-Borícua. Thus, viewing the cosmopolitanized world through the lens of border problematics helps us to better apperceive the dynamics at these points of cultural contact, conflict, and collaboration, whether they be physical or imagined, geopolitical or racialized, within the ummah or beyond—as the next chapter on Puerto Rican Muslims in the context of American empire further illustrates.

# 5
# ¡Pa'lante, inshallah!
## INTERSECTIONAL SOLIDARITIES IN THE SHADOW OF AMERICAN EMPIRE

With oppression manifest, comes insight,
Puerto Rico thrust into darkness, only to see the light.
But Boricuas have hope, we have been in worse situations,
Battling for independence against imperialist nations.

WENDY DÍAZ, *DE PUERTO RICO TO ISLAM WITH LOVE*

STUDENTS BEGAN THEIR STRIKE AT the University of Puerto Rico, Río Piedras (UPRRP) on March 28, 2017. Over the intervening weeks, a range of political activists joined them in protesting a controversial budget cut of $450 million (USD), lack of democratic accountability, and other disputed actions proposed by the Puerto Rico Oversight, Management, and Economic Stability Act (PROMESA) and its Financial Oversight and Management Board, known colloquially as "La Junta." To enforce the UPRRP shutdown, protestors barricaded the campus's *gallito*-emblazoned main gates with delivery pallets, desks, and classroom chairs. If one was following the social-media hashtag #EnLosPortones ("at the gates"), one might have caught a glimpse of Adrián, laying out his *sajjādah* (prayer mat) in front of one of the gates for maghrib prayer at sunset.

Adrián, a staunch *independentista*, was an active and politically engaged street artist in San Juan at the time. Recognized on campus for his striking political paintings, Adrián said he was the only Muslim he knew of who

FIGURE 5.1 *Adrián describes his mural, which was featured on a wall on the campus of Universidad de Puerto Rico Río Piedras during protests in 2017.*

took part. When people asked him about his faith, he pointed to a mural on the wall of one of the campus's parking lots, depicting female freedom fighters—one Palestinian and one Chechen—along with flowers, skulls, and a gunsight trained on Carlos M. García, a prominent member of "La Junta." As he later told me, just weeks after the final protests ended at the UPR campus in Humacao on June 7, this painting symbolized not only his frustration with "La Junta," but also the intersectionality of his faith, global resistance to neoliberal hegemony, and his struggle for Puerto Rican independence. In part inspired by his mural, he said a few student protesters donned "burqas" made from black tee shirts or the black-and-white Puerto Rican resistance flag. "We were fighting for one another, for Puerto Rico, for all those who suffer every day in *la brega*," he said.

Adrián's experience, and the convergence of his faith and resistance politics, helps bring some of the contours of AmeRícan Muslims' political and ethical self-fashioning into focus. AmeRícan Muslim stories like Adrián's illustrate the combination of colonial violence, contradictory representations, state repression, and also the resistance, creativity, resilience, and transformation that simultaneously shape *both* the Puerto

Rican *and* Muslim experience in the shadow of American empire. Furthermore, as this chapter shows, these experiences are inflected and compounded by an array of gendered, sexual, social, cultural, class-based, and political orders.

The story of Puerto Rico has never sat comfortably aside more celebratory narratives of US history. Nor has the story of global Islam. Instead, the plotline of Muslims *and* Puerto Ricans across the nineteenth, twentieth, and twenty-first centuries unfolds in the shadow, and under the influence, of American empire. Thus, the two communities share a story of perseverance, resistance, and resilience in the face of a struggle to reconcile histories of colonization and cultural racism with a strong sense of minoritized identification. At the same time, the two are shaped by their own respective sociopolitical contours, seminal events, and emphases. In AmeRícan Muslim lives, the two narratives are intertwined, revealing a complex and cosmopolitan nexus of solidarity around issues of colonization, racism, oppression, and varying intersectional phobias in the late-modern age.

In this chapter, I share how Puerto Rican Muslims navigate their multiple marginalizations under the specter of American empire and its multivalent raced, gendered, and politicized regimes. Both Muslim and Puerto Rican lives unfold under this shadow in unique and specific ways. But here, I look at the confluence of these minoritizations and their compounding, complicating oppressions. Examining the intersectionality of precarity in AmeRícan Muslim lives helps elucidate the complex cartography of coloniality and subalterity in the late-modern world, allowing me to tease out the concrete ways that the generative frictions produced by colonialism and neocolonialism in AmeRícan Muslim lives are then "spit out in malice," remixed, and otherwise reused to create intersectional solidarities. These solidarities empower Puerto Rican reverts to embody the margins of American empire as a site of resistance and, as a result, to envision and give voice to a more just world they yearn for in the future. To better elucidate these intersectional solidarities, I employ three concepts relevant to broader Puerto Rican and American social, cultural, and political orders: la brega, *encrucijadas*, and *corillos*.

### *La Brega*

In 2020, WNYC Studios and Futuro Studios produced a seven-part podcast series that used narrative storytelling and investigative journalism to reflect and reveal how la brega has, for centuries, given shape to much of Puerto Rican life. In the opening episode, host Alana Casanova-Burgess defined la brega, showing how Borícuas from San Juan to Queens use the term in their everyday lives. She said:

> There's no perfect English translation for this word that Puerto Ricans use all the time, in a way no other Spanish speakers do . . . If you're Borícua and someone asks you how it's going, how you're doing, you might say, "Ah, ya tu sabes—aqui en la brega." Here, making it work, you know, dealing with it, in the struggle. . . . There's an imbalance of power when you're *bregando*, whether it's against your boss or some larger injustice. It's an underdog's word. A brega implies a challenge we can't really solve, so you have to hustle to get around it . . . it's not just about dealing with a problem . . . it can also be finding a way to fight the system . . . or somehow keep moving. There's an edge of creativity, too, it's like an art.[1]

In his essay, "De Cómo y Cuándo Bregar," scholar Arcadio Díaz Quiñonez used la brega as a lens to understand Puerto Rican history, politics, and identification, arguing that there's something about *bregar* that speaks to puertorriquenidad in general.[2] As Meléndez-Badillo wrote, "[f]or Díaz Quiñones, bregar . . . is a strategic practice of working around colonial violence without necessarily publicly opposing or conceding to it."[3] Or, as Casanova-Burgess put it: "Amidst potholes, protests and metaphors . . . [la brega] sometimes asks too much of Borícuas" but at the same time carries with it "an innate sense of hope."

In this chapter, la brega provides a concrete, critical understanding of the social, political, and historical processes that shaped Puerto Ricans' cultural production over the past century and a half. Furthermore, I highlight how AmeRícan Muslims negotiate their way through numerous bregas that affect them as both Puerto Ricans *and* Muslims, including historical racism, urban poverty, oppressive religio-racial orders like Islamophobia, and natural disasters, as well as austerity measures, mass shootings, diasporic disconnects, political unrest, and Puerto Rico's pernicious and persistent precarity vis-à-vis the pressure cooker of American empire. Expressed through a confluence of anti-Brown racism,[4] Islamophobia, traditional and untraditional colonial power, and other minoritizations at work in the US and its environs, AmeRícan Muslims cope with systemic struggles they cannot necessarily solve or fix via solidarities that their quotidian cosmopolitan contexts make available.

### *Encrucijadas*

Second, I employ the concept of encrucijadas to further illuminate the struggle's intersectional aspects. Encrucijadas are "crossroads or intersections of encounter, contact, and interplay which challenge and question, make suffer, or empower and regenerate."[5] They "refer to encountered uncertainties, crucial moments of decision taking, the mere possibility of change, or the troublesome place of multiple oppressions." When I utilize the term, I emphasize the multiple binds and spaces of encounter, division, and generative friction that create both uncertainty and opportunity for AmeRícan Muslims in the context of compounded injustices and long-standing, shared inequalities.

Treating their marginality as both Muslim *and* Puerto Rican in the context of American empire as an encrucijada, their stories reveal not only their struggles but also the various solidarities and intersectional resiliences that materialize in the process of dealing with "oppression manifest," as Puerto Rican Muslim poet Wendy Díaz puts it. Such an intersectional framework facilitates my "ability to perceive the multiplicities, mutually imbricated"[6] and divergently affective nature of AmeRícan Muslim solidarities in a "rapidly changing and increasingly complex" world.[7] Moreover, I suggest the multiple, mingling, reinforcing, and transformative encrucijadas that AmeRícan Muslims grapple with present a complex case through which to consider broader border problematics in late-modern life. The aim in this chapter is not to disentangle them, but to see what new connections and communities they prompt AmeRícan Muslims—and those they struggle with—to create.

### *Corillos*

In light of the many bregas and encrucijadas in AmeRícan Muslim lives, I turn to the Puerto Rican neologism corillo, meaning one's group of friends, or "crew." A slang word used to refer to friends who hang out together (e.g., in Anuel AA and Tego Calderon's "Jangueo"), a corillo is the crew you run with, or a group of people gathered around a shared cause. I employ the term in this chapter to refer to the relationships that AmeRícan Muslims forge in their resistance to the multiple marginalities made manifest within overlapping American political, economic, and social orders.

The correlation I make between corillo and solidarity is underscored by the term's popular use in reggaetón music (e.g., "Que Dios bendiga mi corillo [Mi corillo, mi corillo]" in "Que Dios Bendiga (Remix)" by Arcangel).

Reggaetón, like many Caribbean cultural creations, is the result of mixture, drawing on numerous rhythmic and lyrical lineages to project "a discursive, resonant sound."[8] A hybrid music style mixing Jamaican dancehall and reggae with hip-hop, salsa, and Latin American bomba y plena, reggaetón came to prominence among Panamanian, Jamaican, and Puerto Rican youth in the 1990s. Its "dembow" beats and range of Caribbean aesthetics, not to mention its more contemporary re-mixture of Spanish/English, proved immensely popular in places like Colombia, the Dominican Republic, Brazil, Spain, Italy, and the US, producing global superstars like Daddy Yankee, Ivy Queen, Karol G, and Bad Bunny. Though reggaetón's themes usually revolve around popular motifs of dancing, love, or partying, they also include anecdotes of the performer's life or societal problems shared by artist and fan alike.

Contemporary reggaetón is often associated with its creative and commercial explosion in Puerto Rico and its diaspora. In the mid-1990s, reggaetón took on a particularly Caribbean flare on the archipelago, but also incorporated influences from DiaspoRicans involved with New York City's hip-hop scene.[9] Since then, it has become an unofficial Puerto Rican "'national' soundtrack and the culture's international musical representative."[10] The product of back-and-forth migration, cosmopolitan assemblage, and the struggle of marginalized Puerto Ricans to be heard on the edges of the American empire,[11] reggaetón is also a vehicle to critique and push back against oppressive social constructs, privileged identifications, urban violence, poverty, and political abuses.[12] Reggaetón artists from Calle 13 to Tego Calderón and Bad Bunny use the sonic genre to critique structural racism in the US and Puerto Rico, center Blackness and African diasporic belonging,[13] express and process Puerto Rico's "tumultuous colonial history" and related "shame," and contest its uncertain political status.[14]

When viewed as part of reggaetón's broader political history, the notion of rolling with one's corillo can be associated with solidarity in political activism. While appreciating intersectionality's theoretical weaknesses and blind spots, Puerto Rican Muslims' marginalizations are interconnected and thus compound and transform their experience of oppression. This leads not only to additional complications and tensions but also to opportunities for intersectional solidarity. At encrucijadas like those faced by AmeRícan Muslims, communities and individuals deploy tools at their disposal to challenge and expose oppression, retain collective memory, and navigate the multivalent interstices of power together,[15] imagining new forms of "intersubjectivity premised in relationality and solidarity."[16] By extension, AmeRícan

Muslims' corillos become a way for them to confront their multiple bregas, creating a heterogeneous range of new connections with a diverse array of fellow agitants in their quest for recognition, justice, and equity.

Therefore, if the previous chapters focused on tensions that AmeRícan Muslims face because of their hyphenated identifications (i.e., Muslim in the Puerto Rican community, Puerto Rican in the Muslim community) and the creative reactions they fostered at the margins of such socialities, this chapter looks at the circumstances where their hybrid identifications and the intersectional nature of their oppressions create new partnerships, perspectives, and practices. As will be shown in the accounts that follow, being suspended between peripheries is a messy, painful, and simultaneously empowering process.[17] After all, and as Jürgen Schaflechner argued in relation to South Asia's religious minorities, intersectionality illustrates not only multiple, overlapping oppressions but also how a marginal position might lead to social, political, or cultural capital.[18]

Moreover, the corillos in these vignettes extend beyond particular issues to help AmeRícan Muslims foster collaborations across religious, cultural, and political divides. In a cosmopolitan world of encounter and enmeshed identifications where minoritization is increasingly the norm and everyday experience is shot through with transnational and global realities, scholars must pay attention to how "[m]inoritarian affiliations or solidarities arise in response to the failures and limits of democratic representation, creating new modes of agency, new strategies of recognition, new forms of political and symbolic, as well as affective, representation."[19] Puerto Rican Muslims embody such affiliations and solidarities as they create new modes of agency, fresh strategies of recognition, and innovative forms of political and symbolic representation out of the materials of their mixed, minoritarian identifications. At the same time, the outworkings of these affiliations and solidarities can be messy and limited. This chapter further illustrates these complications, but also shows the possibilities presented to diverse coalitions as they work together to contest economic exploitation, marginalization, oppressive politics, and neocolonization. In the end, I suggest the new corillos that Puerto Rican Muslims create emerge as a key site for political subversion and social rearticulation in the late-modern.

In particular, the intersection of Puerto Rican Muslim's racial and religious identifications reveals the complex ways they deal with the "unresolved contradictions and ongoing provocation" of colonial legacies[20] such as dispossession, racism, and violent loss. Countering notions of "Muslim first" or other forms of identitarian politics in the face of a variety of challenges facing Muslim and Latinx communities in the US, this chapter illustrates an intersectional approach to shared problems. This intersectional approach is not a panacea, nor is it without its tensions and limitations, but given their intersectional identifications and everyday experiences of diversity and difference, AmeRícan Muslims feel they must adopt a convergent approach to the numerous, overlapping issues they face.

## *¡BASTA YA!* ENOUGH IS ENOUGH.

AmeRícan Muslim lives take place under the shadow of American empire. They are forced to contend with colonial violence and the realities of state repression on a daily basis. The reality of empire marks their bodies, psyche, and souls. Furthermore, the imprint of that imperial coin is a two-sided one. On the one side is the ongoing colonial relationship between the US and Puerto Rico, enforced by a range of social, cultural, political, and economic measures. On the other is the perniciousness of anti-Muslim rhetoric and measures in American media, politics, and public discourse, founded in and exacerbated by the US-sponsored global War on Terror. In short, Muslims and Puerto Ricans share a history of colonial rule, racist politics of oppression and marginalization, and current neocolonial exploitation and estrangement. Even though their experiences are not coterminous, they live under the "shared global structures of imperialism."[21]

It is therefore necessary, and illuminating, to analyze AmeRícan Muslim lives within an encrucijada that combines anti-Muslim fear and hostility with US public rhetoric that situates Puerto Ricans as second-class citizens. AmeRícan Muslims are aware of this double-bind. The ways they speak and act, as well as the ways they express and perform their sense of being and belonging in the US and Puerto Rico, are closely linked to the multivalent political realities of American empire. In short, whether because of Islamophobia or imperial policies and recriminations—or the combination thereof—to be an AmeRícan Muslim is to live dangerously in the face of American empire.

### *American Islamophobia*

Anti-Muslim rhetoric, policies, and actions permeate the US and the wider Americas, albeit with varying influences, emphases, and expressions according to context and community. Often known as "Islamophobia," this prejudice includes a range of discriminatory, exclusionary, and violent practices arising from fear and hostility against Muslims and those perceived as Muslims. A form of cultural racism, Islamophobia instigates and imposes animosity toward those coded as "Muslim" and thus, according to Islamophobia's logics, dangerous because of their religion, culture, ethnicity, national identification, or phenotype. Expressed in law, popular culture, health structures, news media, education, politics, business and employment, as well as numerous other areas of culture and society, by actors on the political left *and* right, Islamophobia and anti-Muslim racism take on flesh-and-blood in Muslim lives across the globe. On a daily basis, on trains and buses, at mosques and shopping malls, on social media and in the neighborhoods where they live, work, and breathe, Muslims and those coded as such are verbally, digitally, and physically attacked, threatened, harassed, vandalized, and accused according to Islamophobia's racialized and neocolonial logics.[22]

Since 9/11, the subsequent War on Terror, and the rhetoric surrounding recent US political campaigns, this climate only intensified.[23] Muslims are subject to intrusive government surveillance and profiling programs, detentions and deportations, registration systems, hate crimes, and infringements on freedom of religion in the form of anti-Sharia laws or localized and political resistance to the building of mosques and minarets. This overt hate is often exacerbated by how Muslims lack political representation or other positions in society to properly influence, control, or sway public opinion and popular narratives. What most people think they know about Islam and Muslims comes from media, which frequently frame Muslim lives according to violence and oppression.[24] There is also an associated network of Islamophobic benefactors—social media figures, politicians, activists, authors, and organizations who make money demonizing and dehumanizing Muslims.[25]

Islamophobia and anti-Muslim sentiment have significant impacts on Muslims across Latin America and the Caribbean as well. Historically, Muslims were barred from entering the Americas (e.g., by Spanish colonial authorities in the sixteenth century), limited in their ability to practice their religion, or treated with suspicion as potential rebels, enemies, or underminers of European imperial designs in the hemisphere.[26] Arab migrants to the Americas—Christian, Muslim, and otherwise—also faced racialized discrimination since their first arrival in the hemisphere in the nineteenth century.[27] In the Triple Frontera region, where Argentina, Paraguay, and Brazil meet, Arab Muslims were the targets of undue suspicion as well as unjust interrogations and arrests at the hands of various states, according to what

John Tofik Karam calls the War on Terror's "flexible logic" and its multiple machinations in various American political orders.[28] To different degrees, these historical anti-Muslim prejudices and policies continue to feed into Islamophobic logics today.

Contemporary experiences of Islamophobia in the Americas vary according to context. In Trinidad and Tobago, where media attention has focused on a Muslim-led coup in 1990 and Trinidadians joining ISIS in the 2010s, Muslim youth have reported being negatively impacted by the "bombardment of negative images of Islam" and "prejudices against Muslims."[29] In Guadeloupe, the construction of "difference and 'otherness'" precipitated by the War on Terror led to the unfair treatment of Michel Madassamy, "a local labor activist of East Indian descent" who was compared to Osama Bin Laden.[30] In Mexico, Muslims have faced discrimination and marginalization despite being a small minority. And in 2018, a group of Muslims were denied entry to a hotel in the state of Chiapas because of their religion.[31] Overall, and while there are more instances that could be cited, these examples show how Islamophobia manifests itself in Latin America and the Caribbean, and how Muslim communities across the hemisphere face significant challenges and discrimination within the "tenuous public spheres" shaped by the War on Terror and local political, economic, and social regimes.[32]

In the US, Latinx Muslims often find that combined rhetoric around immigration and religious extremism create a heady mix of Islamophobia, anti-immigrant sentiment, and a host of American fears about crime, disease, and a loss of cultural privilege—what historian Nathaniel Deutsch called the "fear of a brown planet."[33] This multipronged fear is distilled into a consistent through-line in certain sectors of US media, politics, and education,[34] which perpetuate a narrative that the country is deeply threatened by immigration—particularly by the creeping menace of Muslim migrants. In each successive election cycle, immigration becomes a major bone of contention, paired with fears of Islamic terror and infiltration.[35] The combined nativist language that imbues the discourse on these issues can then foster and create overlaps between anti-Muslim and anti-Latinx violence and hate.[36]

Latinx Muslims—AmeRícan Muslims among them—struggle within such an environment. In 2017, when Nabra Hassanen of Virginia was raped and murdered by Darwin A. Martinez Torres, an undocumented immigrant from El Salvador, a robust discussion on Islamophobia within the Latinx community and how it impacts the lives of Latinx Muslims occurred online. Puerto Rican Muslim activist Hazel Gómez wrote that in reaction to the news, "Muslims from other backgrounds have begun to lash out at the Latinx undocumented community to cope. This is not how we can move forward." She continued, "As a Latina Muslim, I feel as if I have to constantly remind Muslims 'Hey, not all Latinos are drug dealers/criminals'" and "then swerve to my Latinx community and be like, 'Hey, not all Muslims are extremists." She concluded, "Both my ethnic community and my religious community need to come together more, drop the stereotyping, and realize we have more in common than not."

AmeRícan Muslims like Gómez shared numerous experiences with Islamophobia and anti-Muslim racism with me during my research. Their stories included overt acts of discrimination, such as hate crimes and employment discrimination, as well as more subtle forms of bias, like the portrayal of Muslims in the media and the public sphere. In 2015, a group of Muslims told me they faced local pushback when they wanted to open a mosque in the town of Bayamón. Likewise, in the summer of 2017, a Puerto Rican Muslim woman claimed she was attacked by a group of men who shouted anti-Islamic slurs at her in the Bronx. During Ramadan 2016, a group of Muslims were harassed while they tried to pray at a public park in San Juan, and in August 2018, a Muslim woman was denied service at a salon in the city of Ponce because of her hijab.

In an interview with Lizza of San Germán (a city in the southwest of Puerto Rico) in 2022, she related how she was asked if she was cold when she began wearing a red-and-white hijab to work. She said:

> When I became a Muslim, I was working in [. . .] an office setting. It took me about three months to feel, to really feel comfortable dressing more Islamically. It took a while . . . so I would only use the hijab on Fridays. When they first saw me, the boss that I used to have, he asked me, "Are you sick? Are you cold? Because you're covered. Do you feel cold?" And I just said it's because I want to use it. But I never said anything about Islam or anything. Because that boss, he was a pastor of a Pentecostal church. I didn't want to go into it. It took me another three months . . . we can say I came out of the closet as a Muslim.[37]

Although she did not find the exchange to be "explicitly Islamophobic," Lizza felt there was an implicit discrimination, or at the very least ignorance about Islam, Muslims, and Muslim sartorial practices at play in the interaction. From that point on, she feared bringing up her religious choices in a context where she knew there was a high probability for misunderstanding, judgment, and possible professional repercussions.

Others shared how they were questioned by family and neighbors after converting. Some were asked whether they were brainwashed by ISIS or were going to "change their name to Osama." Others spoke of being provoked and taunted by neighbors, friends, and family for fasting during Ramadan. In the 2009 documentary film, *New Muslim Cool*, rapper and activist Hamza Pérez detailed a 2006 police raid on his mosque on Pittsburgh's North Side. The raid and its aftermath deeply impacted Pérez and his fellow mosque-goers. They believed they were already under surveillance by the FBI, a well-documented phenomenon that illustrates the federal police force's "sustained fixation on Muslims as the perennial suspects in domestic terrorism," which "continues to pervade counterintelligence driven efforts" in the US.[38] Although the police claimed they were chasing a convicted felon on gun charges, the raid occurred during Friday prayers. Hamza and others in the community were baffled by the invasion. Processing his own pain and confusion, Pérez made it clear in the documentary that Muslims are an "open book" and said, "We don't got nothin' to hide from the FBI."

Aldo, an outspoken, bespectacled activist in the Bronx often seen wearing a black-and-white Palestinian *keffiyeh* around his neck at various marches, public events, and protests in the New York City metroplex, sought to sum up many of his fellow Puerto Rican Muslims' feelings in regard to their experiences with Islamophobia and anti-Muslim racism in a Facebook post in May 2016 titled, "The Tyranny Against Muslims in America." His post, a stream-of-consciousness relation of the oppression he feels and hears from fellow Muslims, is an unrefined and frank protest against the multiple instances of hate—both subtle and overt—related above. It can be read as an abstract for the Puerto Rican Muslim experience with Islamophobia and anti-Muslim racism as a whole. He wrote:

> Muslim Americans and our immigrating population of the Muslim faith are suffering what is a back lash [*sic*] of collateral damage by vicious acts of hate crimes [. . .] most are not even reported due to the fear [. . .] of not being seen as a victim but rather a terrorist. In New York City alone each day Muslim woman [*sic*] walking to schools with their children, jobs, grocery shopping [or] just because they wear a hijab are targets of hate crimes. Where Muslim men wearing their traditional garb or speaking their native language would subject them as targets of hate crime or falsely accused of a terrorist plot. Is

> this a life a [*sic*] freedom and justice in the pursuit of happiness or is this a psychological war fare [*sic*] of fear being placed on Muslim Americans. As a Muslim and Puerto Rican, I see how people after I state that I practice the Islamic faith their faces change as if it were the worst crime in the world but patiently I express my reasons and what is Islam [*sic*] and they get to understand that Muslims and Islam does [*sic*] not hate the United States that [*sic*] rather individuals which falsely may say they practice Islam commit criminal acts which the news exploits as if it were every Muslim in the world.

In conclusion, he wrote, as he often signs off his posts, "UNITY IS THE ONLY SOLUTION FOR OUR VOICES TO BE HEARD." This emphasis on unity and solidarity emerges out of the overlapping experiences of oppression shared by and between Puerto Ricans, Muslims, and Puerto Rican Muslims. It was an oft-repeated theme as I spoke with AmeRícan Muslims, helping form the basis for some of the corillos created to contest and combat the multivalent marginalizations they face under the shadow of American empire.

### *The "oldest colony in the world"*

If Muslim lives must be situated within the context of Islamophobia and its racialized and neoimperial logics, then it is also impossible to understand Puerto Rico or Puerto Ricans without recognizing the colonial reality that has shaped the island's architecture, economics, language, politics, and people for the last five hundred years. In the words of historian Jorell A. Meléndez-Badillo, Puerto Rican history is one of struggle, resistance, and that of "a non-sovereign nation along with its contradictions, hopes, and potential futures."[39] Thus, a brief overview of that condition—with a particular focus on US colonization—is necessary to understand the AmeRícan Muslim experience.

After nearly four hundred years of colonization by the Spanish, the US invaded and occupied Puerto Rico during the Spanish-American War in 1898. Since then, Puerto Rico has remained under US jurisdiction, with the US government possessing the power to pass laws and regulations that determine daily life on the archipelago. Between the 56th (1898) and 117th (2021) Congresses, US federal lawmakers debated more than 140 bills providing for the resolution of Puerto Rico's territorial status, including the Jones-Shafroth Act of 1899, which granted US citizenship to anyone born in Puerto Rico and the still-binding "commonwealth" status from the 1952 Puerto Rican constitutional referendum.[40] Nonetheless, Puerto Rico is still treated as a territory rather than a fully sovereign nation.

As neither a state of the union nor a sovereign republic, but rather a "free associated state" (estado libre asociado), Puerto Rico is a colony in all but name. Without the same representation in Congress afforded to citizens of recognized states, this means that Puerto Ricans do not have the same rights and protections as US citizens, even though they are considered US nationals. Puerto Rico does enjoy a relative degree of political autonomy, a strong national sentiment, and, until recently, a higher standard of living than most colonies. Thus, some call Puerto Rico a "postcolonial colony," and Puerto Ricans "a nation without a state," seeing as the archipelago "belongs to but is not part of the United States."[41]

Today, Puerto Rico's relationship with the US remains a matter of debate and controversy. The "status question," as it is called, has resulted in multiple, overlapping consequences for the archipelago and its diaspora. Some Puerto Ricans advocate for full independence from the US, while others argue for a closer relationship or even statehood. Despite these differences, one thing is clear: the history of US colonialism in Puerto Rico has a profound and lasting impact on the archipelago and its people, and "the Puerto Rican colonial conflict must necessarily take into consideration the various and multiple forms that colonialism entails."[42] For example, the US brought many of its own cultural influences to Puerto Rico—from the prevalence of the English language to the proliferation of Pentecostal churches and fast-food chains like Krispy Kreme or Burger King.

Puerto Rico's colonial status—and by extension Puerto Ricans' marginalized place in American political, social, and cultural orders—was brought into sharp relief in 2017, when Hurricane María struck Puerto Rico and caused widespread damage to the archipelago's infrastructure and economy. The US government's response to the hurricane was widely criticized as inadequate, and many Puerto Ricans felt they were not given the same level of assistance as recognized US states in the aftermath of disaster. In particular, there were well-documented discrepancies between resources allocated to Hurricane Harvey recovery efforts in Texas in August 2017 and those three weeks later in Puerto Rico following Hurricane María.[43]

In addition to during, and in the wake of, natural disasters, American imperialism also shapes various aspects of Puerto Rico's economy and financial standing. Initially, the US invested heavily in Puerto Rico's economy, building infrastructure and attracting foreign investment. This helped modernize and industrialize the archipelago but also led to the concentration of wealth in the hands of elites.[44] Many Puerto Ricans were left behind and struggled to make a living, leading to widespread poverty and inequality. For example, the archipelago was long a hub for the production of pharmaceuticals, thanks to its favorable tax laws and access to the US market. However, the US government used Puerto Rico as a dumping ground for hazardous chemical byproducts and waste, which led to environmental contamination and health problems for many Puerto Ricans. The US's "unfinished colonial experiment and its legacy of racially rooted imperialism"[45] shapes Puerto Rico's real estate market as well. US investors continue to buy up tracts of land or properties on the archipelago and develop them for tourism and other purposes. This leads to the displacement of many Puerto Ricans and the gentrification of certain areas, the concentration of wealth in the hands of resourced elites, and massive outmigration as Puerto Ricans seek better financial security and representation in the US.[46]

Finally, for decades, Puerto Rico has been dependent on massive transfer payments from the US federal government to provide public services (from education to pensions and infrastructure projects), which results in the accrual of massive public debt to US creditors.[47] The territory's escalating debt, combined with a crumbling economy, caused three major credit rating agencies to downgrade Puerto Rico's debt to "non-investment grade," also known as "junk status," in 2014. In 2016, the US Congress passed PROMESA, which established a financial control board of seven unelected officials directly named by the US president to oversee Puerto Rico's financial affairs. The control board was given the power to make decisions concerning the archipelago's budget, including the ability to cut spending in areas like healthcare and education or restructure its debt. But by 2017, Puerto Rico had accumulated more than $70 billion in public debt and more than $50 billion in public pension liabilities. This was the equivalent of almost 70 percent of the territory's gross domestic product (GDP) (as compared to the average debt-to-GDP ratio for federal states, which was around 17 percent).

Unlike recognized states, however, Puerto Rico's government could not file for municipal bankruptcy. Governor Ricardo Rosselló declared a form of bankruptcy in 2017 anyway. Months later, Hurricane María hit Puerto Rico, all but decimating the archipelago's power grid and causing billions of dollars in additional devastation. Eventually, in March 2022, Puerto Rico's government formally exited bankruptcy, completing the largest public debt restructuring in US history. The debt restructuring plan reduced claims against Puerto Rico's government from $33 billion to just over $7.4 billion. While many celebrated the news, it is unlikely the archipelago will be able to access financial markets because of its ongoing "junk status" rating. Furthermore, the PROMESA board is expected to remain in place until Puerto Rico has four consecutive balanced budgets. Many Puerto Ricans feel that the creation of PROMESA was a violation of their sovereignty and that the control board was acting in the interests of US creditors rather than the people of Puerto Rico—hence its colloquial nickname, "La Junta."[48]

The archipelago's liminality and lack of recognition also led to differential and discriminatory treatment at a broader societal level for Puerto Ricans in the US, who face what Carmen Teresa Whalen calls, "a plethora of limited opportunities."[49] For example, in 2017, a national poll reported that 46 percent of US citizens were unaware that Puerto Ricans are fellow citizens.[50] More often than not, they are lumped together with the pre-existing category of other Latinx migrants[51] or considered—as the US Supreme Court put it in 1901—"foreign to the U.S. in a domestic sense." Thus, even if they physically and psychically cross borders, DiaspoRicans remain in the same colonial field. And the nuances, ambivalences, and contradictions of coloniality travel with them.

Altogether, after 405 years of Spanish colonization followed by 127 years of US occupation, Puerto Rico is a Spanish-speaking, Afro-Hispanic, Caribbean nation within the environs, and under the powerful sway, of a broader American imperial order. Thus, at the heart of AmeRícan Muslims' adaptations, affectations, and sense of peoplehood is their reaction and resistance to this ongoing reality. Many Puerto Rican Muslims do not see the US as "the land of the free" but as an empire whose "freedom" for its privileged classes is constituted by colonial power, which leaves those on the margins to struggle in undefined territories and underprivileged circumstances. Thus, Puerto Rican Muslims are already accustomed to living a "double life" as Puerto Ricans.[52] But as converts, they take on additional layers of complicated, and divergent, identifications that further bifurcate and burden their sense of being and belonging. In both cases, however, they do not navigate this ambiguity alone. Some push back from the colonial margins and try to carve out their own distinct place "in between" global identities and local loyalties by banding together with others. This becomes evident in the potency of solidarity expressed by Puerto Rican Muslims with the Palestinian cause.

## "PUERTO RICO CON PALESTINA. PUERTO RICO CON LA INTIFADA."

"We've been here before," Margarita says as she holds a sign with bold, red and green letters exclaiming, *¡Basta ya genocdio!* Variously translated as "enough is enough" or "stop already," *basta ya* is an exclamation of exasperation. And Margarita *is* exasperated. "What I mean is [that] we've done this before," she explains, "when they [the Israeli military] evicted families in Sheikh Jarrah in 2021, when Israel invaded Gaza in 2014, after Hurricane María, when they [the US Navy] bombed Vieques, during the Second Intifada, I was out here, protesting. Enough is enough!" Wearing a loose, floral, floor-length dress, brown jacket, and burgundy head covering, Margarita joined thousands of other Puerto Ricans in November 2023 demonstrating in Brooklyn and Manhattan on behalf of Palestinians, demanding a ceasefire in the Israel-Hamas war. At the march, Puerto Rican flags flew next to Palestinian ones alongside signs reading *Puerto Rico con Palestina* or "Puerto Ricans for Palestine." Other protestors paired keffiyehs, headdresses that have become associated with the Palestinian cause, with black-and-white banners representing Puerto Rican resistance to US colonialism. As an AmeRícan Muslim, Margarita feels compelled to take to the streets. But even before she became Muslim, Margarita possessed a sense of solidarity with people in Gaza and the West Bank. "We share a history of oppression, of being under empire's foot, of being a people without a nation," she says, "so I'll continue to show up until Palestine *and* Puerto Rico are free."

Puerto Rican demonstrations for justice on behalf of Palestinians, and Palestinian solidarity with Puerto Ricans, are nothing new. Forged in their common colonial condition, Puerto Ricans and Palestinians have long spoken up for each other's fight against imperialism and for independence. For example, various Palestinian liberation movements have been part of a wide repertoire of struggles and cross-class collaborations that have marked the Puerto Rican independence movement over the years.[53]

For Puerto Rican Muslims in the archipelago and diaspora, that solidarity takes on additional, resonant meaning. Converts like Ibrahim feel Palestine and Puerto Rico experience analogous forms of oppression and exploitation within broader political, racial, and social orders of American empire. While respecting the distinct differences between their situations, Ibrahim saw parallels between Palestinian experiences in the Middle East and Puerto Ricans' experiences on the archipelago and in the diaspora.

Speaking with me during a work break at a posh Italian restaurant in Santurce—a colorful, artistic neighborhood in San Juan—Ibrahim says, "Puerto Ricans are too small-minded. Maybe it's the colonial situation, but they can't think beyond the island." But the former ballet dancer, BMX biker, skateboarder, and punk rocker, whom I met after being intrigued by his hipster socks at Eid al-Fitr prayers just a couple weeks earlier, grew up reading about Puerto Rico's colonial status. This helped him break out of the archipelago's stranglehold on his mind, he says.

Both academics, his parents provided Ibrahim with a wide array of books through which he perceived himself and the world around him. The first book he remembers reading was *El Manifiesto Comunista* by Karl Marx and Friedrich Engels. Developing a sense of solidarity with various resistance and leftist movements across the globe—from the Zapatistas to Hugo Chávez and the Palestine Liberation Organization (PLO)—Ibrahim became thirsty for understanding the motivations of various "freedom fighters." His parents gave him a Qur'an as a gift around 2011 and told him it was "beautiful literature" he should get to know. Inside, he found much more. "As soon as I began reading it, it changed my life," he says, "I stopped drinking, stopped smoking, stopped eating pork. Then, I decided I better find a masjid. For most converts, Muslims find them. I didn't have Muslim friends. I found the masjid. What started as a sentiment, or a sense of solidarity, led to the shahadah."

With a conspicuous tattoo of Leila Khaled—a prominent member of the Popular Front for the Liberation of Palestine and "icon of the Palestinian liberation movement"[54]—on the inside of his forearm, Ibrahim says he often draws on global solidarities for inspiration and consolation in the midst of la brega. For him, la brega is the daily struggle to provide for his family in Puerto Rico, where an economic crisis was exacerbated by natural disasters and the continual governmental failures and broken promises outlined above. Although he says he would love to study to become "a proper Puerto Rican sheikh," he knows he needs to work. "In this economy, I can't just study," he says. To get by and push back against at what he sees as injustices leveled at the Puerto Rican people, he often draws on Islamic principles and inspiration from fellow Muslims in other parts of the world. He says:

> I grew up as part of the Disciples of Christ [an evangelical "restoration church" with 105 communities in Puerto Rico] and they didn't provide us with real resources for the world. In Christianity, they

> keep spiritual things separate from things like science, mathematics, and politics. In Islam, it's all one thing. It provides *movimiento* for popular political movements. In Puerto Rico, they raise the taxes by 4 percent and all these Christians say nothing. They just wait for the resurrection or hope their bank account will grow miraculously. They just sit there and take it. Islam channels our political energy.

Like Ibrahim, Adrián—introduced earlier—also grew up in a "reading family." After meeting him at jummah at the masjid in Vega Alta, Adrián invited me over to his mom's place for dinner. I obliged and over a meal of *chicharrones de pollo* we talk about his involvement with the Palestinian diaspora community on the archipelago and his political solidarity with their cause. Surrounded by a pile of books ranging from Marx to Foucault and Nelson A. Denis's *Guerra contra todos los puertorriqueños*, we discuss his increasing political engagement over the years and how that led to his eventual conversion to Islam. Raised in what he calls a "leftist, activist" household, he was drawn to the plight of Palestinians from an early age. This is what initially drew him to Islam, he says, "I saw this country of one million people taking on the second largest army in the world and winning, and I wondered what gave them this power. What inspired them." He connected this back to his efforts in the cause of Puerto Rican independence. He dove deep into the stories of anti-colonial movements in Muslim majority countries like Afghanistan and Iran, Palestine and Egypt.

Later that week, while walking around the UPRRP campus, where Adrián took part in the protest action in spring 2017, he shows me some of his "public art interventions." On walls and hallways across the campus, Adrián put the intersectionality of his politico-religious sentiments and solidarities into material, graffitied form. In addition to the painting described at the start of the chapter, Adrián painted a picture of a Palestinian woman holding a flag in one hand and displaying a peace sign with the other. Her eyes shaded with a stylized keffiyeh wrapped around her face, Adrián painted her as a figure of solidarity with the protesting students. At the same time, Adrián says he wanted to express the mutual support of independentistas like himself with the Palestinian cause. Scribbled in red graffiti across the upper-left corner of the mural were the words, "Puerto Rico con Palestina. Puerto Rico con la Intifada." Adrián says he felt both murals—depicting strong Muslim women in places far away—resonated with Puerto Ricans who were fighting against the injustice of their own colonial situation. Despite geographic distance and geopolitical disparities, he says, "we can draw strength from each other and perhaps be inspired that through our struggle we might make a better tomorrow." Referencing Palestine in particular, he elaborates:

> Puerto Rico has a long history of resistance to colonialism and imperialism, and Palestinians have a lot to learn from Puerto Ricans about how to build and sustain a struggle for justice and self-determination. In turn, Puerto Ricans can learn from the Palestinian experience and the strategies and tactics that have been developed to resist occupation and oppression.

Ibrahim and Adrián are far from alone in their solidarities with Palestinian political causes. Nor are they the only converts whose path to Islam began with a sense of resilience in facing, and facing up to, difficult situations in Puerto Rico. Multiple AmeRícan Muslims I spoke with saw echoes and shared sentiments between their political situation and that of other Muslims around the globe, in places like Chechnya, Afghanistan, Iran, and Palestine. The sense of solidarity between them serves as a political, social, and religious alliance rooted in shared experiences of colonization, resistance, and struggles for self-determination.

In particular, they expressed how both Palestine and Puerto Rico are subjected to foreign domination, experiencing comparable forms of oppression and exploitation. Palestine has been under Israeli occupation since 1967, with the Israeli government implementing policies that resulted in the displacement of Palestinians, the confiscation of their land, and the suppression of basic human rights. Similarly, as detailed above, they opined how Puerto Rico has been a territory of the United States since 1898, with the US government imposing its control over the archipelago through various means, including military intervention and economic policies that disadvantaged the Puerto Rican people. In both cases, imperial powers sought to erase the cultural identities of the colonized peoples, imposing their own languages and cultural practices while suppressing local ones. This process of cultural assimilation resulted in both Palestinians' and Puerto Ricans' marginalization and oppression.

Another factor is their shared experience of resistance. Both groups engage in grassroots organizing and political activism in order to assert their rights and challenge the dominant powers that seek to control them. In Palestine, this resistance has been variously configured, including nonviolent protests, civil disobedience, and armed resistance. Palestinian activists also seek to raise awareness of their plight through international solidarity campaigns, seeking support from progressive movements around the world. Similarly, Puerto Ricans have engaged in multiple forms of resistance, including protests, strikes, and armed opposition to the US government, receiving support from progressive movements around the world along the way.

As a result, solidarities between Palestinians and Puerto Ricans have also taken numerous forms, including grassroots organizing, political activism, and cultural exchange. In "Puerto Rican Chicago,"[55] Sara Awartani wrote about how "Puerto Ricans sharpened their political identities in conversation with the struggle for Palestinian liberation," through which they "learned to think and operate within a 'Third World' revolutionary political condition."[56] Elsewhere, Awartani shared how "individuals imprisoned for alleged participation in the Puerto Rican armed clandestine organization Fuerzas Armadas de Liberación Nacional (FALN; Armed Forces of National Liberation),"[57] the YLP,[58] or the Puerto Rican Solidarity Committee (PRSC) "framed Puerto Rico's anti-colonial struggle" within an enlarged and "reimagined geography of liberation,"[59] which drew on, and declared solidarity with, Palestinians' struggle for independence. These struggles simultaneously "disrupted narratives of US exceptionalism" and articulated Palestine "in the Puerto Rican political imaginary."[60] In more recent years, young Palestinians and Puerto Ricans could be seen holding signs of solidarity with regard to each other's respective anti-colonial struggles at public events and marches on college campuses in the US and Puerto Rico.[61]

In the lives of AmeRícan Muslims, the two narratives become intertwined to reveal a complex, and cosmopolitan, nexus of solidarity around issues of independence, being a people without a nation, and facing an intersection of oppressive orders and phobias in the late-modern age. Alim, a New York City–based poet and self-described "social justice activist" who identifies as a Black Puerto Rican Muslim, discussed these intersections online in April 2021. Alim is in his mid-thirties, sports a thick black beard and proudly says he is both "Maoist and Muslim." His multiple allegiances are reinforced by the beret on his head, inspired by those worn by members of the Young Lords Party, but featuring a Puerto Rican flag with a crescent moon and star in place of the typical white star. Behind him on the wall is a portrait of Malcolm X and a black-and-white Puerto Rican flag—created as part of protests against PROMESA and now a general symbol of resistance and grief among Puerto Ricans. Alim told me that his devotion to the Young Lords' legacy, Maoist ideology, and Islamic faith reflects the broader solidarities Puerto Ricans are in search of. "And that search, that search for broader solutions, is about finding a way forward. We have to reject individualism, lean into organizing, build solidarity with our comrades—wherever they are found—and work to the liberation of all," he says. Invoking the Black Panthers, FALN, Latin Kings, PLO, and YLP, Alim said he seeks to combine the received wisdom of those who came before him in order to "develop an advanced method of socialism that exposes the contradictions of the capitalist order." He continues:

> El futuro de Puerto Rico está en nuestras manos [Puerto Rico's future is in our hands]. To defeat the imperialist power, the imperialist classes, we have to form collectives. Make collective decisions to solve the problems that we all struggle against. These groups, our forebears, were always "of the people," not of a particular people. We have a shared cause because we share common oppressors. That's why each time I get in front of my people, I offer a comrade salute, a revolutionary salute, and an as-salamu alaikum. One Lord, one people, staying noble. . . . Pa'lante, siempre pa'lante, [raising his fist] power to the people.

Alim's words about solidarity and common oppressors echo not only those of Adrián, Ibrahim, and Aldo but also those of Alianza Islámica and other Puerto Ricans who have long sought to break away from colonial memories to pursue alternative futures.

## AN EID OBITUARY

Solidarity has been a consistent theme for Puerto Rican Muslim converts across the years. This came to the fore on May 16, 2020, when Rahim Ocasio—a founding member of Alianza Islámica—posted a video to the "Boricuas Embraced by Islam" Facebook page entitled, "Alianza Islamica in NY, celebrating Eid in 1998." As the video begins, a group of children is playing with balloons at the front of what looks like a community event space in a New York City basement. There is a flag with two green bands separated by a single white band with the first line of the shahadah in the middle hanging behind them, a nod to the flag of al-Andalus. All the while, Cuban trombonist and bandleader Generoso Jiménez's "Llegaron del Otro Mundo" blares in the background as the camcorder zooms in on the DJs, who smirk and wave from their setup in the corner of the room. As the camera pans out, Khalil—wearing a blue thawb, dark-rimmed wire glasses, and a black kufi—stands in front of a column bedecked with green and yellow balloons. He smiles a generous, toothy grin and greets the anonymous videographer, "Feliz Ramadan."

It is just after 2 p.m. on January 29, 1998, and Alianza Islámica is hosting a celebration for Eid al-Fitr. Entrees like *arroz con gandules*, pasteles, and a leg of lamb (in place of *pernil* pork) are served alongside desserts like flan and *arroz con dulce*. *Congueros* (conga players) play *tumbaos*, *bombas*, and *guaguancos*, and a DJ spins records in the corner. As already discussed, when Alianza Islámica established themselves, they leveraged and largely adopted a broader Nuyorican and post-colonial Puerto Rican consciousness that was emerging in New York City and its metro area in the 1960s and '70s. In an op-ed for *The Islamic Monthly* in May 2016, Ocasio wrote:

> By the mid to late 1960s, the pacifism of the Civil Rights Movement had given way to restlessness and anger as minority communities grew impatient with the slow progress of social and economic reform. Into this social milieu, four Puerto Rican teenagers from Spanish Harlem—El Barrio . . . became deeply involved with the struggle for social and economic justice for Puerto Ricans on the mainland and freedom and independence for the island of Puerto Rico. We all became involved with the most progressive grassroots movement of the time, The Young Lords Party, and its ancillary organizations. We entered various phases thereafter, two of us even becoming members of the Five Percent Nation, an offshoot of the Nation of Islam. In time, our collective journey brought us to Islam.[62]

The confluence of that Nuyorican consciousness and the blossoming of a distinctly Latinx—and particularly Puerto Rican—radical political and cultural revival were reflected in the Eid celebration in 1998.

Around two minutes into the video, the program officially begins with a choral recitation of "Puerto Rican Obituary" by Pedro Pietri, a prominent member of the YLP. Apologizing in advance for any "offensive language" in the poem, attendees were invited by event leaders to listen for how the poem resonates with their experience as Puerto Ricans *and* as Muslims: "We're hoping, inshallah, you might take the general notion of the poem, which we feel identifies with our Puerto Rican roots and culture and struggles here in America . . ." Then, an ensemble of Alianza Islámica members recites stanzas from the poem, viscerally giving voice to Puerto Ricans'

FIGURE 5.2 *Jorge "Popmaster Fabel" Pabon shows off his Alianza Islámica sweatshirt, featuring symbols of Puerto Rico's Taíno, African, and Spanish heritage, outside of an event in Queens, New York.*

economic, political, and social situation in the US—as citizens whose culture and hearts belong to Borikén, but who struggle living as minorities in the urban centers of the nation that inherited Puerto Ricos's colonial mantle from Spain. As the poem, and its lines about pledging "allegiance to the flag that wants them destroyed" and being "proud to belong to a community of gringos who want them lynched" end, the Alianza Islámica crowd responds: "Takbir! Allahu akbar!"

Influenced by the "revolutionary center of political activism and the struggle for civil rights" around them,[63] the Alianza Islámica story further illustrates the long-standing encrucijadas and corillos created in the midst of AmeRícan Muslim bregando. In this instance, the pressures faced by Puerto Ricans and other minoritized people groups in and around the New York City metro area—and informed by broader Puerto Rican and global anti-colonial discourse—helped them find one another, create new communities, and forge fresh pathways for the pursuit of liberation and justice.

## THREE PUERTO RICAN IMAMS

Alianza Islámica, however, did not last forever. After a fire at their second headquarters in the Bronx, the group dissipated. Yet, their influence and legacy remained. Moreover, Alianza Islámica's founders remained key interlocutors and reference points in the broader Latinx Muslim and Puerto Rican Muslim landscape in the US. Primarily, they served as a source of inspiration and guidance for later generations of AmeRícan Muslim activists who formed their own groups to address new problems facing *su gente*.

I saw this at work in September 2017. I had just left fieldwork in Puerto Rico and was settling into new digs in Harlem. It was then, with distinct dread, that I tracked Hurricane María as it formed in the Atlantic and headed with deadly force toward Puerto Rico. After making landfall near Yabucoa on September 18, the hurricane's 175-miles-per-hour winds and torrential rains ravaged the archipelago. Mobile phone reception and internet were immediately down. Families in the US were cut off from loved ones and no one knew what was happening "back home." As Wendy Díaz said of that September, "the Puerto Rican diaspora in the United States and all over the world watched in horror as their homeland was devastated beyond recognition . . . perhaps the most frustrating ordeal was not being able to communicate with family members to find out if they were safe."[64] Although correspondence was difficult, conversation concerning the archipelago and its people was on overdrive in the US. Amid the furor, AmeRícan Muslims were hyperactive on Facebook: trying to find information, rally support, and quickly collect donations to come to the aid of their brothers and sisters, family, and friends in Puerto Rico.

Once the hurricane struck, none of my contacts got back to me about interviews, and in effect, "fieldwork" as normal went on hiatus. I was but one of thousands from *allá'fuera* waiting for even a shred of news. So, I decided to become a participant in the efforts to raise support and advocate for Puerto Ricans on the archipelago. I attended events, shared donation links on social media, and sent messages to people I knew in Puerto Rico, offering what help I could. It caught my attention, then, when Imam Wesley Lebrón, one of the founders of the aforementioned "Three Puerto Rican Imams" project, posted on the "Boricuas Embraced by Islam" Facebook page soon after the full extent of the storm's devastation became clear. Lebrón explained how, in an effort to connect with, support, and serve family members, friends, and fellow Muslims back on the archipelago, he partnered with fellow Puerto Rican imams Jose "Yusuf" Rios and Daniel Abdullah Hernandez to launch an organization to provide "emergency relief efforts and sustainable projects that addressed and still address the needs of the People of Puerto Rico." They wrote of the project:

> These powerful storms literally hit home for the directors, three Puerto Rican Muslim leaders, and their supporters, who share both their pain and vision, making this a mission of love and solidarity. This project is unique in that it unites various organizations and works collaboratively with others both inside and outside of Puerto Rico, while still working independently in its response. It has successfully brought people together of all faiths and nationalities with the common goal of providing relief to those most affected by the hurricanes and easing some of their hardships (refer to our facebook page for pictures of all the work).

The three imams rushed to Puerto Rico in the aftermath, wearing hats and vests emblazoned with their red and blue logo—including a stylized rendition of the Taíno coquí frog petroglyph—to deliver food, water, household items, and generators to those trying to make their way through the storm's devastation and aftermath.

As part of the Puerto Rican transnational diaspora's efforts "to seek ways to help those in the archipelago,"[65] the Three Puerto Rican Imams worked with various non-Muslim organizations to build homes, serve food, and bring aid to the common cause of "nuestra gente," as Lebrón put it. They partnered with a local Catholic parish to meet pressing community needs in Punto Santiago, Humacao; the mutual aid society La Olla Común to provide breakfast in Río Piedras; Centro de Apoyo Mutuo (CAM) to serve people in Bartolo, Lares; a community kitchen in the infamous La Perla neighborhood in Viejo San Juan; and Agitarte, an organization founded in 1997 in Massachusetts by working-class artists and cultural organizers. They also worked with the Islamic Circle of North America's (ICNA) "Muslims for Humanity" relief agency, in partnership with Centro Islámico del Caribe in Montehiedra and Council on American-Islamic Relations (CAIR) in Florida to meet Muslims' particular needs. Furthermore, they collected donations from Bait-ul Jamaat House of Community in Staten Island and the National Elementary Honor Society—Al Madinah School in Brooklyn, New York. Such corillos, forged in the everyday brega after María's devastation and the widely criticized US federal response, allowed them to serve over five thousand families in over forty-two Puerto Rican municipalities.

With their partners, they were able to provide food packages (including staples like rice, milk, oats, angel hair spaghetti, and beans), generators for a community kitchen, laundry facilities, and a medical clinic in Vieques treating patients after the hospital there shut down, and donations for children with special needs in Moca.

The Three Puerto Rican Imams framed their work within multiple registers, both Islamic and philanthropic. They also leaned on the language of solidarity, described their work as "mutual aid," seeing in it a means of liberation for their people. Yusuf Rios even said their efforts were aimed at bringing unity "between and among oppressed peoples." To that end, and beyond their work in Puerto Rico, the organization went on to pursue and complete projects in other locales, including Hawaii, Guatemala, Haiti, Saudi Arabia, Gaza, and communities in Texas, Ohio, and New Jersey.

For example, in late summer 2021, they shared that they successfully commenced the construction of a well in Gaza. Their stated intention was to not only alleviate immediate concerns but also pursue broader justice initiatives and make a name for Islam—and Puerto Rican Muslims—among those they worked with. Sharing their photos online, they were proud to report that trucks were dropping off pipes and they were already scouting out the location for a second well in the West Bank. Referencing the shared struggle between "Occupied Palestine" and "Occupied Vieques"—a Puerto Rican island once used as a bombing range by the US military and which became a symbol of the archipelago's wider testing ground for "aggressive and exploitative US economic, political, and social policies"[66]—they spoke of the need for concrete solidarity (this time, in the form of a well) among Muslims across the globe.

Whether it is lack of infrastructure in Gaza, acute hunger in Saudi Arabia or Haiti, issues with educational programs and mosque leadership in the US, or natural disasters in the Caribbean, the Three Puerto Rican Imams see their work as a broad effort at uniting the various struggles (bregas) of oppressed peoples and working with others (corillos) in solidarity and mutual aid to address them. The challenge, Rios said, is that oppressed peoples are often divided. "They fight with each other so much they can't focus to come together to see each other as allies and align to address their conditions."[67] Moreover, he emphasized repeatedly the importance of "collective power" in the Three Puerto Rican Imams' work. Rios said their organization was committed to cooperation "in goodness and excellence," mutual aid, mutual consultation, and the careful coordination required to build collective power. He continued:

> To represent the voices and needs of the people, we need to unite for social justice—in Colombia, in Puerto Rico, in Haiti, in Palestine. . . . It's mutual aid and solidarity work that provide the framework and experience for a new social order and community.

The challenge, and opportunity, Rios said, is to constantly resolve

> how [the organization] can bring people of diverse backgrounds and different skill sets together (and the same with various organizations) to collaborate instead of compete and dominate, so we can grow the community to a higher level. The answer? Collaboration, education, and practical participation in collaboration until we get to greater working unity.

Echoing Rios, Lebrón added that to stand up for freedom and stand firm against oppressors, the oppressed need unity. He related this to the Islamic principle of tawhid, or the oneness of Allah and all creation. Quoting the Qur'an and its enjoinders to "stand up for justice" (4:135; 5:8) and injunctions to "enjoin good and oppose evil," (3:110) Lebrón said Islam offers a framework for the pursuit of genuine justice:

> Tawhid teaches us that there is one God and that we are all equal before him. He created us into many tribes and peoples [citing Qur'an 49:13] so that we may know each other and work together for justice. By proposing that the basis for world peace is Allah's oneness (tawhid), Islam provides the basis for the emergence of peace with justice.

To those who feel oppressed, Lebrón encouraged them to be "strong, powerful, and brave." Whatever work they were doing, whatever injustice they were fighting, Lebrón said that Allah sees and hears them. "Stand up and march forward even if by yourself because in reality the one who has Allah is never alone," he said. Thus, what began as a means to address the particular needs that Puerto Ricans faced in the wake of Hurricane María grew to encompass a number of bregas, which were informed by the particular encrucijadas of the AmeRícan Muslim experience, and in turn created new corillos of collective work and action based on a merger of Islamic principles with axioms of social justice work.

In forming partnerships based on the perception of shared struggles—with distinct, contextual expressions and outworkings—the Three Puerto Rican Imams' work recalls that of Alianza Islámica. Similar to Lebrón, Rios, and Hernandez, the leaders of Alianza Islámica felt their mission emerged out of the particular needs of Puerto Ricans in a particular place (New York City) at a particular moment of crisis (in the '80s and '90s). At the same time, they linked their work to wider anti-colonial and antiracist movements for justice and empowerment. Thus, although the Three Puerto Rican Imams' impact is broader and more diffuse, it parallels Alianza Islámica's Puerto Rican founders' motivation to "publicly showcase an expression of Muslim culture that was distinctly Puerto Rican and accurately reflected our contemporary cultural reality" with a result that is "novel yet familiar to both Muslims and non-Muslim alike."[68]

## "UNIDAS POR EL AMOR"

In addition to the marginalizations already mentioned, AmeRícan Muslims are further peripheralized because of additional raced and gendered identifications. Such intersecting identifications are complex, overlapping, and sometimes conflicting sets of simultaneous belonging and *not* belonging, related to representational access to resources of various kinds (organizational, communal, legal, political, etc.). This impacts not only Puerto Rican reverts but also Latinx Muslims as a whole, as Harold Morales wrote:

> A Latino or Muslim may also be a man or a woman; heterosexual or lesbian, bisexual, gay or transsexual; may be Black, White or—Other. A Latino or Muslim may also be a Muslim who has a Latino heritage, a Latino who practices Islam, or a Latino Muslim, the difference here being on what identity is emphasized, marginalized or ignored.[69]

Thus, solidarity work among AmeRícan Muslims can also have its limits, or at least present distinct challenges, when it comes to issues like gender justice or LGTBQI+ politics. With these, AmeRícan Muslims adopt a range of reactions, considerations, and collective actions based on their particular embodied experiences and encounters with political, social, and communal discrimination.[70]

For example, beyond his aforementioned political activism and solidarities, Ibrahim says he also supports LGTBQI+ rights. But only to a degree. Although he does not believe homosexuality is permitted according to the Qur'an or hadith, he says he does not sweat whether a fellow Muslim is gay or not. As he explains, "Nowhere in the Qur'an does it say to hate homosexuals. Sin is sin, like eating pork. All it takes to be a Muslim is the shahadah. Everything else will follow in time." He knows that puts him at odds with most of his fellow mosque-goers at the mezquita in Río Piedras:

> The Muslims on the island are too conservative, too stuck up. Whether it's punk shows or homosexuality, people show up at the masjid and they are received coolly, told that if they become Muslim they have to drop everything right away. Those people never come back to the masjid. That's too harsh, man. When you become a Muslim, you can't just give up your life. It's a gradual thing.

Others take it further, finding friendship and strength through a shared sense of marginalization. One of them is Angelica. A self-described "proud Puerto Rican Muslimah," Angelica advocates for LGBTQI+ rights alongside her outspoken sister in the faith, Sumayah. In a telling photo posted on their respective social media profiles, Angelica and Sumayah pose together at a march held in San Juan in solidarity with the victims of the Pulse Nightclub shooting in Orlando, Florida, in June 2016. Angelica helps hold a flag with a COEXIST logo in rainbow font, bearing the representative symbols of various religious traditions. Next to her, Sumayah wears a rainbow-colored hijab and holds a sign that reads "Sociedad Islámica de Puerto Rico," which she founded in 2002. With the post, Angelica proclaimed they were "unidas por el amor" (united for love). Asked why she not only attended the rally but also proudly—and publicly—posted about it, Angelica says that Puerto Rican Muslims and the LGBTQI+ community must stand united against all forms of hate. For her, the tyranny of Islamophobia and attacks against the LGBTQI+ community are inherently linked. "To end Islamophobia, we have to stand against all kinds of hate crimes," she says.

Beyond rallies, Sumayah takes an active role in the Puerto Rican LGBTQI+ community, having presided at wedding ceremonies in hijab as well as advocating for greater rights and inclusion alongside members of the Colectivo Interreligioso de Mujeres en Puerto Rico (Interreligious

Collective of Puerto Rican Women). Sumayah says she even skipped a community Eid event to take part in a pride march through Viejo San Juan. The result is her increasing ostracism from established Islamic organizations and communities in Puerto Rico. She says, "The imams I used to work with, the partners I had at the local mosques, they've turned their backs on me, published op-eds in the paper denouncing what I do. They've pushed me out."

To find support, Sumayah sought out a range of transnational connections and solidarities with various individuals and groups. Included among them are friends like Angelica in Puerto Rico and fellow activist Vilma in New York City. Sumayah's corillo also includes "fellow Borícua Muslimahs" she knows on Facebook, members of the Nur Ashki al Jerrahi Sufi Order in Mexico City, Mexico, women active in the Women's Piety Movement in Cairo, Egypt, and sympathetic Latinx brothers who are "allies" and advocate for women's rights rather than exacerbating the problem. She even praised those on Facebook who post in solidarity with the #NiUnaMenos ("not one less") movement against gender-based violence or that write about how men should not hit women but go to counseling instead.[71] She says such connections help her form solidarities across the structures of oppression that transcend local communities and national boundaries to impact Muslims across the hemisphere and beyond.[72]

Sumayah admits there is room for disagreement within Islam. Thus, she is willing to work with local mosques and imams again if given the chance. Nonetheless, Sumayah says things need to change:

> The Prophet (PBUH) teaches that we must pursue justice over the rules of religion. For me, when I look at our positions on issues like gay rights, that means a healthier Islam needs to emerge from the conservative forms prevalent today.

Although she draws strength from Muslims who stand with her, Sumayah says she sometimes feels she has more in common with members of the LGBTQI+ community than with other Muslims on the archipelago:

> We know what it is to fight for justice, for inclusion, for the right to exist, to be who we are—Muslim and Puerto Rican, gay and Puerto Rican—no matter our identities. That shared struggle is something I don't have in common with comfortable Muslims who've never known anything else.

## INTERSECTIONALITY IN THE WAKE OF MASS VIOLENCE

Even for those who may not take an active role in campaigning for LGBTQI+ rights, the Pulse Nightclub shooting provided an opportunity for intersectional activism and a juncture for advocating on behalf of Muslim and Latinx minorities of various kinds. Partly, that was because the intersections inherent in the attack itself, as Wilfredo Amr Ruiz shared with me. A US navy veteran and lawyer trained at the University of Puerto Rico and Texas A&M University; Ruiz looks every bit the figure of a Puerto Rican enjoying the Florida lifestyle. One can often find him sporting a *guayabera*, tortoise shell eyeglasses, and a stylish head cap tucked over his curling gray ponytail, which matches his meticulously manicured goatee. As communications director for CAIR in Florida and founder of CAIR *en español*, Ruiz was frequently called into action after the Pulse attack. Then, when Joseph Schreiber, thirty-two, set fire to the Islamic Center of Fort Pierce—where Omar Mateen prayed—on September 11, 2016, in part as a reprisal for the attack and for what he saw as Islam's anti-Jewish, homophobic, and anti-American nature,[73] Ruiz was again on the scene as Florida's Muslims were thrust further into the spotlight.

Amid the "media storm" that followed the shooting,[74] Ruiz frequently spoke to the media, denouncing the "heinous act" and emphasizing how Muslims would be dedicating their "fasting and prayers [to] the victims and their families." He spoke at Latino solidarity events in Orlando, noting that "the vile criminal who perpetrated [the attack] does not represent Islam nor the American Muslim community." He spoke in front of the burned-out section of the Fort Pierce mosque to denounce the individual who struck out at Muslims who not only distanced themselves from the attacker but also raised money ($26,000 USD) and donated blood to the victims of the Pulse attack and their families. As he spoke in front of the blackened hall, Ruiz said of the attack and the intersectional reaction and community organizing that followed it:

> The attack cuts across many communities, many people who are marginalized by society—whether they are gay, Latino, or Muslim. So, the attack meant different things to different people. People who belong to the LGBTQI and Latino communities were significantly affected, Muslims who shared the shooter's background—or the mosque that was attacked by an arsonist as a misdirected reprisal for the shooting. And then, there are people whose identities are in multiple camps.

> That's Puerto Rican Muslims. We are doubly impacted, wrestling with what it means to bridge the Latino community and the Muslim community and respond appropriately to the attack, to help different groups come together in solidarity to fight bigotry against people of all kinds and backgrounds.

As Ruiz shared, the Pulse Nightclub shooting was a particularly powerful encrucijada for Central Florida's Latinx, LGBTQI+, and Muslim communities. Though research shows how media marginalized Latinx and Muslim voices following the attack, focusing instead on LGBTQI+ identifications,[75] there were numerous examples of intersectional activism and solidarity in the shooting's aftermath. Legal scholar Judith E. Koons wrote, "just as forms of oppression are related, so are forms of justice. The Pulse massacre pierced the conscience of the community and illustrated ways relationships of respect can form in a heterogenous public."[76] Koons detailed how social healing, political action, and forms of remembrance were founded in a shared sense of intersectional justice among Latinx and LGBTQI+ community members—and those who associated with both—as they rallied together to advocate for immigration reform or legal protections for sexual minorities.

However, there were limitations to the intersectional potency of such corillos. For example, Florida state officials did "little to acknowledge and act on the historically, economically, and politically driven processes that contribute to LGBTQ+ Latinx populations' vulnerability, resulting in local activist mobilization."[77] Moreover, Muslims were rarely, if ever, mentioned in intersectional analyses of responses to the Pulse attack—despite their frequent, vocal condemnations of the attack and active presence at community solidarity events, as well as increased vulnerability and reception of discriminatory threats and mistreatment after the attack.[78] Partly because the tragedy occurred during the midst of Ramadan, Muslims sprung into charitable action: mobilizing blood drives, setting up GoFundMe campaigns for victims and their loved ones, showing up at events to comfort community members. In particular, Spanish-speaking Muslims and chaplains like Ruiz showed up to be able to connect with the community and grieve by their side.

Rasha Mubarak, a spokeswoman for CAIR in Central Florida who worked alongside Ruiz, said the organization was responding to a number of heightened threats at the time. But more than that, she said, the loss of members of the LGBTQI+ and Latinx community as allies in the fight for justice felt "like the loss of family." She said, "These are people that we go to battle together in the legislative halls against xenophobic legislation. These are people that have stood against Islamophobia, you know. The Muslim community is just mourning and grieving as Floridians."[79] Above all, Mubarak said, to identify as Muslim, Latinx, or LGBTQI+ is to be human:

> Beyond the headlines and hype about Muslims and terrorism, homosexuality and religion, this a story about Orlando, its people, and the intra-personal connections that exist between us. We are Muslim, we are LGBTQ, we are Latinx, but above all we are Orlando strong. There is power in shared pain and we will not let these 49 lives die in vain. [80]

In such an environment, queer Muslims condemned the attacks *and* the response by politicians and others who used it to stir up fear of Islam and Muslims. A student at the University of Florida, Jorge, spoke with me during the 2016 fall semester, a few months following the attack. A vocal social activist on campus, Jorge identifies as a queer, Latinx-Lebanese man from a Muslim family. He spent his whole life in Florida and counts Central Florida as "home." Wearing jean overalls and a baggy white T-shirt, with bleached blond hair and '70s-style gold-rimmed glasses too big for his slim face, Jorge says he watched the story of the Pulse shooting unfold in shock and grief. Having danced in clubs like Pulse with friends, he says:

> It could have been me, not because I am Muslim, but because I am queer. But before the forty-nine bodies were even removed from the building, the attack was being used to justify hatred against Muslims. Hatred against me. The killing of my people is being used to justify the killing of my people. I am scared. I am angry. I am justifiably wondering if there might be another way forward.

He would not, however, let this homophobic attack become a platform for further anti-Muslim rhetoric or violence. "It's time that both parts of me stand together and this event—as horrifying as it is—presents an intersectional moment to do so," he says.

Nonetheless, there were positive intersectional moments Jorge cited as possible ways forward. Even Muslim organizations that were previously quite normative when it came to gender and sexuality began releasing statements after the Pulse shooting that seemed more "inclusive" and "affirming" than ever before, Jorge says. For example, CAIR's National Executive Director at the time, Nihad Awad, sought to make clear in a statement released after the event that "[h]omophobia, transphobia, misogyny, and Islamophobia are all interconnected systems of oppression." He wrote:

> For years, the LGBTQIA community stood shoulder-to-shoulder with the Muslim community as we have faced hate crimes, bigotry, marginalization, and discrimination. . . . Today, we stand firmly and resolutely to declare that this support goes both ways; that we are there for all communities who are the victims of violence and persecution in our country. . . . The liberation of the American Muslim community is inextricably linked with the liberation of all minority groups—Black, Latino, Gay, Jewish, Trans, and every other community that has faced discrimination and oppression in this country. We cannot fight injustice against some groups, and not against others.[81]

For some, this statement signaled a significant shift in the American Muslim landscape on issues of gender and sexuality. They suggested the shift presented an opportunity for those who identified with both "to advocate for their belonging in the larger Muslim community."[82]

Others, however, resisted the statement and the move it implied. They read it as the acquiescence of American Muslims to liberal "grievance culture" over and against traditional readings of Islamic sources and jurisprudence.[83] Still others cited it as evidence of progressive Muslim influence on mainstream organizations like CAIR. Thus, the statement and subsequent reaction to it revealed ongoing tensions among American Muslims regarding LGBTQI+ identifications, normative expressions of Islam and Islamic jurisprudence, and solidarities between mutually marginalized groups. Their perspectives on issues like sexuality and gender, as the above shows, are not monolithic. Instead, they are formed and informed by a range of relational networks, power dynamics, social orders, and notions of being and belonging.[84]

At the same time, Ruiz says, Pulse and its aftermath revealed again to him how Islam preaches a message of peace and solidarity with all peoples on earth. As he said while speaking to the press on September 12 as clean-up crews salvaged what they could after the Fort Pierce fire, Ruiz felt it was no coincidence that one wall survived unscathed within the masjid. That wall was painted with a stylized rendition of Qur'an 49:13, which reads:

> Human beings, We created you all from a male and a female and made you into nations and tribes so that you may know one another. Verily the noblest of you in the sight of Allah is the most God-fearing of you. Surely Allah is All-Knowing, All-Aware.

This, Ruiz said to the journalists gathered around him in the ashen remains, calls out to everyone "with eyes to see" that:

> Allah (SWT) created us for diversity, for being [from] different backgrounds, different countries, different languages, different color-toned skins, different colored eyes, different complexions, different genders, all these different things that he so beautifully gave us . . . to be Puerto Rican, to be Latino, is to be proud to be part of this beautiful country [the United States] and speak the beautiful language of Spanish. I am proud to be who Allah (SWT) created me to be. I am proud to be Puerto Rican and I am even prouder to be Muslim. Alhamdulillah, I can combine the two and it makes something even more exquisite and beautiful. . . . Allah (SWT) in his wisdom created us differently, so we can get to know [one] another. I pray, insha'Allah, such destructive events—this arson and the Orlando tragedy—can help us all get to know one another and not tear us more apart.

The corillos created between these multiple socialities in Orlando endured, at least in part, over the last several years, Jorge says. In response to the shock and trauma of the shooting, multiple communities that would not regularly associate with one another—because of individual prejudice, lack of personal or organizational networking, or otherwise—now attempt to do deep and meaningful work together in Central Florida. Under banners like #OrlandoStrong, Muslims, those who identify with the LGBTQI+ community, Puerto Ricans, and others continue to process what happened and how it shapes their respective socialities and the ways which they intersect and interact. Although the pain lingers and divisions remain, Jorge says the events brought each group closer. "We were able to draw strength from the shared suffering," he says. Looking to the future, he hopes to see more intersectional struggles for justice without the necessity of violence to provoke them.

## CAFECITOS, CORILLOS, AND FURTHER CONSIDERATIONS

After Adrián relocated to Florida in search of work, I invited him for a cafecito at the Black Bean Deli in Orlando's Colonialtown. Taking our seats and sipping our coffees, we start by talking about how Adrián was forced to relocate to Florida after struggling to find stable employment in cash-strapped, hurricane-hit, and financially crippled Puerto Rico. Thankfully, he says, he found not only a job in construction but also a diverse local Muslim community:

> It's different than on the island. It's not perfect. We're not all getting along, but at least we are trying. I've learned more about the ummah in the last six months than I ever did in Puerto Rico. I finally feel like I am connecting.

Then, noting the #OrlandoStrong banner hanging across the street, we turn to discussing the crisscrossing community struggles that can sometimes produce a sense of shared resilience and resistance among different marginalized groups. Asking whether solidarity and intersectional activism bring about real change for Adrián, other Muslims, Puerto Ricans, or AmeRícan Muslims at large, he responds, "Yeah, I think so. At least we feel heard. Unity is the only way forward. It's the only way our diverse voices can be heard, by speaking together."

The above stories foregrounded the intersectional, ambivalent, and sometimes emancipating aspects of being marginal. In addition to Adrián's protests against government corruption and democratic unaccountability in 2017, I shared narratives of AmeRícan Muslims fighting poverty and inequality in "El Barrio" in the 1970s and '80s alongside other minority groups and liberation efforts, others contesting the "status question" in Puerto Rico by forming transregional political solidarities with international Muslim anti-colonial movements, and still others wrestling with gender and LGTBQI+ identifications in the context of lived relationships and complex communities. These stories fleshed out the fluidity of religious and political expressions in the Americas against an ever more cosmopolitan context of exchange and encounter.

Furthermore, and keeping the late-modern age and its various encrucijadas and bregas in mind, I wonder whether AmeRícan Muslim corillos might illuminate some hitherto hidden or underappreciated aspects of the inequalities people face, and connections they make, in a cosmopolitan age. Might they help us reimagine our collective futures? Despite the numerous critiques of intersectionality as a political possibility,[85] and the limits of cosmopolitan assemblages, AmeRícan Muslims' stories might help us chart a different path forward, if ever so tentatively. In other words, I wonder perhaps "with oppression manifest, comes insight" as poet Wendy Díaz put it; or, to invoke Tato Laviera once more, whether "spitting out in malice" and "standing affirmative in action" can spur us to "reproduce a broader answer to the marginality" that threatens to "gobble" up minoritized people groups in the late-modern.

# Conclusion

## "GET TO KNOW ONE ANOTHER"

> Living as we did—on the edge—we developed a particular way of seeing reality. We looked both from the outside and from the inside out. We focused our attention on the center as well as on the margin. We understood both . . . we were a necessary, vital part of the whole.
>
> BELL HOOKS

WHILE WORKING ON THIS MANUSCRIPT, I had an opportunity to conduct an interview with Hazel Gómez.[1] A board member for a network of female Muslim scholars dedicated to educating Muslim women around the world, Hazel discussed how her faith plays a central role in her activism, especially as it pertains to integrating Islamic principles and teachings into her community organizing. Specifically, she quoted the oft-cited Quranic injunction for different people, from different places, to "get to know one another." (49:13) This source, she said, propelled her work and invited others to get to know her story and that of her fellow Puerto Rican and Latinx Muslims. She challenged others to "get to know us" and see AmeRícan Muslims as brothers and sisters in humanity, because:

> Our pain is your pain. . . . Solidarity through philanthropy is a way to get out of our bubbles to genuinely get to know one another. The question is how do we get the broader community to see us? Do we have to wave our hands so that they can see our people are hurting? . . . We need more awareness so that we can have more

access. . . . I'm very Puerto Rican. I'm very Mexican. I'm very Muslim. I want to be known as a whole person.

This book was my attempt to center stories like Hazel's and invite readers to "get to know" AmeRícan Muslims as everyday people navigating the complexities of marginalized being and becoming in the late-modern, cosmopolitan world. To do so, I shared how AmeRícan Muslims resignify what it means to be "Puerto Rican," wrestling with how to communicate and perform their (dis)located identifications in relation to received notions of "race" and "ethnicity." I also included stories of race and the racialization of religion within, and beyond, the US Muslim community, as Puerto Rican reverts encounter, interact with, and negotiate generative frictions with Black, Arab, and other Muslims. There were also stories of how "[m]inoritarian affiliations or solidarities" such as asaBorícua "arise in response to the failures and limits of democratic representation, creating new modes of agency, new strategies of recognition, new forms of political and symbolic, as well as affective, representation . . ."[2] Taking their narratives and lived experiences seriously, I emphasized both their specific struggles and sense of success in navigating the pressures of cosmopolitanization through corillos they form at the encrucijadas of shared bregas. Altogether, AmeRícan Muslims' stories are ones of closures *and* openings; about what can be made of cosmopolitanization's challenges and opportunities in the midst of everyday life.

Like others in the late-modern, AmeRícan Muslims do not live in a "modest, familiar, local, circumscribed and stable" shell, but in a world that is a "playground of universal experiences . . . of encounters and interminglings or, alternatively, of anonymous coexistence and the overlapping of possible worlds and global dangers."[3] Both willingly and unwillingly, AmeRícan Muslims have to rethink their place in, and relation between, their home and the rest of the world. Markers of cosmopolitan existence—traditionally understood as extensive mobility, the capacity to consume many places en route, a curiosity about places, peoples, and cultures, an ability to map one's own society onto the history and geography of the world, semiotic skill to interpret the images of various others, and an openness to other peoples and cultures and a willingness/ability to appreciate some elements of the language/culture of the "Other"[4]—are all characteristic of the lives shared in this book.

Yet, my aim was not to decide whether AmeRícan Muslims are cosmopolitan in a moral or political sense. Instead, it was to examine how their "cross-border moral conceptions and practices" are embedded "within [their] specific lifeworld contexts."[5] The different strategies that AmeRícan Muslims employ to assemble identifications in the midst of hyperdiversity and intimate difference are predicated on the contours of banal experiences, encounters, and engagements with what it means to be and become Muslim, Puerto Rican, and/or AmeRícan. At the same time, their re-engagement with these modes of being as they respond to present circumstances involves the fusion, subversion, and reinforcement of multiple aspects of these identifications, depending on a host of contextual factors. Thus, AmeRícan Muslims' cosmopolitan assemblages reveal the particular tensions, contradictions, and concrete manifestations of cosmopolitan being and becoming. These stories were, at times, incomplete, divergent, and messy. But rather than try and smooth out their complexity and seeming contradiction, or present their lives in toto or with emphasis on analytic precision, I presented them as ontological realities to be encountered and engaged with.

I hope their stories prompt additional research and questions for further consideration in the study of Latinx and Puerto Rican cultures, the Caribbean, American religion, and global Islam. Based on AmeRícan Muslims' stories, how might we further integrate the study of minoritized communities into our understanding of Latinx, Caribbean, and Amerícan cultures? How might we further diversify and disturb the study of "American religion" or religion in the US? How might we better examine the everyday interrelation between race, ethnicity, religion, and politics in the Americas? Or, for that matter, the changeability and transregional entanglements of Latinx and Muslim socialities across the hemisphere? How might centering the Americas—and stories like that of AmeRícan Muslims—help us better integrate Muslims treated as peripheral into our study of global Islam? How might we better let such interlocutors speak for themselves and, perhaps, no longer view them as marginal, but rather as central to the story of Islam?

Finally, how might their perspectives from "the edge," as bell hooks frames it, help us implement strategies to negotiate diversity and difference in the late-modern? As a scholar of religion, I share the conviction that we must do more than critically study cultures, but also learn from them.[6] After spending much of the last decade alongside, with, and learning from AmeRícan Muslims, I came to deeply appreciate how they are quintessential "cosmopolitan strangers" in their own lands, finding a place in the generative frictions between the fissures of joining and cleaving, leaving and arriving, being and belonging. Every day, people like Lebrón, Abdullah, Miriam,

Ilyass, Adrián, and Hazel attempt to bring their whole selves to address the multiple marginalizations they contend with. For each, being on the edge engenders reflection and reform.[7] Thus, their failures and successes, frustrations and breakthroughs, "are critically important under conditions of general social strangeness."[8] While I may not share in their experience nor always agree with their conclusions, I believe they are people making another world possible.

To live in the US and its environs in the twenty-first century is to witness "the cruel unwinding of the American project."[9] Even what works is based on extraction and subtraction from the marginalized and disenfranchised. The unraveling of the project has long been evident in Puerto Rico and is now taking on ever more nefarious forms, as the archipelago's hobbled power grid is privatized, tax breaks are making it a playground for the crypto-rich, education is defunded, corruption is endemic, and displacement and emigration are commonplace. AmeRícan Muslims' stories both reflect these present realities and point to more "liberatory futures for Puerto Ricans . . . in Santurce, Cayey, and Cabo Rojo, or New York City, Orlando, or Milwaukee."[10]

At the same time, we are all living in a reality we are not meant to be living. This is not the promised land. Not in relation to the environment. Not in relation to one another. The economic, education, and healthcare systems we have created are simply not enough. Living as we do in a time of re-entrenched nationalisms, shared international crises, and climate doom; when cities are built but not meant to sustain those who live in them; when women are still not receiving equal pay and recognition; when people work and cannot afford a dignified home; and when deep divisions predicated upon diversity and difference threaten to rend our societies asunder, AmeRícan Muslims' embodied, everyday experiences prompt us to re-examine the global net of human connectivity.

From rural Puerto Rico to the New York City metroplex, the swamps of Gainesville to the beaches of San Juan, I have been drawn to the mundane ways that human relationships hold together, become more intertwined, break apart, or get severed. By paying attention to language and cultural practices, foodways and political perspectives, interclass and intrareligious interactions, I hope I made visible the injustices and ingenuity, local details and global visions, marginality and possibilities of making a better world that constitute everyday AmeRícan Muslim lives. This has required me to turn to where the hurt has been and to learn that what appears at first to be marginal may not actually be so. It may, as I conclude, point to where power is at play, dictating how we relate to each other in such an age and how people create ways of being and belonging in conjunction with, and in opposition to, the humans and environments that surround them.

Our cosmopolitan futures will be made and unmade in the context of everyday relationships; in what we pick up and leave behind in the leftovers of the late-modern; and in how we decide to be and become this people or that people, "Us" or "Them," something beyond or in between. There is, as AmeRícan Muslims show us, immense creative potential and humility to be found in the tension between *nos* and *otras*,[11] insider and outsider, center and margin—in other words, the "what if?" inherent in liminality.[12] Thus, I wonder what they have to teach us all about living in and through the late-modern. Specifically, how we might unfold and discover a new repertoire of imagination for creating and sustaining alternative futures. That repertoire seems all the more invaluable at a time when how we see ourselves, how we believe we belong to one another, and how we see ourselves obligated (or not) to those bonds, will in large part dictate whether we flourish, falter, or fail. We need such re-imagined futures to help us move forward and find a world that is different. One that cares for everybody.

A teleological belief in cosmopolitanism would tell us that the twists and turns of late-modern, neocapitalist globalization will find a positive resolution. But that may not be so. Thus, I hope the perspectives offered here illuminate some of the problems we face, but also our capacity to "get to know one another" and find a way forward together. In the end, I hope it engenders the sentiment evident in the words Hazel shared with me: "As a Borícua Muslim, I am always striving to be a better servant. Because my experience grounds me in both struggle and hopefulness."

# Acknowledgments

AS WITH ALL WORKS OF this nature, this was not a solitary endeavor. I have many to thank for their contributions along the way. First and foremost, I had the humbling honor to sit, learn, laugh, and eat alongside AmeRícan Muslims who shared their stories with me over the course of a decade. I am grateful to each of you for your notes, blessings, warnings, invitations, interventions, and presence in my life. I pray this book honors your stories.

Saying "thanks" does not seem quite enough for those who hosted, helped, or otherwise held my hand during fieldwork. Nonetheless, I'd like to thank Raymond Laureano and family (especially Titi Lucy) in Juana Díaz; George Williams Jr. and Lambda Green in Dorado; Laura Del Olmo and César Piñeiro in San Juan; Livia in Guaynabo; and others who hosted me in Aguadilla, Carolina, and Condado. Thanks are also due to Sumayah and Muhammad for inviting me along for family outings and events and Imam Ahmad for general generosity and some rides here and there (even with the bumper-cruncher, I still trusted you to get us where we needed to go). Additional thanks go to the staff, volunteers, and individuals who welcomed me at mosques across the archipelago, especially to Sheikh Yunus, who regularly opened the doors of his masjid in Vega Alta. Thanks also to the staff at the library of the Centro de Estudios Avanzados de Puerto Rico y El Caribe in San Juan, where I was able to enjoy a respite from the heat in the air-conditioned environs of their reading room. And to Omar: thanks for the shared anthropological musings, meals, and more while we were both researching our respective projects. We've hung out in San Juan, Nassau, New York, and Cairo. Where to next? Maybe (finally) Frankfurt? I'd also like to give a brief shout-out to artists, musicians, journalists, and others who inspired this work, especially Francisco Donoso, who showed me that what it means to belong to a particular place and society emerges from the formation of ambivalent spaces created when cultural identities overlap—a process intensified in an age of "transient borders." In the US, I'd like to thank Ute Kriefall, Matt Popovits, Johnson Rethinasamy, Kelly Sullivan, and Kevin Sharp for arranging housing in Harlem and Queens. Thanks also to Paul in Harrison, New Jersey, Roy in Elizabeth, New Jersey, and Mindy in Boston, Massachusetts. My appreciation also extends to those who welcomed me or showed me around at MAS Queens, the North Hudson Islamic Education Center, the Islamic Cultural Center NYC, the IslamInSpanish studios in Houston, Texas, the Noor Al-Islam Society, the Allah School in Mecca, and Masjid Malcolm Shabazz in New York City. Finally, to Felix, Anibal, and other staff at the Center for Puerto Rican Studies at Hunter College (CentroPR), thank you for your accommodation and assistance.

I am immensely indebted to the institutions and foundations that nourished this project. While at the University of Florida (2014–2019), funding was provided by its Department of Religion; the College of Liberal Arts and Sciences; the Center for Humanities and the Public Sphere; the Center for Global Islamic Studies; and the Spalding Trust in the United Kingdom. In Florida, I could not have pursued this work without input and guidance from Terje Østebø, Anna L. Peterson, Benjamin Soares, Efraín Barradas, David Hackett, Robin Wright, Whitney Sanford, Manuel Vásquez, Gwendolyn Zoharah Simmons, Barbara Mennel, Sophia Krzys Acord, Bhakti Mamtora, Aladdin Al-Ri'fat, Matt Hartley, Megan Geiger, Kerri Blumenthal, Moxy Moczygemba, Jason Purvis, Jeyoul Choi, Victoria Machado, Mark Hoyer, and John Glover. I would also like to thank the many students in my classes at UF, who provided valuable feedback on reports from the field; Bob and Sandy Chitwood for patience, love, and always supporting my writing, especially at the Salt Lick outside Austin, Texas, in 2016; and Jeremy and Rachel Ryder, for moral support, encouragement, and helping me move to Gainesville in 2014.

In Germany (2019–2025), I was able to continue this research thanks to funding and support from the Center for Islam in the Contemporary World (CICW) at Shenandoah University; the Fritz Thyssen Foundation; the Berlin Graduate School Muslim Cultures and Societies; the Affect and Colonialism WebLab at Freie Universität Berlin; and the Muslim Philanthropy Initiative at Indiana University—Purdue University Indianapolis (IUPUI). In particular, I'd like to thank Lars Ostermeier, Giulia Brabetz, Claudia Derichs, Kai Kresse, Nora Lafi, Konrad Hirschler, Antje Müller, Nadja Danilenko, Patrick Franke, Amro Ali, Viktor Ullmann, Udi Raz, Yasmin Ismail, Lucía Cirianni

Salazar, Ingrid Evans, Wikke Jansen, Shariq Siddiqui, Rafia Khader, and Lina Grajales for conversations, support, and interventions along the way.

I am also thankful for the scholars, activists, practitioners, and pioneers who study Islam and Muslim communities in Latin America and the Caribbean. Their interventions and innovations significantly informed this work, and it would not have taken shape without my frequent engagement with them, both in person and online. In particular, I treasure the Latin American and Caribbean Islamic Studies Association (LACISA) and its newsletter, which includes too many people to name here. Consistent co-leaders, collaborators, and contributors in this network include Jorge Araneda, Sara Awartani, Baptiste Brodard, Philipp Bruckmayr, Odette Yidi David, Simon Frey, Luciana Garcia de Oliveira, Cynthia Hernández González, Kevin Funk, John Tofik Karam, Aliyah Khan, Aisha Khan, Harini Kumar, Rahma Maccarone, Arely Medina, Lucas Oliveira Ribeiro, and Lucas Vicente.

Likewise, I remain continually humbled and grateful for collegial support, critical feedback, and generous questions asked by audience members and fellow panelists at numerous venues and organized events over the years, including at the University of Edinburgh (2022), the American Academy of Religion Annual Meeting (2021, 2020, 2019, and 2017), the European Association for the Study of Religion (2021), Universität Tübingen (2021), the International Society for the Sociology of Religion (2021), Humboldt Universität Berlin (2020), Universidad de Puerto Rico Mayagüez (2019), the Caribbean Studies Association (2017), the University of South Carolina (2016), and the Latin American Studies Association (2016).

In the end, I am also immensely grateful that my manuscript found a home with the University of Texas Press, especially in the trusted hands of Kerry Webb. Since she first received my proposal, Kerry was a champion for the project and a kind but "tell it like it is" editor who stewarded the book from proposal to publication with wisdom, keen insight, and a consistent ethic of authorial care. Thanks also to Christina Vargas, Robert Kimzey, Bridget Manzella, Anahi Molina, and the anonymous reviewers who provided feedback. I am humbled by the honor of having this book included in the Joe R. and Teresa Lozano Long Series in Latin American and Latino Art and Culture.

A special thanks is also due to Jack M. Schultz, who was the first to introduce me to ethnography, help me distinguish between culture's variables and theology's conversations, and see the spiritual intimations at work within cultures themselves. I have a feeling he was a blind reviewer on a couple of my articles. Even if he wasn't, his presence is palpable in my words. Such was his influence on my thought and academic trajectory. Rest in peace, Jack.

Finally, words of appreciation are quite impossible to describe my wonderful wife and "editor in chief," Paula Rötscher. This book, believe it or not, is older than our relationship. You've never known me without it taking up space and time in our life. Thank you for journeying with me (literally, in some cases), growing with me, and gifting me patience and perspective along the way.

# Glossary of Terms and Abbreviations

**Adhan** The ritual call to prayer in Islam.

**Ahmadiyya** A messianic Muslim movement founded by Mirza Ghulam Ahmad in Punjab (British-controlled India) in 1899. There are two main factions of Ahmadiyya today: Qadiani and Lahori, the latter who stress Ghulam Ahmad was a restorer of the faith and not a "prophet."

**al-Andalus** The portions of the Iberian Peninsula governed by a series of Islamic governments between 711 and 1492 CE.

**Alianza Islámica** A Latinx Muslim organization founded in East Harlem in 1987.

**Asabiyah** Social solidarity with an emphasis on group consciousness, cohesiveness, and unity. Coined by Ibn Khâldun in his *Muqaddimah.* Sometimes used synonymously with "solidarity" (e.g., asaBorícua is used to refer to solidarity and group consciousness among Puerto Rican Muslims).

**Barrio** Literally, "neighborhood," but used often to refer to a predominately Spanish-speaking quarter of a town or city (e.g., El Barrio is synonymous with portions of East Harlem in New York City).

**Black Hebrew Israelites** A new religious movement claiming that Black Americans are descendants of the ancient Israelites. Some splinter groups are demonstratively xenophobic and misogynistic.

**Bodega** A small grocery shop, especially in a Spanish-speaking neighborhood.

**Borícua/Borikén** Derived from what is said to be the original Taíno (indigenous) name for Puerto Rico, Borikén (alternatively Borinquen, Borinkén, Borinquén) refers to the island and Borícua to Puerto Rican people.

**Botánica** A shop that sells herbal and other traditional remedies, together with charms, candles, and other items used for religious or spiritual purposes.

**Bozales** African enslaved persons in the Americas during the period of Spanish colonial rule brought directly from Africa.

**Brega** In Spanish, literally struggle, quarrel, or dispute. Used colloquially in Puerto Rico to refer to daily struggles and the effort to work around them.

**Council on American-Islamic Relations (CAIR)** A Muslim civil rights and advocacy group.

**Corillo** Puerto Rican slang for friends or a group of friends.

**Coyuntura** Juncture, specifically in relation to time.
**Dawah** Literally, "call." It refers to the "call to Islam" both to non-Muslims and Muslims. Is often used as byword for evangelization and sharing the faith. A da'i is one who calls people to faith.
**Diaspora** Populations or people groups that originated from the same place but were dispersed to different locations (e.g., the Puerto Rican and Palestinian diasporas). Puerto Ricans in the US are sometimes referred to as DiaspoRicans (or Nuyoricans, for those residing in and around the New York City metro area).
**Deen** A way of life, or habit of obedience, often used as a synonym for "religion" by Muslims.
**Dergah** A shrine or tomb built over the grave of a revered religious figure, often a Sufi saint; a Naqshbandi center for the regular practice of *dhikr*, or remembrance.
**Dua** Nonobligatory prayer, supplication, appeal, or other invocation.
**Eid** Literally, "festival" or "feast." Refers to the two primary Islamic holidays of Eid al-Adha (festival of the sacrifice) or Eid al-Fitr (feast of breaking the fast of Ramadan).
**Encruciijada** Crossroads, crossing, or confluence.
**Espiritismo** Literally, "Spiritism." A spiritual belief system based upon the reconciliation of nineteenth-century French spiritualism and, for Puerto Ricans, Taíno healing practices.
**Fiqh** The human attempt to discern divine law based on the interpretation of shariah.
**Fitna** Disunity or discord.
**Five Percent Nation (FPN)** Also known as the Nation of Gods and Earths, it is a Black American movement influenced by Islam founded in 1964 in Harlem by Clarence 13X. Its members emphasize the use of "divine mathematics" for self-realization and empowerment as "gods."
**Fuerzas Armadas de Liberación Nacional** (FALN) A clandestine paramilitary organization that, through direct action and armed resistance, advocated independence for Puerto Rico.
**Hadith** A record of things Prophet Muhammad said, did, or tacitly approved of.
**Hajj** Obligatory pilgrimage to Mecca and Medina, held annually. The lesser, nonobligatory pilgrimage is known as umrah.
**Halal** That which is lawful or permitted, often used in relation to dietary restrictions.
**Haram** That which is unlawful or prohibited, often used in relation to dietary restrictions, but also to holy areas deemed off-limits to some.
**Iftar** Literally, "breakfast." Used to refer to the breaking of the fast every evening during the month of Ramadan.
**Isla** Spanish for "island."
**Islamic Party of North America (IPNA)** Mostly active in the 1970s and the 1980s, the IPNA left a lasting influence on a generation of Black Muslim activists and shaped the formation of Alianza Islámica.
**Islamicate** Associated with regions in which Muslims are culturally dominant but not specifically with the religion of Islam.
**Islamidad** A sense of Latinx Muslim culture and cohesion, shared between Latinx converts to Islam.
**Islamophobia** The irrational fear, hostility, and hatred of Muslims, Islam, and those associated with Islam or assumed to be Muslim, which leads to a range of exclusionary and discriminatory practices in politics, society, and culture.

**Jahiliyyah** Considered a time of "ignorance" prior to monotheism and the recitation of divine law to Muhammad. Also used in modern times to refer to the beliefs and practices of secular modernity.

**Jummah** Refers to obligatory, communal prayers held every Friday.

**Keffiyeh** A traditional headdress worn by men from parts of the Middle East.

**Khutbah** Sermon or speech delivered during Friday midday service, in advance of jummah prayers or as part of special Eid celebrations.

**Kufi** A rounded brimless cap for men, especially of African descent, made of cloth or knitted.

**Ladinos** Blacks, enslaved or otherwise, familiar with the religion, cultures, and languages of the Iberian Peninsula.

**Latin Kings** Also known as the "Almighty Latin King and Queen Nation" (ALKQN, ALKN, LKN), it is the oldest and largest Latinx street gang worldwide with roots stretching back to its foundation by Puerto Ricans in Chicago, Illinois, in 1954.

**Latinidad** A Spanish-language term that refers to the various attributes shared by Latin American people and their descendants.

**Latino American Dawah Organization (LADO)** A pioneering organization founded in September 1997 to promote Islam within the Latinx community.

**LGBTQI+** An abbreviation that stands for lesbian, gay, bi(sexual), transgender, queer, and intersex.

**Madhab** School of legal thought within Islam.

**Madrasah** Educational establishment focused on the teaching of Islamic sciences.

**Masjid** Literally, "mosque." A place of prayer and worship.

**MENA** An abbreviation referring to the regions of the Middle East and North Africa.

**Mezquita** Spanish term for "mosque."

**Mihrab** Ornamental niche set into the wall of a mosque, which indicates the direction to Mecca and thus orients Muslims' prayer.

**Minbar** An ascended space or pulpit from which the imam delivers the khutbah.

**Moors** Berbers from Northwestern Africa who conquered the Iberian Peninsula in 711 CE.

**Morisco** Former Muslim pressured by the Catholic Church in the Iberian Peninsula to convert to Christianity under the threat of death after the Spanish crown outlawed the open practice of Islam in its territories during the sixteenth century.

**Moorish Science Temple of America** A religious organization founded by Noble Drew Ali in the early twentieth century, based on the belief that Black Americans are descendants of the Moabites and thus are "Moorish" by nationality and Islamic by faith.

**Musallah** A place for prayer.

**Muslimah** Term used to refer to a female Muslim.

**Mu'tazilah** Eighth-century school of Islamic philosophy and theology, which emphasized God's absolute uniqueness, unity, and justice. Associated also with use of logic, rationalism, and materialist ethic.

**Nation of Islam (NOI)** Black Muslim organization, which emerged alongside Black nationalist movements in the US and abroad. Considered "heterodox" by some, the Nation of Islam was founded in 1930 by Wallace D. Fard and later led by Elijah Muhammad. It later broke apart into branches led by Warith Deen Mohammad and Louis Farrakhan.

**Palestine Liberation Organization (PLO)** An umbrella political organization representing the Palestinian people in their drive for a Palestinian state, formed in 1964.

**PBUH** Literally, "Peace be upon him." Used after the mention of the Prophet Muhammad's name in everyday parlance.

**Puerto Rico Oversight Management and Economic Stability Act (PROMESA)** A US federal law enacted in 2016 that serves as a custom-made bankruptcy law for Puerto Rico.

**Puertorriqueñidad** A Spanish term referring to the condition or state of being Puerto Rican.

**Quraniyya** A movement within Islam that holds the belief that the Qur'an is the only valid source of religious belief, guidance, and law.

**Ramadan** The ninth month of the Islamic lunar calendar, during which obligatory fasting from eating, drinking, and sexual activity is required during daylight.

**Reconquista** Term used to describe the Christian reconquest of the Iberian Peninsula from the eighth century CE until the fall of the Nasrid kingdom of Granada in 1492 CE.

**Reggaetón** A style of popular music that originated in Panama during the late 1980s, which rose to prominence in the late 1990s and early 2000s through a plethora of Puerto Rican musicians. It evolved from dancehall, with elements of hip-hop as well as Latin American and Caribbean music.

**Reversion** A sometimes preferred term by Muslims to refer to their conversion to Islam.

**Sadaqah** Nonobligatory charity, alms, offerings, or gifts toward a philanthropic end.

**Salafi** Name (derived from *salaf*, "pious ancestors") for a reform movement that developed from the late nineteenth century through to the twenty-first with a focus on purity and piety and the rejection of traditional madhahib in favor of ethical and modernist interpretation of the Qur'an and Sunnah.

**Salah** Obligatory prayer, meant to be performed five times daily.

**Santería** Also known as Regla de Ocha, Regla Lucumí, or Lucumí, it is an Afro-Caribbean religion that combines ancient West African religious practices of the inhabitants of the Yoruba tribe with Catholicism. Predominately practiced in Cuba and other Caribbean nations and their diasporas.

**Shahadah** Recitation of the witness to the Islamic faith. It is seen as a declaration of acceptance of Islam by a convert. It is said twice, once in Arabic and once in the convert's native language, in the presence of at least one other Muslim.

**Sheikh** A pre-Islamic honorific title, meaning "leader" or "notable." Used in relation to religion for someone who possesses learning in religious sciences.

**Souk** Market or marketplace, bazaar.

**Sunnah** The established custom, habits, conduct, precedents, and oral tradition of Muhammad and his Companions. Believed to be a "living Qur'an" that helps establish the norms of practicing Islam and living out the precepts contained in the Qur'an. Considered a primary source of Islamic law.

**SWT** Subhanahu wa ta'ala, "May He be glorified and exalted," conventional Muslim honorific said after referencing Allah.

**Takbir** The phrase "Allahu akbar," which implies that God is greater than anything else that can be named. Part of the call to prayer, it is also used as a chant for religious purposes and as a slogan at political rallies and demonstrations.

**Tariqa** Literally, "path" or "way." Refers to a Sufi order or the spiritual system of a specific master teacher.

**Tawhid** The foundational doctrine of Islam, declaring the absolute oneness, unity, and uniqueness of Allah.

**Thawb** Also referred to as *thobe*, *kandoora*, or *dishdasha*, it is an ankle-length garment, usually with long sleeves, similar to a robe, kaftan, or tunic.

**Tres raíces** Term used to refer to the three "roots" of Puerto Rican culture: Taíno, African, and Iberian/Spanish. Also referred to in regard to individual persons that bear *trigueño* or *trigueña* heritage.

**Ummah** Literally, "community." Refers to the Muslim community, expressing its essential unity and equality.

**Universal Zulu Nation** An international hip-hop awareness and identity movement founded by artist Africa Bambaataa, which aims to revitalize ghetto culture and marginalized ethnic groups through hip-hop.

**Wudu** Obligatory cleansing rituals performed in order to make an adherent pure for ritual purposes. Required for men and women before prayer. Consists of washing the hands, mouth, face, arms, and feet with water. In the absence of water, clay or sand can be substituted.

**Young Lords Party (YLP)** Originally a Chicago-based street gang that became a civil rights and human rights organization. The group aimed to fight for neighborhood empowerment and self-determination for Puerto Rico, Latinos, and colonized people.

**Zakat** Obligatory charity, used for those in need, the propagation of the faith, and for other charitable efforts approved by religious authorities.

# Notes

### Introduction

1. Terms and categories such as Latino, Latina/o, Latinx are "racialized and politicized" concepts, "produced through everyday social interactions in specific historical and geographical settings," writes Sergio M. González in *Strangers No Longer: Latino Belonging and Faith in Twentieth-Century Wisconsin* (University of Illinois Press, 2024), 12–13. Though each has its issues, each can also be helpful. They can, in the words of Héctor Tobar, act as a *connector*, or "alliance of people with similar experiences looking to live in the community of their commonalities." ("Our Migrant Souls." Zócalo Public Square, Los Angeles. June 14, 2024). In this book, I use the term Latinx as it connects the stories of disparate peoples, with various queer, ill-fitting, and non-normative identifications not usually associated with the term "Latino." Thus, it is, in my usage, meant to be a term of inclusivity that takes in the variety of perspectives shared in this book and points to the hidden mixtures and mysteries embedded in Puerto Rican Muslim stories.

2. Christina A. Ziegler-McPherson, *Immigrants in Hoboken: One-Way Ticket, 1845–1985* (The History Press, 2011).

3. Wendy Díaz, "The Fast and the ¡Fiesta! How Latino Muslims Celebrate Ramadan," *Muslim Matters*, May 26, 2019.

4. A significant number of Latinx Muslims (40 percent) call their acceptance of Islam a "reversion" or "return" rather than a conversion. See Gaston Espinosa, Juan Galvan, and Harold Morales, "Latino Muslims in the United States: Reversion, Politics, and Islamidad," *Journal of Race, Ethnicity, and Religion* 8, no. 1 (2017). Although they generally do not claim biological links to Andalusian Muslims, Latinx Muslims do draw on an imagined cultural memory to connect with what they view as their Andalusian *antepasados*. See Harold Morales, "Latinx Muslims, Remembrances of Andalusia, and the Work of Organizing," in Hussein Rashid, Huma Mohibullah, and Vincent Biondo, eds., *Islam in North America: An Introduction* (Bloomsbury Academic, 2023), 112–126. Furthermore, some Latinx Muslims use the term "reversion" as a nod to the notion of *fitrah*, the original state in which humans are created wherein they recognize the innate oneness of God (*tawhid*). See also

Harold D. Morales, *Latino and Muslim in America: Race, Religion, and the Making of a New Minority* (Oxford University Press, 2018), 103–104. In this book, I use both "conversion"/"convert" and "reversion"/"revert" interchangeably, as did most of my interlocutors in the course of our conversations. For more on conversion/reversion terminology and Islamic discourse around the terms, see Matthew J. Kuiper, *Da'wa: A Global History of Islamic Missionary Thought and Practice* (University of Edinburgh Press, 2021), 10–11.

5. Born Lance Taylor in the Bronx, Bambaataa experimented with recorded musical elements such as Latin rock, European disco, funk, punk, and the German electro bands such as Kraftwerk in order to create the ultimate dance environment. His cultural organization, the Universal Zulu Nation, helped spread hip-hop culture throughout the world. See Jonathan Mael, *Harlem World: How Hip Hop's Super Showdown Changed Music Forever* (Johns Hopkins University Press, 2023).

6. Michael Muhammad Knight, *The Five Percenters: Islam, Hip-hop and the Gods of New York* (Simon and Schuster, 2008).

7. Tato Laviera, "AmeRícan," from *Bendición: The Complete Poetry of Tato Laviera* (Arte Público Press, 2014).

8. Laviera, "AmeRícan."

9. Anna Tsing, *Friction: An Ethnography of Global Connection* (Princeton University Press, 2005); Brian Larkin, "Bandiri Music, Globalization, and Urban Experience in Nigeria," *Social Text* 22, no. 4 (2004): 91–112.

10. See Arjun Appadurai, *Modernity at Large: The Cultural Dimensions of Globalization* (University of Minnesota Press, 1996); David Harvey, *The Condition of Postmodernity* (Blackwell Publishing, 1990); and Thomas Tweed, *Crossing and Dwelling: A Theory of Religion* (Harvard University Press, 2006).

11. Doreen Massey, "A Global Sense of Place" in *Space, Place, and Gender* (University of Minnesota Press, 1994).

12. Margaret S. Archer and Jamie Morgan, "Contributions to realist social theory: an interview with Margaret S. Archer," *Journal of Critical Realism* 19, no. 2 (2020): 179–200; Will Atkinson, *Class, Individualization and Late Modernity: In Search of the Reflexive Worker* (Palgrave Macmillan, 2010); Ulrich Beck, "Beyond class and nation: Reframing social inequalities in a globalizing world," *British Journal of Sociology* 58, no. 4 (2007): 679–705; Zygmunt Bauman, *Liquid Times* (Polity Press, 2007); Anthony Giddens, *Modernity and Self-Identity* (Polity Press, 1991); Klaus Rasborg, "From Class Society to the Individualized Society? A Critical Reassessment of Individualization and Class," *Irish Journal of Sociology* 25, no. 3 (December 2017): 229–249.

13. Courtney Bender, *Religion on the Edge: De-centering and Re-centering the Sociology of Religion* (Oxford University Press, 2013); Peter Berger, *The Many Altars of Modernity: Toward a Paradigm for Religion in a Pluralist Age* (Walter de Gruyter/Mouton, 2014); Charles McCrary, "Secularism, Pluralism, and Publics in America," *Oxford Research Encyclopedia of Religion*, May 24, 2018; Michaela Pfadenhauer, "In-Between Spaces. Pluralism and Hybridity as Elements of a New Paradigm for Religion in the Modern Age," *Human Studies* 39 (2016): 147–159.

14. Demetrius Eudell, "From Mode of Production to Mode of Auto-Institution: Sylvia Winter's Black Metamorphosis of the Labor Question," *Small Axe* 20, no. 1 (March): 47–61; Paul Gilroy, *Against Race: Imagining Political Culture Beyond the*

*Color Line* (Harvard University Press, 2000); Achille Mbembe, *Critique of Black Reason* (Duke University Press, 2017); Aníbal Quijano, "Créolisation, Creolization, and Créolité," *Small Axe* 21, no. 1 (2007): 211–219.

15. Peter Berger, "Secularization Falsified," *First Things*, February 2008.

16. Ulrich Beck, *Cosmopolitan Vision* (Polity Press, 2006).

17. Samuel Scheffler, "Conceptions of Cosmopolitanism," *Utilitas* 11, no. 3 (1999): 255. See also Steven Vertovec and Robin Cohen, eds., *Conceiving Cosmopolitanism: Theory, Context and Practice* (Oxford University Press, 2002); Kwame Appiah, *Cosmopolitanism: Ethics in a World of Strangers* (W. W. Norton and Company, 2007); David A. Holinger, *Postethnic America: Beyond Multiculturalism* (Basic Books, 2006); and David A. Holinger, *Cosmopolitanism and Solidarity: Studies in Ethnoracial, Religious, and Professional Affiliation in the United States* (University of Wisconsin Press, 2006).

18. R. J. Holton, *Cosmopolitanisms: New Thinking and New Directions* (Palgrave-Macmillan, 2009); Robert Fine, *Cosmopolitanism* (Routledge, 2009); Stan van Hooft and Wim Vandekerckhove, eds., *Questioning Cosmopolitanism* (Springer, 2010); Win-Chiat Lee, "Cosmopolitanism with Room for Nationalism," *Journal of Moral Philosophy* 9, no. 2 (2012): 279–293; and Craig J. Calhoun, *Cosmopolitanism and Belonging: From European Integration to Global Hopes and Fears* (Routledge, 2007). See also Walter Mignolo, "Cosmopolitanism and the De-colonial Option," *Studies in Philosophy and Education* 29, no. 2 (2010): 111–127 and Amitav Ghosh, "Cosmopolitanisms, Literature, Transnationalisms," in *The Postcolonial and the Global*, ed. Revathi Krishnaswamy and John C. Hawley (University of Minnesota Press, 2007), 178–190.

19. David Inglis and Gerard Delanty, eds., *Cosmopolitanism: Critical Concepts in the Social Sciences* (Routledge, 2011) for a helpful overview.

20. Pnina Werbner, "Vernacular Cosmopolitanism," *Theory, Culture and Society* 23 (2006): 496–498; Mamadou Diouf, "The Senegalese Murid Trade Diaspora and the Making of a Vernacular Cosmopolitanism," in *Cosmopolitanism*, ed. Carol A. Breckenridge et al. (Duke University Press, 2002).

21. Walter D. Mignolo, "The Many Faces of the Cosmo-polis: Border Thinking and Critical Cosmopolitanism," in *Cosmopolitanism*, ed. Carol A. Breckenridge, et al. (Duke University Press, 2002), 160, 174. See also Kwame Appiah, "Identity, Authenticity, Survival: Multicultural Societies and Social Reproduction," in *Multiculturalism: Examining the Politics of Recognition*, ed. Amy Gutmann (Princeton University Press, 1994), 149–163; Nancy Fraser, *Justice Interruptus: Critical Reflections on "Postsocialist" Condition* (Routledge, 1997) and "Rethinking Recognition," *New Left Review* 3 (2000): 107–120; Terje Østebø, "The Question of Becoming: Islamic Reform Movements in Contemporary Ethiopia," *Journal of Religion in Africa* 38, no. 4 (2008): 416–446; and Charles Taylor, "The Politics of Recognition," in *Multiculturalism: Examining the Politics of Recognition*, 25–73.

22. Mitchell Cohen, "Rooted Cosmopolitanism," *Dissent* 39, no. 4 (1992): 478–483.

23. Fuyuki Kurasawa, "A Cosmopolitanism from Below: Alternative Globalization and the Creation of a Solidarity without Bounds," *European Journal of Sociology / Archives Européennes de Sociologie / Europäisches Archiv Für Soziologie* 45, no. 2

(2004): 233–255; Nathaniel Ming Curran, "Neoliberalism From Above and Cosmopolitanism From Below: A Korean-English Meetup Group in the United States," *Communication, Culture and Critique* 14, no. 1 (March 2021): 70–88; James D. Ingram, "Cosmopolitanism from Below: Universalism as Contestation," *Critical Horizons* 17, no. 1 (2016): 66–78; and Rufaro Hamish Mushonga and Vupenyu Dzingirai, "Cosmopolitanism 'from Below' and Claim-Making in the Global South," *Journal of Ethnic and Migration Studies* 49, no. 1 (2023): 156–174.

24. Thomas Thiemeyer and Kwame Appiah, "Cosmopolitanism and Cultural Heritage," in *(Post)Colonialism and Cultural Heritage: International Debates at the Humboldt Forum* (Hanser, 2021), 54–75.

25. Steven Vertovec and Robin Cohen, eds., *Conceiving Cosmopolitanism: Theory, Context and Practice* (Oxford University Press, 2002); David A. Holinger, *Cosmopolitanism and Solidarity: Studies in Ethnoracial, Religious, and Professional Affiliation in the United States* (University of Wisconsin Press, 2006).

26. Beck, *Cosmopolitan Vision* and Dilip M. Menon, "Walking on Water: Globalization and History," *Global Perspectives* 11, no. 1 (May 2020): 12176.

27. Other words often used interchangeably with this conceptualization include urbane, sophisticated, worldly, or multicultural, which are morally linked to a neoliberal world order.

28. Mara A. Leichtman and Dorothea Schulz, "Introduction to Special Issue: Muslim Cosmopolitanism: Movement, Identity, and Contemporary Reconfigurations," *City & Society (Washington, D.C.)* 24, no. 1 (2012): 1; Steven Vertovec and Cohen Robin, eds. *Conceiving Cosmopolitanism* (Oxford University Press, 2003), 8–14.

29. Leichtman and Schulz, "Introduction," 2. See also Aaron M. Hughes, *Theorizing Islam: Disciplinary Deconstruction and Reconstruction* (Acumen Publishing Ltd., 2012), 107.

30. For example, as defined by Bruce Lawrence, Muslim cosmopolitans are "world affirming," life endorsing, and open to change. See Ali Mian, *The Bruce Lawrence Reader: Islam Beyond Borders* (Duke University Press, 2021), 6.

31. Beck, *Cosmopolitan Vision* and Thiemeyer and Appiah, "Cosmopolitanism."

32. Kai Kresse, "Interrogating 'Cosmopolitanism' in an Indian Ocean Setting: Thinking Through Mombasa on the Swahili Coast," in *Cosmopolitanisms in Muslim Contexts: Perspectives from the Past*, ed. Derryl N. MacLean and Sikeena Karmali Ahmed (University of Edinburgh Press, 2013), 31–50 and "On the Skills to Navigate the World, and Religion, for Coastal Muslims in Kenya," in *Articulating Islam: Anthropological Approaches to Muslim Worlds*, ed. Kostas Retsikas (Springer, 2012), 77–99.

33. Beck, *Cosmopolitan Vision*, 44.

34. See also the concept of "Islam *mondaine*" or a "worldly Islam" in Benjamin Soares and Filippo Osella. "Islam, Politics, Anthropology," *Journal of the Royal Anthropological Institute* 23, no. 1 (2009), S8.

35. Ulf Hannerz, "Cosmopolitanism," in *A Companion to the Anthropology of Politics*, ed. David Nugent and Vincent Joan (Blackwell; 2004), 69–85.

36. Engseng Ho, "Names beyond Nations: The Making of Local Cosmopolitans," *Études Rurales* 163/164 (2002): 215–231 and *The Graves of Tarim: Genealogy and Mobility across the Indian Ocean* (University of California Press, 2006). See also

Samuli Schielke, "Second Thoughts about the Anthropology of Islam, or How to Make Sense of Grand Schemes in Everyday Life," *Zentrum Moderner Orient Working Papers*, no. 2 (2010): 1–16.

37. Alina Kokoschka, "The Thing with Islam: Material Culture beyond the Museum Display Case and the Cabinet of Curiosities," trans. Todd Sekuler, in *Muslim Matters*, ed. Omar Kasmani and Stefan Maneval (Berlin: Revolver Publishing, 2016), 77.

38. Thiemeyer and Appiah, "Cosmopolitanism," 71.

39. Kevin Funk, *Rooted Globalism: Arab–Latin American Business Elites and the Politics of Global Imaginaries* (Indiana University Press, 2022) and Kira Huju, "The Cosmopolitan Standard of Civilization: A Reflexive Sociology of Elite Belonging among Indian Diplomats," *European Journal of International Relations* 29, no. 3 (2023): 698–722.

40. Humboldt Forum, *(Post)Colonialism and Cultural Heritage*, 118.

41. Ada María Isasi-Díaz, "Lo Cotidiano: A Key Element of Mujerista Theology," *Journal of Hispanic / Latino Theology*, 10, no. 1 (Aug. 2002) 5–17.

42. Tsing, *Friction*.

43. Anjali Prabhu, *Hybridity: Limits, Transformations, Prospects* (SUNY Press, 2007), 3. See also Shalini Puri, *The Caribbean Postcolonial: Social Equality, Post/Nationalism, and Cultural Hybridity* (Palgrave Macmillan, 2004) and Najnin Islam, "Creolization," in *Global South Studies: A Collective Publication with The Global South*, January 4, 2023.

44. Bill Ashcroft, "Archipelago of Dreams: Utopianism in Caribbean Literature." *Textual Practice* 30, no. 1 (2015): 89–112.

45. Immanuel Maurice Wallerstein, *World-Systems Analysis: An Introduction* (Duke University Press, 2004), 23–24.

46. Ashcroft, "Archipelago of Dreams," 90.

47. Ibid.

48. Benítez-Rojo, *The Repeating Island*, 20.

49. See Niall Finneran and Christina Welch, *Materialities of Religion: Spiritual Traditions of the Colonial and Post-colonial Caribbean* (Routledge, 2024).

50. Homi K. Bhabha, *The Location of Culture* (Routledge, 1994), 173.

51. Stuart Hall, "Negotiating Caribbean Identities," *New Left Review* 1, no. 209 (Jan/Feb 1995).

52. H. Adlai Murdoch, "Creolization, Hybridity and Archipelagic Thinking: Interrogating Inscriptions of Postcolonial Agency," *The Cambridge Journal of Postcolonial Literary Inquiry* 10, no. 1 (2023): 104–120. For more on thinking with the Caribbean about the modern and late-modern, see Kim Williams-Pulfer, *Get Involved! Stories of Bahamian Civil Society* (Rutgers University Press, 2024).

53. Jon Butler, Grant Wacker, and Randall Balmer, *Religion in American Life: A Short History* (Oxford University Press, 2011), xvi.

54. Schielke, "Second Thoughts."

55. Ronald Takaki, *A Different Mirror: A History of Multicultural America* (Seven Stories Press, 2012), 4–5.

56. Thomas Tweed, *Re-telling U.S. Religious History* (University of California Press, 1997).

57. Ramón A. Gutiérrez, *When Jesus Came, the Corn Mothers Went Away: Marriage, Sexuality, and Power in New Mexico, 1500–1846* (Stanford University Press, 1991).

58. Pew Research Center, "U.S. Religious Landscape Survey: Religious Affiliation," (Feb. 2008), 5.

59. See Ryan P. Jordan, "Race and Religion in the United States," *Oxford Research Encyclopedias: Religion*, April 26, 2017.

60. J. F. Schwaller, *A History of the Catholic Church in Latin America: From Conquest to Revolution and Beyond* (New York University Press, 2011). See also J. G. Young, *Mexican Exodus: Emigrants, Exiles, and Refugees of the Cristero War* (Oxford University Press, 2015).

61. Anna L. Peterson and Manuel Vásquez, *Latin American Religions: Histories and Documents in Context* (NYU Press, 2008), 2.

62. Lloyd D. Barba, "Latin American and US Latinx Religion," in *Bloomsbury Religion in North America* (Bloomsbury, 2021), accessed August 16, 2023, http://dx.doi.org/10.5040/9781350898813.006.

63. B. J. Thornton, "Changing Landscapes of Faith: Latin American Religion in the Twenty-First Century." *Latin American Research Review* 53, no. 4 (2018): 858.

64. See Lee M. Penyak and Walter J. Petry, eds., *Religion in Latin America: A Documentary History* (Orbis Books, 2006); Henri Gooren, ed., *Encyclopedia of Latin American Religions*, Vols. 1–2 (Springer, 2019); and Gustavo Morello, S. J., *Lived Religion in Latin America* (Oxford University Press, 2021). For research on the "Protestantization" of Latin American Christianity, see David Martin, *Tongues of Fire: The Explosion of Protestantism in Latin America* (Blackwell, 1990); David Stoll, *Is Latin America Turning Protestant? The Politics of Evangelical Growth* (University of California Press, 1990); Virginia Garrard-Burnett and David Stoll, eds., *Rethinking Protestantism in Latin America* (Temple University Press, 1993); R. Andrew Chesnut, *Competitive Spirits: Latin America's New Religious Economy* (Oxford University Press, 2003); C. Garma Navarro *Pentecostalismo en Iztapalapa y la Ciudad de México* (Universidad Metropolitana, Iztapalapa, 2004); Timothy Steigenga and Edward L. Cleary, eds., *Conversion of a Continent Contemporary Religious Change in Latin America* (Rutgers University Press, 2007); David Smilde, *Reason to Believe: Cultural Agency in Latin American Evangelicalism* (University of California Press, 2007); Todd Hartch, *The Rebirth of Latin American Christianity* (Oxford University Press, 2014).

65. Virginia Garrard-Burnett, *Protestantism in Guatemala: Living in the New Jerusalem* (University of Texas Press, 1998) and Timothy H. Wadkins, *The Rise of Pentecostalism in Modern El Salvador: From the Blood of the Martyrs to the Baptism of the Spirit* (Baylor University Press, 2017).

66. Edward L. Cleary, *The Rise of Charismatic Catholicism in Latin America* (University Press of Florida, 2011).

67. Appadurai, *Modernity at Large*.

68. Tweed, *Crossing and Dwelling*, 62.

69. The literature on these various traditions is too vast to cite here. However, for a helpful review of these interventions and the relevant works associated with them, see Frank Usarski, "Editorial: The International Journal of Latin American Religions," *International Journal of Latin American Religions* 1, no. 1 (2017): 1–4.

70. Peterson and Vásquez 2008, 254. See also Ken Chitwood, *The Muslims of Latin America and the Caribbean* (Lynne Rienner Publishers, 2021), 7.

71. Kristy Nabhan-Warren, "Hispanics and Religion in America," *Oxford Research Encyclopedia of Religion*, March 3, 2016, accessed August 29, 2024, https://oxfordre.com/religion/view/10.1093/acrefore/9780199340378.001.0001/acrefore-9780199340378-e-79.

72. Alicia Schmidt Camacho, *Migrant Imaginaries: Latino Cultural Politics in the U.S.-Mexico Borderlands* (New York University Press, 2008), 12.

73. See Josh Jelly-Schapiro, *Island People: The Caribbean and the World* (Vintage, 2016); Edna Acosta-Belén and Carlos E. Santiago, *Puerto Ricans in the United States: A Contemporary Portrait* (Lynne Rienner Publishers, 2006); Antonio Benítez-Rojo, *The Repeating Island: The Caribbean and the Postmodern Perspective* (Duke University Press, 1992); Sidney Mintz, "Ethnic Difference, Plantation Sameness," in *Ethnicity, Social Structure, and National Identities in the Caribbean: Essays in Honor of Harry Hoetink*. ed. G. Oostindie (Macmillan, 1996), 39–52.

74. Aida Negrón de Montilla, *Americanization in Puerto Rico and the Public School System* (Editorial Universitaria, 1971); Samuel Silva Gotay, *Protestantismo y política en Puerto Rico, 1898–1930: Hacia una historia del protestantismo evangélico en Puerto Rico* (Editorial de la Universidad de Puerto Rico, 1997); Samuel Cruz, *Masked Africanisms: Puerto Rican Pentecostalism* (Kendall Hunt Publishing, 2005); G. Espinosa, *Latino Pentecostals: Faith and Politics in Action* (Harvard University Press, 2014), 192–232; Angel Santiago-Vendrell, "Give Them Christ: Native Agency in the Evangelization of Puerto Rico, 1900 to 1917," *Religions* 12, no. 3 (2021): 196. See also Ramón Grosfuguel, *Colonial Subjects: Puerto Ricans in a Global Perspective* (University of California Press, 2003) on the "message of salvation and progress" and Protestantization's links to (post)colonial capitalism. For more on the latter, see Acosta-Belén and Santiago, 185, and Jorge Juan Rodríguez, "The Colonial Gospel in Puerto Rico: Protestant Missionaries as Agents of Empire," *Christian Century*, January 3, 2017.

75. Pew Research Center, "Religion in Latin America," November 13, 2014, accessed January 13, 2024, https://www.pewresearch.org/religion/2014/11/13/religion-in-latin-america/#religious-affiliations-of-latin-americans-and-u-s-hispanics.

76. Ennis B. Edmonds and Michelle A. González, *Caribbean Religious History: An Introduction* (New York University Press, 2010).

77. Margarita Fernández Olmos and Lizabeth Paravisini-Gebert, *Creole Religions of the Caribbean: An Introduction from Vodou and Santeria to Obeah and Espiritismo* (New York University Press, 2003); Bettina Schmidt, *Caribbean Diaspora in the USA: Diversity of Caribbean Religions in New York City* (Routledge, 2008); and Diana Espírito Santo and Anastasios Panagiotopoulos, *Beyond Tradition, Beyond Invention: Cosmic Technologies and Creativity in Contemporary Afro-Cuban Religions* (Sean Kingston Publishing, 2015).

78. A Creole, Afro-Hispanic spiritual healing practice with roots in the United States, Europe, Africa, and the indigenous Taíno Caribbean. See Fernández Olmos and Paravisini-Gebert, *Creole Religions*, 171.

79. Fernández Olmos and Paravisini-Gebert, *Creole Religions*, 222.

80. Edil Torres Rivera, "Espiritismo: The Flywheel of the Puerto Rican Spiritual Traditions," *Interamerican Journal of Psychology* 39, no. 2 (2005): 295–300; Raquel

Rombert, "'Today, Changó Is Changó': How Africanness Becomes a Ritual Commodity in Puerto Rico." *Western Folklore* 66, no. 1/2 (2007): 75–106; Bettina E. Schmidt, "Meeting the Spirits: Puerto Rican 'Espiritismo' as Source for Identity, Healing and Creativity," *Fieldwork in Religion* 3, no. 2 (2008): 178–194; Marie Rivera Díaz, "Santería y espiritismo: ¿dos alas de un mismo pájaro?" *Tinta Digital*, June 26, 2017, https://tintadigital.upra.edu/santeria-y-espiritismo-es-lo-mismo; and M. Carolina Zerrate, Sara B. VanBronkhorst, Jaimie Klotz, et al., "Espiritismo and Santeria: a Gateway to Child Mental Health Services among Puerto Rican families? *Child Adolescent Psychiatry Mental Health* 16, no. 3 (2022), https://doi.org/10.1186/s13034-022-00439-0. These practices are also evident within the diaspora, see Acosta-Belén and Santiago, 16–17.

81. While systematic or up-to-date demographic data may not be readily available, evidence of small communities can be found, for example, in the establishment of synagogues in Condado, a Chabad center in Isla Verde, Buddhist centers in Miramar, and Caparra Terrace in San Juan, etc. On the Puerto Rican Rastafari community, see Omar Ramadan-Santiago, "*Dios en Carne*: Puerto Rican Rastas Choosing Black / Refusing White," *Transforming Anthropology* 30, no. 2 (2022): 107–121 or "Constructing Spiritual Blackness," *New West Indian Guide / Nieuwe West-Indische Gids* 95, 1–2 (2021): 33–56.

82. David Flores, "Latinx Religious Nones," in *Bloomsbury Religion in North America*, edited by Lloyd D. Barba (Bloomsbury Academic, 2023).

83. Pew Research Center, "The Shifting Religious Identities of Latinos in the United States," May 7, 2014, https://www.pewresearch.org/religion/2014/05/07/the-shifting-religious-identity-of-latinos-in-the-united-states. For more recent information on Latinx religious affiliation in the US, see Pew Research Center. "In US, Decline of Christianity Continues at Rapid Pace: An Update on America's Changing Religious Landscape," October 17, 2019, https://www.pewforum.org/2019/10/17/in-u-s-decline-of-christianity-continues-at-rapid-pace.

84. Pew Research Center 2014. For texture on the religious experience of Puerto Ricans in the US, see also Christina T. Williams, "Que Se Sepa: Perspectives from the Puerto Rican Diaspora in Hartford" (senior thesis, Trinity College Hartford, 2013).

85. Hosffman Ospino, *Hispanic Ministry in Catholic Parishes: A Summary Report of Findings from the National Study of Catholic Parishes with Hispanic Ministry* (Trustees of Boston College, 2014).

86. Manuel J. Gaxiola-Gaxiola, "Latin American Pentecostalism: A Mosaic within a Mosaic." *Pneuma: The Journal of the Society for Pentecostal Studies* 13, no. 1 (1991): 107–129; Arlene Sanchez-Walsh, *Latino Pentecostal Identity: Evangelical Faith, Self, and Society* (Columbia University Press, 2003), Juan Francisco Martínez, *Sea la Luz: The Making of Mexican Protestantism in the American Southwest, 1829–1900* (University of North Texas Press, 2006); Néstor Medina and Sammy Alfaro, eds., *Pentecostals and Charismatics in Latin American and Latino Communities* (Palgrave MacMillan, 2015); Daniel Ramírez, *Migrating Faith: Pentecostalism in the United States and Mexico in the Twentieth Century* (University of North Carolina Press, 2015); Mark Mulder, Aida Ramos, and Gerardo Martí, *Latino Protestants in America: Growing and Diverse* (Rowman and Littlefield, 2017); Arlene Sanchez-Walsh, *Pentecostals in America* (Columbia University Press, 2018); Jonathan E. Calvillo, *The*

*Saints of Santa Ana: Faith and Ethnicity in a Mexican Majority City* (Oxford University Press, 2020); Lloyd D. Barba, *Sowing the Sacred: Mexican Pentecostal Farmworkers in California* (Oxford University Press, 2022)

87. Samiri Hernández Hiraldo, *Black Puerto Rican Identity and Religious Experience* (University Press of Florida, 2006).

88. Juan Flores, "Reclaiming Left Baggage: Some Early Sources for Minority Studies," *Cultural Critique*, no. 59 (2005): 187–206.

89. María del Mar Logroño Narbona, Paulo G. Pinto, and John Tofik Karam, *Crescent Over Another Horizon: Islam in Latin America, the Caribbean, and Latino U.S.A.* (University of Texas Press, 2015).

90. Morales, *Latino and Muslim in America*, 211.

91. See Hisham Aidi, "Let Us Be Moors: Islam, Race and 'Connected Histories,'" *Middle East Report*, no. 229 (2003): 42–53; Patrick D. Bowen, "Conversion to Islam in the United States: A Case Study in Denver, Colorado," *Intermountain West Journal of Religious Studies* 1, no. 1 (2009): 42–64 and "The Latino American Da'wah Organization and the 'Latina/o Muslim' Identity in the United States," *Journal of Race, Ethnicity and Religion*, vol. 11, no. 1 (2009): 1–23; and Morales, *Latino and Muslim in America*.

92. Morales, *Latino and Muslim in America*.

93. Stephanie Londono, "Immigrant Latinas and their Shahadah in Miami" (master's thesis, Florida International University, 2014); Cynthia Hernández González, "¿En quiénes pensamos cuando hablamos de las mujeres musulmanas? La develación de nuestra mentalidad colonizada," *Latin America and Caribbean Islamic Studies Newsletter* 2, no. 2 (January 2022): 11–24.

94. See Aidi, "Let Us Be Moors" and Hjamil A. Martínez-Vasquez, *Latina/o Y Musulmán: The Construction of Latina/o Identity among Latina/o Muslims in the United States* (Wipf & Stock Publishers, 2010);"The Act of Remembering: The Reconstruction of U.S. Latina/o Identities by U.S. Latina/o Muslims," in *Decolonizing Epistemologies: Latina/o Theology and Philosophy*, ed. Ada María Isasi-Díaz and Eduardo Mendieta (Fordham University Press, 2012), 127–150; and "Dis-covering a Historical Consciousness: The Creation of a U.S. Latina/o Muslim Identity," in del Mar Logroño Narbona, Pinto, and Karam, *Crescent Over Another Horizon*, 255–275.

95. SpearIt, "God Behind Bars: Race, Religion and Revenge," *Seton Hall Law Review* 37, no. 1 (January 12, 2007): 497–525 and *American Prisons: A Critical Primer on Culture and Conversion to Islam* (First Edition Design Publishing, Inc., 2017).

96. Ken Chitwood, "Muslim AmeRícans: Puerto Rican Muslims in the USA and the Need for More Cosmopolitan Frames of Analysis in the Study of Islam and Muslim Communities in the Americas," *International Journal of Latin American Religions* 3 (2019): 413–434.

97. Morales, *Latino and Muslim in America*.

98. SpearIt, "God Behind Bars;" Aidi, "Let us Be Moors"; Morales, *Latino and Muslim in America*; and Patrick D. Bowen, "Conversion to Islam in the United States: A Case Study in Denver, Colorado," *Intermountain West Journal of Religious Studies* 1, no. 1 (2009): 42–64.

99. Bowen, "Conversion" and "The Latino American Da'wah Organization and the 'Latina/o Muslim' Identity in the United States," *Journal of Race, Ethnicity and Religion* 11, no. 1 (2010): 1–23.

100. Martínez-Vasquez, *Latina/o Y Musulmán*; Abbas Barzegar, "Latino Muslims in the United States: An Introduction," *Journal of the High Plains Society for Applied Anthropologists* 23, no. 2 (2003).

101. Barzegar, "Latino Muslims;" Bowen, "Conversion;" Martínez-Vásquez, *Latina/o Y Musulmán*; Ken Chitwood, "Islam en Español: The narratives, demographics, & reversion pathways of Latina/o Muslims in the U.S.," *University of Waikato Islamic Studies Review* 1, no. 2 (Fall 2015): 35–54; Juan Galvan, *Latino Muslims: Our Journeys to Islam* (Self-published, 2017).

102. Espinosa, Galvan, and Morales, "Latino Muslims," 4–5. Similar to how "hispanidad" helped Nuevomexicanos in the American Southwest regain "some degree of control over symbols of their identity" (John Nieto-Phillips, *The Language of Blood: The Making of Spanish-American Identity in New Mexico, 1880s-1930s* (University of New Mexico Press, 2004), 171–172) "Latino Islamidad" serves as "a sentiment, a sensibility, and a self-perception" that empowers Latina/o Muslims in the US, as a counterpoint to other dominant cultures.

103. Martínez-Vasquez, *Latina/o Y Musulmán*, 12.

104. Omar Ramadan-Santiago, "Insha'Allah, Ojalá, Yes Yes Y'all: Puerto Ricans (Re)Examining and (Re)Imagining Their Identities through Islam and Hip Hop," in *Islam and the Americas*, ed. Aisha Khan (University Press of Florida, 2015), 115–140.

105. Morales, *Latino and Muslim in America*, 7.

106. Brett Hendrickson, *Mexican American Religions: An Introduction* (Routledge, 2022), 175–176.

107. Espinosa, Galvan, and Morales, "Latino Muslims."

108. Aliyah Khan, *Far from Mecca: Globalizing the Muslim Caribbean* (Rutgers University Press, 2020).

109. This literature is too broad to cite sufficiently here but can be further explored through resources like the "American Muslim Bibliography" from the Latin America and Caribbean Islamic Studies Association (https://www.lacisa.org).

110. Khan, *Far From Mecca*, 279.

111. Jorge Duany, *Puerto Rico: What Everyone Needs to Know* (Oxford University Press, 2017), 1.

112. Francio Guadeloupe, *Black Man in the Netherlands* (University Press of Mississippi, 2022), xxii.

113. Marisel C. Moreno, *Crossing Waters: Undocumented Migration in Hispanophone Caribbean and Latinx Literature & Art* (University of Texas Press, 2022).

114. Jorge Duany, "Dominican Migration to Puerto Rico: a Transnational Perspective," *Centro Journal* 17, no. 1 (Spring, 2005): 242–269 and "Reconstructing Racial Identity: Ethnicity, Color, and Class among Dominicans in the United States and Puerto Rico," *Latin American Perspectives* 25, no. 3 (1998):147–172.

115. Duany, *Puerto Rico: What Everyone Needs to Know*, 3.

116. An Yountae, "A Decolonial Theory of Religion: Race, Coloniality, and Secularity in the Americas," *Journal of the American Academy of Religion* 88, no. 4 (December 2020): 947–980.

117. Ziauddin Sardar ed., *Critical Muslim 35: The Muslim Atlantic* (Hurst Publications, 2020). See also Aisha Khan, "Realising a Muslim Atlantic," *The Maydan*, July 16, 2020.

118. Scott S. Reese, "Islam in Africa/Africans and Islam," *Journal of African History* 55 (2014): 17.

119. Talal Asad, "The Idea of an Anthropology of Islam," *Qui Parle* 17, no. 2 (Spring–Summer 2019): 10–11.

120. Magnus Marsden and David Henig, "Muslim Circulations and Networks in West Asia: Ethnographic Perspectives on Transregional Connectivity," *Journal of Eurasian Studies* 10, no. 1 (January 2019): 11.

121. See Jesse Weaver Shipley, Jean Comaroff, and Achille Mbembe, "Africa in Theory: A Conversation Between Jean Comaroff and Achille Mbembe, *Anthropological Quarterly* 83, no. 3 (Summer 2010): 653–678.

122. Claudia Derichs, "Shifting Epistemologies in Area Studies: From Space to Scale," *Middle East—Topics & Arguments* 4 (May 2015): 29.

123. Miriam Cooke and Bruce B. Lawrence, eds., *Muslim Networks: From Hajj to Hip Hop* (University of North Carolina Press, 2005).

124. Gilles Deleuze and Félix Guattari, *A Thousand Plateaus: Capitalism and Schizophrenia*, trans. Brian Massumi (University of Minnesota Press, 1987).

125. Julia Verne, *Living Translocality Space, Culture and Economy in Contemporary Swahili Trade* (Stuttgart: Franz Steiner Verlag, 2012) and Michael Muhammad Knight, *Muhammad's Body: Baraka Networks and the Prophetic Assemblage* (University of North Carolina Press, 2020).

126. del Mar Logroño Narbona, Pinto, and Karam, *Crescent Over Another Horizon*, 3.

127. Kris Manjapara, *Age of Entanglement: German and Indian Intellectuals across Empire* (Harvard University Press, 2014), 6 and 291.

128. See Beck, *Cosmopolitan Vision* and Mara Leichtman, *Shii Cosmopolitanisms in Africa: Lebanese Migration and Religious Conversion in Senegal* (Indiana University Press, 2015).

129. Farah Bakaari, "Islam and Its Others," in *Across the Worlds of Islam: Muslim Identities, Beliefs, and Practices from Asia to America*, ed. Edward E. Curtis IV (Columbia University Press, 2023), 27.

130. Nile Green, *Global Islam: A Very Short Introduction* (Oxford University Press, 2020), 7.

131. Chitwood, *The Muslims of Latin America and the Caribbean*, 13–14.

132. Shahab Ahmed, *What Is Islam? The Importance of Being Islamic* (Princeton University Press, 2015) and Ali Mian, "Shahab Ahmed's Contradictions," *Der Islam* 97, no. 1 (2020): 239–240.

133. Green, *Global Islam*, 17.

134. Deleuze and Guattari, *A Thousand Plateaus*, 198.

135. Jasbir K. Puar, *Terrorist Assemblages: Homonationalism in Queer Times* (Duke University Press, 2017). The idea of assemblage, of course, is related to the concept of bricolage. See Claude Levi-Strauss, *The Savage Mind* (University of Chicago Press, 1966), 24, and Véronique Altglas, "'Bricolage': reclaiming a conceptual tool," *Culture and Religion* 15, no. 4 (2014): 475–489.

136. Puar, *Terorist Assemblages*, 295.

137. Avtar Brah, *Cartografías de la diáspora: Identidades en cuestión* (Traficantes de Sueños, 2011).

138. Ahmed, *What Is Islam?* and Robert W. Hefner, "An Alternative View of the Modern Islamic: Indonesian Perspectives on Shahab Ahmed's Balkans-to-Bengal Legacy," *The Maydan*, June 19, 2018.

139. Verne, *Living Translocality Space, Culture and Economy in Contemporary Swahili Trade*, 23–25.

140. Mian, "Shahab Ahmed's Contradictions," 240.

141. Halal versions substitute the fried pork skin, opting instead for everything from onions to plantain chips, chicken, or cheese.

142. Cruz Miguel Ortíz Cuadra, *Eating Puerto Rico: A History of Food, Culture, and Identity*, trans. Russ Davidson (The University of North Carolina Press, 2013), 149.

143. Ken Chitwood, "Ethnographic Journalism and the Public Understanding of Religion," *Bulletin for the Study of Religion* 52, no. 3 (2024): 88–101.

144. Ken Chitwood, "On Eid 2017, a Peek into the Lives of Puerto Rican Muslims," *The Conversation*, June 23, 2017.

145. What some call a "patchwork ethnography." See Gökçe Günel, Saiba Varma, and Chika Watanabe, "A Manifesto for Patchwork Ethnography," Society for Cultural Anthropology, June 9, 2020.

146. Guadeloupe wrote, "I do not make any sharp distinction between fieldwork and life. There is no beginning and end of reflection. For me, anthropology is a discipline of infinitely rehearsing life experiences with others on and off the job, behind and in front of the computer," in *Black Man in the Netherlands*, xxxiv–xxxv.

147. Joel Antonio Blanco-Rivera, "The Forbidden Files: Creation and Use of Surveillance Files Against the Independence Movement in Puerto Rico," *The American Archivist* 68, no. 2 (Sept. 2005): 297–311; Pedro A. Cabán, "Puerto Rico: State Formation in a Colonial Context," *Caribbean Studies* 30, no. 2 (Jul.–Dec., 2002): 170–215; Marisol LeBrón," *Carpeteo* Redux: Surveillance and Subversion against the Puerto Rican Student Movement," *Radical History Review* May 1, 2017; 2017 (128): 147–172; Claudia Sofía Ojeda Rexach, "Ojos en la espalda, vigilándome: Carpeteo, Police Surveillance, and the Negative Space of Colonial Liberalism in Mid-Twentieth Century Puerto Rico," (thesis, Haverford College, 2021).

148. Arshad Imitaz Ali, "Citizens under Suspicion: Responsive Research with Community under Surveillance," *Anthropology and Education Quarterly* 47, no. 1 (March 2016): 78–95 and "Off the Record: Police Surveillance, Muslim Youth, and an Ethnographer's Tools of Research," *Equity & Excellence in Education* 51, nos. 3–4 (2018): 431–449; Sabrina Alimahomed-Wilson, "When the FBI Knocks: Racialized State Surveillance of Muslims." *Critical Sociology* 45, no. 6 (September 2019): 871–887; Sara Kamali, "Informants, Provocateurs, and Entrapment: Examining the Histories of the FBI's PATCON and the NYPD's Muslim Surveillance Program," *Surveillance and Society* 15, no. 1 (2017).

149. See Ken Chitwood, "An Ethnographic Turn in Comparative Theology?", *Ecclesial Practices* 8, 2 (2021): 199–215.

150. Anne Marie O'Conner, "Emergence of a Hybrid Culture," *Los Angeles Times*, April 29, 1997.

151. Ken Chitwood, "Houston's Hispanic Imam Bridges Cultures," *Houston Chronicle*, July 5, 2012.

152. Ilan Kapoor, "Hyper-self-reflexive development? Spivak on representing the Third World 'Other'," *Third World Quarterly* 25, no. 4 (2004), 627–647.

153. Lisa Jane Disch, *Hannah Arendt and the Limits of Philosophy: With a New Preface* (Cornell University Press, 1996).

154. To ensure participants' welfare and rights were upheld according to federal and state laws, local policies, and ethical principles, my research underwent review at the University of Florida and Freie Universität Berlin.

155. Julio César Torres, Ricardo Olivero Lora, "Nuyorican Básquet," Documentary Film, 2020; Antonio Sotomayor, *The Sovereign Colony: Olympic Sport, National Identity, and International Politics in Puerto Rico* (University of Nebraska Press, 2016).

156. Kristy Nabhan-Warren and Natalie Wigg-Stevenson, "Situating the 'Crisis of Representation' in Ethnographic Approaches to Theology and Working Toward Community-Centered, Dialogic Approaches," *Ecclesial Practices* 8, 2 (2021): 123–128.

157. Gayatri Spivak, *The Post-colonial Critic: Interviews, Strategies, Dialogues*, S. Harasym, ed. (Routledge, 1990), 42.

158. Elaine A. Peña, *Performing Piety: Making Space Sacred with the Virgin of Guadalupe* (University of California Press, 2011), 3.

159. Ulf Hannerz, "Being There . . . and There . . . and There! Reflections on Multi-Site Ethnography," in *Ethnographic Fieldwork: An Anthropological Reader* (2nd ed.) ed. Antonius C. G. M. Robben and Jeffrey A. Sluka (Wiley-Blackwell, 2012), 399–408; Elizabeth McAlister, *Rara! Vodou, Power, and Performance in Haiti and its Diaspora* (University of California Press, 2002); Paul Christopher Johnson, *Diaspora Conversions: Black Carib Religion and the Recovery of Africa* (University of California Press, 2007); Cristina Rocha and Manuel A. Vásquez eds., *The Diaspora of Brazilian Religions* (Brill, 2013); Donizete Rodrigues, F. M. Mendes, "O Processo Identitário na Primeira Igreja Batista de Marília/SP: um estudo antropológico do modelo de discipulado apostólico," in *Expressões Religiosas de um Brasil Plural: Estudos contemporâneos*, ed. Marcos Vinicius de Freitas Reis, Fábio Py, Diego Omar Silveira, (Fonte Editorial, 2018), 205–230; and Martijn Oosterbaan, Linda van de Kamp, Joana Bahia, eds., *Global Trajectories of Brazilian Religion: Lusopheres* (Bloomsbury Academic, 2019); Peña, *Performing Piety*.

160. George Marcus, "Ethnography in/of the World System: The Emergence of Multi-Sited Ethnography," *Annual Review of Anthropology* 24 (1995): 95–117.

161. The vast majority of interviews were with Muslims who identify as "Puerto Rican." I also conducted interviews with Palestinian, Egyptian, Black, and other Muslims who did not identify as "Puerto Rican." I must also note that most of my interactions and interviews were with men. Of my 111 interviews, only 24 were with women.

162. Ken Chitwood and Khadijah Taylor, "AmeRícan Muslims," Affect and Colonialism Web Lab, accessed January 14, 2023, https://affect-and-colonialism.net/video/american-muslims.

163. Ken Chitwood and Hazel Gómez, "'We Carry All These Different Hijabs'" *Journal of Muslim Philanthropy and Civil Society* 7, no. 2 (Fall 2023): 70–77 and Ken Chitwood, "From Puerto Rico to Palestine, with Solidarity," *The Revealer*, March 2024.

164. Margarethe Kusenbach, "Street Phenomenology: The Go-Along as Ethnographic Research Tool," *Ethnography* 4, no. 3 (2003): 455–485 and Richard M. Carpiano, "Come Take a Walk with Me: The 'Go-Along' Interview as a Novel Method for Studying the Implications of Place for Health and Well-Being," *Health & Place* 15, no. 1 (2009): 263–272.

165. See also Ken Chitwood, "Halāl Habichuelas: Food, Belonging, and the Conundrums of Being a Puerto Rican Muslim," *Journal of the American Academy of Religion* 90, no. 4 (December 2022): 916–936.

166. Anne Kirstine Hermann, "An Ethnographic Journalism," *Journalism—Theory Practice and Criticism* 17, no. 2 (2016): 260–278.

167. Manuel Castells, "Materials for an Exploratory Theory of the Network Society," *British Journal of Sociology* 1, no. 51 (January/March 2000).

168. Madelina Nuñez and Harold D. Morales, "Latinx Muslim Digital Landscapes: Locating Networks and Cultural Practices," in *Cyber Muslims: Mapping Islamic Digital Media in the Internet Age*, ed. Robert Rosenahl (Bloomsbury, 2022), 84–99.

169. Jacqueline H. Fewkes, "Piety in the Pocket: An Introduction," in *Anthropological Perspectives on the Religious Uses of Mobile Apps*, ed. Jacqueline H. Fewkes (Springer, 2019), 10.

170. Harold P. Morales contends that while regionally diverse, Latinx Muslims create a pan-Latinx Muslim "brand" fostered via online communities, which is frequently picked up by mass media and further marginalizes those who do not empathize with these narrow narratives of what it is to be Latinx Muslim. See Harold Morales, *Religion and American Cultures: An Encyclopedia of Traditions, Diversity, and Popular Expression*, Gary Laderman and Luis D. León, vol. 4 (ABC-CLIO), 11.

171. Maurizio Telli, Francesco Pisanu, and David Hakken, "The Internet as a Library-of-People: for a Cyberethnography of Online Groups," *Forum Qualitative Sozialforschung* 8, no. 3 (2007): 283–301.

172. Christine Hine, "The E3 Internet: Embedded, Embodied, Everyday Internet," in *Ethnography for the Internet: Embedded, Embodied and Everyday* (Bloomsbury, 2015), 19–54.

173. Ken Chitwood, "Latinx Muslims 'Like' One Another: An Ethnographic Exploration of Social Media and the Formation of Latinx Muslim Community," in *Anthropological Perspectives on the Religious Uses of Mobile Apps*, ed. Jacqueline H. Fewkes, 83–104. See also Nina Grønlykke Mollerup, "'Being There', Phone in Hand: Thick Presence and Ethnographic Fieldwork with Media," *EASA Media Anthropology Network's 58th e-Seminar* (2017.)

174. Robert V. Kozinets, *Netnography* (Sage Publications, 2010).

175. John Postill and Sarah Pink, "Social Media ethnography: the digital Researcher in a Messy Web," *Media International Australia* (2012): 1–14.

176. Christine Hine, *Virtual Ethnography* (Sage Publications, 2000).

**Chapter 1: *Coyunturas* and Contingent Lineages**

1. James Baldwin, "Black English: A Dishonest Argument," 1980, as quoted in Raoul Peck, "I Am Not Your Negro," 2016.

2. A dojo is a dedicated space for martial arts or meditative training and learning.

3. Variously translated as "judgment," "custom," or "religion," this term is often used to refer to the practice of one's religion, submission to the law and customs of Islam, or to following *shariah*.

4. Salafi is a label derived from the term *salaf* (meaning "pious ancestors"), and refers to a reform movement that first emerged at the turn of the twentieth century. While the Salafi movement is broad and the identity contested, Salafis tend to emphasize the restoration of what they deem "pure" Islamic jurisprudence, sole adherence to the Qur'an and Sunnah, the rejection of *madhahib*, and the restoration of the unity of the ummah. For a helpful history overviewing the development of Salafism, see Henri Lauzière, *The Making of Salafism: Islamic Reform in the Twentieth Century* (Columbia University Press, 2016).

5. Episodes and information about the program can still be found on Facebook, at "Muslim Topics USA with your host Mualana Yusef Ali Abdullah," accessed September 5, 2023, https://www.facebook.com/p/Muslim-Topics-USA-with-your-host-Mualana-Yusef-Ali-Abdullah-100069448162779/?paipv=0&eav=AfZyUrkn4KTMBjjBFlR_4Pr6gj8yktRfrLmqPoSAUzp-hHZRhDiYPMFUeay5CTTFU5M&_rdr.

6. Juan F. Caraballo-Resto, "¿Islam *en* Puerto Rico o Islam *de* Puerto Rico?: Prácticas Identitarias entre Conversos/as al Islam en Puerto Rico," *Revista Ámbito de Encuentros* 12, no. 2 (2019): 7–29.

7. Patricia Silver, *Sunbelt Diaspora: Race, Class, and Latino Politics in Puerto Rican Orlando* (University of Texas Press, 2020), 22.

8. Jorell A. Meléndez-Badillo, *The Lettered Barriada: Workers, Archival Power, and the Politics of Knowledge in Puerto Rico* (Duke University Press, 2021), 179.

9. Ibid.

10. Vincent L. Wimbush, Lalruatkima, and Melissa Renee Reid, eds., *MisReading America: Scriptures and Difference* (Oxford University Press, 2013), 3.

11. Jorell Meléndez-Badillo, *Puerto Rico: A National History* (Princeton University Press, 2024), 155.

12. Kevin Funk, *Rooted Globalism: Arab–Latin American Business Elites and the Politics of Global Imaginaries* (Indiana University Press, 2022), 139.

13. Ibid.

14. Beck, *Cosmopolitan Vision*, 8.

15. Khan, "Realising a Muslim Atlantic."

16. Baldwin, as quoted in Peck, "I Am Not Your Negro."

17. Caraballo-Resto, "¿Islam *en* Puerto Rico . . . ?" There was a massive outmigration of people from Puerto Rico between 2010 and 2020, with the archipelago losing 11.8 percent of its population across the decade.

18. Espinosa, Galvan, and Morales "Latino Muslims."

19. Ramadan-Santiago, "Insha'Allah/Ojalá," 122. See also Michael A. Gomez, *Black Crescent: The Experience and Legacy of African Muslims in the Americas* (Cambridge University Press, 2005), 12, and Leslie B. Rout Jr., *The African Experience in Spanish America* (Markus Wiener Publishers, 2003), xiv–xv.

20. The call to Islam, both from within and beyond the Muslim community.

21. Caraballo-Resto, "¿Islam *en* Puerto Rico . . . ?" See also Soraya Asad Sánchez, "La Presencia Árabe en San Juan, Puerto Rico (1910–1940)" (PhD diss., Centro de Estudios Avanzados de Puerto Rico y El Caribe, 2016); Ken Chitwood, "Latinx

Muslims 'Like' One Another;" Omar Ramadan-Santiago, "Introduction of Islam to Sixteenth-Century Puerto Rico," in *Encyclopedia of Latin American Religions*, ed. Henri Gooren (Springer Reference, 2019); Lourdes Enid Saez, 'Hay Moros en la Costa: The Imprint and Legacy of Islam in Puerto Rico and the Fiestas De Santiago Apostol' (PhD diss., Arizona State University, 2017); Héctor Antonio Morales Rivera, "Representación del islam en Puerto Rico : creyentes, la prensa, y su trayectoria en la Isla : 1993–2015," (master's thesis, Universidad de Puerto Rico Río Piedras, 2022); and Wendy Díaz, "Rediscovering Puerto Rico's Lost Islamic History: Islamic Influence at Isla del Encanto," *Islamic Horizons*, Sept/Oct 2023: accessed September 5, 2023, https://islamichorizons.net/rediscovering-puerto-ricos-lost-islamic-history.

22. See Acosta-Bélen and Santiago, *Puerto Ricans in the United States*; Jorge Duany, *Blurred Borders: Transnational Migration between the Hispanic Caribbean and the United States* (University of North Carolina Press, 2011), 48–61; and Jorge Duany, *The Puerto Rican Nation on the Move: Identities on the Island and in the United States* (University of North Carolina Press, 2003).

23. Laviera, "AmeRícan."

24. Duany, *The Puerto Rican Nation on the Move*, 23.

25. E.g., as it is used by Dominican musician Juan Luis Guerra in his song, "Ojalá que llueva café"—"I hope it rains coffee."

26. Federico Corriente, *Dictionary of Arabic and Allied Loanwords: Spanish, Portuguese, Catalan, Galician and Kindred Dialects* (Brill, 2008). It should be mentioned that the word has cognates in other regional languages as well, including *oxalá* in Portuguese.

27. See Saez, "'Hay Moros en la Costa.'"

28. David Morgan, *Visual Piety: A History and Theory of Popular Religious Images* (University of California Press, 1999), 195.

29. Chitwood, *The Muslims of Latin America and the Caribbean*, 50.

30. Ramadan-Santiago, "Introduction of Islam to Sixteenth-Century Puerto Rico," 2.

31. Anouar Majid, *We Are All Moors: Ending Centuries of Crusades against Muslims and Other Minorities* (University of Minnesota Press, 2009), 10.

32. Alan Mikhail, *God's Shadow: Sultan Selim, His Ottoman Empire, and the Making of the Modern World* (Liveright, 2020). See also Paul Gilroy, *The Black Atlantic: Modernity and Double-Consciousness* (Harvard University Press, 1993).

33. Gomez, *Black Crescent*, 13.

34. From *Cedulario Indiano Recopilado por Diego de Encinas*, vol. I, 455, as quoted in Karoline P. Cook, *Forbidden Passages: Muslims and Moriscos in Colonial Spanish America* (University of Pennsylvania Press, 2016), 56.

35. See Majid, *We Are All Moors*.

36. Cook, *Forbidden Passages*, 5. See also Arely Medina, "Islam in Mexico: Diversity, Accommodations, and Perspectives on Approach," *International Journal of Latin American Religions* (2023), https://doi.org/10.1007/s41603-023-00193-x.

37. The cases in Puerto Rico are few and underwhelming in detail, but there could be more to discover in archives. It is possible, given further research, that Moriscos, like "crypto-Jews," could have practiced their faith on the periphery of the concentrated centers of power in San Juan. See Ezratty, Harry, "Crypto Jews in Puerto Rico Welcomed by Reform Community," *Society For Crypto Judaic Studies*,

accessed November 21, 2015, http://bechollashon.org/heart/index.php/articles/789; Jacobs, J., *Hidden Heritage: The Legacy of the Crypto-Jews* (University of California Press, 2002).

38. Saez, "'Hay Moros en la Costa,'" 38.

39. Irene Silverblatt, *Modern Inquisitions: Peru and the Colonial Origins of the Civilized World* (Duke University Press, 2004); Carolyn Dean, *Inka Bodies and the Body of Christ: Corpus Christi in Colonial Cuzco, Peru* (Duke University Press, 1999); Jennifer Scheper Hughes, panel presentation, "Rethinking Islamic Studies," American Academy of Religion Annual Meeting, Atlanta, GA: November 20, 2015. See also Chitwood, *The Muslims of Latin America and the Caribbean*, 49–74.

40. See Saez, "'Hay Moros en la Costa.'"

41. Aidi, "Let Us Be Moors," 42–53. See also Ken Chitwood, "Islam en Español"; "Halāl Habichuelas"; and "'A Place of Our Own': Puerto Rican Muslims and their Architectural Responses as Quadruple Minorities on the Margins," *International Journal of Islamic Architecture*, Special Issue: Hinterland Forces: Architectural Responses at the Margins, ed. Angela Andersen (July 2022) 267–292.

42. Patrick D. Bowen, "U.S. Latina/o Muslims Since 1920: From 'Moors' to 'Latino Muslims,'" *Journal of Religious History* 37, no. 2 (2013), 165–184; Christina Civantos, *The Afterlife of Al-Andalus: Muslim Iberia in Contemporary Arab and Hispanic Narratives* (SUNY Press 2017); and Charles Hirschkind, *The Feeling of History: Islam, Romanticism, and Andalusia* (University of Chicago Press, 2020).

43. Chitwood, "Islam en Español."

44. Facebook post by Mutah "Napoleon" Beale on September 10, 2022, https://www.facebook.com/lifeofanoutlaw.

45. Díaz, "Rediscovering Puerto Rico's Lost Islamic History."

46. Hjamil A. Martínez-Vázquez, "The Act of Remembering: The Reconstruction of U.S. Latina/o Identities by U.S. Latina/o Muslims," *Decolonizing Epistemologies: Latina/o Theology and Philosophy*, Transdisciplinary Theological Colloquia (FUP) (New York, NY, 2011; online edition, Fordham Scholarship Online, September 20, 2012), accessed September 6, 2023, https://doi.org/10.5422/fordham/9780823241354.003.0007.

47. Some of the material here was originally published in Ken Chitwood, "The Enduring Legacy of Black Muslims in the Americas," *New Lines Magazine*, January 20, 2022.

48. Greg Gandin, *The Empire of Necessity: Slavery, Freedom, and Deception in the New World* (Macmillan Publishers, 2015).

49. Ayla Amon, "African Muslims in Early America: Religion, Literacy, and Liberty," Smithsonian Institute, https://nmaahc.si.edu/explore/stories/african-muslims-early-america.

50. Gomez, *Black Crescent*, 43.

51. William F. Keegan, "Destruction of the Taino" in *Archaeology*. January/February 1992, pp. 51–56; Irvine Rouse, *The Tainos: Rise and Decline of the People Who Greeted Columbus* (Yale University Press, 1992), 150–168; Noble David Cook, "Sickness, Starvation, and Death in Early Hispaniola." *The Journal of Interdisciplinary History* 32, no. 3 (2002): 349–386.

52. Ramadan-Santiago, "Introduction of Islam."

53. Gomez, *Black Crescent*, 12.

54. Ramadan-Santiago, "Insha'Allah/Ojalá," 122.

55. Saez, "Hay Moros en la Costa," 85.

56. Specifically, a 1493 law against the importation of "Muslims, Jews, and infidels" and a 1505 law that prohibits Black enslaved Muslims, or those raised with a Moorish person, to come to Hispaniola—whether from Iberia, North Africa, or sub-Saharan Africa). See Saez, "Hay Moros en la Costa," 86.

57. Saez, "Hay Moros en la Costa," 79ff.

58. Diouf, *Servants of Allah*, 38, 211.

59. Ibid., 50, 241.

60. Fernando Picó, *History of Puerto Rico: A Panorama of Its People* (Markus Wiener Publishers, 2011), 51–94.

61. Saez, "Hay Moros en la Costa," 79ff.

62. Ramadan-Santiago, "Insha'Allah/Ojalá," 122.

63. Ramadan-Santiago, "Introduction of Islam to Sixteenth-Century Puerto Rico."

64. For a helpful, public-facing overview of these practices, see Sylviane Diouf, "Muslims in America: A Forgotten History," *Al Jazeera*, February 10, 2021.

65. Delmonte, "Cubans Searching for a New Faith in a New Context," 191–192.

66. Saez, chapters 3–4. See also Brent Singleton, "The Ummah Slowly Bled: A Select Bibliography of Enslaved African Muslims in the Americas and the Caribbean," *Journal of Muslim Minority Affairs*, vol. 22, no. 2 (2002).

67. Gomez, *Black Crescent*; and Diouf, *Servants of Allah*, 179–210.

68. See Johnson, *Diaspora Conversions*.

69. Numerous authors took up this theme. See, for example, José Luis Gonzaléz in *El País De Cuatro Pisos y Otros Ensayos* (Rió Piedras: Ediciones Huracán, 1989) and Juan Flores in *Divided Borders: Essays on Puerto Rican Identity* (Arte Público Press, 1993).

70. Marta I. Cruz-Janzen,"Out of the Closet: Racial Amnesia, Avoidance, and Denial—Racism among Puerto Ricans." *Race, Gender & Class* 10, no. 3 (2003): 64, http://www.jstor.org/stable/41675088.

71. Yeidy M. Rivero, *Tuning Out Blackness: Race and Nation in the History of Puerto Rican Television* (Duke University Press, 2005).

72. Ileana Rodriguez-Silva, *Silencing Race: Disentangling Blackness, Colonialism, and National Identities in Puerto Rico* (Palgrave Macmillan, 2012).

73. Yomaira C. Figueroa-Vásquez, *The Survival of a People* (Duke University Press, forthcoming).

74. Hilda Lloréns, *Making Livable Worlds: Afro-Puerto Rican Women Building environmental Justice* (University of Washington Press, 2021).

75. Grace Asiegbu, "Blackness in Puerto Rico," *Medill Reports Chicago, Puerto Rico 2020, Social Justice, Winter 2020*, accessed September 8, 2023, https://news.medill.northwestern.edu/chicago/blackness-in-puerto-rico and Cruz-Janzen,"Out of the Closet," 64.

76. Hilda Lloréns, "Identity Practices: Racial Passing, Gender, and Racial Purity in Puerto Rico." *Afro-Hispanic Review* 37, no. 1 (2018): 29–47.

77. Maritza Quiñones Rivera, "From Trigueñita to Afro-Puerto Rican: Intersections of the Racialized, Gendered, and Sexualized Body in Puerto Rico and the U.S. Mainland." *Meridians* 7, no. 1 (2006): 162–82, http://www.jstor.org/stable/40338721.

78. Stuart Hall, "New Ethnicities [1988]," in *Selected Writings on Race and Difference*, ed. Paul Gilroy and Ruth Wilson Gilmore (Duke University Press, 2021), 246–256.

79. Guadeloupe, *Black Man in the Netherlands*.

80. W. E. B. DuBois, *The Souls of Black Folk: Essays and Sketches* (Johnson Reprint Corp, 1968), xxii.

81. See also Hilda Lloréns and Maritza Stanchich, "Water Is Life, but the Colony Is a Necropolis: Environmental Terrains of Struggle in Puerto Rico," *Cultural Dynamics* 31, no. 1–2 (February 2019): 81–101. See also Erika Matthews, "Race, Health, and the Environment in Puerto Rico," ArcGIS Story Map, https://www.arcgis.com/apps/Cascade/index.html?appid=8a3f53b28b844c2eaa35b2a167ede473; and Hilda Lloréns, "Racialization Works differently Here in Puerto Rico, Do Not Bring Your U.S.-centric Ideas about Race Here!" *Black Perspectives*, March 3, 2020.

82. Jocelyn Fenton Stitt, *Dreams of Archives Unfolded: Absence and Caribbean Life Writing* (Rutgers University Press, 2021), 41.

83. Yomaira C. Figueroa-Vásquez, *Decolonizing Diasporas: Radical Mappings of Afro-Atlantic Literature* (Northwestern University Press, 2020).

84. C. Eric Lincoln, "The American Muslim Mission in the Context of American Social History," in *The Muslim Community in North America*, ed. Earle H. Waugh, Baha Abu-Laban, and Regula B. Qureshi (University of Alberta Press, 1983), 219.

85. There are significant exceptions to this rule. Among others cited in this book, see Nancie Gonzalez, *Dollar, Dove, and Eagle: One Hundred Years of Palestinian Migration to Honduras* (University of Michigan Press, 1992); Ignacio Klich, "The Chimera of Palestinian Resettlement in Argentina in the Early Aftermath of the First Arab Israeli War and Other Similarly Fantastic Notions," *The Americas* 53 (1996): 15–43; Xavier Abu Eid, "Al-Lajiun (Al-Falasteen-ioun fi Amrika Al-Lataniyah wa Al-bahith Ain Al- A'tiraf" [Palestinian Refugees in Latin America and the Search for Recognition], *Resource Center for Palestinian Residency and Refugee Rights*, 21–22 (2010): 1; Hebat El Attar, "Una *Intifada* Literaria. Mahfud Massis: El Poeta Palestino-Chileno" [A Literary Intifada. Mahfud Massis: The Palestinian-Chilean Poet], *E.I.A.*, 21 (2010): 77–95; Juan Abugattas, "The Perception of the Palestinian Question in Latin America," *Journal of Palestine Studies* 11 (1982): 117–128; Edward B. Glick, "Latin America and the Palestine Partition Resolution," *Journal of Inter-American Studies* 1 (April 1959): 211–222; Bruce Hoffman, *The PLO and Israel in Central America: The Geopolitical Dimension* (Rand, 1988); Ignacio Klich, "Latin America, the United States and the Birth of Israel: The Case of Somoza's Nicaragua," *Journal of Latin American Studies* 20 (1988): 389–432; Regina Sharif, "Latin America and the Arab-Israeli Conflict," *Journal of Palestine Studies* 7 (1977): 98–122; John Tofik Karam, *Another Arabesque: Syrian-Lebanese Ethnicity in Neoliberal Brazil* (Temple University Press, 2007); Cecilia Baeza, "Women in Arab-Palestinian Associations in Chile: Long Distance Nationalism and Gender Mixing," *Al-Raida*, 133–134 (2011): 18–32; Pilar A. Varagas and Luz Marina V. Suaza, *Mujeres árabes de Colombia* [*Arab Women from Colombia*] (Planeta, 2011); Lily Pearl Balloffet, *Argentina in the Global Middle East* (Stanford University Press, 2020).

86. Mary M. Kritz and Douglas T. Gurak, "International Migration Trends in Latin America: Research and Data Survey," *International Migration Review* 13, no. 3 (Autumn 1979): 407–427.

87. Peter Mandaville, *Global Political Islam: An Introduction* (Routledge, 2010), 292, 279.

88. Chitwood, *The Muslims of Latin America and the Caribbean*, 97–126.

89. Kevin Funk, in his book *Rooted Globalism*, talks about how "place-less logics do not precisely replace, but rather coexist alongside place-based mental frameworks, including in the mind of the same individual." This is what he calls "rooted globalism." See Ken Chitwood and Kevin Funk, "Spotlight on Kevin Funk: Rooted Globalism," *Latin America and Caribbean Islamic Studies Newsletter* 3, no. 3 (May 2023), 32–39.

90. Soraya Asad Sánchez, Arab American Institute Foundation, "Puerto Rico," accessed November 1, 2015, https://d3n8a8pro7vhmx.cloudfront.net/aai/pages/7706/attachments/original/1431630809/PuertoRico.pdf?1431630809.

91. "La Presencia Árabe en San Juan, Puerto Rico (1910–1940)." May 2016, Centro de Estudios Avanzados de Puerto Rico y El Caribe under the direction of Dra. Amalia Alsina Orozco, 139.

92. Ibid., 2.

93. Roberto Marín-Guzmán and Zidane Zéraoui, *Arab Immigration in Mexico in the Nineteenth and Twentieth Centuries: Assimilation and Arab Heritage* (Instituto Tecnológico de Monterey and Augustine Press, 2003) and Roberto Marín-Guzmán, *A Century of Palestinian Immigration into Central America: A Study of their Economic and Cultural Contributions* (University of Costa Rica, 2000).

94. Juan F. Caraballo-Resto, "Palestinian Muslims as a 'Middle-Man Minority Group' in San Juan, Puerto Rico" (undergraduate thesis, University of Puerto Rico, 2003).

95. Alia Farid, "Elsewhere," December 2023, film, sculpture, and textile, Chisenhale Gallery, London, accessed November 2024, https://chisenhale.org.uk/project/alia-farid/#elsewhere-second-gallery-close.

96. A version of this appeared in Chitwood, *The Muslims of Latin America and the Caribbean*, 118–121.

97. Sherez Mohamed, Carolina González, and Antje Muntendam. "Arabic-Spanish Language Contact in Puerto Rico: A Case of Glottal Stop Epenthesis," *Languages* 4, no. 4: 93 (2019), https://doi.org/10.3390/languages4040093.

98. Baeza, "Palestinians in Latin America," 59–72.

99. They also made their way to Hawaii, Ohio, Massachusetts, and more recently places such as Texas, California, Georgia, and California. For an overview of these migrations and background on the experience of Puerto Rican Muslims in each of these places, see Carmen Teresa Whalen and Víctor Vásquez-Hernández eds., *The Puerto Rican Diaspora: Historical Perspectives* (Temple University Press, 2005). See also Victor Vásquez-Hernández, *Before the Wave: Puerto Ricans in Philadelphia, 1910–1945* (Centro Press, 2017).

100. Jennifer Hinojosa, Nashia Román, and Edwin Meléndez, "Puerto Rican Post-Maria Relocation by States," CENTRO - Center for Puerto Rican Studies, March 2018. In some sense this brings the Florida–Puerto Rico connection full circle over the last five hundred years, starting with Juan Ponce de León's initial foray into *La Florida* from the western ports of Puerto Rico in 1513.

101. Patrick D. Bowen, "Early U.S. Latina/o - African-American Muslim Connections: Paths to Conversion." *Muslim World* 100, no. 4 (October 2010): 390–413.

See also Patrick D. Bowen, "The Latino American Da'wah Organization and the 'Latina/o Muslim' Identity in the United States." *Journal of Race, Ethnicity and Religion*, 1, no. 11 (September 2010): 1–23.

102. Morales, *Latino and Muslim in America*, 28–36.

103. See Ken Chitwood, "Muslim AmeRícans: Puerto Rican Muslims in the USA and the Need for More Cosmopolitan Frames of Analysis in the Study of Islam and Muslim Communities in the Americas," *International Journal of Latin American Religions* 3, no. 2 (2019): 413–434.

104. Duany, *Blurred Borders*, 63.

105. Bowen, "Early U.S. Latina/o. See also Bowen, "The Latino American Da'wah Organization and the 'Latina/o Muslim' Identity in the United States."

106. Zain Abdullah, *Black Mecca: The African Muslims of Harlem* (Oxford University Press, 2013).

107. Morales, *Latino and Muslim in America*, 28–36.

108. Bowen, "Early U.S. Latina/o," 397.

109. Ibid., 405.

110. Ibid., 408.

111. Knight, *The Five Percenters*, 327.

112. Bowen, "Early U.S. Latina/o," 408.

113. Knight, *The Five Percenters*, 230.

114. Roel Meijer ed., *Global Salafism: Islam's New Religious Movement* (Oxford University Press, 2013), 13.

115. Olivier Roy, *Globalized Islam: The Search for a New Umma* (Columbia University Press, 2004).

116. David J. Dodd and Damon Pearson, "Black Gods in Red Bank: The Five Percent Nation in Central New Jersey," *Journal of Gang Research* 10, no. 1 (Fall 2002): 66–74.

117. Aidi, "Let Us Be Moors."

118. At the same time, as much as Puerto Rican Muslims were part of the Black Muslim experience in the US, they were also marginalized from it and chose to maintain a certain distance.

119. Juan Galvan, *Alianza Islamica: Spanish Harlem's Islamic Odyssey* (Publishing Experts, LLC, 2024).

120. Morales, *Latino and Muslim in America*, 36.

121. Umar Abdur-Rahim Ocasio, "Why Alianza Islamica?" *Alianza Islamica*, no. 0 (April/May/June 1987), 1.

122. Ibid., 3.

123. Galvan, *Alianza Islamica*, 122.

124. Ibid., 17.

125. These departments are from pp. 11–12 of Alianza Islamica, Inc.'s "By-Laws" from 1992, provided courtesy of Rahim Ocasio.

126. Anonymous, "Alianza, Here for the Community," a printout from Alianza Islámica's personal archives.

127. Andrés Torres and José E. Velázquez, eds., *The Puerto Rican Movement: Voices from the Diaspora* (Temple University Press, 1998).

128. Acosta-Belén and Santiago, *Puerto Ricans in the United States*, 151.

129. Sara Awartani, "'You Have Living Legends among You': Commemorating the Fiftieth Anniversary of the Chicago Young Lords," *Kalfou* 6, no. 1 (2019), https://doi.org/10.15367/kf.v6i1.238.

130. Acosta-Belén and Santiago, *Puerto Ricans in the United States*, 151.

131. Miguel Melendez and Jose Torres, *We Took the Streets: Fighting For Latino Rights With the Young Lords* (Rutgers University Press, 2005).

132. Johanna Fernández, *The Young Lords: A Radical History* (University of North Carolina Press, 2021).

133. Darrel Enck-Wanzer, ed., *The Young Lords: A Reader* (New York University Press, 2010) and Hiram Maristany, "Mapping Resistance: The Young Lords in El Barrio," a public art project available at https://www.mappingresistance.com/home.

134. José Ramón Sánchez, *Boricua Power: A Political History of Puerto Ricans in the United States* (New York University Press, 2007).

135. Gabriel Haslip-Viera and Sherrie Baver, *Latinos in New York: Communities in Transition* (University of Notre Dame Press, 1996); Gabriel Haslip-Viera, Felix V. Matos Rodriguez, and Angelo Falcon, *Boricuas in Gotham: Puerto Ricans in the Making of Modern New York City* (Markus Wiener Publishers, 2004); and Vicky Muniz, *Resisting Gentrification and Displacement: Voices of Puerto Rican Women of the Barrio* (Routledge, 1998).

136. Danny "Khalil" Salgado, "Stories of Some of the Early 'Latino' Muslims," *Islamic Horizons* (January/February 2020): 28–29.

137. Galvan, *Alianza Islamica*, 79–80.

138. Ibid., 2, 7.

139. So important was Malcolm X to the New York YLP that in the first issue of its paper, *Palante*, published in New York City (in late 1969), their initial biographical feature was not on a great Puerto Rican leader, but on Malcolm X and the relevance of his legacy. See http://darrel.wanzerserrano.com/2015/05/19/the-young-lords-and-malcolm-x/?fbclid=IwAR3xPm32wzNtgaL-GL9N3iX7yKCaNshtbHFtVgjvBH3eN9GEu0HsYYL_FJE.

140. Morales, *Latino and Muslim in America*, 38.

141. Ibid.

142. Ibrahim González, "Latino Muslims in El Barrio," *Somos: Revista panislámica de Alianza Islámica* 1, no. 1 (Spring 1993), 2.

143. Morales, *Latino and Muslim in America*, 39.

144. Ibid., 36.

145. Al-Hajj Yusuf Abdul Rahman Padilla-Alvarez, "A Historical Review of Bani Saqr," Alianza Islamica Blog, February 2016, https://alianzaislamica.org/a-historical-review-of-bani-saqr.

146. Galvan, *Alianza Islamica*, 11–12.

147. The testimony must also be seen as part of Alianza Islámica's wider efforts to legitimate itself as a critical historical node in the Latinx Muslim narrative in opposition to those who later claimed Centro Islámico in Houston, Texas was the "first" Latinx-specific Muslim mosque in the US. See Morales, *Latino and Muslim in America*, 44–74.

148. Ari Goldman, "Sayedah Khadijah Faisal is Dead; Co-founder of Mosque Was 93," *New York Times*, September 10, 1992.

149. Kambiz GhaneaBassiri, *A History of Islam in America* (Cambridge University Press: 2010), 250.

150. Ocasio, however, would continue to speak fondly of the IPNA, citing their organizational premises as inspirations for Alianza. In particular, he includes the IPNA along with the Jamaati Islami and the Ikhwan (Muslim Brotherhood) for giving shape to the organization's constitution. See Galvan, *Alianza Islamica*, 31.

151. Whalen and Vásquez-Hernández, *The Puerto Rican Diaspora*, 237.

152. Ibid., 41–42.

153. Ramon Ocasio, "Alianza Islamica: The True Story," *The Islamic Monthly*, March 14, 2016.

154. Ibid.

155. Galvan, *Alianza Islamica*, 1.

156. Morales, *Latino and Muslim in America*, 42.

157. Bowen, "Early U.S. Latina/o," 392–393, 397.

158. Morales, *Latino and Muslim in America*, 44ff.

159. Ibid.

160. See Espinosa, Galvan, and Morales, "Latino Muslims in the United States."

161. Morales, *Latino and Muslim in America*, 165–198.

162. Todd M. Johnson and David R. Scroggins, "Christian Missions and Islamic Da'wah: A Preliminary Quantitative Assessment," *International Bulletin of Missionary Research*, 29, no. 1 (January 2005): 8–11.

163. Daniel Abdullah Hernandez and Mujahid Fletcher shared how they regularly spend time on trips to support masjids in these countries, to train da'is there, or to call Latina/os to Islam themselves. Hernandez also raised funds and support for an Islamic Learning Center he wanted to launch in Moca, Puerto Rico.

164. Alejandra Molina, "Centro Islámico, a hub for Latino Muslims near and far, breaks ground on expansion during Ramadan," Religion News Service, April 15, 2022.

165. This is based on conversations about research conducted by Benjamin McDowell at Columbia International University in 2021.

166. See Chitwood, "Latinx Muslims 'Like' One Another," and Morales and Nuñez, "Latinx Muslim Digital Landscapes."

167. Morales, *Latino and Muslim in America*, 165–198.

168. Ibid., 39.

**Chapter 2: "I will never deny I'm Borícua"**

1. Hilda Lloréns, *Imaging The Great Puerto Rican Family: Framing Nation, Race, and Gender during the American Century* (Rowman and Littlefield, 2014).

2. Gonzaléz, *El País De Cuatro Pisos y Otros Ensayos.*

3. Flores, *Divided Borders*. See also controversial notions like *insularismo* in the reprint of Antonio Salvador Pedreira's *Insularismo: An Insight into the Puerto Rican Character* (New York: Ausubo Press, 2007) or ideas about the "chaos" of the Caribbean and its "island of paradoxes" in Antonio Benítez-Rojo, *The Repeating Island: The Caribbean and the Postmodern Perspective* (Duke University Press, 1997).

4. Jean-François Bayart, *L'Illusion identitaire* (Fayard, 1996).

5. Judith Butler, "Performative Acts and Gender Constitution: An Essay in Phenomenology and Feminist Theory," in *Performing Feminisms: Feminist Critical Theory and Theatre*, ed. Sue-Ellen Case (Johns Hopkins University Press, 1990).

6. Michel Foucault, "3. Morality and Practice of the Self," in *History of Sexuality Vol. 2: The Use of Pleasure*, ed. Robert Hurley (Vintage Books, 1990); Edward Demenchonok, "Michel Foucault's Theory of Practices of the Self and the Quest for a New Philosophical Anthropology," in *Peace, Culture, and Violence*, ed. Fuat Gursozlu (Brill Publishers, 2018), 218–247; and Sergey S. Horujy, *Practices of the Self and Spiritual Practices: Michel Foucault and the Eastern Christian Discourse*, ed. Kristina Stoeckl, trans. Boris Jakim (Eerdmans, 2014). For an application of this concept in the Puerto Rican case, see Flores, *Divided Borders*.

7. Bawaka Country, et al., "Co-Becoming Bawaka: Towards a Relational Understanding of Place/Space," *Progress in Human Geography* 40, no. 4 (2016): 455–475.

8. Asad Sánchez, "La Presencia Árabe en San Juan, Puerto Rico (1910–1940)."

9. Jon M. Chu, *In the Heights*. Warner Bros, 2021.

10. In "On the Hispanophone Caribbean Question," Vanessa Pérez-Rosario highlights "the question of the possibility of return and highlighting the circular migration that animates Caribbean life" in particular. *Small Axe 20*, no. 3/51 (2016): 21–31.

11. Bawaka Country et al., "Co-Becoming Bawaka" and Bruce Robbins and Paulo Lemos Horta, eds., *Cosmopolitanisms* (NYU Press, 2017).

12. Magdalena López and María Teresa Vera-Rojas, "Introduction: New Theoretical Dialogues and Critical Reflections on Hispanic Caribbean Studies," in *New Perspectives on Hispanic Caribbean Studies*, ed. Magdalena López and María Teresa Vera-Rojas (Palgrave Macmillan, 2020), 1.

13. "We're all in the Caribbean, if you think about it," wrote Junot Díaz, drawing on Stuart Hall's notion that the Caribbean is the original "home of hybridity." See Díaz, *The Brief Wondrous Life of Oscar Wao* (Riverhead Books, 2008), as quoted in Joshua Jelly-Schapiro, *Island People: The Caribbean and the World* (Knopf, 2016), 1. See also Stuart Hall, "Negotiating Caribbean Identities," *New Left Review* 209 (1995): 3–14.

14. Jelly-Schapiro wrote "The Caribbean has been anything but marginal to the making of our modern world" (*Island People*, 16). It is anything but marginal to the making of the late-modern as well.

15. Kokoschka, "The Thing with Islam," 77.

16. Talal Asad, "The Idea of an Anthropology of Islam."

17. Vernon Schubel, *Religious Performance in Contemporary Islam: Shi'i Devotional Rituals in South Asia* (University of South Carolina Press, 1993), 160.

18. Kokoschka, "The Thing with Islam," 77.

19. Guadeloupe, *Black Man in the Netherlands*, xxv.

20. Michael Jackson, *The Wherewithal of Life: Ethics, Migration, and the Question of Well-Being* (University of California Press, 2013), 70. See also Russel McCutcheon ed., *Fabricating Identities* (Equinox Publishers, 2017). See also Jelly-Schapiro, *Island People*, 16.

21. Sandra Ruiz, *Ricanness: Enduring Time in Anticolonial Performance* (New York University Press, 2019).

22. Meléndez-Badillo, *Puerto Rico*, 113. See also Catherine Marsh Kennerly, *Negociaciones culturales: Los intelectuales y el proyecto pedagógico del estado muñocista* (Ediciones Callejón, 2008).

23. Love Lazarus Sechrest, *Race and Rhyme: Rereading the New Testament* (Eerdmans Publishing, 2022), 38–39.

24. Terje Østebø, *Islam, Ethnicity, and Conflict in Ethiopia: The Bale Insurgency, 1963–1970* (Cambridge University Press, 2020), 35.

25. Sherina Feliciano-Santos, *A Contested Caribbean Indigeneity: Language, Social Practice, and Identity within Puerto Rican Taíno Activism* (Rutgers University Press, 2021).

26. Arlene M. Dávila, *Sponsored Identities: Cultural Politics in Puerto Rico* (Temple University Press, 1997), 7.

27. Feliciano-Santos, *Contested Caribbean Indigeneity*, loc. 171.

28. Ibid., 14.

29. Feliciano-Santos, *Contested Caribbean Indigeneity*, loc. 295.

30. Juan F. Caraballo-Resto, "Ritualizing Orientalism and Philo-Semitism: The Task of Making God Exist in Puerto Rico," *International Journal of Latin American Religions* 4 (2020): 81.

31. Ibid.

32. Asad-Sánchez, "La Presencia Árabe."

33. Dávila, *Sponsored Identities*, 16–17.

34. Meléndez-Badillo, *Puerto Rico*, 3.

35. William F. Keegan, *Taíno Indian Myth and Practice: The Arrival of the Stranger King* (University Press of Florida, 2007); Fatima Bercht, Estrellita Brodsky, John Alan Farmer, and Dicey Talor, eds., *Taíno: Pre-Columbian Art and Culture from the Caribbean* (Monacelli Press, 1998); and Rouse, *The Tainos*.

36. Meléndez-Badillo, *Puerto Rico*, 13.

37. Duany, *Puerto Rico*, 11.

38. There are those who interpret these claims as inauthentic and problematic. On the discourse around "Taíno extinction," see: Maximilian C. Forte, "Extinction: The Historical Trope of Anti-Indigeneity in the Caribbean," *Issues in Caribbean Amerindian Studies* 6, no. 4 (August 2004–August 2005); Lynne Guitar, "Documenting the Myth of Taíno Extinction," *Kacike: Journal of Caribbean Amerindian History and Anthropology* (December 2002), https://ia800309.us.archive.org/5/items/KacikeJournal/GuitarEnglish.pdf; Gabriel Haslip-Viera, *Race, Identity and Indigenous Politics: Puerto Rican Neo-Tainos in the Diaspora and the Island* (CreateSpace Independent Publishing Platform, 2013); Yolanda Martínez-San Miguel, "Taíno Warriors? Strategies for Recovering Indigenous Voices in Colonial and Contemporary Hispanic Caribbean Discourses," *CENTRO: Journal of the Center for Puerto Rican Studies* 23, no. 1 (2011): 197–215; among others.

39. Meléndez-Badillo, *Puerto Rico*, 13, 20.

40. Ibid., 41.

41. Some cite a 2002 mitochondrial DNA (mtDNA) study of eight hundred Puerto Ricans that found that 61 percent of the Puerto Rican population has Taíno mtDNA. The study also confirmed that the genetic pool of Puerto Ricans is a mix of European/Spanish, Amerindian/Taíno, and African lineage. See Gabriel Haslip-Viera, *Race, Identity and Indigenous Politics*, 2013.

42. Duany, *Puerto Rico*, 12.

43. Angela Gonzales, "The (Re)Articulation of American Indian Identity: Maintaining Boundaries and Regulating Access to Ethnically Tied Resources," *American Indian Culture and Research Journal* 22, no. 4 (1998): 199–225.

44. Jorge Duany, "Review: The Rough Edges of Puerto Rican Identities: Race, Gender, and Transnationalism," *Latin American Research Review* 40, no. 3 (2005): 177–190. See also Juan Flores, John Attinasi, and Pedro Pedraza Jr., "Puerto Rican Language and Culture in New York City," in *Caribbean Life in New York City: Sociocultural Dimensions* (The Center for Migration Studies of New York, Inc., 1987): 222–234.

45. Feliciano-Santos, *Contested Caribbean Indigeneity*, loc. 503.

46. Rosario Ferré Ramírez de Arellano, "Memorias de *Maldito amor*," Dianna Niebylski, ed. (Fondo de Cultura Económica, 2006): 107–112.

47. Eduardo J. Aguiar, "The Legacy of Frank Bonilla," CENTRO film, https://vimeo.com/30896177.

48. Carlos Quiles, *Un boricua en la luna: Juan Antonio Corretjer en la comunidad puertorriqueña de Chicago* (Batey Urbano, Mariana Editores, 2008).

49. This is derived from language in the Downes v. Bidwell Supreme Court decision, in which US territories like Puerto Rico were described as such.

50. Caraballo-Resto, "¿Islam *en* Puerto Rico o Islam *de* Puerto Rico?"

51. Charles E. Littlefield, "The Insular Cases," *Harvard Law Review* 15, no. 3 (1901): 169–190.

52. Portions of this section were published in Chitwood, *The Muslims of Latin America and the Caribbean*, 1–3.

53. For visuals of these celebrations in the past, see Ricardo E. Alegría, *Las Fiestas de Loíza Santiago Apóstol: A Documentary Film*, San Juan: Instituto de Cultural Puertorriqueña, 1949.

54. Samiri Hernández Hiraldo, "If God Were Black and from Loíza": Managing Identities in a Puerto Rican Seaside Town," *Latin American Perspectives* 33, no. 1 (2006): 66–82. For more from Hernández Hiraldo on religion and Black Puerto Rican identifications, see *Black Puerto Rican Identity and Religious Experience* (University Press of Florida, 2006).

55. Chitwood, *The Muslims of Latin America and the Caribbean*, 2 and 55f.

56. Alejandro Escalante, "The Long Arc of Islamophobia," *Journal of Africana Religions* 7, no. 1 (2019): 179–180, 184; see also Sherman Jackson, *Islam and the Blackamerican: Looking Toward the Third Resurrection* (Oxford University Press, 2005), 101–102.

57. Escalante, "The Long Arc of Islamophobia."

58. Judith Butler, *Excitable Speech: A Politics of the Performative* (Routledge, 1997) and Judith Butler and Athena Athanasiou, *Dispossession: The Performative in the Political* (Polity Press, 2013).

59. Espinosa, Galvan, and Morales, "Latino Muslims in the United States."

60. Benítez-Rojo, *The Repeating Island.*

61. Feliciano-Santos, *Contested Caribbean Indigeneity*, loc. 295.

62. Meléndez-Badillo, *The Lettered Barriada*, 17.

63. Feliciano-Santos, *Contested Caribbean Indigeneity*, loc. 205.

64. Ramadan-Santiago, "Insha'Allah, Ojalá," 115.

65. Jennifer Maytorena Taylor, *New Muslim Cool*, PBS, 2009.

66. José Osvaldo Reyes, "Familismo y geografía en Puerto Rico: algunas reflexiones," *Voces Desde El Trabajo Social* 4, no. 1 (2016): 59–76.

67. Yamil Avivi, "Puerto Rican Muslims in Post-9/11 Documentaries" Authenticity, Cultural Identity, and Communal Belonging," in *New Approaches to Islam in Film*, ed. Kristian Petersen (Routledge, 2021), 52–67.

68. A version of the following section originally appeared in Chitwood, "'A Place of Our Own.'" The analysis was also referenced in Alice Fordham, "No victor but God," a Kerning Cultures podcast episode originally aired on March 18, 2021.

69. Ramadan-Santiago, "Insha'Allah/Ojalá," 118.

70. Aidi, "Let Us Be Moors: Islam, Race and 'Connected Histories'" and Martínez-Vásquez, *Latino y Musulmán*.

71. R. Brooks Jeffery, "The Islamic Legacy in the Built Environment of Hispano-America," in *The Bloomsbury Reader on Islam in the West*, ed. Edward E. Curtis IV (Bloomsbury Academic, 2015), 40.

72. Rafael López Guzmán and Rodrigo Gutiérrez Viñuales, coordinators, *Alhambras: Arquitectura Neoárabe en Latinoamérica* (Almed Ediciones, 2017). See also *The Islamic Design Module in Latin America: Proportionality and the Techniques of Neo-Mudejar Architecture* (McFarland, 2004).

73. Ibid.

74. Ibid.

75. Rodrigo Gutiérrez Viñuales, "El orientalismo en el imaginario artístico y urbano de Iberoamérica. Exotismo, fascinación e Identidad," in *El Orientalismo Desde el Sur*, ed. José Antonio González Alcantud (Anthropos, 2006), 255–256. Regarding Mercado de las Carnes, see also the National Register of Historic Places Inventory, listing reference number 86003199. Other locales were identified during fieldwork in Puerto Rico in 2015, 2017, and 2018.

76. Gernot Böhme, *Architektur und Atmosphäre* (Fink, 2006) and Rainer Kazig, "Atmosphären. Konzept für einen nicht repräsentationellen Zugang zum Raum," in *Kulturelle Geographien: Zur Beschäftigung mit Raum und Ort nach dem Cultural Turn*, ed. Robert Pütz and Christian Berndt (Transcript Verlag, 2007), 167–187.

77. Ken Chitwood, "Dreams of al-Andalus: Latinx Muslims Re-Imagining Race as Quadruple Minorities," in *Routledge Handbook of Islam and Race*, ed. Zain Abdullah (Routledge, 2024).

78. Michael J. Fischer, "Ethnicity and the Post-Modern Arts of Memory," in *Writing Culture*, ed. James Clifford and George Marcus (University of California Press, 1986), 195.

79. Aidi, "Let Us Be Moors," and "The Interference of al-Andalus: Spain, Islam, and the West," *Social Text* 24, no. 1 (2006), 67–88. See also Su'ad Abdul Khabeer, "Africa as Tradition in U.S. African American Muslim Identity," *Journal of Africana Religions* 5, no. 1 (2017): 26–49.

80. Aidi, "Let Us Be Moors"; Bowen, "U.S. Latina/o Muslims Since 1920"; Eric Calderwood, *On Earth or in Poems: The Many Lives of Al-Andalus* (Harvard University Press, 2023); Christina Civantos, *The Afterlife of Al-Andalus: Muslim Iberia in Contemporary Arab and Hispanic Narratives* (SUNY Press, 2017); and Chitwood, "Dreams of al-Andalus."

81. A previous version of this section originally appeared in Chitwood, "Halāl Habichuelas."

82. Johan Fischer, "Branding Halal: A Photographic Essay on Global Muslim Markets," *Anthropology Today* 28, no. 4 (2012): 18–21.

83. David M. Freidenreich, *Foreigners and Their Food: Constructing Otherness in Jewish, Christian, and Islamic Law* (University of California Press, 2011), 144.

84. Jacqueline Fewkes, "'Siri is Alligator Halal?': Mobile Apps, Food Practices, and Religious Authority Among American Muslims," in *Anthropological Perspectives on the Religious Uses of Mobile Apps*, ed. Jacqueline Fewkes (Palgrave Macmillan, 2019), 112.

85. Ruth Jatziri Linares García, "Women in Islam in Mexico," in *Springer Encyclopedia of Latin American Religions*, ed. Henri Gooren (Springer Reference, 2018), 1636–1642.

86. See García Canclini, *Consumidores y ciudadanos: Conflictos multiculturales de la globalización* (Grijalbo, 1995); Jose Martí, "Nuestra América," *Revista Illustrada*, New York, 1891; Shalini Puri, *The Caribbean Postcolonial: Social Equality, Post-nationalism, and Cultural Hybridity* (Palgrave Macmillan, 2004).

87. DuBois, *The Souls of Black Folk*.

88. Ortíz Cuadra, *Eating Puerto Rico*, 249.

89. Ibid., 258.

90. S. Zubaida and R. Tapper, eds., *A Taste of Thyme: Culinary Cultures of the Middle East* (Tauris, 2001).

91. Ortíz Cuadra, *Eating Puerto Rico*, 162.

92. Arjun Appadurai, "How to Make a National Cuisine: Cookbooks in Contemporary India," *Comparative Studies in Society and History* 30 (1988): 3–24.

93. Von Díaz, "This Wildly Popular Blogger Shows How Halal Food Is Adapting to America," *The Kitchn*, May 24, 2019.

94. Mian, "Shahab Ahmed's contradictions."

95. Ahmed, *What Is Islam?*

96. Freidenreich, *Foreigners and Their Food*.

97. Roberto Márquez, ed. and trans., *Puerto Rican Poetry: An Anthology from Aboriginal to Contemporary Times* (University of Massachusetts Press, 2006), xxxvi.

98. María Acosta Cruz, *Dream Nation: Puerto Rican Culture and the Fictions of Independence* (Rutgers University Press, 2014), 110.

99. Felicia Fahey, "Beyond the Island: Puerto Rican Diaspora in 'America' and 'América,'" *University of Michigan Library* 3, no. 1 (2001).

100. Rafael Ocasio, *Race and Nation in Puerto Rican Folklore: Franz Boas and John Alden Mason in Porto Rico* (Rutgers University Press, 2020).

101. The Bronx-born poet María Teresa ("Mariposa") Fernández coined the term "Diasporican" in her celebrated 1993 poem of the same name.

102. Edna Acosta-Belén, "Haciendo patria desde la metrópoli: The cultural expressions of the Puerto Rican diaspora," *Centro Journal* 21, no. 2 (2009): 49–83. See also Miranda J. Martinez, *Power at the Roots: Gentrification, Community Gardens, and the Puerto Ricans of the Lower East Side* (Lexington Books, 2010).

103. Acosta Cruz, 111.

104. Quiara Alegría Hudes, *My Broken Language: A Memoir* (OneWorld, 2021), 101–102.

105. Jorge Duany, "Nation on the Move: The Construction of Cultural Identities in Puerto Rico and the Diaspora," *American Ethnologist* 27, no. 1 (2000): 5–30.

106. In Roberto Márquez, *Puerto Rican Poetry*, xx.

107. Ibid., xx.

108. Adrian Florido, "For Those Missing Puerto Rico, A Song About Dreaming of Home," KUOW Radio, June 20, 2019.

109. Farzana Akhter, "Looking Backward to a Distant Land: South Asian Diaspora and Function of Nostalgia in 'Silver Pavements, Golden Roofs,' 'Mrs. Sen's' and *The Inheritance of Loss*," *South Asian Review* 41, nos. 3–4 (2020): 373–386; Lukasz Dominik Pawelek, "The Role Of Nostalgia In The Literature Of The Caribbean Diasporas—Linking Memory, Globalization And Homemaking," (PhD diss., Wayne State University, January 1, 2015).

110. Erik López, "Nostalgic *Jíbaro*: A Structure of Loss in U.S. Puerto Rican Literature," *Label Me Latina/o* 4 (Fall 2014): 1–13.

111. Carlos Vargas-Ramos, ed., *Race, Front and Center: Perspectives on Race among Puerto Ricans* (Centro Press, 2017).

112. Akhter, "Looking Backward to a Distant Land," 374.

113. Lisa Funnell and Klaus Dodd, *Geographies, Gender and Geopolitics of James Bond* (Palgrave Macmillan, 2017), loc. 139.

114. Ibid.

115. The "island of enchantment," proudly printed on each state-issued license plate.

116. Carmen Cila Rodríguez, "¡Un agricultor de nueve años de edad!: Carlos Emanuel Guzmán, un jíbaro de nueva estirpe," *La Perla del Sur* 29, no. 1443 (27 July 2011).

117. Carla M. Santamaría López, *Boricuas isleños y nuyorriqueños: La construcción de identidades puertorriqueñas a través de la poesía de la calle* (dissertation, State University of New York at Albany, 2011).

118. Østebø, *Islam, Ethnicity, and Conflict in Ethiopia*, 35.

119. Ibid.

120. Ibid. One can also see similar dynamics in some Indo-Guyanese Muslim literature, highlighted by Aliyah Khan in *Far From Mecca*, 149.

121. See Ralph Penny, "The Hispanophone Caribbean," in *Volume 3: An International Handbook of the Science of Language and Society*, ed. Ulrich Ammon, Norbert Dittmar, Klaus J. Mattheier, and Peter Trudgill (De Gruyter, 2006), 2081–2082. And on Spanish-Arabic diglossia in Puerto Rico, see Sherez R. Mohamed, "Language Contact in Puerto Rico: Realizations of Vowel Sequences in Arabic-Spanish Bilinguals," (PhD diss., Florida State University, 2020).

122. Beck, *Cosmopolitan Vision*, 93.

123. Meléndez-Badillo, *Puerto Rico*, 73.

124. Ibid., 74.

125. For an overview of the Foraker Act and life under early US colonial rule, see José Trías Monge, *Puerto Rico: Las penas de la colonia mis antigua del mundo* (Editorial de la Universidad de Puerto Rico, 2005), 40–79.

126. Ana Celia Zentella, "Returned Migration, Language, and Identity: Puerto Rican Bilinguals in Dos Worlds/Two Mundos." *International Journal of the Sociology of Language* 84 (1990): 84.

127. Amílcar Antonio Barreto, *The Politics of Language in Puerto Rico* (University Press of Florida, 2001).

128. Rafael Pérez Torres, *Movements in Chicano Poetry: Against Myths, Against Margins* (Cambridge University Press, 1995), 277.

129. Ibid., 233.

130. With that said, Spanish and English (as well as "Spanglish" on the island or "Nuyorican" in certain parts of the diaspora) coexist within the Puerto Rican cultural repertoire. See Library of Congress, "Yo Soy (I am): The Historical Trajectory of Language in Puerto Rico," accessed September 30, 2023, https://guides.loc.gov/language-in-puerto-rico/introduction?fbclid=IwAR2KLEUQ5PlZteTFunKjgAX4DLccjneAmzIwjjoMn4t4s56jvWwoVe-v5o4.

131. Barreto, *The Politics of Language in Puerto Rico*, xx.

132. Edwin M. Lamboy, "Language and Identity Construction: Can We Talk about a *New* Puerto Rican in the United States?" *Selected Proceedings of the 13th Hispanic Linguistics Symposium*, ed. Luis A. Ortiz-López (Cascadilla Proceedings Project): 70–80.

133. Sánchez, "La Presencia Árabe."

134. See also Pedro López Pagán, "La Huella Islámica" *Primera Hora, a tu manera cooltura*, May 11, 2006, 81.

135. Sánchez, "La Presencia Árabe," 239–253. For example, agricultural (*aceite, arroz, azúcar, naranja, zanahoria*), architectural (*alcalde, mezquita* [not from mosquito as some people assert], *barrio*), astronomy (*acrab, nadir*), topography (place names), mathematics (*algebra, cifra, algoritmo*).

136. Sánchez, "La Presencia Árabe," 199. "Con la información obtenida en esta investigación podemos señalar que el árabe fue el cuatro grupo étnico en integrarse a nuestra cultura. Es decir, el árabe es parte fundamental del mismo."

137. Similar sentiments were expressed outside of Puerto Rico, albeit less so. While most mosques that Puerto Rican Muslims attend in the US have the khutbah in English alone or in both Arabic and English, those that offered Spanish-language messages were lauded (for example, the NHIEC in New Jersey or IslamInSpanish's Centro Islámico in Houston, Texas).

138. Sheldon Pollock, "Cosmopolitan and Vernacular in History," in *Cosmopolitanism*, ed. Carol A. Breckenridge, et al. (Duke University Press, 2002), 15–53.

139. Ibid., 47.

140. To borrow the language of Mucahit Bilici as he discussed English as a language of Islam and Muslims in the US in *Finding Mecca in America: How Islam Is Becoming an American Religion* (University of Chicago Press, 2012), 73

141. Jorge Araneda, "Las ilusiones y los padecimientos de la emigración. El caso de los inmigrantes árabes musulmanes Levantinos a Chile 1930–1950," *Tabula Rasa* 22 (2015): 125–146.

142. Carlos Jair Martínez Albarracín,"El Contacto De Lenguas Árabe-Castellano En Colombia: Lenguas En Contacto Y Bilingüismo." *Revista Digital* 3 (2011): 1–12; "La Lengua Árabe En San Andrés Isla." *Anthropology and Linguistics. Languages of the World* 40 (2011).

143. Mónica Vianney Ramírez Rodríguez, "Inmigrantes Del Medio Oriente En San Luis Potosí: Primeras Tres Décadas Del Siglo XX" (master's thesis, El Colegio de San Luis, 2010).

144. Philipp Bruckmayr, "Arabic and Bilingual Newspapers and Magazines in Latin America and the Caribbean," *Historical Aspects of Printing and Publishing in Languages of the Middle East* (2013): 245–269.

**Chapter 3: *An ummah en vaivén***

1. Green, *Global Islam*, 9, 17.

2. Chitwood, *Muslims of Latin America and the Caribbean*, 15–17; Marsden and Henig, "Muslim Circulations and Networks in West Asia: Ethnographic Perspectives on Transregional Connectivity."

3. Erik Bleich and A. Maurits van der Veen, *Covering Muslims: American Newspapers in Comparative Perspective* (Oxford University Press, 2022).

4. Ilyse Morgenstein Fuerst, "Job Ads Don't Add Up: Arabic + Middle East + Texts ≠ Islam," *Journal of the American Academy of Religion* 88, no. 4 (December 2020): 915–946.

5. Susanne Schröter, *Allahs Karawane: Eine Reise durch das islamische Multiversum* (C. H. Beck, 2021), 11.

6. For the latter, see Jennifer Taylor and Mustafa Davis, "Redneck Muslim," documentary short, https://www.theatlantic.com/video/index/566348/redneck-muslim.

7. Schröter, *Allahs Karawane*, 13.

8. Curtis, *Across the Worlds of Islam*, 1.

9. Ibid.

10. Asad, "The Idea of an Anthropology of Islam." See also Ovamir Anjum, "Islam as a Discursive Tradition: Talal Asad and His Interlocutors." *Comparative Studies of South Asia, Africa and the Middle East* 27, no. 3 (2007): 656–672.

11. Wendy Shaw, *What is "Islamic" Art? Between Religion and Perception* (Cambridge University Press, 2019), 332.

12. Ibid.

13. John Tofik Karam, *Manifold Destiny: Arabs at an American Crossroads of Exceptional Rule* (Vanderbilt University Press, 2021), 8. See also Dipesh Chakrabarty, *Provincializing Europe: Postcolonial Thought and Historical Difference - New Edition* (Princeton University Press, 2008).

14. Thiago Henrique Mota, "Review of The Muslims of Latin America and the Caribbean," *European Review of Latin American and Caribbean Studies* 115 (January-June 2023): 6.

15. See Tobi Matthiesen, *The Caliph and the Imam: The Making of Sunnism and Shiism* (Oxford University Press, 2023); Hugh Kennedy, *The Historical Atlas of Islam* (Brill, 2001); and Malise Ruthann and Azim Nanji, *Historical Atlas of Islam* (Harvard University Press, 2004).

16. Espinosa, Galvan, and Morales's "Latino Muslim Survey" reported that 91 percent of Latinx Muslims identify as Sunni, 6 percent as Shi'i, and less than 9 percent as both Sufi and Sunni. Furthermore, less than 9 percent self-identified as Salafi or Wahhabi. See Espinosa, Galvan, and Morales, "Latino Muslims in the United States: Reversion, Politics, and Islamidad," 25.

17. See Monique Bernards and John Nawas, "The Geographic Distribution of Muslim Jurists during the First Four Centuries AH," *Islamic Law and Society* 10, no. 2 (2003): 168–181, http://www.jstor.org/stable/3399250.

18. Aaron W. Hughes, "Why is Islam so Different in Different Countries?" *The Conversation*, February 18, 2016, https://theconversation.com/why-is-islam-so-different-in-different-countries-51804.

19. Sandra Cañas Cuevas, "The Politics of Conversion to Islam in Southern Mexico," in *Islam in the Americas*, ed. Aisha Khan (University of Florida Press, 2015), 163–185; Camila Pastor de María y Campos, "Guests of Islam: Conversion and the Institutionalization of Islam in Mexico," in *Crescent Over Another Horizon: Islam in Latin America, the Caribbean, and Latino USA*, ed. María del Mar Logroño Narbona, Paulo G. Pinto, and John Tofik Karam (University of Texas Press, 2015), 144–189; Michelle Romero Gallardo, "Allah Made me Indian: Narratives of Divine Determination of the Self Among Muslim Tzotzils in Southern Mexico," Religion and Power Conference, Gainesville, FL, March 17, 2018; and Arely Medina, "Conversion to Islam in Mexico," in *Encyclopedia of Latin American Religions*, ed. Henri Gooren (Springer, 2019), 363–366.

20. The idea of *la nación en vaivén* (the nation on the move) is used to describe the "back and forth" of Puerto Ricans moving between the island, the continental United States, and other countries. It also signifies an ongoing connection to "Puerto Rican-ness"—a national identity and culture that is transported, adapted, and stateless, but not lost. See Jorge Duany, *La nación en vaivén: identidad, migración, y cultura popular en Puerto Rico* (Ediciones Callejón, 2010); Mónica Fernandez Martins, "La gran familia puertorriqueña: la nación en vaivén," *Polifonía* 6, no. 1 (2016): 101–114; and Frank Espada, "Nation on the Move," https://exhibits.library.duke.edu/exhibits/show/espada/introduction.

21. Shaw, *What is Islamic Art?*, 327.

22. Aejaz Ahmad Rather, "Sacred Spaces as Markers of Disputes: Ahmadiyya Claims on Rozabal Shrine and Political Intervention in Kashmir," *Social Scientist* 49, no. 3/4 (March–April 2021): 57–68.

23. S. Alejandra Sotomayor and Rolando Macías, "Humanity First: Serving Mankind and its work in the Caribbean." Latin America and Caribbean Islamic Studies Association Colloquium, May 30, 2024.

24. E.g., stabbing a woman if she denigrates the Prophet, permitting a man to strike a woman in certain instances, specifically as it relates to the interpretation of the Arabic term *daraba* as "to hit" in al-Nisa 4:34. It has been variously translated as to strike, hit, disregard, part from, separate from, or to cut off contact with. Mohamed Mahmoud divides up the interpretation of this verse, and the term of debate in particular, into two camps: classical and neo-traditionalist scholars who use what he calls the "limitation strategy" by permitting wife-beating but only under limited circumstances and "without causing harm." However, there are Muslim feminist scholars who argue that they cannot condone wife-beating under any circumstance, using what he calls the "virtual abrogation strategy." Mohamed Mahmoud, "To Beat or Not to Beat: On the Exegetical Dilemmas over Qur'ān, 4: 34," *Journal of the American Oriental Society* 126, no 4 [2006]: 544–545. Progressive scholars such as amina wadud in *Qur'an and Woman: Rereading the Sacred Text from a Woman's Perspective* (Oxford University Press, 1999), Asma Barlas and David Raeburn Finn in *Believing Women in Islam: A Brief Introduction* (University of Texas Press, 2019), and Laleh Bakhtiar, "The Sublime Quran: The misinterpretation

of Chapter 4 Verse 34," *European Journal of Women's Studies* 18, no. 4 (2011): 431–439, propose new meanings of the word.

25. Overall, Puerto Rico has higher rates of gender-based violence than the mainland US. In 2018, the territory reported more than one woman murdered per week, on average, which is approximately double the per-capita rate of the US. For more on the state of domestic abuse in Puerto Rico, see Maria Natal, "Intimate Partner Violence Experiences Among Puerto Rican Mothers," *Journal of Interpersonal Violence* 37, nos. 5–6 (2022): NP2626-NP2651; Lillian Perlmutter, "Deadly Violence Against Women in Puerto Rico Is Surging During Lockdown," *Vice*, December 8, 2020; Ángel Villafañe-Santiago, José Serra-Taylor, María I. Jiménez-Chafey, and Carol Y. Irizarry-Robles, "Family and Intimate Partner Violence Among Puerto Rican University Students," *Revista Puertorriqueña de Psicología* 30, no. 1 (Jan.–June 2019): 70–81.

26. Also referred to as Quranism, Qur'anism, or a Quran-centric approach to Islam.

27. Univision, "Angélica Molina: Primera mujer musulmana candidata en Puerto Rico," July 29, 2016.

28. Jesús is referring to the case of Larycia Hawkins. For more details, see Christine Hauser, "Wheaton College Professor Is Put on Leave After Remarks Supporting Muslims," *New York Times*, December 17, 2015.

29. Now closed, though some signage remained in September 2023.

30. One of the Afro-Cuban religious traditions, Santería, or Regla de Ocha, La Regla de Ocha-Ifá, or La Regla de Lukumí, is also prevalent among Puerto Ricans. Typically practiced in private ritual communities rather than public worship spaces, many practitioners and initiates have home altars where an Orisha is often represented by stones—embodiments of the divine power—placed alongside other sacred emblems inside lidded calabash gourds, bowls, tureens, or jars. Each Orisha also has their own foods, Patakís, or sacred stories (myths), numbers, colors, dances, and drum rhythms. According to Marguerite Fernández Olmos and Lizabeth Paravisini-Gebert, "In the Caribbean, the creolization process led to the creation of distinctly Cuban and Puerto Rican varieties of Spiritism [philosophical, religious, and healing notions that emerged in Europe and North America in the nineteenth century]—Espiritismo—and, in the diaspora of the United States, Santerismo. A Creole spiritual healing practice with roots in the United States, Europe, Africa, and the indigenous Taíno Caribbean, Espiritismo amplified and transformed European Spiritism in its travels back and forth from the Old World to the New." *Creole Religions of the Caribbean: An Introduction from Vodou and Santería to Obeah and Espiritismo* (New York University Press, 2003), 171.

31. Adela Suliman, "Sufi Sect of Islam Draws 'Spiritual Vagabonds' in New York," September 23, 2016.

32. Bakaari, "Islam and Its Others," 27.

33. Ulrike Freitag, "Preface," in *Muslim Worlds—World of Islam?* (Leibniz-Zentrum Moderner Orient, 2019), 5.

34. Ibid.

35. See Dietrich Reetz, "Traveling Islam—Madrasa Graduates from India and Pakistan in the Malay Archipelago," Liebniz-Zentrum Moderner Orient Working Papers no. 8, 2013.

36. See Rebekka King, *Key Categories in the Study of Religion: Contexts and Critiques* (Equinox Publishers, 2021).

**Chapter 4: Between *ummah* and *asaBorícua***

1. "Our Mission," Ta'Leef Collective, accessed November 23, 2018, https://www.taleefcollective.org/our-mission.

2. Marcia Hermansen, "American Sufis and American Islam: From Private Spirituality to the Public Sphere," in *Islamic Movements and Islam in the Multicultural World: Islamic Movements and Formation of Islamic Ideologies in the Information Age* (Russian Federation, Kazan Federal University Publishing House, 2014), 189–208; and Farooq Maseehuddin, *Religious Debates Doth Not a Community Make: North American Muslim Counterpublics and the Limits of Community* (master's thesis, University of Alberta, 2017).

3. Following Charles Hirschkind, *The Ethical Soundscape: Cassette Sermons and Islamic Counterpublics* (Columbia University Press, 2009).

4. In 2019, the Ta'leef Collective's founder Usama Canon was permanently removed from leadership after allegations of "professional misconduct" by the organization's board of directors. Aysha Khan, "Ta'leef Collective cuts ties with founder over alleged misconduct," Religion News Service, November 7, 2019.

5. Umar Faruq Abd-Allah, "Islam and the Cultural Imperative," The Oasis Initiative, accessed October 24, 2023, https://www.theoasisinitiative.org/islam-the-cultural-imperative. See also Muhammad Khalifa and Mark A. Gooden, "Between Resistance and Assimilation: A Critical Examination of American Muslim Educational Behaviors in Public School," *The Journal of Negro Education* 79, no. 3 (2010): 308–323; and Walaa Quisay, *Neo-Traditionalism in Islam in the West: Orthodoxy, Spirituality and Politics* (Edinburgh University Press, 2023), 148–174.

6. Ibid.

7. Al-Bukhari, Hadith 1623, 1626, 6361 Sahih of Imam Muslim also refers to this sermon in Hadith number 98. Imam al-Tirmidhi mentioned this sermon in Hadith nos. 1628, 2046, 2085. Imam Ahmed bin Hanbal gave the longest and perhaps most complete version of this sermon in his Masnud, Hadith no. 19774.

8. Caraballo-Resto, "¿Islam *en* Puerto Rico . . . ?"

9. Mónica Cappas, "La comunidad musulmana en Puerto Rico: ¿la conocemos?" *Revista Cuenta Gotas*, April 9, 2020.

10. Jamillah A. Karim, "To Be Black, Female, and Muslim: A Candid Conversation about Race in the American Ummah," *Journal of Muslim Minority Affairs* 26, no. 2 (2006): 225–233; Bruce A. Collet, "Islam, National Identity and Public Secondary Education: Perspectives form the Somali Diaspora in Toronto, Canada," *Race Ethnicity and Education* 10, no. 2 (2007): 131–153; Jamillah Karim, *American Muslim Women: Negotiating Race, Class, and Gender within the Ummah* (New York University Press, 2008); Sylvia Chan-Malik, "'Common Cause': On the Black-Immigrant Debate and Constructing the Muslim America," *Journal of Race, Ethnicity, and Religion* 2, no. 8 (May 2011): 1–39; Imam Luqman A. Ahmad, *Double Edged Slavery: How African American Muslims Have Been Colonized* (Independently Published, 2016); Hishaam Aidi, "Let Us Be Moors"; Dawn-Marie Gibson, *A History of the Nation of Islam: Race, Islam, and the Quest for Freedom* (Bloomsbury, 2012);

Hishaam Aidi, "Jihadis in the Hood: Race, Urban Islam and the War on Terror," *Middle East Research and Information Project 224* (Fall 2002).

11. Gerard Delanty, "The Cosmopolitan Imagination: Critical Cosmopolitanism and Social Theory," *British Journal of Sociology* 57, no. 1 (April 2006), 25–47.

12. Tsing, *Friction*, 1.

13. Ibid.

14. Magnus Marsden, "Muslim Cosmopolitans? Transnational Life in Northern Pakistan," *Journal of Asian Studies* 67, no. 1 (Feb 2008): 213–247.

15. Aisha Khan, *The Deepest Dye: Obeah, Hosay, and Race in the Atlantic World* (Harvard University Press, 2021), 172.

16. Ibid., 173.

17. Ibid., 182.

18. Ibid., 176.

19. Scott Morrison, "'Os Turcos': The Syrian-Lebanese Community of São Paulo, Brazil," *Journal of Muslim Minority Affairs* 25, no. 3 (2005): 435.

20. Mian, "Shahab Ahmed's Contradictions," 239.

21. Aisha Khan, *Calaloo Nation: Metaphors of Race and Religious Identity among South Asians in Trinidad* (Duke University Press, 2004), 5.

22. Ibid., 225.

23. Mian, "Shahab Ahmed's Contradictions," 241.

24. Feliciano-Santos, *Contested Caribbean Indigeneity*, 21.

25. Ibid.

26. Michael W. Jennings, ed., *Walter Benjamin: Selected Writings Volume 4, 1938–1940* (Harvard University Press, 2003), 243.

27. J. Andrew Bush, *Between Muslims: Religious Difference in Iraqi Kurdistan* (Stanford University Press, 2020).

28. Terje Østebø and Benedikt Pontzen, "Introduction: the Formation of Religious Minorities in Muslim Africa," *Islamic Africa* 13 (2022): 115–132.

29. Moustafa Bayoumi, *This Muslim American Life* (New York University Press, 2015); Juliette Galonnier, "The racialization of Muslims in France and the United States," *Social Compass* 62, no. 4 (2015): 570–583; Kambiz GhaneaBassiri, *A History of Islam in America* (Cambridge University Press, 2010); Steve Garner and Saher Selod, "The racialization of Muslims," *Critical Sociology* 41, no. 1 (2015): 9–19; Zareena Grewal, *Islam is a Foreign Country* (New York University Press, 2013); Jeffrey Guhin, "Colorblind Islam: The Racial Hinges of Immigrant Muslims in the United States," *Social Inclusion* 6, no. 2 (2018): 87–97; Amir Hussain, *Muslims and the Making of America* (Baylor University Press, 2016); Michael Muhammad Knight, "Converts and Conversions," in *The Cambridge Companion to American Islam*, ed. Juliane Hammer and Omid Safi (Cambridge University Press, 2013), 83–97.

30. Wilfred Cantwell Smith, *Toward a World Theology: Faith and Comparitive History* (Orbis Books, 1981), 4–5 and 27–28.

31. Østebø and Pontzen, "Introduction," 116.

32. This description not only parallels my framing of the process of cosmopolitanization but also echoes the theorization of global flows and religious traditions by the likes of Thomas Tweed in *Crossing and Dwelling* and Manuel A. Vásquez, "The Limits of the Hydrodynamics of Religion," *Journal of the American Academy of Religion* 77, no. 2 (2009): 434–445.

33. Stephen F. Dale, *The Orange Trees of Marrakesh* (Harvard University Press, 2015), 5.

34. Ibid.

35. Ibid., 26.

36. Ibn Khaldûn, *The Muqaddimah: An Introduction to History*, trans. Franz Rosenthal (Princeton University Press, 1967), 111.

37. Abdesselam Cheddadi, *Ibn Khaldûn L'homme et le théoricien de la civilization* (Gallimard, 2006); Abdesselam Cheddadi, *Ibn Khaldûn Le Livre des Exemples, Histoire des Arabes et des Berberes du Magreb* (Gallimard, 2012); Claude Horrut, *Ibn Khaldûn, un islam des 'Lumieres'?* (Editions Complexe, 2006); Mushin Mahdi, *Ibn Khaldun's Philosophy of History* (Routledge, 2017); Syed Farid Atlas, *Ibn Khaldun* (Oxford University Press, 2013).

38. Ruthven and Nanji, *Historical Atlas of the Islamic World*, 12–13. See also Holly Donahue Singh, "Love and Care at the Margins of Future Generations," in *Across the Worlds of Islam*, 177–178.

39. Robert Irwin, *Ibn Khaldun: An Intellectual Biography* (Princeton University Press, 2018).

40. Khaldûn, 111.

41. Gelner quoted in Ruthven and Nanji, *Historical Atlas of Islam*, 12.

42. E. I. J. Rosenthal, *Political Thought in Medieval Islam: An Introductory Outline* (Cambridge University Press, 1962), 87–91.

43. Magid Shihade, "Asabiyya—Solidarity in the age of Barbarism: An Afro-Arab-Asian Alternative. *Current Sociology* 68, no. 2 (2020): 263–278.

44. Østebø and Pontzen, "Introduction," 127.

45. On the idea(l) of the ummah among non-nation-state groups like al Qaeda and al-Dawla al-Islamiyya (a.k.a. Islamic State, ISIS, ISIL), see works like Asef Bayat ed., *Post-Islamism: The Changing Faces of Political Islam* (Oxford University Press, 2013); Jeevan Deol and Zaheer Kazmi, eds., *Contextualizing Jihadi Thought* (Columbia University Press, 2011); Faisal Devji, *Landscapes of the Jihad: Militancy, Morality, Modernity* (Cornell University Press, 2005); Azza Karam, ed., *Transnational Political Islam: Religion, Ideology, and Power* (Sterling Press, 2004); Peter Mandeville, *Global Political Islam* (Routledge, 2007); David J. Wasserstein, *Black Banners of ISIS: The Roots of the New Caliphate* (Yale University Press, 2017). See also Hassan al-Turabi, "Islam as a Pan-National Movement and Nation-States."

46. 'Abdul Mannân 'Omar, *Dictionary of the Holy Qur'an* (Noor Foundation, 2006), 32.

47. Mohamad Jebara, *Muhammad, the World-Changer: An Intimate Portrait* (St. Martin's Press, 2021), 79.

48. Gerhard Bowering, Patricia Crone, Mahan Mirza, eds., *The Princeton Encyclopedia of Islamic Political Thought* (Princeton University Press, 2012), 107.

49. Benedict Anderson, *Imagined Communities* (Verso Books, 2016).

50. Ahmet T. Karamustafa, "Community," in *Key Themes in the Study of Islam*, ed. Jamal L. Elias (Oneworld Publications, 2014), 95.

51. Juliane Hammer, *Palestinians Born in Exile: Diaspora and the Search for a Homeland* (University of Texas Press, 2005), 4.

52. Ibid., 1, 2, and 222.

53. Wesley Lebron, "My Battle for Peace of Mind," in *Latino Muslims: Our Journeys to Islam*, ed. Juan Galvan, 212.

54. Ibid.

55. Su'ad Abdul Khabeer, *Muslim Cool: Race, Religion, and Hip Hop in the United States* (New York University Press, 2016), 13.

56. Ibid.

57. Sunan Abi Dawud 5121, book 43, hadith 349.

58. Gloria E. Anzaldúa, *Borderlands/La Frontera: The New Mestiza* (Aunt Lute Books, 1987); José David Saldívar in *Border Matters: Remapping American Cultural Studies* (University of California Press, 1997); Homi K. Bhabha, "Frontlines / borderposts," in *Displacements: Cultural Identities in Question*, ed. Angelika Bammer (Indiana University Press, 1994); Bhabha, *The Location of Culture*.

**Chapter 5: *¡Pa'lante, inshallah!***

1. Alana Casanova-Burgess, "What Is La Brega?" WNYC Studios and Futuro Radio, podcast audio, February 24, 2021, https://www.wnycstudios.org/podcasts/la-brega/articles/what-la-brega.

2. Arcadio Díaz Quiñones, et al., "De Cómo y Cuándo Bregar (2000)," in *Antología Del Pensamiento Crítico Puertorriqueño Contemporáneo*, ed. Anayra Santory Jorge and Mareia Quintero Rivera, (CLACSO, 2018), 379–424, https://doi.org/10.2307/j.ctvnp0jr5.17.

3. Meléndez-Badillo, *Puerto Rico*, 24.

4. Though "Brown" is used to describe a disparate range of people—Latinx, Indigenous, Asian, Middle Eastern—and "Black" could be used to describe Puerto Ricans, I use "Brown" here to refer to a general fear of Brown-skinned peoples, in this case including both Puerto Ricans and Muslims.

5. I opt for the Spanish term here, but I draw on the theoretical framing of the Brazilian Portuguese *encruzilhada* as put forth by the Maria Sibylla Merian Centre (Mecila) in "*Encruzilhadas* of Conviviality-Inequality: Re-Generating Suspensions, Struggles, and Openings," Mecila Annual Meeting and Young Researchers Forum, November 8–10, 2021.

6. Funk, *Rooted Globalism*, 110.

7. Jocelyn M. Boryczka and Jennifer Leigh Disney, "Intersectionality for the Global Age," *New Political Science*, 37:4 (2015): 447.

8. Raquel Z. Rivera, Wayne Marshall, Deborah Pacini Hernandez eds., *Reggaeton* (Duke University Press, 2009).

9. Juan Flores, *From Bomba to Hip-Hop: Puerto Rican Culture and Latino Identity* (Columbia University Press, 2000); Nina Vásquez, "Sin la diáspora, no hay reggaetón," *Hasta Bajo Project*, October 25, 2022, https://www.hastabajoproject.com/post/sin-la-diáspora-no-hay-reggaetón; and Jonathan Mael, *Harlem World: How Hip Hop's Super Showdown Changed Music Forever* (John Hopkins University Press, 2023).

10. Frances Negrón-Muntaner and Raquel Z. Rivera, "Reggaeton Nation," *North American Congress on Latin America (NACLA) Magazine*, March 13, 2008.

11. Cruz Garcia and Nathalie Frankowski, "Loudreading in Post-colonial Landscapes (to the Beat of Reggaeton)," *Avery Review* 48 (June 2020), https://averyreview.com/issues/48/loudreading.

12. Zaire Dinzey Flores, "De la disco al caserío: Urban Spatial Aesthetics and Policy to the Beat of Reggaetón," *Centro Journal* 20, 2 (2008): 35–69.

13. Petra R. Rivera-Rideau, *Remixing Reggaetón: The Cultural Politics of Race in Puerto Rico* (Duke University Press, 2015).

14. Alison Torres-Ramos, "Displays of Colonial Shame in Puerto Rican Reggaetón," *Fast Capitalism* 12, no. 1 (2015): 81–88. For more on these themes, see also the "Bibliografía" at the *Hasta Bajo Project*, accessed December 7, 2023, https://www.hastabajoproject.com/b.

15. In this section I am relying on analysis from Francesca Sobande and layla-roxanne hill, *Black Oot Here: Black Lives in Scotland* (London: Bloomsbury Academic 2022), 20ff, and William A. Calvo-Quirós, *Undocumented Saints: The Politics of Migrating Devotions* (Oxford University Press, 2022), 20, as well as the notions of "spiritual activism" and *Nepantla* politics as described by Anzaldúa in *Borderlands/La Frontera*.

16. M. Jacqui Alexander, *Pedagogies of Crossing: Meditations on Feminism, Sexual Politics, Memory, and the Sacred* (Duke University Press, 2006).

17. Stephanie Elizondo Griest, *All the Agents and Saints: Dispatches from the U.S. Borderlands* (University of North Carolina Press, 2019), 234.

18. Jürgen Schaflechner, "Populism of the Precarious: Marginalization, Mobilization, and Mediatization of South Asia's Religious Minorities," Anthropology Group Lecture, Freie Universität Berlin, November 25, 2020.

19. Robbins and Lemos Horta, eds., *Cosmopolitanisms*, 145.

20. James Tully, "The Struggles of Indigenous Peoples for and of Freedom," in *Political Theory and the Rights of Indigenous Peoples* ed. Duncan Ivison, Paul Patton, and Will Sanders (Cambridge University Press, 2000), 40. See also Makere Stewart-Harawira, *The New Imperial Order: Indigenous Responses to Globalization* (Bloomsbury Academic, 2013).

21. Sara C. Awartani, "Solidarities of Liberation, Visions of Empire: Puerto Rico, Palestine, and the U.S. Imperial Project, 1967–1999" (PhD dissertation, George Washington University, August 2020), 104.

22. Bobby S. Sayid, *A Fundamental Fear: Eurocentrism and the Emergence of Islamism* (Zed Books, 2004); Deepa Kumar, *Islamophobia and the Politics of Empire* (Haymarket Books, 2012) and "Rightwing and Liberal Islamophobia: The Change of Imperial Guard from Trump to Biden," *South Asian Review* 42, no. 4 (2021): 408–412; Todd H. Green, *The Fear of Islam: An Introduction to Islamophobia in the West* (Fortress Press, 2015); Gallup, "Islamophobia: Understanding Anti-Muslim Sentiment in the West," accessed December 8, 2023, https://news.gallup.com/poll/157082/islamophobia-understanding-anti-muslim-sentiment-west.aspx; Natalie Doyle and Irfan Ahmad, eds., *(Il)liberal Europe: Islamophobia, Modernity and Radicalization* (Routledge, 2019); Jordan Denari Duffner, *Islamophobia* (Orbis Books, 2021); and Khaled A. Beydoun, *American Islamophobia: Understanding the Roots and Rise of Fear* (University of California Press, 2019).

23. Louise Cainkar, "Islamophobia and the US ideological infrastructure of white supremacy," in *The Routledge International Handbook of Islamophobia*, ed. Irene Tempi and Imran Awan (Routledge, 2019), 239ff.

24. Bleich and van der Veen, *Covering Muslims*.

25. Wajahat Ali, et al., "Fear, Inc.: The Roots of the Islamophobia Network in America," Center for American Progress Report, August 26, 2011.

26. Cecília L. Mariz and Rodrigo Freston, "Islam in Latin America," in *The Cambridge History of Religions in Latin America*, ed. Virginia Garrard-Burnett, Paul Freston, and C. S. Dove (Cambridge University Press, 2016), 714–722; Sophia Rose Arjana, *Muslims in the Western Imagination* (Oxford University Press, 2015). See also Cook, *Forbidden Passages*; Diouf, *Servants of Allah*; Gomez, *Black Crescent*; and Escalante, "The Long Arc of Islamophobia."

27. Ignacio Klich and Jeffrey Lesser, "Introduction: 'Turco' Immigrants in Latin America," *The Americas* 53, no. 1 (1996): 1–14; Joaquín Viloria de La Hoz, "Los 'Turcos' De Lorica: Presencia De Los Árabes En El Caribe Colombiano, 1880–1960" (Universidad de los Andes, 2004); Scott Morrison, "'Os Turcos': The Syrian-Lebanese Community of São Paulo, Brazil," *Journal of Muslim Minority Affairs* 25, no. 3 (2005): 423–438; Jorge Araneda,"Nuevas agendas para una antigua migración: La migración siria, libanesa y palestina desde una mirada Latinoamericana." *LASA Forum* 47, no. 1 (2016): 15–20.

28. John Tofik Karam, "Crossing the Americas: The U.S. War on Terror and Arab Cross-Border Mobilizations in a South American Frontier Region," *Comparative Studies of South Asia, Africa and the Middle East* 31, no. 2 (2011): 251–266 and *Manifold Destiny: Arabs at an American Crossroads of Exceptional Rule* (Vanderbilt University Press, 2021).

29. Halima-Sa'adia Kassim, "Forming Islamic Religious Identity among Trinidadians in the Age of Social Networks," in *Crescent Over Another Horizon*, 246.

30. Yarimar Bonilla, "Between Terror and Transcendence: Global Narratives of Islam and the Political Scripts of Guadeloupe's Indianité," in *Islam and the Americas*, 141–162.

31. Rukhsana Qamber, "Anti-Islamic Bias in Sources on Latin America: Preliminary Findings," *Islamic Studies* 42, no. 4 (2003): 651–685; and Susana Mangana, "Averting Islamophobia in Latin America: The Media Coverage: From Orientalism to New Fears and Positive Counter-Constructions," *Doha* 12 (2019): 131–142.

32. Chitwood, *Muslims of Latin America and the Caribbean*, 151–180.

33. Nathaniel Deutsch, "Fear of a Brown Planet: Pan-Islamism, Black Nationalism, and the Tribal Twenties," in *Islam and the Americas*, 92–114.

34. Mabel Sanchez and Shafiqa Ahmadi, "Latinx Muslims," in *Islamophobia in Higher Education*, ed. Shafiqa Ahmadi and Darnell Cole (Routledge, 2020), 21.

35. Ken Chitwood, "Muslim Asylum Seekers Face a Unique Plight at the US-Mexico Border," *New Lines Magazine*, April 6, 2023.

36. Alejandro Beutel, "How Trump's Nativist Tweets Overlap with Anti-Muslim and Anti-Latino Hate Crimes," *Southern Poverty Law Center Magazine*, May 18, 2018.

37. Chitwood and Taylor, "AmeRícan Muslims."

38. Sabrina Alimahomed-Wilson, "When the FBI Knocks: Racialized State Surveillance of Muslims," *Critical Sociology* 45, no. 6 (2019): 871–887.

39. Meléndez-Badillo, *Puerto Rico*, xiii and xv.

40. For a helpful historical overview and other information related to Puerto Rico's "commonwealth" status and how Puerto Rican citizenship was formed

and functions, see the Puerto Rico Status Archives Project (PRSAP), https://scholarscollaborative.org/PuertoRico.

41. Duany, *Puerto Rico*, 2.

42. José Atiles-Osoria, "Colonial State Terror in Puerto Rico: A Research Agenda," *State Crime Journal* 5, no. 2 (2016): 220–241.

43. Fenton Stitt, *Dreams*, 135. For more, see Yarimar Bonilla and Marisol LeBrón, eds., *Aftershocks of Disaster: Puerto Rico Before and After the Storm* (Haymarket Books, 2019).

44. Julian Go, *American Empire and the Politics of Meaning: Elite Political Cultures in the Philippines and Puerto Rico during U.S. Colonialism* (Duke University Press, 2008).

45. Christina Duffy Burnett, Burke Marshall, eds., *Foreign in a Domestic Sense: Puerto Rico, American Expansion, and the Constitution* (Duke University Press, 2001).

46. Damaris Suárez, Víctor Rodríguez Velásquez, and Omaya Sosa Pascual, "A Nightmare for Puerto Ricans to Find a Home, While Others Accumulate Properties," Centro de Periodismo Investigativo, December 19, 2022; and Coral Murphy Marcos and Patricia Mazzei, "The Rush for a Slice of Paradise in Puerto Rico," *New York Times*, January 31, 2022.

47. Rocío Zambrana, *Colonial Debts: The Case of Puerto Rico* (Duke University Press, 2021).

48. Pedro Cabán, "PROMESA, Puerto Rico and the American Empire," *Latino Studies* 16 (2018): 161–184.

49. Carmen Teresa Whalen, *From Puerto Rico To Philadelphia: Puerto Rican Workers and Postwar Economies* (Temple University Press, 2001), 137.

50. Morning Consult, "National Tracking Poll #170916," September 22–24, 2017, accessed December 11, 2023, https://morningconsult.com/wp-content/uploads/2017/10/170916_crosstabs_pr_v1_KD.pdf.

51. Fenton Stitt, *Dreams*, 134.

52. Duany, *Blurred Borders*, 103.

53. Meléndez-Badillo, *Puerto Rico*, 135–136. See also Margaret M. Power, *Solidarity across the Americas: The Puerto Rican Nationalist Party and Anti-imperialism* (University of North Carolina Press, 2023).

54. Sarah Irving, *Leila Khaled: Icon of Palestinian Liberation* (Pluto Press, 2012).

55. See Mirelsie Velázquez, *Puerto Rican Chicago: Schooling the City, 1940–1977* (University of Illinois Press, 2022).

56. Sara Awartani, "Puerto Rico, Palestine, and the Politics of Resistance and Surveillance at the University of Illinois Chicago Circle," in *Critical Dialogues in Latinx Studies: A Reader*, ed. Ana Y. Ramos-Zayas and Mérida M. Rúa (New York University Press, 2021), 197–210.

57. Sara Awartani, "In Solidarity: Palestine in the Puerto Rican Political Imaginary," *Radical History Review* 128 (2017): 199–222.

58. Enck-Wanzer, *The Young Lords*, 67.

59. Sara Awartani, "Puerto Rican Freedom Dreaming: Solidarity and the Radical Protest Tradition," *Society and Space*, February 25, 2020.

60. Awartani, "In Solidarity." See also Sara Awartani, "Weaponizing Solidarity: Puerto Rico, Palestine, and US Counterterrorism in the 1980's," American Studies Association Annual Meeting, New Orleans, LA, November 4–6, 2022.

61. E.g., the "Occupied Lands, Scattered Diasporas: Puerto Rican and Palestinian" film series held at Café Teatro Batey Urbano in Chicago's westside Humboldt Park community in January 2012 or pro-Palestine marches in Puerto Rican Chicago in May 2021, when tensions flared over the eviction of Palestinian families in Sheikh Jarrah, East Jerusalem, and Israeli authorities fired rockets on Gaza, killing 256 Palestinians (including 66 children). See Hugo Balta, "Many Puerto Ricans See Solidarity With Palestinians," *The Chicago Reporter*, May 21, 2021.

62. Ocasio, "Alianza Islamica: The True Story."

63. Morales, *Latino and Muslim in America*, 36.

64. Wendy Díaz, "Puerto Rican Imams Step Up for Puerto Rico," *The Muslim Link*, October 9, 2017.

65. Meléndez-Badillo, *Puerto Rico*, 191.

66. Ed Morales, *Fantasy Island: Colonialism, Exploitation, and the Betrayal of Puerto Rico* (Bold Type Books, 2019), 47.

67. March 15, 2021, https://www.facebook.com/3PuertoRicanImams/photos/3064857853756005.

68. Morales, *Latino and Muslim in America*, 39.

69. Harold Morales, "Latino Muslim By Design," 23. See also Kimberlé Crenshaw, "Mapping the Margins: Intersectionality, Identity Politics, and Violence Against Women of Color," *Stanford Law Review* 43, no. 6 (1991): 1241–1299; Richard Delgado and Jean Stefancic, *Critical Race Theory: An Introduction* (New York University Press, 2001); and David Ingram, *Rights, Democracy, and Fulfillment in the Era of Identity Politics: Principled Compromises in a Compromised World* (Rowman & Littlefield, 2004).

70. This parallels, in many ways, "the performance of bodily endurance against US colonialism through different measures of time" among Puerto Ricans in general. See Ruiz, *Ricanness*.

71. Three Puerto Rican Imams, 2020, "Real men don't hit women," Facebook, November 20, 2020, https://www.facebook.com/3PuertoRicanImams/photos/2726875004220960; Three Puerto Rican Imams, 2021, "3 Puerto Rican Imams contra la violencia de genero," Facebook, May 8, 2021, https://www.facebook.com/3PuertoRicanImams/photos/2846232568951869.

72. For more on women's experiences in other Latin American contexts, see Sdenka S. Alfaro, "Presencia E Identidad De La Mujer Musulmana En América Latina," *Shia News Association*, June 16, 2019; Margot Badran, "Feminismo Islámico En Marcha," *Clepsydra, Revista de Estudios de Género y Teoría Feminista* (2010): 69–84; Cecilia Baeza, "Women in Arab-Palestinian Associations in Chile: Long Distance Nationalism and Gender Mixing." *Al-Raida* (133–134, 2011): 18–32; Claudia L. Castro Flores,"Allah En Masculino Y Femenino: Formas Diferenciadas De Interpretar Y Practicar El Islam En México" (master's thesis, El Colegio de México, 2012); Sandra Cañas Cuevas, "The Politics of Conversion to Islam in Southern Mexico," in *Islam and the Americas*, ed. Aisha Khan (University Press of Florida, 2015), 163–185; Ruth Jatziri García Linares, "La Construcción De Una Identidad Religiosa, El Caso De Las Mujeres Del Centro Educativo De La Comunidad

Musulmana," in *La Investigación Social En México*, vol. 2, ed. Tomás Serrano Áviles, B., Jaciel Montoya Arce, Pablo Jaso Salas, Abigail Moreno Jiménez (Universidad Autónoma del Estado de Hidalgo, 2012), 1561–1574; Cynthia Hernández González, "Más Alla Del Matrimonio: La Sexualidad Desde La Mirada Y Corporeidad De Sus Creyentes Latinx-Musulmanxs" (PhD thesis, Centro de Investigaciones y Estudios Superiores en Antropología Social, Ciudad de Mexico, 2019); Arely Medina and Ruth Jatziri García Linares, eds., "Islam: Una Perspectiva Global Y Local," Special issue, *Revista Ruta Antropológica* 6 (2017); Angélica Schenerock, "Más Allá De Velos Y Peinados: Las Reelaboraciones Étnicas Y Genéricas De Las Chamulas Musulmanas Sufis En San Cristóbal De Las Casas," *LiminaR* 2 (2, 2004): 75–94; Sylvie Taussig and Yolotl Valadez, "Le Mariage Islamique En Amérique Latine: Dévelоppement Et Enjeux," *Les cahiers de l'Islam*, September 29, 2018; Pilar A. Varagas and Luz Marina V. Suaza, *Mujeres Árabes De Colombia* (Planeta, 2011); Mayra S. Valcarcel, "Women Embracing Islam in Buenos Aires: Unsubmissive Femininities on the Move," *International Journal of Latin American Religions* 6 (2022): 420–448.

73. Schreiber posted on Facebook in July 2016 that "All Islam is radical," and all Muslims should be treated as terrorists and criminals.

74. Bleich and van der Veen, *Covering Muslims*, 88f.

75. Doug Meyer, "An Intersectional Analysis of LGBTQ Online Media Coverage of the Pulse Nightclub Shooting Victims," *Journal of Homosexuality* 67, no. 10 (2020): 1343–1366.

76. Judith E. Koons, "Pulse: Finding Meaning in a Massacre Through Gay Latinx Intersectional Justice," *Scholar* 19, no. 1 (2017), https://ssrn.com/abstract=2841534.

77. Nolan Kline and Christopher Cuevas, "Resisting Identity Erasure after Pulse: Intersectional LGBTQ+ Latinx Activism in Orlando, FL," *Chiricu* 2, no. 2 (2018): 68ff.

78. Hannah Thompson, "Muslim Community Response to the Pulse Nightclub Shooting," Orange County Regional History Center, December 20, 2021.

79. Ibid.

80. Steven Thrasher, "Latino community mourns Pulse shooting victims: '90% were Hispanic,'" *The Guardian*, June 14, 2016; and Matthew Rodriguez, "Latino, LGBTQ Muslims in Orlando Are Grieving the Pulse Shooting," *Yahoo! Finance*, June 15, 2016, accessed January 10, 2024, https://finance.yahoo.com/news/latino-lgbtq-muslims-orlando-grieving-171417852.html?guccounter=1.

81. Nihad Awad, "Muslim Leader: Homophobia and Islamophobia Are Connected Systems of Oppression," *TIME*, June 14, 2016.

82. Alisa Perkins, "Muslims at the American Vigil: LGBTIQ Advocacy, Religion, and Public Mourning," *The American Journal of Islamic Social Sciences* 36 no. 4, (Fall 2019): 27–60.

83. Ismail Ayer, "American Muslims and Islam Drift Apart," A Good Tree, March 7, 2017, accessed January 10, 2024, https://agoodtree.net/2017/03/07/american-muslims-and-islam-drift-apart.

84. For a further example of the tensions at play, see Wendy Díaz, "I Am an Imam and My Brother Is Gay: Navigating the Intersection of Religion and Family: An Interview with Imam Wesley Lebron," Sound Vision, July 19, 2023, accessed January 10, 2024, https://www.soundvision.com/article/i-am-an-imam-and-my-brother-is-gay-navigating-the-intersection-of-religion-and-family.

85. Particularly how it reifies and stabilizes identifications that are often in flux and whether or not overlapping group identifications are useful in advocating for change in the public sphere. For various critiques of intersectionality, see Barbara Foley, "Intersectionality: A Marxist Critique," *New Labor Forum* 28, no. 3 (2019): 10–13; Anna Carastathis, "The Invisibility of Privilege: A Critique of Intersectional Models of Identity," *Les ateliers de l'éthique / The Ethics Forum* 3, no. 2 (2008): 23–38; Lisa Downing, "The Body Politic: Gender, the Right Wing and 'Identity Category Violations,'" *French Cultural Studies* 29, no. 4 (2018): 367–377; Rekia Jibrin and Sara Salem, "Revisiting Intersectionality: Reflections on Theory and Praxis," *Trans-Scripts* 5 (2015): 7–24; Jennifer C. Nash, "Re-Thinking Intersectionality," *Feminist Review* 89, no. 1 (2008): 1–15; Maria Rodó-Zárate and Marta Jorba, "Metaphors of Intersectionality: Reframing the Debate with a New Proposal," *European Journal of Women's Studies* 29, no. 1 (2022): 23–38; Salla Aldrin Salskov, "A Critique of Our Own? On Intersectionality and 'Epistemic Habits' in a Study of Racialization and Homonationalism in a Nordic Context," *NORA—Nordic Journal of Feminist and Gender Research* 28, no. 3 (2020): 251–265.

**Conclusion**

1. Chitwood and Gómez, "'We Carry All These Different Hijabs.'"
2. Robbins and Lemos Horta, *Cosmopolitanisms*, 145.
3. Beck, *Cosmopolitan Vision*, 6.
4. Bronislaw Szerszynski and John Urry, "Cultures of Cosmopolitanism," *Sociological Review* 50, no. 4 (2002): 42–43.
5. John Tomlinson, *Globalization and Culture* (Polity Press, 1999), 42.
6. Shaw, *What is Islamic Art?* 330.
7. Bakaari, "Islam and Its Others," 40.
8. Esperança Bielsa, "The Cosmopolitan Stranger," in *Cosmopolitanism in Hard Times*, ed. Vincenzo Cicchelli and Sylvie Mesure (Brill, 2020), 263.
9. Tobar, "Our Migrant Souls."
10. Meléndez-Badillo, *Puerto Rico*, 215.
11. Anzaldúa, *Borderlands/Las Fronteras*, 281–282.
12. Vernon James Schubel, "Let the Margins Be the Center," in *Across the Worlds of Islam*, 257.

# Index